D1765755

Strategic Sourcing of Information Systems

Wiley Series in Information Systems

PREVIOUS VOLUMES IN THE SERIES

Boland & Hirschheim: *Critical Issues in Information Systems Research*
Schäfer: *Functional Analysis of Office Requirements—A Multiperspective Approach*
Mumford & MacDonald: *XSEL's Progress—The Continuing Journey of an Expert System*
Swanson & Beath: *Maintaining Information Systems in Organizations*
Friedman: *Computer Systems Development—History, Organization and Implementation*
Huws, Korte & Robinson: *Telework—Towards the Elusive Office*
Lincoln: *Managing Information Systems for Profit*
Silver: *Systems that Support Decision Makers—Description and Analysis*
Irving & Higgins: *Office Information Systems Management Issues and Methods*
Cotterman & Senn: *Challenges and Strategies for Research in Systems Development*
Walsham: *Interpreting Information Systems in Organisations*
Watkins & Eliot: *Expert Systems in Business and Finance—Issues and Applications*
Lacity & Hirschheim: *Information Systems Outsourcing—Myths, Metaphors and Realities*
Österlie, Brenner & Hilbers: *Total Information Systems Management—A European Approach*
Ciborra & Jelassi: *Strategic Information Systems—A European Perspective*
Knights: *Managers Divided*
Krcmar: *EDI in Europe*
Lacity & Hirschheim: *Beyond the Information Systems Outsourcing Bandwagon—The Insourcing Response*
Ward: Strategic Planning for Information Systems
McKeen & Smith: *Management Challenges in IS—Successful Strategies and Appropriate Action*
Ciborra: *Groupware & Teamwork—Invisible Aid or Technical Hindrance?*
Remenyi, Sherwood-Smith with White: *Achieving Maximum Value from Information Systems—A Process Approach*
Wigand: *Information, Organisation & Management—Expanding Markets Corporate Boundaries*
Galliers and Baers: *Information Technology & Organizational transformation—Innovation for the 21st Century Organization*
Willcocks & Lacity: *Strategic Sourcing of Information Systems—Perspectives and Practices*

Strategic Sourcing of Information Systems

Perspectives and Practices

Edited by

LESLIE P. WILLCOCKS
Templeton College, University of Oxford

and

MARY C. LACITY
University of Missouri, St Louis

JOHN WILEY & SONS
Chichester · New York · Weinheim · Brisbane · Singapore · Toronto

Baffins Lane, Chichester,
West Sussex PO19 1UD, England
National 01243 779777
International (+44) 1243 779777
e-mail (for orders and customer service enquiries):
cs-books@wiley.co.uk
Visit our Home Page on http://www.wiley.co.uk
or http://www.wiley.com

Other Wiley Editorial Offices

John Wiley & Sons, Inc., 605 Third Avenue,
New York, NY 10158–0012, USA

WILEY-VCH Verlag GmbH, Pappelallee 3,
D-69469 Weinheim, Germany

Jacaranda Wiley Ltd, 33 Park Road, Milton,
Queensland 4064, Australia

John Wiley & Sons (Asia) Pte Ltd, 2 Clementi Loop #02–01,
Jin Xing Distripark, Singapore 129809

John Wiley & Sons (Canada) Ltd, 22 Worcester Road,
Rexdale, Ontario M9W 1L1, Canada

Library of Congress Cataloging-in-Publication Data
Strategic sourcing of information systems : perspectives and practices
edited by Leslie P. Willcocks, Mary C. Lacity.
p. cm. — (Wiley series in information systems)
Includes bibliographical references and index.
ISBN 0-471-97787-X
1. Electronic data processing departments—Contracting out.
I. Willcocks, Leslie P. II. Lacity, Mary Cecelia. III. Series.
HF5548.2.S87 1997
658'.05–dc21 97–17401
CIP

British Library Cataloguing in Publication Data
A catalogue record for this book is available from the British Library

ISBN 0-471-97787-X

Typeset in 10/12pt Palatino by Vision Typesetting, Manchester
Printed and bound in Great Britain by Bookcraft (Bath) Ltd
This book is printed on acid-free paper responsibly manufactured from sustainable forestation, for which at least two trees are planted for each one used for paper production.

Contents

Contributors

Soon Ang Head of the Human Resource and Quality Division and Deputy Director of the Information Management Research Center at Nanyang Business School, Nanyang Technological University, Singapore. She gained her PhD at the University of Minnesota, USA. She has published widely in such journals as *Information Systems Research* and *Communications of The ACM* and is on the editorial boards of ISR and JISE. Research interests include cross-national perspectives on information services outsourcing, the impact of foreign employment outsourcing and the role of guanxi networks in labour mobility.

Uday Apte Associate Professor of MIS at Southern Methodist University, Dallas, USA. He holds a PhD from The Wharton School where he previously taught for eight years. Research interests include service operations and MIS. His published research articles have won several awards. He has ten years of management experience in the financial services industry, and has consulted with several major corporations.

Paul W. Beamish Royal Bank Professor of International Business, Western Business School, The University of Western Ontario, London, Ontario, Canada N6A 3K7. Paul has published widely in leading journals and is also the Editor-in-Chief of the *Journal of International Business Studies*. His research has been focused on organizational alliances.

Myun J. Cheon College of Business Administration of University of Ulsan at Ulsan, Korea. He has a PhD from The University of South Carolina, an MBA from Indiana State University, USA, and a BBA from Keimyung University, Korea. His primary areas of interest include outsourcing of IS functions and IS security.

JONATHAN CRONK Senior manager, and a Research Associate at Canterbury Business School at the University of Kent.

THOMAS CLARK Professor at and Dean of the College of Business at Louisiana State University. His current research involves the study of multicultural issues in IS design and operation, the nature and evolution of decision support systems, the value of information in decision processes, the effects of outsourcing on IS functions and the effects of technology on work groups and organizations. He holds a DBA from The Florida State University, an MBA from Arizona State University and AB in Biological Sciences from Mercer University.

DONALD L. DAWLEY Assistant Professor of MIS in the Department of Decision Sciences and MIS at Miami University, Oxford, Ohio, USA. In addition to IS outsourcing, especially offshore development, his research interests are in the areas of strategic applications of information systems, executive information and decision support, and end user computing.

RAMY ELITZUR Associate Professor in the Faculty of Management at the University of Toronto. Ramy's research focuses on the application of game theory to issues in executive compensation, financial accounting and information systems.

VARUN GROVER Associate Professor in the Management Science Department of University of South Carolina, Columbia, USA. He has over 60 refereed papers published on outsourcing, reengineering, strategic information systems, the management of information systems and telecommunications. A co-edited book is *Business Process Change* (Ideal Publishing). He received an Outstanding Achievement Award from the Decision Science Institute, and is a member of AIS, TIMS and DSI.

JAAK JURISON Assistant Professor and Deputy Chair of Information and Communication Systems at the Graduate School of Business Administration, Fordham University, USA. He holds a doctorate from The Claremont Graduate School, USA. His research interests include management of IT benefits and international IT issues. He has published numerous papers and co-edited two books: *Productivity in the Office and Factory*, and *Information Technology in a Global Business Environment*.

ROBET KLEPPER Associate Professor of MIS at the School of Business at Southern Illinois University at Edwardsville, USA. He holds a PhD in economics from the University of Chicago. His research interests include IS outsourcing, technology transfer to Eastern Europe and career paths of senior IS executives. Author of *Information Systems Outsourcing* (1997).

MARY C. LACITY Assistant Professor of MIS at the University of Missouri-St. Louis, USA, a research associate of Templeton College, Oxford University, and Americas Editor for the *Journal of Information Technology*. She has published two books (with Rudy Hirschheim)—*Information Systems Outsourcing: Myths, Metaphors, and Realities* (1993) and *Beyond the Information Systems Outsourcing Bandwagon: the Insourcing Response* (1995). Her articles have appeared in journals such as the *Harvard Business Review, Sloan Management Review, Journal of MIS*, and *Journal of Strategic Information Systems*.

LEON A. DE LOOFF Research Associate at the Department of Information Systems at Delft University of Technology and has a degree in Information Systems (MSc). He lectures in courses on Information Economics and Information Management. His research interests include organizational and economic aspects of information management. He took part in the Ernst & Young/ICIS Doctoral Consortium 1994 and presented at the IRMA 1996 International Conference.

BARBARA L. MARCOLIN Associate Professor at the Faculty of Management, The University of Calgary, Calgary, Alberta, Canada, T2N 1N4. She received her degree from the Western Business School, at the University of Western Ontario. Dr Marcolin has conducted research into end user sophistication, end user implementation, and end user complaint processes. She has published articles in several journals, such as the *Journal of Systems Management* and the *Business Quarterly*.

GORDON MCCRAY Assistant Professor of IS in the Wayne Calloway School of Business and Accountancy at Wake Forest University. His research interests centre around IT planning and leveraging investments in IT. He is completing his PhD from Florida State University, and holds the MBA degree from Stetson University and a BS in Physics from Wake Forest University.

KERRY MCLELLAN Research Associate at the National Centre for Management Research and Development, Western Business School, although is currently pursuing other interests with a consulting practice exploring the choices for deploying technology to support business strategies. Kerry's research has been focused on Information System Outsourcing and telecommunications technology in firms within North America and Europe.

T. M. RAJKUMAR Assistant Professor of MIS in the Department of Decision Sciences and MIS at Miami University, Oxford, Ohio, USA. In addition to information systems outsourcing his research interests are in multimedia, data communications, object oriented systems.

TAPIO REPONEN Professor in the Department of Information Systems Science and Rector at the Turku School of Economics and Business Administration, Finland. He is a member of several Editorial Boards and has served on programme committees for many international conferences. He has acted as consultant for business planning and information management for several Finnish companies, and has published over a hundred papers on strategic planning and IS, organizing the IS function and investment planning.

JOHN SHARP Professor of Management in the Canterbury Business School, University of Kent, UK. His research interests include IS strategy, and investment decision making for manufacturing systems. He has published widely on decision modelling, forecasting investment appraisal, and manufacturing systems.

HARRY SCARBROUGH Lecturer in Industrial Relations in the Warwick Business School at the University of Warwick, UK. Harry has researched and published widely in the areas of information systems and organization studies. Co-authored titles include *The Management of Expertise* (1996) and *Technology and Organization* (1992). His current interests are focused on the management of so-called 'knowledge assets' in organizational contexts.

MARION G. SOBOL Professor, has taught Management Information Sciences at Southern Methodist University, Dallas, USA for 20 years. She is a Fellow of the Decision Sciences Institute, and holds an MA and PhD from the University of Michigan. She has worked at the Survey Research Centre, Metropolitan Life Insurance Company and Rutgers University, and is the co-author of four books and many refereed papers. Her research interests include validation of statistical models, survey research techniques, and economic analyses of computerization.

JAMES T. C. TENG Associate Professor in the Management Science Department of the College of Business Administration at the University of South Carolina. His research interests are in the areas of IS outsourcing, data resource management, DSS and business process redesign. He received an Outstanding Achievement Award from the Decision Science Institute in 1992, and has published over 40 research papers in leading IS journals.

SEE-KIAT TOH Senior Lecturer in the Division of Business Law, Nanyang Business School, Nanyang Technological University, Singapore. He has been its Programme Director but is currently on leave serving as president of the Consumers' Association of Singapore and town councillor of Eunos Pasir Ris Town. He is also attached to Arthur

Loke and Partners, practising banking, commercial and computer law.

LESLIE P. WILLCOCKS Fellow in Information Management and University Lecturer in Management Studies at Templeton College, Oxford University. He is Editor-in-Chief of the *Journal of Information Technology*, and holds Visiting Professorships in Information Systems at Universiteit van Amsterdam and at Erasmus University, Rotterdam. He is co-author of ten books including *A Business Guide to IT Outsourcing* (1994), and *Investing in Information Systems* (1996). His research interests are reflected in refereed papers in journals such as *The Harvard Business Review, Sloan Management Review, Long Range Planning* and *Journal of Management Studies*.

ANTHONY WENSLEY Associate Professor of Management at the University of Toronto. He is also a Visiting Senior Research Fellow at the University of Central Lancashire and was a Visiting Fellow at the Australian National University, Canberra, in March 1996. He has worked for many years in the field of knowledge-based systems and has during the past few years begun to explore the application of game theory to issues in information systems strategy.

ROBERT ZMUD Professor and Thomas L. Williams, Jnr. Eminent Scholar in Management Information Systems in the Information and Management Science Department at the College of Business, Florida State University. He is also Editor-in-Chief of *MIS Quarterly*, and has published numerous books and academic papers. His current research interests focus on the impact of IT in facilitating a variety of organizational behaviours and on organizational efforts involved with planning, managing, and diffusing IT. Both his PhD (University of Arizona) and his MS (MIT) degrees are in management.

Wiley Series in Information Systems

Series Preface

The information systems community has grown considerably since 1984, when we first started the Wiley Series in Information Systems. We are pleased to be part of the growth of the field, and believe that this series of books is playing an important role in the intellectual development of the discipline. The primary objective of the series is to publish scholarly works which reflect the best of research in the information systems community.

As the information systems field matures, there is an increased need to carry the results of its growing body of research into practice. The series desires to publish research results that speak to important needs in the development and management of information systems and our editorial mission recognises explicitly the need for research to inform the practice and management of information systems. *Strategic Sourcing of Information Systems* takes a fresh look at the area of IT outsourcing and asks the key question of not whether IT should be outsourced, but where and how can business leverage be achieved through utilising the rapidly developing market for IT services. The book answers this question by providing a forum of current thinking by prominent scholars and practitioners from around the world. The areas of focus of the book include selective outsourcing, total outsourcing, total insourcing, offshore development and the establishment of an IT department as a trading agency.

Introduction – The Sourcing and Outsourcing of IS: Shock of the New?

LESLIE P. WILLCOCKS AND MARY C. LACITY

"Disaggregating corporate activities into manageable intellectual clusters—called service activities—is the crux of reconceptualizing organizational structures, the management of intellect, and the interlinkage of corporate organizations with the 'new alliance' modes of external competition." *James Brian Quinn, Intelligent Enterprise*

"Outsourcing is a method of rebuilding the focus of the organization so that you focus on what is important to the organization, and not what is important to the traditional IT world." *CIO, oil multinational*

"Essentially, with outsourcing, I believe you get a better service as a customer than you did as a boss; I can think about the strategy objective, and not worry about the day-to-day work." *Logistics Director, major retail company*

"We believe no major long-term deal signed in 1992 will run its full course. Most of those large outsourcing deals are built on voodoo economics." *Ray Manganelli, CEO Gateway Information Services*

During the 1980s, American Airlines, American Hospital Supply (now Baxter), Merrill Lynch, and McKesson provided the exemplars for the management of information technology (IT) and systems (IS). (Note: throughout the terms IT and IS will be used interchangeably). These companies testified to the competitive advantage that can be achieved through the successful exploitation of IT. A host of competitive advantage frameworks sought to formalize and further legitimate the strategic potential of IT (Feeny and Ives, 1989; Ives and Learmonth, 1984; McFarlan, 1984; Porter and Millar, 1985). In 1989, Kodak outsourced its information technology functions to IBM, Businessland and DEC (Applegate and Montealegre, 1991; Brown and Eckerson, 1990; Hovey, 1991). This event publicized an alternative exemplar for the management of IT (Loh and Venkatraman, 1992a). Kodak was the first visible Fortune 500 company to argue that IT was primarily a commodity best handled by expert vendors, rather than a coveted strategic asset. Even Max Hopper—American Airline's symbolic figurehead of the strategic potential of IT—claimed in 1990 that the old models of competitive advantage no longer apply because IT is too easily replicated to create a sustainable competitive advantage (Hopper, 1990). Therefore, senior executives should seek to minimize the IT costs, perhaps by outsourcing to a third party vendor.

The new exemplars for IT management include British Petroleum, British Aerospace, Continental Bank, Continental Airlines, First Fidelity Bank, General Dynamics, The UK Inland Revenue, McDonnell Douglas, National Car Rental, Sears and Xerox (Collins, 1996; Cross, 1995; Ganz, 1994; Harrar, 1993; Huber, 1993; Melymuka, 1994; Moad, 1993). Since these mega-deals were signed a number of changes have begun to emerge. Most notably, the increased competition in the IT outsourcing market, more niche players, and a mounting customer experience base have given customers opportunities to negotiate and leverage deals in different ways. At the same time this has meant that the environment has become more muddled with diverse trends, options and terms. However, as more companies, and public sector organizations, jump on the outsourcing bandwagon, practitioners are gaining ample experiences of outsourcing "successes" that lead to, for example, lower IT costs, increased service levels, and more flexible IT management, as well as outsourcing "failures", that lead perhaps to increasing IT costs, decreased service levels, and/or inflexibility (see Lacity and Hirschheim 1993, 1995; Willcocks and Fitzgerald, 1994 and Chapters 7 and 12 for documented cases of outsourcing successes and failures). Enough evidence is now being accumulated to analyse and assess practices through several theoretical perspectives. One possibility may be the eventual adoption of one common, powerful theoretical perspective on outsourcing. Through this, academics and practitioners could well come to share a language to explain factors associated with successful and unsuccessful IS outsourcing experiences and so be able to provide guidelines for practice.

It is clear, however, that we are some way from such an outcome. In practice the outsourcing market for third party management of IT assets and services has continued to grow, with estimated 1994 global revenues of US $ 49.5 billion probably exceeding $70 billion by the end of 1998, and on some accounts reaching US $ 121 billion in the year 2000. In the USA the

Outsourcing Institute's 1996 survey of 1200 companies indicated that 50 per cent of all companies with IT budgets of $US 5 million or more were either outsourcing or evaluating the option. They also reported that one-twelfth of IT dollars spent in 1995 flowed through an outsourcing contract (IDC, 1992; IDC, 1996 reported on 20 May, http://www.outsourcing.com; Willcocks, Lacity and Fitzgerald, 1995). By 1996 the European market was about US$ 8 billion, with the United Kingdom being the biggest at £1.7 billion revenues with an estimated annual growth rate of about 24 per cent (Holway, 1996; Willcocks and Fitzgerald, 1994).

Along with its growth in the industrialized economies, and the diversity of approaches and experiences it has engendered, so information systems outsourcing has become increasingly the subject of considerable debate amongst academics and practitioners alike. Patterns are difficult to discern with, for example, some commentators suggesting an inexorable, accelerating trend toward more and more IS being outsourced, marking a fundamental change in the way organizations need to be run. Still others point to continuity as well as change, and the more typical, widespread use of selective outsourcing rather than of the high profile large-scale, long-term partnering arrangements often styled as "strategic alliances". In this book we seek to contribute to these and related discussions by collecting together a range of theoretical and empirical studies. In a later part of this Introduction we will also assess current trends and future issues.

The studies in this book are informed by a wide range of theoretical perspectives. Most of these perspectives are taken from related disciplines/fields of study, then applied critically to the analysis of IS outsourcing. Several chapters attempt to build new theory specifically for the study of IS sourcing. Many of the studies are also based on case study and/or survey research into IS outsourcing practices and outcomes. Taken together the chapters make a significant contribution in both theoretical and empirical work. Not surprisingly, in varying degrees they touch upon many debates and issues of considerable contemporary interest. In this Introduction we will outline and comment on the shape of these debates and the chapters that embody them.

OUTSOURCING: TOWARDS NEW FORMS OF ORGANIZATION

Throughout this book the working definition of information systems (IS) outsourcing is the handing over to third party management of IT/IS assets, resources and/or activities for required result. The definition in Clark, Zmud and McCray's chapter complements this where they describe outsourcing as the delegation, through a contractual arrange-

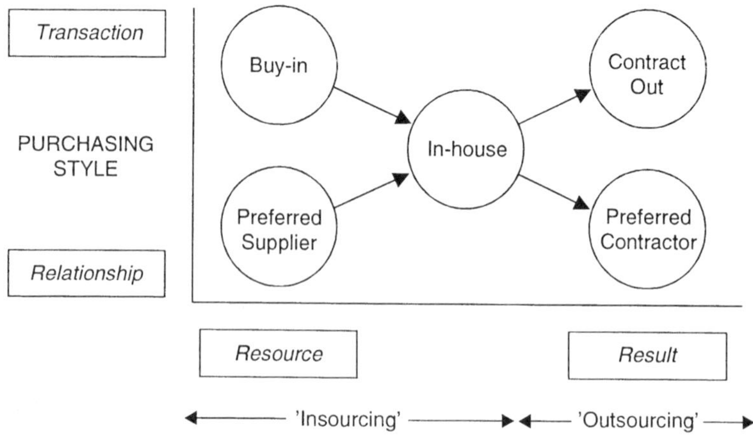

Source: Adapted from Lacity *et al.* (1996).

Figure I.1 *Clarifying Sourcing Options*

ment, of all or any part of the technical resources, the human resources and the management responsibilities associated with providing IT services, to an external vendor. To provide further clarity Figure I.1 illustrates our own view, derived from our research experiences, of the different possible relationships an organization can have with the external market for IS services (Lacity, Willcocks and Feeny, 1996).

In general, sourcing contracts can be categorized along two dimensions—purchasing style and purchasing focus. In Figure I.1 "transaction" style refers to one-time or short-term contracts with enough detail to be the original reference document. "Relationship" style refers to less detailed, incentive contracts based on the expectation that the customer and vendor will do business for many years. With a resource option, companies buy vendor resources, such as hardware, expertise or software, but manage the delivery of the IT activity themselves. With a result option vendors manage the delivery of the IT activity to provide the company with specified results. As a result four distinct contracts emerge. Only two of these—contract-out and preferred contractor—are, on our definition, outsourcing contracts.

Contract-out Strategy

Here the vendor is responsible for delivering the result of the IT activity. We have found that this strategy is most successful when organizations can clearly define their needs in an airtight contract. In practice this is not always an easy thing to achieve.

Preferred Contractor Strategy

Following this approach, organizations contract long term with a vendor to help mediate risk. The vendor is responsible for the management and delivery of an IT activity. To ensure vendor performance the organization constructs an incentive-based contract to ensure shared goals. As one example of the possibilities, in May 1990 Philips Electronics transferred its 183 software development and support staff to a new company, Origin, at the time part-owned with Dutch software house BSO. Origin's main business was providing services back to Philips, as well as on the open market (Willcocks, 1995).

Buy-in Strategy

Some organizations also "buy-in" from the external market, typically to meet a temporary resource need, for example for programmers for the latter stages of a development project. In these cases the organizations are often unsure of the exact hours needed to complete the coding, so they sign contracts that specify the skills required and cost per person.

Preferred Supplier Strategy

This strategy takes the buy-in approach further, with an organization seeking to develop a long-term close relationship with a vendor in order to access its resources for ongoing IT activities. An incentive-based contract defines complementary goals. For example, one company we researched engaged a preferred supplier to provide contract programmers whenever needed. The company was offered a volume discount in exchange for not going out to bid when it needed programmers. The vendor was motivated to perform because it relied on a steady stream of revenue. In both buy-in and preferred supplier strategies the client organization is hiring resources but it, not the vendor, is responsible for managing those resources to required result. In Figure I.1, therefore, we label these two strategies as "insourcing".

We have found that retained in-house capabilities (also defined in Figure I.1 as part of "insourcing") play a critical role, even when organizations are spending most of their IT budget on contracting out or preferred contractors. There are vital capabilities that need to be maintained in-house in order to mitigate risks inherent in IS outsourcing, namely:

- the ability to track, assess and interpret changing IT capability and relate this to organizational needs;
- the ability to work with business management to define the IT requirements over time;
- the ability to identify appropriate ways to use the market, specify and manage IT sourcing; and
- the ability to monitor and manage contractual relations.

In more recent, complementary research we have found that outsourcing forms part of a broader picture of emerging changes in the shapes of IS functions in organizations. What seems to be emerging is an IS function with four vital "faces" or roles: managing external supply, governance, identifying and delivering business requirements and providing the technical capacity the business needs. The research throws up nine key in-house capabilities and related skill sets to deliver on these roles. It also posits the need for a smaller but high-performance in-house team than previously operated in most organizations (Feeny and Willcocks, 1997).

In practice, as Part II of this book reveals, research shows organizations operating various models and approaches to how IT is used, and different mixes and degrees to which types of outsourcing, insourcing and in-house options are operated. We focus on whether there may be emerging best practices and ways forward amidst this confusing state of affairs at a later point in this Introduction. However, it can be said that increasingly we are seeing organizations using simultaneously all five modes of sourcing their various IT/IS requirements, a potential mode of operation posited in our published case of Energen—a composite of a range of researched case histories, and also demonstrated to a considerable degree in practice in the case of British Petroleum (see below. Also Cross, 1995; Lacity, Willcocks and Feeny, 1995).

On a broader front, large-scale IS outsourcing has been portrayed as symptomatic of larger, more permanent changes in the way organizations need to be focused, organized and managed. There is already a strong literature arguing the case that organizations need to focus on their core competences and activities, while contracting out that work which the market can do more cost-effectively, or that acts as a distraction from core activity (for examples only see Pralahad and Hamel, 1990, Quinn, 1992). Where does IT fit into this debate amongst organizational strategists? In some cases, and for a variety of reasons, senior executives have been inclined to perceive most, if not all of their IT not as a core competence but as an undifferentiated commodity that could be easily outsourced (Lacity, Willcocks and Feeny, 1996). Such predilections, however, tend to ignore an ongoing debate in the core competency literature itself about the ways in which information-based assets embodied in assemblies of skills and technologies can themselves form core competencies differentiating a company in terms of organizational efficiencies and its offering to customers (Quinn, 1992). In practice organizations so far have resolved these debates in different ways, with many retaining IS mostly in-house, others going down a "total" outsourcing route, while the vast majority of the more than 50 per cent of organizations that outsource have taken a selective route, typically outsourcing less than 24% of their IT budget (Collins and Millen, 1995; PA Consulting, 1996; Lacity and Willcocks, 1996a).

Amongst practitioners the return to core competencies argument is frequently made to support the case for outsourcing some or most of IS, but in fact, it also represents one of up to 20 reasons cited for undertaking IS outsourcing (Lacity, Hirschheim and Willcocks, 1994; Willcocks and Fitzgerald, 1994). When deciding whether or not to outsource, each stakeholder's perceptions and interests tend to bring a mix of financial, business, technical and political factors into play. In Chapter 1 Thomas Clark Jr., Robert Zmud and Gordon McCray provide a coherent account of the many factors and forces that influence the decision to outsource. Our own research suggests that four general drivers seem to be operating:

1. *Bandwagon effect.* IS outsourcing is often a response to the hype and publicity surrounding the subject—a bandwagon effect leads to senior managers asking: "Why don't we outsource IT/IS?"
2. *Cost reduction/containment.* Outsourcing has also often been a response to tough economic and competitive climates, and the need to cut, or at least to control costs. And indeed, as a variety of other research indicates, cost reduction remains the most frequently cited reason for undertaking IS outsourcing.
3. *New forms of organization and management.* We can find many examples where outsourcing represents an explicit strategy, or can be interpreted as a reactive move as part of larger and longer term changes in how organizations are structured and managed (see for examples Chapter 7; also PA Consulting, 1996). In addition to the core competencies argument, later in this book Kerry McLellan, Barbara Marcolin and Paul Beamish point to IS outsourcing being a response to developments in various forms of strategic networks

creating emerging "intermediate" forms of organization between the markets and hierarchy models with which we are more familiar.
4. *The IS "Money Sink"*. Finally, IS outsourcing may reflect the desire of senior managers to get rid of a troublesome function that finds it difficult to demonstrate its business value (Earl and Feeny, 1994; Willcocks, 1996).

It is clear that these forces or drivers as outlined above and in Chapter 1 will be applied through salient stakeholders own perceptions, interests and decision-making processes. The result has already been a variety of practices and ways in which organizations and IS departments have changed their forms as a result of IS outsourcing in combination with other factors. Willcocks (1995) provides several detailed examples of this variety, and also discusses where the outsourcing trend may be heading. Of course, in the longer run offshore outsourcing trends as detailed in Chapters 9 and 13 could have even more radical impacts on the nature of work and organization in industrialized economies, though both chapters note that the possible scope and advantages for offshore outsourcing are hardly unlimited. On the other hand both Chapter 11—with its case histories of outsourcing and subsequent insourcing—and Chapter 12, with its analysis of an IS outsourcing failure, perhaps bring further food for thought to the debate around whether IS outsourcing will be a long-term growing trend, whether large-scale outsourcing is the most appropriate form of outsourcing and whether IS outsourcing is driving or symptomatic of moves toward new forms of organization.

Our first chapter provides a further overview of these issues, together with a positioning of the other chapters and debates in the book. The particular contribution of Thomas Clark Jr., Robert Zmud and Gordon McCray comes from the interview programme they carried out with 63 executives representing a range of industries. Their research was motivated by the quest for the contextual variables that influence IS sourcing decisions and experiences. They found these variables to be complex and varied, but found four sets of "forces"—technology, technology management, industry and organizational—to be very influential. Their chapter details the many factors which their respondents considered as making the case for and against outsourcing, develops a preliminary framework for making sourcing decisions and also provides a detailed discussion, derived from their interview programme, on how outsourcing relationships can be managed.

THEORIZING OUTSOURCING: TRANSACTION COSTS AND BEYOND

One vital debate that Chapter 1 touches upon is the degree to which various theoretical perspectives are more (or less) useful, in explaining outsourcing outcomes and providing guidelines for practice. A dominant perspective found in the literature has been that of Transaction Cost Theory (TCT) as propounded by Williamson (1975, 1979, 1985, 1996). Several academics, such as Beath (1983), Klepper (1993), Lacity and Hirschheim (1993), and to a limited extent Bensaou (1993) and McFarlan and Nolan (1995), have proposed that TCT provides one theoretical framework for describing and explaining the IS outsourcing phenomenon. Our own research found a significant number of residuals (experiences not explained by TCT) and anomalies (experiences that contradict TCT) that challenged the applicability of TCT to the IS outsourcing context (Lacity and Willcocks, 1995). We found that residuals and anomalies existed because the nature of IT/IS outsourcing decisions tend to violate many TCT assumptions. We noted, however, that TCT proponents could explain the residuals and anomalies by appealing to TCT exceptions, such as uncertainty and small number of suppliers, or to ambiguities in TCT language. We also noted what Hodgson (1994) described as the "regrettable malleability" of TCT constructs. TCT seemed cast as a high level general theory, its uncalibrated constructs permitting empirical data to be fitted to support the theory all too easily. This becomes especially problematic where, as in several IS outsourcing studies we have reviewed, TCT is assumed to be a fully explanatory theory and few tests of its predictiveness in terms of outsourcing success or failure are carried out. This finding also raised the question, not pursued in detail here, whether other non-IT focused empirical studies actually corroborate transaction cost economics, as Williamson suggests, or also raise more questions than they answer. In fact, reviews of the limited number of empirical studies are hardly decisive (Hodgson, 1994; Joskow, 1991; Shelanski, 1991), and suggest that at the very least alternative explanatory hypotheses should be considered.

We focus initially on transaction cost economics because it has become a major starting point for those studying IS outsourcing. Furthermore, many of the chapters in this book touch on TCT and its importance in helping to understand the IS outsourcing phenomenon. In Chapter 2 Varun Grover, James Teng and Myun Cheon add to the debate by providing a detailed overview of several alternative theoretical models of outsourcing. While these include resource-based theory, resource-dependence theory, transaction cost and agency cost theories, the authors advance the debate even further by putting forward a contingency model for IS outsourcing. They invite further expansion of the model as well as its use as a guide for future empirical research. Thomas Clark, Robert Zmud and Gordon McCray also show how:

> "if rational cost-economizing behaviour defines one end of the spectrum, then viewing decision outcomes as the result of power and politics defines the other ... the two perspectives are not, however, mutually exclusive."

Leon De Loof, in Chapter 8, also shows how additional theories and frameworks, including coordination theory and perspectives gleaned from the competitive strategy and microeconomics literatures, can be usefully employed in the process of setting up a research design for subsequent empirical work on IS outsourcing.

Much of this indicates both the potential richness but also the dangers of theoretical confusion and complexity in the possible routes forward. There are dangers as well as advantages inherent in theoretical eclecticism. One issue is the degree to which the theories utilized are compatible or can be developed to be so. A second is the extent to which the theories selected are appropriate for the phenomena studied. Here the guidelines the authors offer for good theory in Chapter 2 are worth noting, though perhaps they are more relevant for positivist than interpretive research:

> "The function of a theory, then, fulfil the objectives of prediction (knowledge of the outcome) and understanding (knowledge of the process) regarding the relationships among the variables of interest ... a good theory enables one to predict what will happen given a set of values for certain variables, and to understand why this predicted value should result ... [and] ... enables one to determine whether the theory is constructed such that empirical refutation is possible."

A third issue is the degree to which theories are brought into Information Systems studies from other disciplines uncritically, in particular without bringing to bear the various debates around the theory present in its original discipline. Our own view is that this certainly has been happening frequently with Transaction Cost Theory (Lacity and Willcocks, 1995).

A further approach is to apply two or more different theories to a phenomena, examine the findings from each separately then compare and contrast the findings. Lacity and Hirschheim (1993), for example, did this in case study work, utilizing Transaction Cost Theory and a political model derived largely from Pfeffer (1981). One other approach is to apply one internally consistent set of propositions and perspectives that has been widely utilized in other, similar fields of study. This is the position adopted in Chapter 3 where Ramy Elitzur and Anthony Wensley make a persuasive case for applying Game Theory to the analysis and explication of IS outsourcing contracts. Here the authors provide a review of two-person non-co-operative games and stress the importance of the information structure of two-person games. They then provide a general game-theoretic interpretation of many key aspects of IS outsourcing arrangements. These include different ways of determining fees, the effects of transferring assets, and issues concerning risk-sharing relationship management, technology upgrading and contract duration. Finally they indicate how a principal-agent model can provide insights into IS outsourcing arrangements. On this reading, Game Theory would seem to offer a potentially rich theoretical framework for studying IS outsourcing, and what is now needed is to put it to work empirically, to test its applicability, to see if it can be developed further for IS studies, and to discover the type and quality of insights it can yield.

The authors in this book make at least three further distinctive theoretical contributions.

1. *Organizing knowledge*. In Chapter 4, Harry Scarbrough proposes a different theoretical perspective for understanding IS outsourcing, that is: "viewing it not as the product of a decision process, but, more fundamentally, as a particular way of organizing knowledge". Scarbrough points out that focusing exclusively on the motives and outcomes of IS outsourcing, or even on the decision processes themselves, fails to address critical questions to do with the way IS knowledge is communicated, organized and applied. From this perspective outsourcing and insourcing are neither good nor bad in themselves but represent responses to the problems of organizing different kinds of knowledge important in the initial sourcing decisions but also in the long-run effectiveness of the contractual arrangements produced. Scarbrough proceeds firstly by revising Williamson's transactional model. This involves redefining transactions, and accounting much more fully for the roles of knowlege, innovation, and knowledge communication/transfer in IS outsourcing arrangements. A particular strength of this chapter is the way in which the author then applies these theoretical developments to five case studies concerned with the organization of IS knowledge.
2. *Risk-return in IS outsourcing*. Jaak Jurison, in Chapter 6, also provides a theoretical paper in working through, once again, transaction cost theory assumptions but this time together with modern theory of investments and finance. He arrives at a decision-making model for

IS outsourcing in conditions of risk. In practice Jurison integrates a risk and return model with transaction cost economics, thus enriching the perspective TCT can provide on IS outsourcing. This is important because in all too many evaluations, risk is given inadequate attention (Willcocks, Lacity and Fitzgerald 1995). Furthermore, the model can be used not just to assess outsourcing against in-house options, but also for assessment of competing vendors. Jaak Jurison also points out, correctly, that the risk and return model is not restricted in its applicability to TCT but can also provide a rich framework for analysing decisions from political and agency theory perspectives, and can also be applied to assessing the degree of risk where there are conflicts between client and vendor goals.

3. *Partnering and relationships in IS outsourcing*. Finally, there is also a theoretical contribution made by Robert Klepper in Chapter 10. The importance of partnering and relationships in IS outsourcing is widely acknowledged amongst researchers and practitioners alike. However, as far as IS outsourcing is concerned, there has been all too little rigorous analysis of what makes for successful and less successful relationships and the affect this can have on the long-term viability of the contractual arrangements. In practice, along with Henderson (1990), Robert Klepper provides one of the few reasonably robust and academically derived frameworks for the study of relationships in IS outsourcing. It is significant that in order to do so, Klepper, after reviewing other contributions, needs to move to the Dwyer, Schurr and Oh (1987) model from the marketing literature. Klepper also demonstrates the usefulness and applicability of this model through two case studies. In fact, the issues he deals with have been widely theorized and studied in the industrial networks and marketing fields, and it may well be that further insight can be gained from applying and adapting other work. As one example Kumar and Willcocks (1996) and Willcocks and Kern (1997) have put forward the interaction approach developed by the IMP Group (1990) for the study of buyer-seller relationships. In these two contributions it is used in the study of relationships between client and vendor organizations in the cases of USA-India offshore outsourcing and "strategic partnering" between EDS and the United Kingdom Inland Revenue.

REVEALING IS OUTSOURCING PRACTICE

Given the relative immaturity of the IS outsourcing market, and the lack of experience of many client organizations in dealing with IS outsourcing, we still need a continuing flow of empirical evidence, not least in order to assess the viability of explanatory theoretical frameworks, to provide insight into how outsourcing arrangements unravel, as opposed to the declared expectations (Lacity, Hirschheim and Willcocks, 1994), and also as some basis for testing out any prescriptions for good practice. Part II adds significantly to the already extant complex picture on how IS outsourcing is being practised. Additionally Chapters 1 and 4 also contain some rich empirical work. Together the studies covered in these chapters are international in scope, having been carried out in the USA, India, Finland, Canada, Singapore and Europe, including the Netherlands and United Kingdom. The book reveals detail on six main practice issues, on which we will now comment briefly.

Outsourcing Alliances: North American Evidence

The main studies of the North American scene, where the IS outsourcing trend started earlier and has grown at the fastest rate, are found in Chapters 1, 7 and 9. As indicated above, Chapter 1 provides an overview of IS outsourcing developments in the USA. In Chapter 7 Kerry McLellan, Barbara Marcolin and Paul Beamish provide additional empirical material in their in-depth study of seven outsourcing alliances in the US/North American banking industry. In general the outsourcing contracts had been signed in the late 1980s for a five to ten year period. In all cases, at least 75 per cent of the IS budget was outsourced, representing a major organizational change for these firms. Their particular focus is on the financial and strategic motivations behind these outsourcing arrangements. They found financial motivations as a key part of the IS outsourcing decision—two financial institutions had disappointing financial performance before outsourcing, and one was experiencing clear financial difficulties—but there were also important strategic motivations that influenced each of the seven decisions. This chapter is highly useful as a sectoral-based study that adds to the picture on major long-term outsourcing collaborations. It also serves to position the more iconoclastic work presented by Paul Strassmann (1995a and b). In analysing companies frequently mentioned in the press for their outsourcing actions, he concluded that there was a strong correlation between heavy outsourcing of IT and a company's prior financial position and headcount reduction strategy:

> "corporations that outsourced heavily were economic losers heading into the outsourcing act. ... the losers were casting off IT because they were already shrinking their firm."

Interestingly, the majority of cases cited by Strassmann refer to contracts signed after 1990, while McLellan, Marcolin and Beamish studied contracts starting in the 1977–90 period. Their last deal—First Fidelity Bank and EDS, August 1990—is not mentioned in the Strassmann study.

To further this debate it is worth commenting on our own research findings on "total" outsourcing successes and failures (Lacity and Willcocks, 1996). We investigated 61 sourcing decisions in USA and Europe; 14 of these were total outsourcing decisions of the sort investigated by McLellan, Marcolin and Beamish, and also Strassmann. Our particular focus was on success and failure. We measured this by comparing outcomes against participant expectations; against "anticipated cost savings" since cost savings were cited as a major expectation in 85 per cent of cases, and there were clear financial outcomes in 53 of the sourcing decisions; and against satisfaction factors, for example service levels maintained or better, low levels of dispute, decision to renew contract. In discounting all those deals where the outcome was not clear, or where it was too early into the contract to tell, of 14 total outsourcing decisions two could be adjudged successful and five unsuccessful. This contrasted remarkably with the selective sourcing record where out of 32 decisions 22 were successful, and only four were unsuccessful (Lacity and Willcocks, 1996). Clearly this is becoming a very interesting area of academic study, especially given the drive amongst many vendors and some companies for large-scale outsourcing and long-term deals.

The Insourcing Option

A further debate—investigated in detail empirically by Lacity and Hirschheim (1995)—relates to how far in-house departments can match, or even surpass, vendor performance. Some have argued (for example Earl, 1996) that IS outsourcing is not only high risk, but may also, in most cases, be unnecessary. Indeed there is mounting empirical evidence to show that companies can achieve required cost reductions internally without outsourcing. As one example, Bergstrom (1991) found companies reducing data centre costs by 17–25 per cent a year without outsourcing. Lacity and Hirschheim (1995) added to this evidence by showing how, in six insourcing cases drawn from different industrial sectors in the USA, cost reductions of between 20–54 per cent combined with headcount reductions of 21–51 per cent were achieved. A qualification to their finding is that there is invariably a cost-service trade-off involved: it is not possible to achieve a Rolls Royce service at a

Chevrolet price. However, this is quite frequently a finding in cases of IS outsourcing, as the authors point out in their earlier work (see Lacity and Hirschheim, 1993). The argument for insourcing is further pursued in the empirical work in Chapter 11, as will be discussed below.

Effective IS Users and Outsourcing

The other detailed empirical analysis of US developments is in Chapter 9, by Marion Sobol and Uday Apte. Their study of US-based organizations investigates, amongst other issues, what type of companies are more likely to outsource IS; what is being outsourced; what are the reasons advanced for and against outsourcing; who initiates and who makes the final decision. These results help to give more detail to what organizational practices are in the outsourcing arena. The authors also make a new contribution in their examination of domestic versus "global" (i.e. US firms outsourcing to non-US vendors) outsourcing. "Global" or offshore outsourcing is very much a developing field but has been the subject of little study so far. While the authors' work is restricted to looking at US firms, their chapter does manage to shed a great deal of light on the reasons why organizations may choose to undertake—or not—"global" outsourcing. One interesting finding is that the median cost saving needed for US-based outsourcing emerged as 20 per cent, while for global outsourcing it was 30 per cent —presumably reflecting the higher risks associated with offshore outsourcing, but also, perhaps revealing the predominant driver of global outsourcing, at least in the early 1990s.

Offshore Outsourcing

This debate is taken further in Chapter 13 on offshore IS outsourcing, where the focus is on the possibilities for US firms. T. Rajkumar and Donald Dawley provide a detailed overview study of the risks, benefits and conditions under which offshore software development in India is practicable for US firms. A particular strength of their study is to present the issues from both client and vendor market perspectives. It is useful to compare this chapter with the detailed findings of Kumar and Willcocks (1996). They analysed longitudinally a 1993–96 case of outsourcing by Holiday Inns, Atlanta to an Indian supplier. Apart from large cost savings, they found that IT could be an enabling technology co-ordinating the work between USA and India, though in this case the control possibilities of IT were not fully utilized, to the detriment of the project's progress. They also found that offshore outsourcing provided positive benefits in terms of round-the-clock work by taking advantage of time zone differences. Furthermore, and somewhat ironically, offshore outsourcing reduced interpersonal problems arising from cultural differences when client and vendor staff initially worked together in Atlanta more on an insourcing basis. The study also found that the move to offsite development could not work without substantive contract maintenance mechanisms, and these were somewhat lacking in the case investigated.

Studying Outsourcing Failure

One remaining chapter in Part II provides a detailed outsourcing case history. In Chapter 12 Soon Ang and See Kiat-Toh investigate a software outsourcing failure, and thus provide further evidence of the risks in outsourcing outlined by Jurison in Chapter 6, and some evidence supporting the argument for insourcing. However, on the researchers' analysis, failure could be related to critical hierarchical elements missing from the contract. Authority relations were unclear in the outsourcing arrangements in terms of assignment of duties and responsibilities, project scope and authority over personnel changes. Furthermore the rule-based incentive system lost its effectiveness as project costs soared and time schedules slipped badly. The cost of the project was poorly estimated and the price was fixed with one vendor without considering other bids. Dispute resolution mechanisms were poor, while standardized operating procedures and documentation for the project were lacking. There are many learning points in this study, and the way it was carried out, for researchers and practitioners alike. Not only do the authors demonstrate the importance of carrying out a *post mortem* on a failed project, but they also indicate critical factors that need to be taken into account in outsourcing arrangements in order to mitigate risk.

The IS Department as Vendor

In Chapter 11, Tapio Reponen provides a longitudinal study of six cases of a special form of outsourcing—where a new outsourcing enterprise is developed from an internal IS department. Our own work has found this a difficult venture to engage in, at least in economies where there are highly developed and competitive vendor marketplaces already extant, as in, for example, the USA and UK. Usually the new vendor is very dependent on its own parent company for business for several years (Willcocks, Fitzgerald and Lacity, 1996). Reponen researched cases in Finland in the period 1987–94. In two cases, in changed circumstances, the experiment was curtailed and the IS department recreated in-house. The study found that it took at least two years to stabilize operations in the newly-created vendor companies. The most important influencers of success included the ability to obtain outside sales, together with four personnel-related factors, namely: the motivation, customer orientation, cumulative experience and efficiency of the IT professional staff comprising the outsourced enterprise.

Some support for both outsourcing and insourcing occurs in the two detailed case studies the researcher provides. In the case of a wholesale-retail chain it was reorganization, changing technology platforms and a merger that resulted in the IS function being variously outsourced and insourced at different times. In the case of a construction company the IS department became an external vendor that became subject to rationalization. Six years later network and financial services were re-established in-house and the rest sold to a software house. A major merger, and the way it handled IT issues then re-established the credibility of the in-house operation which grew in size with only programming and computer operations being outsourced. This study by Tapio Reponen is highly useful for demonstrating the advantages gained from investigating longitudinal and historical dimensions by means of case studies. It also provides detailed examples of how IT/IS requirements should be considered as dynamic over time, and how a range of contingent factors rarely allow outsourcing or insourcing to be final, let alone complete solutions to sourcing IS capability. (Further support for this argument can also be found in Lacity, Willcocks and Feeny, 1995.)

ARE THERE EMERGING MANAGEMENT PRINCIPLES?

The book also seeks to make a contribution to providing guidelines for how to conduct outsourcing assessments, assess vendors and manage outsourcing arrangements. Of course a feature is that each chapter provides, in addition to its main focus and to a varying degree, some guidelines and principles for practitioners (see in particular Chapters 1, 3, 6, 11 and 13). Our own research work has also suggested a range of prescriptions in these areas. Thus a 1996 paper provided a number of matrices to enable a sourcing assessment to be carried out through examining the primary business, technical and economic factors emerging from an analysis of case studies and survey responses (Lacity,

Willcocks and Feeny, 1996). We have also suggested a range of guidelines on assessment issues and on managing the contract and vendor once the deal has been agreed (see for example Lacity and Hirschheim, 1995; Willcocks, Lacity and Fitzgerald, 1995). We have, of course, not been alone in this (see for examples only Buck-Lew, 1992; Loh and Venkatraman, 1992b; McFarlan and Nolan, 1995). As research proceeds, so ever new or more detailed guidelines will be seen to emerge. Thus our own most recent research suggests, amongst other things, that selective sourcing is the key to rightsourcing; that senior executives, acting without IT's input make poor outsourcing decisions; that internal IT departments should be allowed to compete with external vendor bids; and that shorter (less than four years) contracts are more successful than longer contracts (Lacity and Willcocks, 1996).

This will not be the end of the research story, especially as the types of outsourcing, what the market can offer, and client maturity are already changing over time. For the moment, however, the chapters in the book provide additional detail on two main areas of prescription:

Decision Frameworks

In Chapter 5 Jonathan Cronk and John Sharp add to the literature by offering a further strategic framework for the outsourcing decision. They suggest how core competence and segmentation analyses of the IT function can be carried out, including analysis of infrastructure activity and the management of the technology life cycle. A particular contribution is their adaptation and use of the Perry, Stott and Smallwood (1993) model for making sourcing decisions in both private and public sectors. The public sector is particularly under-studied and under-represented in terms of management prescription (but see Lacity and Willcocks, 1997). Cronk and Sharp provide a useful development by introducing into IS analysis the notion of Leading Competence Advantage (LCA). An LCA on a particular aspect of IS activity exists in a public sector organization where there are no potential external IS suppliers with greater competence in performing that activity. The notion replaces that of an IS activity in a private sector being a "critical differentiator", that is giving a firm competitive advantage over rival firms.

Leon De Loof's research described in Chapter 8 is particularly welcome for providing further insight into practice in a European—in this case Dutch—context. As indicated above, it is clear that the US outsourcing market is by far the biggest and most advanced and that in Europe the United Kingdom represents the biggest and the fastest developing market. However, there does seem to have been a slow increase in outsourcing across the more developed European economies, particularly in public sector organizations (IDC, 1996 reported on 20 May, http://www.outsourcing.com; PA Consulting, 1996). Leon de Loof carried out an analysis of 23 IS outsourcing arrangements in six, mainly public sector, organizations. He produces a wealth of detail on the reasons for outsourcing, who made the decisions, the size of outsourcing, how bids were organized, the management of the outsourcing process, and the results organizations were getting. He, too, derives a sourcing decision framework from his empirical work.

Partnering and Relationships

Once an outsourcing deal has been agreed, how it is managed and the quality of the relationship between client and vendor staff become important factors in the outcomes gained. Robert Klepper devotes Chapter 10 to the partnering issue and his highly useful review of partnering studies in the management literature finds that social exchange theory underlies many of the contributions. He then utilizes work by Ring and Van de Ven (1994) and Dwyer, Schur and Oh (1987) to show how partnerships in IS outsourcing may be studied, but also built and sustained. The development of this work on aspects of partnering in IS outsourcing is critically needed given, firstly, the rising number of long-term "total" outsourcing contracts in the 1990s in the developed economies, and, secondly, as indicated above, the relatively few extant studies that have dealt in detail with partnering specifically in the IS outsourcing context (for examples see Henderson, 1990; McFarlan and Nolan, 1995; Willcocks, 1995; Willcocks and Kern, 1997). As already argued, following Robert Klepper's lead, there may well be many extant useful theories and frameworks to be found in alternative, non-IS literatures; the strategic alliance and marketing literatures would seem to be particularly replete with work done on the partnering issue.

SOURCING AND OUTSOURCING: TRENDS AND FUTURE ISSUES

Having examined the contribution made by this book to understanding IS outsourcing developments, it remains to consider what current trends are and where they may lead. Here we will consolidate points made earlier, comment on what is emerging good practice, and suggest the future critical issues that are ripe for study and practitioner attention.

Selective IS Sourcing

Although the large multi-million dollar long-term deals make headlines, research has systematically unveiled that selective IS sourcing is much the more common practice, a trend we expect to continue (Lacity, Willcocks and Feeny, 1995). In addition to Chapter 9, the following surveys found selective sourcing as the most common practice:

- In a survey of 300 IS managers in the US, on average less than 10 per cent of the IT budget was outsourced (Caldwell, 1996a).
- A survey of 110 Fortune 500 companies found that 76 per cent spent less than 20 per cent of the IT budget on outsourcing, and 96 per cent spent less than 40% (Collins and Millen, 1995).
- A survey of 365 US companies found that 65 per cent outsourced one or more IT activities, but only 12 outsourced IT completely (Dekleva, 1994).
- A survey by IDC found that "in the United States, outsourcing takes around 17 per cent share of the IT services market" (Foley, 1993).

Sears, Roebuck, and Co. provides an example of selective sourcing. As at 1997 Sears had two contracts—one contract with ISSC for distributed systems and the help desk, and one contract with Advantis (a joint venture between Sears and IBM) for mainframes. Sears has been focusing the new internal IT staff on development of new applications while the IT vendors manage the "old world". As its Senior Systems Director stated: "The more mundane IS functions we outsource, the better we can leverage our resources" (*Chainstore Age Executive*, 1996).

A further feature worth commenting on is that most organizations are successful with their selective sourcing strategies. Success is defined here as meeting expected sourcing objectives. In practice only a few studies have assessed expected outcomes against actual outcomes:

- In a survey of 110 Fortune 500 companies, Collins and Millen (1995) found that 95 per cent realized increased flexibility, 95 per cent focused in-house staff on IS core competencies, 86 per cent realized personnel cost savings, and 88 per cent improved service.
- Lacity and Willcocks (1996) studied 61 sourcing decisions, including total outsourcing, total insourcing, and selective sourcing. We interviewed over 150 senior executives, IT managers, IT staff, business managers, and vendors, as well as collected requests-for-proposals, bid analysis reports, contracts and many other documents. Although there were 15 reasons given for sourcing decisions, cost reduction was the most prevalent (80 per cent), followed by

> service improvements (59 per cent). We found that 85 per cent of selective sourcing decisions met customers' expected cost savings, whereas only 29 per cent of total outsourcing decisions and 67 per cent of total insourcing decisions met expected cost savings.

Other surveys did not include a measure of success, but instead asked respondents for expected outcomes. For example, in a survey of 48 of 100 US companies on *Computerworld*'s Premier 100 list, 90 per cent expected to save money with their sourcing decisions (see Chapter 9). Other important expectations, in order of rank, included reduced need to hire IS professionals, improved cost predictability, and improved focus on strategic use of IT.

Why is selective sourcing successful? Information technology spans a variety of activities in terms of business contribution, integration with existing processes, and level of technical maturity. Such diversity demands tailored solutions. Typically, no one vendor or internal IT department possesses the experience and economies of scale to perform all IT activities most effectively. While some activities, especially stable IT activities with known requirements, may be easily outsourced, other IT activities require much management attention, protection and nurturing to ensure business success.

In 1996–7 the types of IT services most commonly outsourced continued to be low-level and/or routine, IT activities, with the exception of applications development. In the US, surveys indicate that the types of services most commonly outsourced are contract programming, education and training, PC maintenance, disaster recovery, applications development, and data entry. Although surveys rank-order the most commonly outsourced IT activities differently, these same activities surface again and again (Apte, Sobol *et al.*, 1997; Dekleva, 1994; Grover, Cheon and Teng, 1996). No surveys found that companies outsource strategic planning, environmental scanning, or customer liaisons, and surveys generally indicate that 60 per cent of applications are still developed in-house. Several studies have now found that outsourcing low-level and/or routine IT activities has been generally successful. Grover *et al.* (1996) conducted two surveys (n=68 and n=188) and correlated the types of IT functions outsourced with perceived success. They found a high rate of perceived success associated with outsourcing systems operations and telecommunications, but outsourcing applications development, end user support, and systems management "did not lead to increased satisfaction" (p. 103).

We found that selective sourcing was highly successful because deals were short-term (Lacity, Willcocks and Feeny, 1996). Short-term contracts were preferable to long-term contracts because:

1. technology and business conditions could not be predicted for more than three years; thus contracts became increasingly outdated as time progressed;
2. short-term contracts motivated vendor performance because vendors realized customers could have switched suppliers when the contract expired;
3. short-term contracts allowed companies to recover and learn more quickly from mistakes.

In addition we found that it was easier for participants to outsource technically mature activities because they understood how to cost and evaluate such activities and could thus negotiate a sound contract (Willcocks and Fitzgerald, 1994). In essence, "technically mature" IT activities had become "routine".

Transitional Outsourcing

Transitional outsourcing is the practice of temporarily outsourcing during a major transition to a new technology. Transitional outsourcing has been gaining momentum as a solution to, for example, the resource shortage caused by the advent of client/server computing. Companies do not have the staff to simultaneously run legacy systems while building new client/server applications.

One of the first highly-advertised cases of transitional outsourcing was Sun Microsystems. In 1993, Sun Microsystems signed a three-year, $27 million dollar outsourcing contract with CSC. CSC ran Sun's legacy systems while Sun's staff built client/server systems. By 1997 similar deals have included the following:

- Elf Alochem signed a four-year, $4.3 million contract with Keane, a Boston company. Keane maintains Elf Alochem's accounting systems (which run on a range of platforms) while Alochem's internal staff develops a migration to client/server (Heichler, 1995).
- Owens-Corning Fiberglass signed a five-year, $50 million contract with Hewlett-Packard. HP maintains the legacy systems while the Owens-Corning IS staff implements SAP (which runs on a client/server platform) in 75 sites worldwide (King, 1995).
- NASDAQ stock exchange outsourced legacy systems to Tate Consulting Services (Bombay, India) while the NASDAQ IT staff develops client/server (Guterl, 1996).

In general, transitional outsourcing has been experienced as successful. Legacy systems are technically mature, and thus customers can negotiate a sound support contract for a short period of time. In addition, customers who focus in-house staff on the development of new technologies often "buy-in" vendor resources to supplement in-house skills. This strategy worked well in the cases Willcocks and Fitzgerald (1994) studied because the in-house staff provided the needed business perspective, while the vendor transferred technical skills during the project. By the time the new systems were complete, significant organizational learning had occurred so that the customer was able to support the new technology themselves, or in some cases, negotiate a sound maintenance contract. Subramanian and Lacity (1997) studied first-time implementations of client/server. In each of the three companies studied, the system was developed successfully in-house, but outside expertise was hired in to evaluate the technical plan, train the IS staff, or help with the conversion.

We would expect this transitional sourcing strategy to continue to be adopted as good practice in the type of circumstances described above. Transitional outsourcing is a form of selective sourcing. As at 1997, selective sourcing continued to be the practice most companies pursued, and the success rate for this strategy appeared to be high. Given the diversity of assets, skills, and capabilities required to provide the diversity of IT activities, selective sourcing enables organizations to seek the best sourcing option for given IT activities. Selective sourcing creates an environment of competition which overcomes organizational impediments to improvement and motivates performance. Selective sourcing also provides flexibility to adapt to changes, allows companies to capitalize on organizational learning, and is less risky than total outsourcing.

Selective sourcing, however, does have one major limitation: the transaction costs associated with multiple evaluations, multiple contract negotiations, and multiple vendors to manage and coordinate. Some organizations have rejected selective sourcing for this reason, and instead seek total outsourcing solutions, with fewer evaluations, fewer contracts (although the remaining contracts are wider in scope and longer in duration), and fewer vendors to manage and coordinate. Having noted earlier the problems with traditional total outsourcing contracts, we further document the problems associated with fixed-price, exchange-based, total contracts and discuss pioneering companies that are trying to reduce the risks of total outsourcing through creative contracts and alliances.

"Total" IS Outsourcing

Throughout the 1990s the press was increasingly reporting on major fixed-price, exchange-based, long-term, total IT outsourcing deals that were being renegotiated. In practice few of this type of total IT outsourcing deals are reaching maturity without major stumbling blocks. Increasingly conflicts have been resolved through contract renegotiations, or in some cases, through early termination. Examples of contract renegotiations include:

- Enron renegotiated its seven-year, $2 billion contract (signed in 1989) with EDS after three years—the original contract improperly defined baseline services and service levels.
- When First Union acquired First Fidelity, it renegotiated a ten-year contract between First Fidelity and EDS because the contract did not meet the needs caused by the change in business (O'Heney, 1996).
- TransAlta almost terminated their $75 million outsourcing deal to DEC due to poor customer service, but the newly-appointed VP decided to renegotiate because he feared terminating the service during a software roll-out (*CFO Magazine*, 1996).
- Xerox and EDS renegotiated their $3.2 billion, 10-year contract only two years into the contract (Hoffman, 1996). The original Xerox contract was partially modelled on Chase Manhattan's contract (Burch, 1994).
- Chase Manhattan Bank was reported to be renegotiating its $90 million per year contract with AT&T (signed in 1994) after the contract impeded the success of an acquisition (Hoffman, 1996b).

A high rate of renegotiation has been so prevalent that some customers have been including renegotiation stages in the original contract. For example, California Federal Bank's long-term contract with Alltel Information Services was designed as a "Protocol of Change". The Executive Vice President for the bank stated that: "Our contract is written so that we can easily add to or reduce the scope without going through arduous negotiations". (Reported in O'Heney, 1996.)

There are also examples of contract termination:

- Zale Corp signed a ten-year deal with ISSC in 1989. After Zale recovered from bankruptcy in 1994, they decided to terminate the ISSC contract early and find another vendor. Zale signed a letter of intent with SHL Systemhouse in May 1996. The proposed contract will be a "performance-based" contract in which SHLs earnings will partly depend on Zale's performance. The idea is that IT is so critical to a retailer's success, that the vendor's profits should be tied to the customer's profits (Caldwell, 1996a).
- Chase Manhattan Bank terminated its contract with Fiserv for check

processing when it got in the way of their merger with Chemical. Chase paid Fiserv $15 million to terminate the contract (O'Heney, 1996).

- Lacity and Hirschheim (1993) studied one chemical company that terminated a seven-year contract prematurely due to unexpected excess fees and poor service. The company rebuilt an IT department by purchasing mid-range technology and "buying back" 40 former IT employees from the vendor. In another instance, a manufacturing company terminated an outsourcing contract in one of their subsidiaries when IT costs rose to 4 per cent of sales in that subsidiary. The company migrated the subsidiary's systems to the parent company's data centre.

Some companies have been *avoiding* contract renegotiations by beginning long-term relationships with short-term contracts. For example, Cigna began what they hoped to be a long-term relationship with Entex Information Systems with a one-year contract (see below). Other companies have been *planning* for renegotiations within the original contract by including annual or bi-annual renegotiation clauses (Menagh, 1995).

As discussed earlier, organizations most likely to outsource on a large scale have tended to be in poor financial situations, had poor IS functions, and/or had IS functions with little status within their organizations. The findings of Strassmann (1995a) and Lacity and Willcocks (1996), discussed earlier, have some support from the following:

- In a sample of 55 major US corporations, Loh and Venkatraman (1992a) found that outsourcing was negatively related to IS performance and positively related to IS costs.
- Arnett and Jones (1994) surveyed 40 CIOs to determine the structural features which distinguish companies that outsource IT from companies that insource. They found that companies that outsourced were characterized by: lower CEO involvement in IT, CEOs who do not personally use a computer, and heads of IS who are several reporting levels from the CEO.

Our own assessment of trends is that many total outsourcing deals have been entered into by client organizations from a position of weakness, and that, unfortunately, outsourcing cannot typically transform a weak organization into a strong one. Thus in a general study of over 200 alliances, Bleeke and Ernst (1995) found that alliances failed when weak companies partnered with strong companies. In another study of 37 companies comprising over 500 interviews, Kanter (1994) found that

- Value-added Outsourcing—"combining strengths to market IT products/services"
- Equity Holdings—"we own a piece of each other"
- Multi-sourcing—"one contract, multiple suppliers"
- Co-sourcing—"performance-based contracts"
- Spin-offs—"internal IT departments go to market"
- Creative Contracting—"tougher shoppers"

Figure I.2 *IS Sourcing—Emerging Practices*

both partners must be strong in order for the alliance to work. Alliances work when each "partner" brings something to the table—something we are seeing more organizations trying to achieve in "value-added" outsourcing.

New Approaches to Large-scale Outsourcing

Several new strategic sourcing trends have been emerging in the 1995–7 period, would seem to be accelerating, and will provide new challenges and opportunities for study. These trends are shown in Figure I.2.

Valued-added Outsourcing

Customers have been looking for "value-added" from their IT outsourcing suppliers. With value-added outsourcing, the "partners" combine strengths to add value, such as selling jointly-developed products and services to the external marketplace. Because each partner shares in the revenue generated from external sales, the partnership is not based on an exchange, but rather an alliance with shared risks and rewards.

One of the biggest deals touted as a "value-added" deal was the Xerox-EDS contract. Unlike many other large total outsourcing deals, Xerox was not in a position of financial weakness when they negotiated the contract. At the time of the contract signing, the President of EDS and CEO of Xerox commented:

> "We realized that each of our companies brought to the table specific best-in-class capabilities that enabled a level of performance that neither could achieve independently. This is a case of two technology companies enabling one another to achieve a shared vision for adding value for their customers." (*reported on 10 October 1996 on WWW at http://www.xerox.com/PR/NR950321-EDS.html*)

In this case, value-added took the form of future shared revenues for the development and sale of a global electronic document distribution service.

Other examples of value-added contracts include:

- Kodak and IBM formed Technology Service Solutions to provide multivendor PC maintenance and support services to the manufacturing industry.
- Mutual Life Insurance of New York and CSC market software and services to the insurance industry.
- Andersen Consulting and Dow Chemical formed a strategic alliance in which the partners plan to sell any systems developed for Dow to external customers. The services are being offered through three alliance centres—two in the US and one in Belgium—which encompass Dow Chemicals $100 million per year investment in IS consulting, projects, and applications support (Moran, 1996).

Value-added deals promise to overcome many of the limitations of fixed-fee, exchange-based contracts, but the partners must truly add value by offering products and services demanded by customers in the market. They must possess distinctive advantages in the marketplace to achieve success. In some cases customers have used the term "value-added" to describe their "exchange-based" contracts when they hoped to gain something extra by outsourcing with a particular vendor. For example, in one case a large aerospace company signed a multi-billion dollar outsourcing contract for ten years in 1994. The company selected the vendor because it has major contracts with other aerospace companies. The customer believed this company would "add value" because of access to software and services in the aerospace industry. But the deal was an exchange-based contract. The vendor was (and is) not free to share products and services from other clients. Some time into the contract, the IT Services Director claimed:

> "Yes, [the vendor] can achieve all the things that were proposed—but where is this famous 'added-value' service? We are not getting anything over-and-above what any old outsourcer could provide."

Equity Holdings

One of the major limitations of the traditional exchange-based contract is that the customer and vendor had no shared risk and reward. The vendor's profits were based on maximizing their profit given the fixed-fee and by charging excess fees for services beyond the contract. The customer's profits were based on trying to get as many services as possible for the fixed fee, hoping for free upgrades and access to new technology. To tie their futures together more closely, some companies have been buying each other's stocks. These include vendors buying client's stock, clients buying vendor's stock, or both parties taking stake in the formation of a new entity (Lacity and Hirschheim, 1997).

For example, in 1996 Swiss Bank signed a 25-year outsourcing deal with Perot Systems worth $6.25 billion. The partners agreed to sell client/server solutions to the banking industry. The bank had an option to acquire up to 25 per cent shares in Perot Systems and Perot Systems would acquire a share of a European software company—Systor AG—owned by the bank (O'Heney, 1996). Subsequently 520 Swiss Bank employees joined forces with about 200 Perot System employees. Swiss Bank retained sole control of all security-related functions, proprietary applications and hardware, while the alliance covered global operations, management and system engineering functions (Schmerken and Goldman, 1996).

There are other examples of equity-holding deals:

- Delta Airlines and AT&T(NCR) formed TransQuest to provide IT solutions to the airline/travel industry. Under the $2.8 billion, ten-year agreement, Delta transferred 1100 employees and 3000 applications to TransQuest while NCR contributed 30 employees, software and cash. Their goal was to generate $1 million a year for the 50-50 partnership. In 1996, however, the joint venture was terminated with Delta bringing everything back in-house. A 1996 article speculated that NCR's inexperience with large-scale professional service deals was a major contributing factor to the early termination (Hoffman, 1996b).
- In 1996 Telestra (Australia's telecommunications company) was negotiating to outsource its IT to ISSC, which in turn would outsource its network operations and management to Telestra. Additionally, Telestra would take a 26 per cent stake in ISSC. In Canada, Bell Canada and IBM Canada were reportedly negotiating a similar kind of deal (Hirschheim, 1996).

Time is needed to test the viability of these new jointly-owned entities. While the mechanism of truly shared risks and rewards does overcome the previous conflict of exchange-based contracts, these new entities must have a core competence so they can attract external customers. In essence, equity deals are "value-added" deals with the additional incentive of shared ownership. In some companies we are currently studying, these new entities still gain nearly all their revenue earnings from the original customer.

Multi-sourcing

In 1995, Cross described the multi-vendor outsourcing strategy of British Petroleum. Rather than totally outsource to one vendor, BP hired three suppliers under an umbrella contract which obligated the suppliers to work together:

> "We decided against receiving all our IT needs from a single supplier as some companies have done, because we believed such an approach could make us vulnerable to escalating fees and inflexible services. Instead, we sought a solution that would allow us both to buy IT services from multiple suppliers and to have pieces delivered as if they came from a single supplier." (*Cross, 1995*).

BP reported that this sourcing strategy reduced the IT staff by 80 per cent, and reduced IT operating costs from $360 million in 1989 to $132 million in 1994.

In July 1996, JP Morgan announced a similar multi-vendor strategy. JP Morgan signed a seven-year, $2.1 billion dollar contract with four major vendors. Computer Sciences Corporation (Pinnacle Alliance) became responsible for the coordination of CSC and three other vendors: Andersen Consulting, AT&T Solutions, and Bell Atlantic Network Integration. JP Morgan transferred 45 per cent of its IT staff—over 900 people—to the alliance firms. These 900 people joined the 600-plus staff of the alliance firms devoted to the contract. The alliance became responsible for data centres, midrange computers, distributed computing, and voice and data services. The contract was stated to be about 30 per cent of Morgan's $1 billion annual IT budget. JP Morgan has kept IT strategy, application development and support, and vendor management in-house. The contract was expected to save JP Morgan $50 million annually (*Wall Street and Technology*, July 1996). Although cost savings were a driving factor, JP Morgan executives claimed that the real impetus was to help retain its leading edge in technology, provide better service to end-users, together with an internal focus on new applications. According to Hoffman (1996a), the contract is based on "a flexible team approach in which JP Morgan sets the strategic direction."

In our view, with multi-sourcing, the risks of going with a single supplier are mitigated but replaced to a degree by additional time and resources required to manage multiple suppliers. In both cases, the key to multi-sourcing is vendor co-ordination and management. In the BP case, there were initial difficulties in getting the vendors to work together. BP hit upon a plan to provide seamless service whereby one of its three suppliers served as a primary contractor at each of its eight business sites. Its job was to coordinate the services provided by the three suppliers to the businesses supported by that site. Framework agreements allowed business managers at each of the eight major sites to negotiate with the IT suppliers for customized services. BP has noted that the suppliers worked well together to deliver day-to-day service, in part because they were so interdependent. However:

> "They are also rivals competing for our future business. As a result they are reluctant to share, for example, best practices with one another." (*Cross, 1995*).

The JP Morgan case also shows a multiple supplier approach, but in this case, one contractor is made the principal contractor throughout, whereas in BP each contractor has a principal role in at least some part of BP. The JP Morgan approach simplifies the administrative pattern; the BP case develops greater interdependence among suppliers. JP Morgan also chose to retain more of its staff and functions in-house. It is fairly clear that both firms would find it difficult to recreate its original IT function if this were required. But in BPs case, total outsourcing is, as at 1997, almost irrevocable. This makes risk mitigation on vendor management even more critical than in the JP Morgan case.

Co-sourcing: Performance-based Contracts

The largest IT outsourcing supplier, EDS, has pioneered a new term in the customer-vendor relationship: "co-sourcing"™. According to EDS vice-chairman Gary Fernades:

> "Co-sourcing goes beyond marginal reductions in IT costs to the effective alignment of IT assets and expenditures with business objectives. The result is the enhancement for the entire enterprise." (*reported in Moran, 1996*)

An example of co-sourcing is EDS's contract with a US pharmaceuticals company in which the rate of payment is based on EDS' ability to reduce the development and registration process for new drugs. The change in EDS' focus was being supported by an internal retraining effort. In 1996 *Fortune* magazine (Kirkpatrick, 1996) reported that EDS employees were being taught to focus more on customer service, a programme referred to by insiders as EDS going to "charm school". However, even in 1997 co-sourcing was still a new concept accounting for only a small percentage of revenues. In 1996, Ted Shaw, VP of EDS' banking services division, noted "EDS is still primarily a fee-based outsourcing business" (O'Heney, 1996).

Other outsourcing companies have also been offering performance-based contracts as customer demand has grown. In 1996 Perot Systems announced a deal with Citibank in which Perot Systems would share in the revenues of Citibank's Travel Agency Commission Settlement system (Caldwell, 1996c). In 1996 Perot Systems' "performance-based" contracts still accounted for only a small percentage of total business.

As at 1997, EDS has been and remains the marketleader in the IT outsourcing arena. In 1984 when EDS was sold to General Motors, EDS was largely hindered by GM's large bureaucracy. In June 1996, EDS became its own company, free to pursue its own strategies. Would this new freedom help transform EDS? Perhaps EDS' new culture, combined with their strong IT practices (such as consolidation, standardization, and volume-purchasing power), could enable them to focus more on customer service and less on making a profit from fee-based deals. But EDS still had to deliver on its existing fee-based contract obligations, amounting to $US 80 billion over 10 years (Kirkpatrick, 1996). The question that is then raised for any supplier in such a position is: can co-sourcing coexist with the supplier's ongoing fixed-fee commitments?

Spin-offs

The idea of tranforming an internal IT department into an external entity is certainly not new, but the practice continued into 1997. A "spin-off" allegedly empowers the IT entity to behave like a vendor. Freed from the bureaucratic restraints associated with being a support function, spin-off companies can focus on a marketing mentality, one which delivers good customer service at competitive prices. In the past, spin-offs generally have not been successful. For example, Mellon Bank, Sears Roebuck, Kimberly-Clark and Boeing had only limited success with their spin-off IT companies (Venkatraman, 1997). On the other hand, European-based multinational Philips Electronics successfully spun off both its development and operations functions in the 1990s (Willcocks, 1995). Some companies continue to undertake this approach. Thus in 1996 the CIO of Baxter announced plans to move 500 employees and 80 per cent of its systems to a spin-off company (Alexander, 1996). Swiss Bank had also planned a spin-off until the CFO steered the company towards an alliance with Perot Systems (see above).

In our assessment past experiences suggest that spin-offs are only successful if they have a core competency to attract external customers. One of the notable exemplars of a successful spin-off has been American Airline's SABRE unit. American Airlines already had a strong product with many external customers in the form of their renowned airline reservation system. The viability of spin-offs by other organizations will also depend on whether they have a viable product to attract external customers.

Creative Contracting

Increasingly client organizations are examining options and shopping around for better deals. For example, Ameritech studied outsourcing for 15 months before awarding a ten-year, multi-billion dollar contract to IBM (Verity, 1996). In addition to longer evaluations, some client organizations have been adopting more creative contracting practices.

One such practice is the inclusion of a customer-written contract with the request for proposal. For example, when Elf Alochem, a Philadelphia chemical company, searched the market in 1995 for an IT outsourcing vendor, they took a novel approach by sending out a completed contract along with the request for proposal. The contract enabled the company to specify accurately what they wanted from an outsourcing vendor, as well as provide all vendors with precise information to make an informed bid. The four-year, $4.3 million contract was awarded to Keane, a Boston company. Keane contracted to maintain Elf Alochem's accounting systems running on a range of platforms while Alochem's internal staff planned and developed a migration to client/server (Heichler, 1995).

A second growing practice is to provide for competitive bidding for services beyond the contract. Customers have become increasingly aware of the threat of giving the power of a sole supplier to the outsourcing vendor. Customers are protecting themselves by including contract clauses that specify that the customer will competitively bid any service beyond the contract. Specifically, customers hope to ensure vendor motivation and competitive pricing. However, competition does not always protect the customer. Consider the following two examples taken from our recent research. In the first case where an aerospace company went outside of their multi-billion dollar outsourcing contract, the vendor refused to support the entire function:

> "Our contract says we can go elsewhere. When [the vendor] wanted to charge us $2500 to upgrade each of our HP workstations to two gigabyte hard drives, we went elsewhere and bought them for $1000. Now [the vendor] won't support our machines because we put somebody elses hardware in them." *User manager, Aerospace Company (Year 2 into a ten-year contract)*

From the vendors' perspective, they could not assure the quality of products or services delivered outside the original contract. In a similar circumstance, one petroleum company awarded a large-scale development effort to a company other than their primary contractor. After the system was developed, the vendor refused to run the application on their mainframes unless they were awarded the support contract.

A third growing practice has been that of flexible pricing. The term "flexible pricing" has been used to cover a variety of pricing mechanisms, including vendor-cost-plus pricing, market pricing, fixed-fee-adjustments-based-on-volume-fluctuation pricing, or preferred-customer pricing. Some customers have been negotiating for a share in the vendor's savings. By 1997 customers had become well aware that unit costs can fall 20–30 per cent annually, and increasingly they have wanted this reflected in the vendor price. Some customers now track vendor costs with "open book accounting" clauses and demand a percentage of vendor savings. Other customers are relying on annual third-party benchmarks to assess current market prices. Some customers have clauses to adjust their fixed-price fee based on volume fluctuations. Some customers have clauses to reduce their fees based on prices charged to the vendor's other preferred customers. Most pricing adjustments appear to occur annually rather than monthly due to the costs associated with measuring and agreeing upon such adjustments.

A fourth development has been that of beginning long-term relationships with a short-term contract. As one example, in the mid-1990s executives at Cigna Healthcare of Atlanta Georgia wanted a long-term relationship with their IT outsourcer, Entex Information Services. Cigna, however, pushed for a one-year contract even though Entex would be required to make significant investments in Cigna, without any future guarantees. But the short-term contract served to motivate both sides—Entex wanted the renewal to reap their investment, Cigna wanted renewal rather than incurring the costs of switching to a new outsourcer. The strategy worked well for both companies, as the contract and relationship were subsequently extended (Guterl, 1996).

Implications for Research

These developments, together with the trends, successes and relative failures in selective, transitional and total outsourcing, point to a very large research agenda for strategic IS sourcing. Clearly, all these contracting options and approaches need to be closely monitored to determine the critical success factors, and the circumstances in which different outcomes occur. Ongoing research on a case and survey basis needs to be conducted in different sectors and economies on the already established themes of how sourcing decisions are made, the critical elements of sourcing strategy, how vendor bids are assessed, contracts constructed, the assessment regimes operated and needed before and after contracts are signed, and how contracts and relationships are, and should be, managed. It will be particularly interesting to monitor how the newer approaches to IS sourcing turn out over the course of specific contracts.

Past research has also neglected three themes now emerging as critical. One is greater exploration of vendors, their strategies, competencies and the changing nature of the vendor marketplace. A recent paper leading the way here is that of Michell and Fitzgerald (1997). A second issue particularly poorly understood by vendors and client organizations alike, but acutely important for large-scale outsourcing arrangements, is that of client-vendor relationships, how they are formed, developed and sustained. Willcocks and Kern (1997) have recently attempted to develop work in this area by studying the ten-year EDS-Inland Revenue deal in the United Kingdom.

A third area is that of key capabilities and skills that need to be retained in-house whatever IS sourcing arrangements are decided upon. This is particularly acute because organizations have, up to 1997 at least, tended not to be very strategic in the handling of the human resource implications of their sourcing decisions (Willcocks, Feeny and Islei, 1997). All too frequently there has been a tendency, particularly in cases of large-scale outsourcing, to view what remains in-house as some sort of "skeleton crew" or "residual organization", usually staffed by some form of contract manager and an IT director with a few additional staff to monitor the contract and provide some liaison with user managers and staff. In our own research we have found examples where this has been precisely the case and avoidable problems have resulted.

Additionally, the wider human resource issues surrounding outsourcing are often underplayed. For example, in one public sector organization we researched, the vendor transferred over most of the client's competent IS staff, and made clear which staff were not wanted. This not only embittered retained staff; it also meant that they became responsible for managing and monitoring the vendors performance. The result was a soured relationship, disputes and continuous complaints about vendor service levels and quality. In several other cases we have researched, retained staff found themselves carrying out work and functions they thought had been outsourced, and found little time to devote to what they believed to be their main tasks under the new arrangements (Willcocks and Currie, 1997). On retained management capability the words of Max Hopper, vice-president of IS at American Airlines, may still be worth noting:

> "For us outsourcing makes sense. My fear is that some companies which are looking at outsourcing still don't really understand information systems, and they don't know what is required to run IS. For them outsourcing is a cop-out." (*quoted in Willcocks and Fitzgerald, 1994*)

Hopefully the developing research base, including the work represented in this volume, will serve to make this scenario less frequently the case.

CONCLUSION

The chapters in this book make a number of contributions to our understanding of the IS outsourcing phenomenon and point to many ways forward on both its research and management. They emphasize two things embodied in the title of the book—that the primary focus for practice needs to be on sourcing IS, of which outsourcing is only a component; and that the development of strategy in IS sourcing remains key—strategy in the sense of a long-term, integrated, dynamic approach. It is clear that IS sourcing will continue to be of major interest to practitioners, and that the research and academically-based studies represented here are a source of more rigorous, more objectively carried out and thought-through analyses than those generally available in the more popular trade literature and press, and also often from the marketing departments of interested parties on the supply side.

To some degree such a provision serves to define at least one of the purposes of academic research in the field of IS outsourcing. One would be surprised if practitioners did not gain something, and in some cases a great deal, from reading these studies, recognizing, of course, that learning on outsourcing must be a continuous process in what is now a fast-moving field.

A further purpose must be to continue to push forward on the theoretical front, whether this is to develop a more integrated and internally consistent theoretical lense, the identification and adaptation of relevant theory from other disciplines, and/or the application of a number of different theoretical perspectives to the study of the outsourcing field. It is also clear that the IS outsourcing trend is growing and its contextual variables highly dynamic. Therefore there is a continuing need for ever more empirical studies, whether utilizing for example positivist or interpretative, qualitative or quantitative, case study or survey-based, snapshot or longitudinal research approaches. This, of course, does not exhaust the options.

Finally, is IS outsourcing so different that it requires a distinctive theoretical framework for its study? There is a practitioner version of this question. One thing we are regularly asked is: is IS outsourcing different from outsourcing anything else? Our own—research-based—answer is: No in many ways, but Yes on five counts:

1. IT evolves rapidly; this surrounds IT/IS sourcing decisions with a high degree of uncertainty.
2. The underlying economics of Information Technology changes rapidly. Although price/performance improvements occur in every industry for example, in few industries do the underlying economics shift as fast as IT.
3. The penetration of Information Technology to all business functions is becoming ubiquitous: unlike many other products and services IT cannot be easily isolated from other organizational functions.
4. The switching costs to alternative Information Technologies and IT suppliers are high, and sometimes prohibitive.
5. Many potential and actual customers are still highly inexperienced in Information Technology outsourcing. This can put them at a significant disadvantage when negotiating and running contracts with outsourcing vendors.

Except possibly for the fifth item, it is doubtful whether these distinctive characteristics of IT/IS will recede in the next five years, and indeed it is likely that several, especially items one, two and three, will heighten in that period of time. All these points serve to render questions relating to sourcing IT/IS capability highly problematic. If the chapters we have collected together in this book serve to illustrate this, by doing so they also demonstrate why the IS outsourcing phenomenon is worthy of distinctive study. In theory, as our different contributors make clear, there are a number of options, of course. A *synthesis* of the debate may lead to supplementing a major theory set—for example transaction cost theory or game theory—with additional theories to increase its explanatory powers in the context of IT outsourcing. Or alternatively, following the argument of distinctiveness, we as a discipline may seek to develop a more narrow, but IT-specific, theory to explain and predict IS sourcing behaviours. Whatever directions are now pursued if, together, the chapters represent some further advances in perspectives and in understanding practice, then we and the contributors will have helped towards understanding and dealing with some key issues in the IS field.

REFERENCES

Alexander, S. (1981) Spin-Off Doctors, *Computerworld*, 8 April, **30**, 15, 77.

Applegate, L. and Montealegre, R. (1991) Eastman Kodak Company: Managing Information Systems Through Strategic Alliances, Harvard Business School Case 9-192-030, Harvard Business School, Cambridge, Massachusetts.

Apte, U. *et al.* (1997) IS Outsourcing Practices in the USA, Japan, and Finland: A Comparative Study. *Journal Of Information Technology*, **12**, 4.

Arnett, K. and Jones, M. (1994) Firms that Choose Outsourcing: A Profile, *Information and Management*, Vol. 26 179–188.

Beath, C. (1983) Strategies For Managing MIS Projects: A Transaction Costs Approach, in *Proceedings of the Fourth International Conference on Information Systems*, December, 133–147.

Bensaou, M. (1993) Interorganizational Cooperation: The Role of Information Technology—An Empirical Comparision of US and Japanese Supplier Relations, in *Proceedings of the Fourteenth International Conference of Information Systems*, Orlando, Florida, December, 117–127.

Bergstrom, L. (1991) *The Ins and Outs of Outsourcing*, Darien: Real Decisions Corporation.

Bleeke, J. and Ernst, D. (1995) Is Your Strategic Alliance Really a Sale? *Harvard Business Review*, January–February, 97–105.

Brown, B. and Eckerson, W. (1990) Kodak Turns Nets over to IBM and DEC; Farming out Net Operations Can Trigger Staffing Issues, *Network World*, **7**, 3, 15 January, 1, 4, 61, 63.

Buck-Lew, M. (1992) To Outsource or Not? *International Journal of Information Management*, 12, 3–20.

Burch, B. (1994) Xerox Turns Nets Over to EDS in $3.2 Billion Deal, *Network World*, **11**, 26, 19.

Caldwell, B. (1996a) The New Outsourcing Partnership, *Information Week*, 585, 24 June, 50–64.

Caldwell, B. (1996b) We Are the Business, *Information Week*, 28 October, 36–50.

Caldwell, B. (1996c) IT Management: Perot's Pact, *Information Week*, 28 October, 112.

CFO Magazine (1996) For Better or Worse, July, 47–50.

Chainstore Age Executive (1996) Sears' Prudent Move, **72**, 8 August, 46.

Collins, T. (1996) Sears Strikes £344 million 'No Tender'' FM Deal', *Computer Weekly*, 18 January, 1.

Collins, J. and Millen, R. (1995) Information Systems Outsourcing by Large American Industrial Firms: Choices and Impacts, *Information Resources Management Journal*, **8**, 1, Winter, 5–13.

Cross, J. (1995) IT Outsourcing: BP's Competitive Approach, *Harvard Business Review* **73**, 3, 94–104.

Dekleva, S. (1994) CFOs, CIOs, and Outsourcing, *Computerworld*, **28**, 20, 16 May, 96.

Dwyer, F., Schurr, P. and Oh, S. (1987) Developing Buyer-Seller Relationships, *Journal of Marketing*, 51, 11–27.

Earl, M. (1996) The Risks of Outsourcing IT, *Sloan Management Review*, **37**, 3, 26–32.

Earl, M. and Feeny, D. (1994) Is Your CIO Adding Value? *Sloan Management Review*, Spring, **35**, 3, 11–20.

Feeny, D. and Ives, B. (1989) In Search of Sustainability—Reaping Long Term

Advantage from Investments in Information Technology, *Journal of Management Information Systems*, **7**, 1, Summer, 27–46.

Feeny, D. and Willcocks, L. (1997) The IT Function: Changing Capabilities and Skills, in Willcocks, L., Feeny, D. and Islei, G. (eds), Managing IT as a Strategic Resource, Maidenhead: McGraw Hill.

Foley, A. (1993) Hong Kong Busks Asia Services Trend, *Computerworld*, Hong Kong, 13 May, 1, 56.

Ganz, J. (1994) Outsourcing: The Scam May Be On You, *Computerworld*, 18 April, 41.

Grover, V., Cheon, M. and Teng, J. (1996) The Effect of Service Quality and Partnership on the Outsourcing of Information Systems Functions, *Journal of Management Information Systems*, **12**, 4, 89–116.

Guterl, F. (1996) How to Manage Your Outsourcer, *Datamation*, **42**, 5, 1 March, 79–83.

Harrar, G. (1993) Outsource Tales, *Forbes*, 7 June, 37–42.

Heichler, E. (1995) Unique Contract Helps Outsourcing Process, *Computerworld*, **29**, 14, 3 April, 75.

Henderson, J. (1990) Plugging into Strategic Partnerships: The Critical IS Connection, *Sloan Management Review*, Spring, 7–18.

Hirschheim, R. (1996) Current Trends in IT Outsourcing, presentation at International Conference of Information Systems, Cleveland, Ohio, 17 December.

Hodgson, G. (1994) Corporate Culture and Evolving Competences: An Old Institutionalist Perspective on the Nature of the Firm, paper presented at The Conference of Transaction Cost Economics and Beyond, Erasmus University, Rotterdam, Netherlands, June.

Hoffman, T. (1996a) JP Morgan to save $50 million via Outsourcing Pact, *Computerworld*, **30**, 21, 20 May, 10.

Hoffman, T. (1996b) NCR Grounded in Delta Venture, *Computerworld*, 1 July, 8.

Holway, R. (1996) The 1996 Holway Report, reported in Jones, R., Software and Services Sector Flourishing in UK. *Computer Weekly*, 6 June, 22.

Hopper, M. (1990) Rattling SABRE—New Ways to Compete on Information, *Harvard Business Review*, **68**, 3, May–June, 118–125.

Hovey, V. (1991) Presentation to the University of Houston's Information Systems Research Center, Houston University, Houston, 22 January.

Huber, R. (1993) How Continental Bank Outsourced Its "Crown Jewels", *Harvard Business Review*, **71**, 1, January–February, 121–129.

IDC (1992) *Outsourcing Options in Europe*, Watford UK: The Yankee Group Europe.

IMP Group (1990) An Interaction Approach, in Ford, D. (ed.), *Understanding Business Markets: Interaction, Relationships And Networks*, London: Academic Press.

Ives, B. and Learmonth, J. (1984) The Information System as a Competitive Weapon, *Communications of the ACM*, **27**, 12, December, 1193–1201.

Joskow, P. (1991) The Role of Transaction Cost Economics in Antitrust and Public Utility Regulatory Policies, *Journal of Law Economics and Organization*, 7, special issue, 53–83.

Kanter, R. (1994) Collaborative Advantage: The Art of Alliances, *Harvard Business Review*, July–August, 96–108.

King, J. (1995) Owens-Corning hands over Legacy Gear to HP, *Computerworld*, **29**, 26, 1, 12.

KirkPatrick, D. (1996) This Tough Guy Wants to Give You a Hug, Fortune,

14 October. 170–178.

Klepper, R. (1993) Efficient Outsourcing Relationships. Paper at the *Outsourcing of Information Systems Services Conference*, University of Twente, the Netherlands, 20–22 May.

Kumar, K. and Willcocks, L. (1996) Offshore Outsourcing: A Country Too Far?, *Proceedings of the Fourth European Conference in Information Systems*, Lisbon, June.

Lacity, M. and Hirschheim, R. (1993) *Information Systems Outsourcing: Myths, Metaphors, and Realities*, Chichester: Wiley.

Lacity, M. and Hirschheim, R. (1995) *Beyond The Information Systems Outsourcing Bandwagon*, Chichester: Wiley.

Lacity, M. and Hirschheim, R. (1997) What Problems are Organizations Solving with IT Outsourcing?, in Currie, W. and Galliers, R. (eds), *Rethinking MIS*, Oxford: Oxford University Press.

Lacity, M., Hirschheim, R. and Willcocks, L. (1994) Realizing Outsourcing Expectations: Incredible Expectations, Credible Outcomes, *Information Systems Management*, Fall, 7–18.

Lacity, M. and Willcocks, L. (1995) Interpreting Information Technology Sourcing Decisions from a Transaction Cost Perspective: Findings and Critique, *Accounting, Management and Information Technology*, **5**, 3/4, 203–244.

Lacity, M. and Willcocks, L. (1996) Best Practices in Information Technology Sourcing, *Oxford Executive Research Briefing* No. 2, Templeton College, Oxford.

Lacity, M. and Willcocks, L. (1997) The Sourcing of Information Systems: Examining The Privatization Option in US Public Administration, *Information Systems Journal* (forthcoming).

Lacity, M., Willcocks, L. and Feeny, D. (1995) IT Outsourcing: Maximize Flexibility and Control, *Harvard Business Review*, May–June, 84–93.

Lacity, M., Willcocks, L. and Feeny, D. (1996) The Value of Selective IT Sourcing, *Sloan Management Review*, **37**, 3, 13–25.

Loh, L. and Venkatraman, N. (1992a) Diffusion of Information Technology Outsourcing: Influence Sources and the Kodak Effect, *Information Systems Research*, 334–358.

Loh, L. and Venkatraman, N. (1992b) Determinants of Information Technology Outsourcing: A Cross-sectional Analysis, *Journal of Management Information Systems*, 9, 7–24.

McFarlan, W. F. (1984) Information Technology Changes the Way You Compete, *Harvard Business Review*, **62**, 3, May–June 98–103.

McFarlan, W. and Nolan, R. (1995) How to Manage an IT Outsourcing Alliance, *Sloan Management Review*, **36**, 2, 9–24.

Melymuka, K. (1994) Is There Life After Outsourcing?, *Computerworld*, 16 May, 89–96.

Menagh, M. (1995) Driving a Hard Bargain, *Computerworld*, **29**, 32, 7 August, 69–76.

Michell, V. and Fitzgerald, G. (1997) The IT Outsourcing Marketplace: Vendors and Their Selection, *Journal of Information Technology*, **12**, 3, 130–148.

Moad, J. (1993) Inside an Outsourcing Deal, *Datamation*, 15 February, 20–27.

Moran, N. (1996) Outsourcing Begins, *Chemical Week*, **158**, 32, 21 August, 31–32.

O'Heney, S. (1996) Outsourcing is Hotter than Ever, *ABA Banking Journal*, **88**, 5 May, 44–54.

PA Consulting (1996) 1996 International Strategic Sourcing Survey, PA Consulting, London.

Perry, L., Stott, R. and Smallwood, W. (1993) *Real Time Strategy: Improvising Team Based Planning for a Fast-changing World*, New York: John Wiley.

Pfeffer, J. (1981) *Power in Organizations*, Marshfield, Mass: Pitman Publishing.

Porter, M.E. and Millar, V. (1985) How Information Gives You Competitive Advantage, *Harvard Business Review*, **63**, 4, July–August, 149–160.

Pralahad, C. and Hamel, G. (1990) The Core Competence of the Corporation, *Harvard Business Review*, 63, 79–91.

Quinn, J. (1992) *Intelligent Enterprise: A New Paradigm for a New Era*, New York: The Free Press.

Ring, P. and Van de Ven, A. (1994) Development Processes of Cooperative Relationships, *Academy of Management Review*, **19**, 1, 90–118.

Schmerken, I. and Goldman, K. (1996) Outsourcing Megadeals: Drive the New IT Economy, *Wall Street and Technology*, **14**, 4, 36–41.

Shelanski, H. (1991) Empirical Research in Transaction Cost Economics: A Survey and Assessment, Department of Economics, University of California, Berkeley, December (mimeo).

Strassmann, P. (1995a) Outsourcing—A Game For Losers, *Computerworld*, 21 August, 75.

Strassmann, P. (1995b) *The Politics of Information Management*, New Canaan, USA: Information Economics Press.

Subramanian, A. and Lacity, M. (1997) Managing Client Server Implementations: Today's Technology, Yesterday's Lessons, *Journal of Information Technology*, **12**, 2 (forthcoming).

Venkatraman, N. (1997) Beyond Outscourcing Managing IT Resources as a Value-Center, *Sloan Management Review* **38**, 3, 51–64.

Verity, J. (1996) Let's Order Out for Technology, *Business Week*, 13 May, 47.

Wall Street and Technology (1996) JP Morgan to Outsource One-third of its Technology to Vendor Alliance, *Wall Street and Technology*, **14**, 7, 12.

Willcocks, L. (1995) Collaborating To Compete: Strategic Partnerships In IT Outsourcing?, *Oxford Institute of Information Management Research and Discussion Paper*, Templeton College, Oxford.

Willcocks, L. (1996) *Investing in Information Systems: Evaluation and Management*, London: Chapman and Hall.

Willcocks, L. and Currie, W. (1997) IT Outsourcing in the Public Sector: Towards the Contractual Organization?, *British Journal Of Management* 8 special issue S107–120.

Willcocks, L., Feeny, D. and Islei, G. (eds) (1997) *Managing IT as a Strategic Resource*, Maidenhead: McGraw Hill.

Willcocks, L. and Fitzgerald, G. (1994) *A Business Guide to Outsourcing IT. A Study of European Best Practice in the Selection, Management and Use of External IT Services*, Business Intelligence, London.

Willcocks, L., Fitzgerald, G. and Lacity, M. (1996) To Outsource IT or Not? Research on Economics and Evaluation Practice, *European Journal of Information Systems*, September, **5**, 3, 143–160.

Willcocks, L., Lacity, M. and Fitzgerald, G. (1995) IT Outsourcing in Europe and The USA: Assessment Issues, in Doukidis, G. *et al.* (eds), *Proceedings of the Third European Conference in Information Systems*, Athens, 1–3 June.

Willcocks, L. and Kern, T. (1997) IT Outsourcing as Strategic Partnering: The Case of the UK Inland Revenue, *Proceedings of the Fifth European Conference in Information Systems*, Cork, Ireland, June.

Williamson, O. (1975) *Markets and Hierarchies: Analysis and Antitrust Implications. A Study in the Economics of Internal Organization*, New York: The Free Press.
Williamson, O. (1979) Transaction Cost Economics: The Governance of Contractual Relations, *Journal of Law and Economics*, **22**, 2, October, 233–261.
Williamson, O. (1985) *The Economic Institutions of Capitalism*, New York: The Free Press.
Williamson, O. (1996) *The Mechanisms of Governance*, Oxford: Oxford University Press.

PART I

Perspectives

1

The Outsourcing of Information Services: Transforming the Nature of Business in the Information Industry

THOMAS CLARK, ROBERT ZMUD AND GORDON MCCRAY

INTRODUCTION

A significant and, to many, surprising movement has been afoot in the executive suites of both public and private organizations. A question being asked more and more loudly by chief executives is: "What has all of our investment in information technology really gotten us?" As information technology (IT) professionals scramble for a precise answer that has eluded them for years, the senior executives have become increasingly impatient for an understandable response. A clear and compelling answer has become the "holy grail" for IT managers, consultants and scholars alike.

At the same time, truly fundamental changes in the structure of the information services (IS) industry have been taking place. During the 1990s organizations have been downsizing their IS staffs, replacing technically-oriented IT managers with executives from core areas of the business, experiencing a remarkable reduction in the acquisition costs of new technology, and increasingly looking outside the organization for information services (IS) solutions. Into this situation appears a

Strategic Sourcing of Information Systems.
Edited by L. P. Willcocks and M. C. Lacity.

representative of an information services vendor with the message: "We'll take over your IS responsibilities, provide you with stable, predictable costs over a long period of time and give you world-class service to meet your needs". As a senior executive, would you be interested in the message? Of course. As an IT executive would you be just as interested? As observed by Caldwell (1992b), support is mixed:

> "Outsourcing? We tried it 25 years ago. Only then we called it using a service bureau. And, where are all those service bureaux today? Out of business, that's where."
>
> "Outsourcing? I'll bet there's a newly-minted CIO involved. It seems that every company that is outsourcing has a CIO who is saying all the right things and doing all the wrong ones."
>
> "I decided that operating IS had evolved to the point where it was a commodity. There were suppliers to run the engine; and, much to our surprise, we found we could also save money."

As suggested in the Introduction to this book, the decision to contract with an IS vendor for a substantial portion of any firm's IT services is a critical strategic choice for the firm. Critical, because for profit maximization, the vendor would like to establish a contractual arrangement of eight to ten years which is a very long time frame given today's high velocity technological environment. Additionally, this decision is fraught with emotional arguments, difficult questions and complex links with many organizational processes. The purposes of this chapter are to review the structure of this important decision, to analyse the competing forces involved, and to prescribe executive guidelines. As such it provides an overview of the issues that later chapters will deal with in more detail.

CONCEPTUAL BACKGROUND

Economists have, for many years, pondered the make-or-buy decision, both as a topic in itself and as but one of a variety of available sourcing options. Consequently, a large literature now exists that addresses the relative merits and pitfalls of various sourcing strategies. For the most part, this work has focused upon the identification of appropriate sourcing strategies given a very limited set of contextual variables.

Drawing from this literature, if we envision a spectrum of motivations for acquiring the requisite IT services from an outside vendor, two prominent bodies of work define the ends of that spectrum. On the one hand, there exists the notion that the decision to outsource is based wholly upon a desire to minimize the costs associated with providing the necessary IT services. Perhaps the most visible contributor to this line of reasoning has been Williamson (1979, 1981) and his work on transaction cost theory.

Transaction cost theory holds that the firm considering the outsourcing option will behave in a cost-economizing way, and this will involve consideration of two costs: transaction costs (those costs associated with planning, adapting and monitoring task completion—Williamson, 1979), and production costs (those costs directly associated with the handling of the task—see Walker and Weber, 1987; Williamson, 1979, 1981). As defined by Williamson, a transaction "occurs when a good or service is transferred across a technologically separable interface" (Williamson, 1981). Relative to insourcing, outsourcing is often posited to have lower production costs, yet higher transaction costs. Conceptually this is a reasonable assumption since, if production is rationally shifted outside the firm, the direct costs of production are reduced for the client firm. Significantly, however, transaction cost theory holds that there will exist a greater likelihood of opportunistic behaviour on the part of the outside vendor than would be expected from internal sources, thus giving rise to the need (and associated costs) to more closely monitor and perhaps control the outside vendor. Given these opposing costs, Williamson has suggested the most efficient strategy for acquiring goods or services given the frequency with which the good or service is demanded, and the degree of asset specificity associated with the transaction (Lacity and Hirschheim, 1993; Williamson, 1979).

If rational, cost-economizing behaviour defines one end of this spectrum, then viewing decision outcomes as the result of power and politics defines the other. Indeed, to view the make-or-buy decision through the lens of power and politics is to focus primarily upon the "power of the IS department, the vested interests of different stakeholder groups, and the political tactics they may enact to sway decisions in their favour" (Lacity and Hirschheim, 1993; Pfeffer, 1981). Thus, this perspective would leave us with a decision situation in which various constituents in the decision process—even internal actors—tend primarily to their own welfare or, in other words, exhibit opportunism.

For the interested reader, the work of Lacity and Hirschheim (1993) provides a more detailed comparison between these two perspectives. Chapters 2 and 4 in the present volume also provide a more detailed description and critique of the use and limitations of transaction cost theory for analyzing and understanding IT outsourcing decisions and outcomes. We should note here, however, that the cost-ecomomizing and political perspectives are not mutually exclusive. Rather, each contributes significantly to a more informed understanding of the trend toward the outsourcing of IT services. Alone or taken together, these perspectives fail to capture the scope and complexity of the actual decision context or process associated with the outsourcing of IT services.

What can be said with certainty is that the outsourcing of IT services is an increasing trend—sufficiently increasing, in fact, to merit *very* close attention. What is not so easily said, however, is why this trend is emerging. Economists, decision scientists and IS researchers have grappled with the outsourcing issue, attempting to carve out of extant theory and anecdotal evidence a more accurate depiction of this decision context. Researchers, in fact, have addressed a number of issues close to the outsourcing issue, as well as several related to IT and its evolution in the marketplace. For example, an increase in the incidence of firms pursuing a co-operative strategy in IT and IS development has long been predicted (Clemons and Knez, 1988). Given the difficulty of sustaining competitive advantage via IT, co-operative IT and IS development via a consortium hedges against insufficient returns to the lone innovator while allowing the individual firm to perform competitively. This would suggest, then, that for commodity-like IT, firms will increasingly engage in co-operative efforts toward the development of such technologies. Subsequent research, though not focused upon IT, supports this notion that, indeed, co-operation occurs "within a competitive context" between firms (Kogut, 1989), and further supports the notion that it is the potential of reciprocity, both desirable and otherwise, that at least contributes to the stability of such relationships. Interestingly, this same research suggests a positive relationship between the number of ties between firms and the stability of the co-operative relationship.

As discussed previously, transaction cost theory has provided the reference point for a good deal of the research and discussion of the outsourcing phenomenon. It should not be construed from this, however, that researchers and practitioners alike have failed to recognize motivations beyond cost minimization. Indeed, several authors have explored other determinants in sourcing decisions. Ouchi (1980), for example, relates performance ambiguity and goal incompatibility to the choice of "mechanisms of control". Kogut and Zander (1992) depart significantly from the transaction cost perspective, instead viewing the make-or-buy decision as one predicated upon existing internal expertise or knowledge, irrespective of threats of opportunism. Perhaps the more compelling research findings have been those that find support for transaction cost theory and, at the same time, identify other decision factors (Walker and Weber, 1984; Montverde and Teece, 1982). While this research generally finds support for the effect of transaction costs, threats of opportunism, and transaction cost theory in general, it fails to identify it as the primary motivating force in the outsourcing decision. Rather, findings suggest the most influential force is quite simple: Which firm is the most efficient producer?

Finally, IS researchers have themselves wrestled with the outsourcing issue. Much of this literature has addressed the pros and cons of the outsourcing of IT services, providing would-be outsourcing clients with laundry lists of associated benefits and caveats. For examples, see Johnston and Lawrence (1988), Kelly (1990), Lyons *et al.* (1990), Rosenthal and Salzman (1990), and Gupta and Gupta (1992). Recently, however, IS researchers have taken steps toward developing a more complete understanding of what motivates and influences the IT outsourcing decision. Early findings have proven most interesting. Loh and Venkatraman (1992), for example, found that as a historical event, the Kodak-IBM outsourcing deal marks the beginning of the current outsourcing revolution, and the forming of this specific relationship is held more to account for the subsequent trend toward the outsourcing of IT services than the efforts of outsourcing vendors to promote that trend. The implications of this finding are most intriguing since they imply that organizations tend to do as their colleagues do, particularly in very complex decision situations such as whether or not to outsource.

Indeed, it is just such findings that are likely to lead us to a broader understanding of the decision to outsource IT services. Surely there are myriad forces at work in this decision context beyond that captured by transaction cost theory, agency theory, and notions of power and politics. The findings of Loh and Venkatraman (1992) raise questions about these "other" factors without explicitly addressing them. The issue at hand is the determination of what these factors, or motivations, are, and then the explication of these factors through rigorous empirical research.

RESEARCH METHODOLOGY

It is the quest for the aforementioned contextual variables that motivates this chapter. In order to uncover as many factors as possible, 63

Table 1.1 *Interviewee Representation by Industry*

Industry	Number of interviewees
Financial services	4
Manufacturing & distribution	6
Consumer services & retail	11
Information services providers	6
Government	1
Health	1
Public utility	2

in-depth interviews with executives about the "outsourcing" option were conducted. In discussions with interviewees, we broadly defined the term outsourcing to mean the delegation, through a contractual arrangement, of any part of, or all, the technical resources, the human resources and the management responsibilities associated with providing IT services to an external vendor. Interviews were conducted over a period of two years. In a number of the interviews more than one individual was present. Generally, the interviewees included chief information officers (CIOs) and other senior information systems executives within firms acquiring information services and marketing executives within those firms providing information services. The decision structure was discussed with three senior managers of large providers of IS services. There was a special effort to gain access to those industries, firms, and personalities (both proponents and opponents of outsourcing) associated with outsourcing in the press. In addition, three meetings were held with 22 IBM employees (executives and consultants) familiar with various aspects of the outsourcing phenomenon. Categorization of the interviews is shown in Table 1.1.

WHAT'S GOING ON?

The mid-1990s interest in IS outsourcing has accelerated an already expanding definition of what an information service is and who may provide such services. The phrase *information services* now embraces virtually all types of computer and communications technologies and all types of activities associated with the acquisition, development, implementation and management of these technologies. Today, highly-competent third-party providers generally are available to undertake most, if not all, of the IS activities currently being handled by an internal IS organization. Table 1.2 provides a listing, certainly not exhaustive, of such services. Firms today clearly have the potential to outsource all or

Table 1.2 *Information Services Activities*

Data center installation/operations/maintenance
Data storage
Facilities management
Hardware and software maintenance
LAN support
Network design/operations/maintenance/control (voice/data)
PC support
Professional services (consulting, planning, technology assessment)
Programming services
Remote operations
Security and disaster recovery
Service center (transaction processing or MIPS utility)
Software development process (any or all phases)
Staff and/or user training
Systems installation and integration
Systems software

some of their internal IS activities for the short term, intermediate term or long term, by business unit or by geographical area.

The decision to source IS internally or externally is clearly strategic in nature, being treated as such by all of the individuals with whom we have discussed the topic. In today's complex organizations and volatile business environment, information services impacts virtually every organizational function and touches, in some way, virtually every organizational process. In many organizations, the information infrastructure is the mechanism that enables the organization to exist. This would be true in investment firms, insurance companies and banks. For example, with First Tennessee Corporation, the decision to outsource was viewed as one of necessity for the bank to remain competitive. (Wilder, 1989b):

> "To compete against larger banks, we either had to become a partner of a larger bank or find a technology partner. . . . [an OS vendor] will provide the technology that we will need to compete and they will help us cut costs. The contract will also allow us to spend more time on the strategic part of our jobs rather than the actual operating part."

Since effective management of the IS development, deployment and employment cycle is so important, it may be surprising to many that a variety of firms have chosen to acquire part or all of their IS from outside the organization. Nonetheless, over the last three years, the occurrence of IS outsourcing has been increasing at a rapid rate. Although specific figures are confounded by broad variations in the nature of the information technologies and services included within the definition used in collecting and aggregating data, dramatic growth is evident. Between 1988 and 1994, the growth rate of the outsourcing market has grown at nearly 14 per cent with a market revenue of approximately $50 billion in 1994 (*Computerworld*, 1990). By any account, the make-or-buy decision has been a part of the managerial landscape for decades. It is relatively new, however, to the strategic management of IT. The remarkable growth of the outsourcing of IT services has been attributed to a changing economic environment in which several factors are newly influencing sourcing strategies (Barreyre, 1988 see also Introduction). Our research generally confirms the existence of forces posited in the literature and identifies several not uncovered in our examination of that literature. These other factors will undoubtedly receive further attention as research on the outsourcing of IT services begins to tackle the inherent complexity of the outsourcing decision context.

As shown empirically (Loh and Venkatraman, 1992), and as discussed in the Introduction, the existent interest in outsourcing in 1989 was accelerated by Kodak's highly publicized agreements to purchase IT services from IBM, Digital Equipment Corporation and Businessland. Then Director of Corporate IS, Katherine Hudson's strong stand regarding the topic caused many executives to reconsider their own positions on the outsourcing option (Layne, Caldwell, Garvey *et al.*, 1989; Wilder, 1989a):

> "It is not in Kodak's best interest to be investing in all the infrastructure it takes to run the data center. ... If it doesn't contribute to the core business strategy, I don't want to own it."

As noted earlier, there exists a strong market outlook for IS outsourcing that will undoubtedly bring in new providers and those interested in the services they offer. By the Mid-1990s, the typical IS executive spent about 12.6 per cent of his or her budget to external providers (McMullen, 1990; Willcocks, Fitzgerald and Lacity, 1996). The success of IBM's outsourcing unit, ISSC, further illustrates the power of this new market force. From the initial entry in 1989 through formation of the subsidiary to the present time, ISSC has grown dramatically continuing through 1995/6 for which a 75 per cent increase was predicted (Caldwell and Krass, 1992). In addition to being a dramatic revenue generator, the unit has transformed the way IBM traditionally has done business. The nature of the outsourcing market requires rapid response and flexibility to deal with customers. ISSC possesses these attributes, and its success in the marketplace has caused many to launch the ISSC model as the "new IBM", a set of independent units operating in tightly-focused market segments.

Caution in all strategic decisions is sound management. The increasing interest in IS outsourcing, therefore, must be tempered with the observation that the decision to outsource, as is the case with all strategic decisions, is very specific for a given firm and particular situation. For example, the brokerage firm of T. Rowe Price, which traditionally had outsourced the majority of its IS activities, has re-emphasized the internal handling of IS activities in order to better apply its information resources to those areas where these resources can add value to the business. Still, the firm recognizes that its outsourcing background has created a culture for tight management control within its IS function—a "culture" often found lacking with internal IS groups. This and related experiences, such as those of Avon and Texaco (both of whom decided not to outsource after intensely considering the option), indicate that an interesting off-shoot of the "outsourcing movement" is that internal IS groups are being challenged to become their firm's "provider of choice" in competition with outside vendors. In the case of Avon Products, extensive and thorough analyses of the outsourcing alternative led to decisions not only *not* to outsource but to consolidate operations internally—a move projected to save the company a million dollars annually. This is, of course, selection of what we will term the insourcing rather than outsourcing alternative while re-engineering the firm's information infrastructure to attain many of the benefits identified within vendors' proposals.

WHAT'S INVOLVED IN THE DECISION?

In general, the interest currently shown in the outsourcing of services is driven by a recognition that a large portion of a firm's costs are in overhead categories (65–75 per cent for the typical manufacturing firm) and that most of these overhead costs are "bought" from internal service groups. Since outside service vendors potentially offer (a) greater economies of scale, (b) greater economies of scope, (c) greater expertise and (d) greater flexibility (Quinn, Doorley and Paquette, 1990), the decision to buy outside rather than inside is one that should be carefully evaluated by all firms. One need only consider the success of ADP, a provider of flexible payroll handling systems, to understand the forces involved. ADP offers its clients a number of benefits, including greater expertise in payroll handling, higher quality and quantity of payroll services, and lower payroll costs via economies of scale, tighter control of fixed costs, and fewer overhead expenses. These benefits would be difficult for any firm to ignore.

Given today's rapid technological changes and advances, many firms may be able to lower their risks and better leverage their internal assets by avoiding investments in vertical integration and focusing on managing "intellectual" systems instead of workers and machines. One needs to ask, activity by activity, "Are we able to compete with the world's best with each one of our internal activities?" If not, outsourcing may significantly improve a firm's long-term position. Stated simply and assuming cost effectiveness, the key for a firm is to identify and strive to off-load those activities for which no strategic advantage exists and, similarly, to shed those internal activities that are weaker than if obtained from outside suppliers. Research suggests that technologies that can be described as commodities are better candidates for outsourcing than more firm-specific assets (Williamson, 1981), owing to a lesser likelihood of opportunistic behavior on the part of the outsourcing vendor. Implementing such a strategy in a given firm, however, is a very challenging assignment. For example, a very simple management posture might be to outsource all activities except those crucial to its strategic position in order that available capital (financial and human) can be focused on those strategic activities. While appealing, such a posture grossly understates the difficulty in *identifying a firm's strategic activities* and does not allow for those situations where it might be, in fact, best to outsource a strategic activity, *if an effective governance mechanism is devised.*

Companies that strategically exploit outsourcing opportunities build their business strategies around a deep knowledge of a few highly developed core competencies (see also Chapters 5 and 8). As a result, management and professional staff focus on what they do best, avoid distractions, and are able to leverage the organization's resources far beyond what traditional, vertical integration strategies allow. Consequently, the firm is more likely to develop and maintain competitive advantages derived from outstanding depth in selected human skills, logistics capabilities, knowledge bases or other service strengths that competitors cannot easily reproduce, leading to both demonstrable value for the customer and sustainable competitive advantage. To summarize, then, an effective outsourcing strategy involves aggressively seeking ways to eliminate or substantially limit (via outsourcing) asset investments associated with the internal provision of activities *where a firm cannot attain competitive superiority and where high-quality, cost-effective service providers are recognized.* This notion is developed in more detail in later chapters.

THE FORCES INVOLVED

As we mentioned, the forces "driving" the current allure of IS outsourcing are complex and varied. The competing alternatives, situation-specific economics, and the myriad things that a manager must consider combine to make the decision extremely complex, as are most decisions of a strategic nature. With all strategic decisions, there exists a set of dominant forces that combine to drive decision outcomes. For the outsourcing decision, these forces are in the areas of technology, technology management, industry considerations and organizational considerations.

Technology Forces

The technology forces are of two types: those that have enabled vendors to provide improved services and those that induce firms to seek the services offered by vendors. We will call the first category *service enablers* and the second category *demand enhancers*.

Service Enablers

With the maturing of the computer and communications industries and with the growing experiences of firms regarding the use of information technologies, many information products and services have become commodity-like. In fact, a *Wall Street Journal* article of 1991 offered the position that all computers as well as associated services and products had become commodities (*Wall Street Journal*, 5 September 1991). A product or service can be considered a *commodity* when a common functionality exists across customers and/or clients, particularly firms within a specific industry, and when reliable, high-quality performance levels are widely available at competitive prices. As commodities rarely represent strategic assets and as they tend to cluster together in economy-of-scale sizes, it is often economically beneficial to purchase them from vendors. The purchase of global telecommunications networking solutions is a recent example in the IS context. In this case as in most others, competition is based on both service levels and price-performance ratios.

Advances in both automated systems management tools and telecommunications have also made it possible to physically separate the management, operation and delivery of many information services. With such separation, a firm's choices regarding the sourcing of information services greatly expands, and the inherent risk is sharply reduced.

Demand enhancers

A second set of technology forces is that creating demand for the external handling of a firm's information services. First, in the last decade, we have seen continuing decreases in the price/performance ratio of most information technologies. Coupled with this has been a growing base of competence in most organizations' capabilities to envision and successfully apply these technologies. Subsequent increases in the volume and complexity of firms' uses of information services and products have associated with them increases in the cost and complexity of the required technological infrastructure. Katherine Hudson's earlier remarks (page 52) are a good illustration of this. Second, the high rates of technological advancement associated with many information technologies are coupled with equally rapid obsolescence rates, which greatly increase the risk involved in investing heavily in an internal technological infrastructure. Third, this growing demand for information services has occurred during a long period in which the supply of human resources adequately trained in the skills associated with newer technologies is declining (Carroll and Wilke, 1989). This presents organizations with the dual problem of not being able to recruit sufficient specialists in critical skill areas and an oversupply of specialists skilled in technological areas that are rapidly becoming obsolete. Consequently, firms are increasingly receptive to opportunities to gain access to the facilities, services and expertise provided by external vendors as well as to opportunities to off-load those technological resources, both artifacts and humans, which do not fit their evolving technological strategies. As one example, a protracted inability to hire the human resources needed to meet their rapidly expanded IS workload proved to be a primary factor in National Car Rental's decision to outsource much of its IS activity to EDS (Kirkpatrick, 1991).

Technology Management Forces

Three forces reflect the changing nature of information services management in many firms. First, as mentioned above, the expanding portfolio of information services and products being applied in today's organizations has increased IS-related expenses to the point where they have become very visible to senior management. Since it is often difficult to quantify the business value derived from investments in information technology (infrastructure investments in particular), senior managers are increasingly attracted to various options offering comparable services at lower costs. For example, consider the comment of the CIO of a major bank (obtained during an anonymous interview):

> "I became a hero when I outsourced our data center operations because the boss, for the first time, could predict IS costs and plan for them. ... and it didn't hurt when the vendor bought our equipment, providing a short-term 'shot' to the bottom line."

Second, business acumen, interpersonal skills and political adeptness are becoming at least as important as technical skills in managing information technology. As a result, many of the individuals being brought into CIO positions have strong business backgrounds in addition to (or, in some cases, rather than) technology backgrounds. Further, ultimate responsibility for technology management seems to be moving from those who control the technology to those who control the application or who control the business unit within which the application is implemented. As a result, those individuals responsible for deciding whether to source information services internally or externally are increasingly doing so from a business rather than a technological perspective. The movement toward treating IS as a commodity has accelerated the effects of such forces.

Third, the general trend to disperse information technology resources and information services management responsibilities from the central IS group to divisional IS groups and to line management has decreased the required size and scope of the central IS group in most organizations. In certain firms, an overcapacity in centrally-located IS resources, both artifacts and humans, has resulted. Naturally it follows that the organization will examine available alternatives, such as outsourcing, for eliminating this unneeded capacity. In addition, as many external service providers are experiencing difficulty increasing their resource capacities, the opportunity to quickly gain access to needed IS resources has created, and continues to create some very interesting business opportunities (Booker, 1990; Anthes, 1991). As one example, even after consolidating three large data centers into one, First American Bankshares found that it still had capacity not being used. At the same time, as it happened, Perot Systems Corporation was actively expanding its processing capacity in the Washington, D.C. area, where First American's data center was located. What transpired was an arrangement where Perot Systems took over all the IS functions of the bank, including applications development and maintenance, data center operations, and telecommunications. A similar situation unfolded for Sun Refining and Marketing Company and Andersen Consulting. After decentralizing IS to move staff closer to business units, Sun was left with excess capacity, personnel and building space. As Jack Donohue, Director of IS, stated, "We had a good building and a staff capable of more than we asked." As a result, the firm began to look for someone "...who'd value staff and the center." Such a partner turned out to be Andersen Consulting when it acquired Sun's Dallas Computer Center, hired its employees and managed the firm's data processing and SNA backbone network.

Industry Forces

Three distinct industry forces can be identified. First, a general overcapacity (often in "older" technologies) of information services resources has emerged in certain information-intensive industries. A sustained period of technological development in any technology-intensive area tends to create overcapacity as the technology matures and improves its price/performance characteristics. This is seen most readily within the banking industry (Steiner and Teixeira, 1990). US banks, in general, have installed far more capacity to process industry transactions than is needed, particularly for wholesale activities, such as payment and funds transfer, cash management and securities products. As a result, in the wholesale banking business, many banks seem to be moving toward what looks increasingly like head-to-head technology-based competition with each other. The opportunity thus arises for a bank to dramatically reduce its costs by outsourcing wholesale services to third-party providers, which may in fact be other banks. Such industry overcapacities, however, are generally invisible to individual firms.

The second industry force is the rapid emergence of third-party vendors offering reliable, affordable services across a wide breadth of information technology products and services. Early empirical research has found that a high degree of technological flux is positively associated with the outsourcing of goods and services when the vendor marketplace is relatively competitive (Walker and Weber, 1987). Given that few barriers of entry exist for this industry, and that the technological marketplace is experiencing a high degree of flux, it is expected that this trend will continue. Increasing demand will most certainly result in an acceleration in both the growth of existing vendors and the formation of new start-ups. Instances of IS outsourcing can only be expected to increase as these vendors compete in their efforts to attract and keep clients, further enhancing the support of the process. As mentioned earlier, it is particularly interesting that in a number of outsourcing deals, the vendors have acquired from the client far more technological and human assets than would be required to service the client's IS needs. While off-loading such assets is certainly attractive to the clients, the opportunities provided to these vendors to obtain massive amounts of processing power and human expertise only underscore the rapid development and future expected growth of the information services industry.

A third industry effect, and one which might not be as obvious as the first two, is the impact of the growth taking place in this new industry on the supply of individuals who possess skills in high demand technology areas. Current hiring trends suggest that the IS services vendors are attracting, through high salaries and advancement potential, much of the technical and managerial talent that exists, as well as that being produced. This is occurring at a time when there are fewer college majors in Management Information Systems and Computer Science as well as, at least up to 1997, fewer people in the 18–23 year age group and at a time where older IS workers with outdated skills are being displaced. This increased competition for human talent only can be expected to intensify the current shortage of human resources mentioned earlier.

Organizational Forces

The final two forces reflect general organizational trends affecting many firms. First, an increased concern for competitiveness along with a requirement to service large amounts of corporate debt brought about because of the financial frenzies of 1980s has led many, if not most, firms to issue a broad mandate for management to reduce costs and otherwise "run lean". Managers with such a concern naturally would be attracted to those expenses, such as many information services-related expenses, which have recently increased and whose direct benefits are often difficult to visualize and justify. Many observers, in fact, claim this force is the dominant explanation for the rapid interest in IS outsourcing. While this may very well be the primary motive for many outsourcing deals, it certainly is not for others. This is perhaps best seen with the very profitable decision by NationsBank to outsource much of its IS activities to Perot Systems (Wilder, 1991). Second, an increased concern for the globalization of business has further intensified the use of information technology products and services as a means of coping with increased business competitiveness, volumes and distances. Such increases only stand to intensify many of the other forces discussed above.

A FRAMEWORK FOR THE OUTSOURCING DECISION

The industry press has tended to examine the *outsourcing issue* around two opposing views:

1. Outsourcing is a beneficial and reasonable way to manage the information technology and services of a firm, either because a major asset can be shifted in the balance sheet, or because a management headache can be eliminated or because the firm can gain access to another firm's core competencies.
2. Outsourcing is a poor alternative to a firm's internal management of information technology and services because it is tantamount to selling your ''birthright'' and, at best, is appropriate only as a Band-Aid for companies ''on the ropes''.

The real answer in the outsourcing decision, as is most often the case with any strategic decision, lies somewhere between the two extremes. Outsourcing can make a lot of business sense for some companies if it is done right; it can be disastrous if it is the wrong course for another company.

The Case for Outsourcing

Nine classes of potential benefits that arise from effective IS outsourcing emerged from our interviews. While each is described separately below, it is important to recognize the strength of the interrelations. While the order in which these benefits are presented reflects the frequency of mention, no sense of relative importance is intended. The relative importance of a benefit will vary for different firms and for different situations in the same firm. The benefits side of the outsourcing equation is compelling because most of what was mentioned is fairly easy to quantify. This is not the case with the converse, *not outsourcing*.

Reducing Costs and/or Infusing Cash

The most direct and immediate benefits associated with outsourcing are those associated with reducing expenses by obtaining external services at a cost less than a firm's internal costs to provide those services, and with obtaining cash through either the sale of assets or transfer of IS staff to an external vendor. There are numerous paths through which such benefits might materialize, including but not limited to: (i) disengaging the firm from costly, outdated technological resources; (ii) transforming information services from a fixed asset, which is hard to justify during business slowdowns, to a variable expense, which more easily can be reduced or increased according to business requirements; (iii) reducing staffing levels and transferring personnel to a vendor, or reducing overhead expenses (administration, office space, power, air conditioning and so forth); and, (iv) leveraging purchasing power with vendors. Further short-term economic benefits also may arise from the increased flexibility and more favorable tax implications of obtaining information services out of operating budgets rather than capital budgets.

Developing Information Technology Applications More Rapidly

Off-loading IS activities to a vendor enables a firm to focus its internal resources and energies on those IS activities which remain internally. Such a strategy is particularly attractive when scarce internal resources are being applied to mundane or support activities rather than being directed toward activities that focus on the core business mission or that otherwise enable business strategies to be more effectively pursued. One executive termed this the "greening of IS", which for him meant a stronger focus on those elements that could be directly tied to profit. An increasingly common example of this benefit finds a firm wishing to move from a mainframe-based architecture to a client-server architecture contracting with a IS vendor to operate and maintain (and possibly purchase) the mainframe-based infrastructure and its associated applications while the firm's own IS staff migrates these applications to the new architecture.

Improving Service Quality and Productivity

Often, the quality and productivity of information technology or services improves after they have been outsourced. This occurs for numerous reasons. For example, the vendor may (i) have access to more current technological environments; (ii) have more qualified or more motivated personnel; (iii) provide a greater breadth of services; (iv) have better management systems with which to co-ordinate or control the provision of services; and (v) simply be more committed than internal staff to making the alliance with the customer work well. This latter point was mentioned frequently by the executives from the major IS outsourcing vendors, who believed the key to their long-term viability lay in excellent customer service. Witness the experience of J. P. Morgan (Horwitt, 1992):

> "What really sealed the decision in our minds was the willingness of [our vendor] to step up and contract with us for performance guarantees on the network as well as to make modifications to their public service offering to meet our management, security and reporting needs to ensure that our use was secure and monitorable."

In addition, work quality and productivity realized from a firm's internal IS staff often increases after a major portion of the firm's IS activities have been outsourced. This occurs because the internal staff is more sharply focused and organized more compactly—a common result from a firm's examination of the outsourcing alternative. In fact, as mentioned earlier, significant reorganizations, consolidations and reductions do occur after an examination of the outsourcing alternative, even when the final decision is that of not outsourcing. In these instances, the managers involved emphasized the benefit they obtained from determining and/or obtaining information about IS quality and productivity in order to make an appropriate decision regarding the outsourcing alternative.

Gaining Access to Leading-edge Technologies

Developing close relationships with external vendors enables a firm not only to utilize the vendor's technologies but also to tap into the vendor's links into other technology providers and users. Thus, the firm may be able to gain access to leading-edge technologies faster and less expensively than otherwise. One manager with whom we spoke, for example, used a consulting firm to establish a CASE capability in his firm. The firm's staff worked closely with the consultants to develop a series of applications with the IEF tool. The consultants "transferred" knowledge in the process. Also, as firms making effective use of outsourcing should have less capital tied up in aging technologies, these firms generally have more funds available for acquiring newer technologies needed internally.

Reducing Technological Risk and Increasing Technological Flexibility

If much of a firm's technological infrastructure is shifted to a vendor, the vendor rather than the firm must bear the risks of both technological obsolescence and variable services demand. As the vendor provides the investment for this infrastructure, it is easier for a firm to move to a different or improved infrastructure (in order to exploit new technologies or strategic opportunities) either with the same vendor or with a different vendor.

Implementing Change More Rapidly

Quite often, it is more effective or much easier for an information services vendor to implement a radical (managerial, technical or organizational) change than it would be for an internal IS group. There are two reasons for this. First, the vendor might simply have more expertise and experience with a particular initiative and with managing change initiatives. Second, the vendor is under far less pressure to bend to the bureaucracy or politics of an organization. The use of consultants or systems integrators was mentioned by a number of the executives interviewed as an effective strategy to implement changes that otherwise would be very difficult to effect through purely internal channels.

Assessing Current Information Management Capabilities

The existence of external service vendors provides a readily available "reality check" on the quality and cost of a firm's internal capabilities to handle a certain information services activity. Just the process of conducting a feasibility study contrasting internal versus external sourcing can be of great managerial benefit. One executive said that he frequently brought in consultants for specific projects to "keep the troops on their toes" by providing a point of reference for current thinking and practices. As previously noted, results from such interventions by vendors serve as a basis for many types of organizational changes. In fact, a number of the major IS service providers are recognizing the value added by such "reality checks" and, hence, are reluctant to invest in the analysis to develop a strong bid unless they believe the client is truly serious about the "outsourcing option".

Enhancing the Status of the Senior Information Services Executive

Through IS outsourcing, it is possible for senior information services executives to dramatically reduce their firms' short-term information services expenses and investment base and to both broaden and redirect their personal organizational role to reflect a more strategic business orientation. The political value of such benefits alone are sufficient to induce many managers to consider the outsourcing alternative. One manager interviewed believed it was "one way to turn around a career" and another cited specific examples of this. The political context of the outsourcing decision also has been clearly recognized by the vendors. Here, however, the implications play out differently. All of the vendor executives interviewed believed it best to deal with either the chief executive or operating officer of a firm rather than the chief information officer. It was consistently stated by vendors that the CIO is often too protective of internal functions, even when the benefits of outsourcing could clearly be recognized. The vendor executives had a strategy of making the CIO "a winner" even though their primary emphasis was with senior management.

Easing the Information Services Management Tasks of Senior Management

By its nature, IS outsourcing makes the associated costs much more visible and provides the potential to manage these services in a fashion similar to many other corporate functions. As might be expected, such benefits are especially attractive to the senior executive who has become disenchanted with a CIO's inability to demonstrate the business value being obtained from the firm's investment in information technology.

Recent work has added to this picture with Lacity, Hirschheim and Willcocks (1995) and Willcocks and Fitzgerald (1994) finding a range of financial, business, technical and political objectives being pursued by the organizations they studied (see also Chapter 7).

The Case Against Outsourcing

It is rare to experience opportunities in organizational life where the managerial actions taken to produce benefits are not also associated with potential risks. This is most certainly the case with IS outsourcing. For example, the senior IS executives in one major firm which out-sourced solely for cost-based motives now are very concerned that senior management tends to view IT from a pure cost perspective. Further, while their IS costs have dropped 25 per cent, they are not certain what proportion of the reduction can actually be attributed to the outsourcing arrangement. In addition, most managers seriously considering the IS outsourcing alternative continue to be nagged by the question " . . . and, if the outsourcer can provide this service at a reduced cost [or, an increased benefit], why can't *I* do it?" Most CIOs with whom we talked attempted a comparative analysis to answer the question, but such efforts quickly return to the issue of IS benefit which is difficult to measure. Costs then would dominate the analysis and internal costs are difficult to assess because of complex overhead allocation methods.

While the benefits described above make the appeal of IS outsourcing quite apparent, five classes of negative consequences also exist. What is most interesting is that moves to embrace outsourcing in order to obtain these benefits also have the potential to produce negative consequences. As was the case with benefits, these negative consequences are listed in the order of the frequency in which they were noted.

Increased Costs

Over the long term, it is questionable whether or not a vendor can deliver information services at lower costs than those experienced by a well-managed, well-equipped and well-staffed internal IS function. Since the profitability of outsourcing to the vendor lies in the size of a long-term price/cost differential, the vendor is unlikely to pass all productivity improvements to the client firm, as predicted by Williamson (1975), among others. Further, unexpected (and, hence, often unaccounted for) costs often arise (Due, 1992). Three such costs are first, vested pension and insurance plan compensation being paid to employees transferred to a vendor, second, software license transfer fees paid to software houses in order for a vendor to continue running client software, and finally, the considerable contract administration and governance costs incurred in most arrangements (Walker and Weber, 1987). Again, establishing a clear picture of internal costs is difficult.

Increased Risk

To the extent that the decision to outsource is a manifestation of organizational risk taking, it is a decision of extreme complexity. Certainly, senior executives must recognize that they are encountering risk in any strategic decision. Yet risk and firm performance, it has been suggested, are actually co-dependent (Bettis, 1982; Baird and Thomas, 1985), thus furthering complexity. Whenever an agent performs tasks for a principal, the principal always bears the risk of the agent not completing the task as expected or of being less vigilant than would be the principal. And, when vendors outsource their contractual responsibilities to secondary vendors, it can become very difficult to pinpoint responsibility for particular activities.

Another well-documented source of risk that arises is the potential that the vendor may not act in the client's best interest but may instead opt for "solutions" that benefit the vendor more than the client (Eisenhardt, 1989). In addition, as a vendor's staff is naturally less sensitive to a client's culture, tradition and business strategies, instances of customer or user dissatisfaction are likely to arise. All of these forces are related to the risk of decline in quality of IS services. Consider, for example, the case of a large southern US company that outsourced a major portion of its IS activities. The firm's managers eventually given the responsibility for planning and implementing the outsourcing relationship were not involved in the planning for or negotiation of the contract. More seriously, they were new to the firm and, hence, had no first-hand experience of the exceptional level of service and support that had traditionally been given to the operating managers and employees in the firm. As a result, the internal functions had become accustomed to immediate response and exceptional computer service. The outsourcing vendor only provided a support group that was about 40 per cent of the size of the former in-house staff. When the vendor began to cut services, the firm's relationship managers responded very poorly to employee complaints, because they simply had no idea of what the internal users had come to expect. While the firm was able to get out of the contract, rebuilding an internal support group proved to be both difficult and costly.

A related issue that repeatedly arose in the interviews with client firms was that many of the vendors that constitute the growth segment of the information services industry are relatively young and new providers are regularly springing up. Thus, doubts about vendors' competence, resource base, responsiveness and long-term viability do exist. In the same context, risk that a vendor will not be able to respond to a rapid change in business conditions because of the core competencies required does exist. It is a risk also faced by the firm, but when change is required, it is more rapidly accomplished when the firm does not have to renegotiate a complex contract or help a vendor understand the nature of the new business needs.

An honest assessment of the downside risk of IS outsourcing is all too often neglected. Even when the downside risk is considered, a valid assessment is difficult to develop. For example, Enron Corporation, a $13.5 billion energy company, decentralized its IS operations after signing a $750 million outsourcing contract with EDS in 1988 (Caldwell, 1992a). The changing nature of the business and subsequent decentralization of management demanded a new IS solution. In response to these events, EDS and Enron—at considerable costs to both firms—have found themselves "renegotiating" the contract virtually since its inception. The subject of risk in outsourcing decisions is pursued further by Jaak Jurison in Chapter 6.

Loss of Internal Technical Knowledge

Every company depends increasingly on knowledge about business processes and technologies, management and technical skills, information about customers and suppliers, and the vast tacit understanding about the company and its activities that are bound up in the experience and intuition of its employees. It is through tapping and managing, as a whole, this base of *intellectual capital* that a company is able to create sustainable competitive advantage. An increasingly important area of knowledge, perhaps the area whose importance is increasing the fastest in many industries, is that associated with information technology development and deployment, and information services management. Under the best of circumstances, this is a difficult area to measure and factor into the outsourcing equation.

Whenever a service is outsourced to a vendor, the client loses some understanding of the service over time. Whenever vendors undertake innovative services for a client, much of the new knowledge to be gained remains with the vendor and is not transferred to the client. If a significant amount of information services are outsourced and if the client firm takes no steps to counter this loss of expertise, it may not only find itself lacking technical specialists who understand the firm's business needs but also lacking in business managers or professionals who remain aware of the business and strategic roles of information technology. Even more importantly, the firm is very likely to lose its ability to keep abreast of technological advances as any internal capacity to absorb new knowledge about information technology and information services will slowly dissipate. This issue was mentioned as a particularly vexing one by several executives.

Loss of Flexibility

If a firm becomes locked into long-term outsourcing contracts, it can be very difficult to reverse the decision to outsource, as the firm would have to rebuild its internal technological infrastructure. Many of the executives who have participated in major outsourcing deals were consistent in their belief that the firm simply could never go back. Those who *have* gone back support the difficulty of doing so. The reasons for the problems were varied but predictable. First and perhaps foremost are the costs involved. Second, attracting needed staff becomes very difficult, and third, the length of time required to restructure can make it prohibitive. The experience of Freeport-McMoRan is illustrative (Caldwell, 1992b): "We need to completely swap out the old environment." Six months after signing an outsourcing contract, the company discovered the world's largest single known deposit of gold and shortly thereafter acquired the largest sulfur deposits in North America. These discoveries redefined the company's business and related IS needs. It is shifting outsourcing vendors, at some expense, to take advantage of newer IT support concepts and technologies.

Also, given the nature of the contractual relations, vendors may find it very difficult to respond to significant workload increases/decreases or to a desire to readjust priorities, or to move in new technological directions. Instances where major shifts along such lines have occurred necessitated renegotiating the contract and, in some cases, canceling portions of contracts—both of which may require penalty payments. Renegotiating alone can be quite difficult because of changed expertise and the evolving nature of all business alliances.

Our examination of the concept of flexibility *as it relates to IS outsourcing* has resulted in the identification of three distinct categories of flexibility concerns. Table 1.3 contains definitions of these categories along with important considerations for each. The nature of flexibility and requirements for it must be carefully evaluated by each firm depending upon its competitive situation.

Increased Information Services Management Complexity

Often, the initial motivation to consider an outsourcing arrangement is driven by the naïve assumption that information services management needs will be simplified by delegating these responsibilities to an external vendor. What has actually occurred, instead, is that management responsibility for information services has been replaced by management responsibility for the vendor's performance. It is quite likely that the absolute level of management complexity being faced may increase, and it will most certainly be of a very different nature. In particular, procurement and contract management will become much more important and complex. In managing both an internal IS staff and a vendor staff, responsibilities must be negotiated among each, conflicts over these responsibilities are likely to flare periodically, and the potential for compensation inequities and procedural differences always exist.

One of the more consistent findings of the study was a recognition by most interviewees that the *governance costs* associated with managing outsourcing relationships were typically ignored or incorrectly evaluated in analyzing the desirability of a potential alliance. Both vendors and clients stressed that extensive efforts were required to "make this thing work". Several of the managers interviewed indicated that they had hired contracting executives to replace outsourced IS executives. A common strategy finds consultants being hired to advise clients in both their contractual negotiations with vendors and their management of the outsourcing arrangement once it has commenced. Many, if not most, of the governance costs are hidden in a firm's administrative infrastructure and thus are very difficult to identify. Even when the costs are recognized, they have proven hard to measure.

A variety of approaches for managing an outsourcing arrangement

Table 1.3 *Flexibility Structure*

Category	Definition	Time frame	Source
Flexibility	The ability of a firm to quickly redeploy its existing technology and knowledge to react to ongoing business challenges	Short term	Excess capacity
Adaptability	The ability of a firm to effectively restructure its business strategies and processes by employing existing technology in new and innovative ways in order to respond to competitive forces	Short or medium term	New capabilities
Evolvability	The ability of the firm to transform its technological infrastructure in order to incorporate new generations of technology	Medium or long term	R&D funding Forecasting ability

was encountered, with the five predominant management models shown in Table 1.4. The broad definition of what constitutes an outsourcing instance is illustrated by the range of examples given in the table. In some cases, managers were satisfied with management arrangements; in others, they were not. However, no systematic patterns arose to provide general management guidelines as to the most effective means of managing an IS outsourcing arrangement. As with most complex situations, the management process was contingent on the specific circumstances of the client, vendor and situation.

MANAGING THE ALLIANCE

While there are a number of methods and approaches for managing an outsourcing alliance, one thing seems clear. A firm's senior management must plan and control outsourcing coalitions so that the firm does not become overly dependent on, and hence dominated by, its partners. Even when an outsourcing arrangement involves information services crucial to a firm's continued business success, this can be accomplished by strategically controlling critical aspects of the process by which the

Table 1.4 *Outside Services Management Models*

Management model	Description	Predominant use
User managed	A functional manager controls the entire project. Usually the manager has made a contract without IS involvement	Specific project examples —Financial IS product — Marketing IS product —Production control
IS managed	IS personnel manage all phases of the intervention	Specifications project Systems RFP development Contract administration
Vendor managed	Outside personnel manage all aspects of the intervention	Specific projects Data centre operations
Commitee managed	Personnel from the outside agent, internal IS staff and users jointly manage. The leadership can come from any group or is shared	Specifications project Data centre operations Software projects Network operations
Mixed management	People from different agencies and organizations manage different parts of the intervention. Leader usually comes from internal IS staff	Contract administration Wide variety of projects Data center Network

services are obtained. How does one "strategically control" a fully-contracted but crucial service? By establishing *strategic partnerships* with the vendors providing each service while *simultaneously maintaining alternative competitive sources* for these services. Strategic partnerships exist when the alliance becomes a constituent element of each firm's business strategy and each firm adds to its core competencies through the relationship. In those situations where such possibilities are limited, it still becomes possible to develop a strategic partnership by allowing the vendor to take an equity position in the client firm. The issue of partnering is dealt with in more detail by Robert Klepper in Chapter 10.

Traditionally, *contracts* have been the primary vehicle through which IS outsourcing relationships have been governed. The role of contracts is to prevent, by stipulating acceptable behavior at the outset of the transaction-specific relationship, either the vendor or client from realizing too large a portion of the gains from the relationship. Contracts, however, are not panaceas. The mere specification of contracts represents a significant expense. The threat of *ex post* opportunistic behavior also looms large for all parties involved, even within the seeming security of a contractual relationship (Klein *et al.*, 1978). Furthermore, proving violation of a contract is costly, thereby potentially limiting the usefulness of contracts. Because contingent performance is costly to stipulate and even more difficult for courts to administer, contracts typically contain few such provisions and as a result, tend to be inflexible mechanisms for governing exchange. Further complicating the use of contracts is the difficulty of verifying what the outsourcing vendor is doing and determining, on an ongoing basis, whether the goals of the vendor are consistent with those of the client (Eisenhardt, 1989). In addition, differences in risk-taking behavior between the outsourcing vendor and client may exacerbate such goal inconsistencies.

The greater the complexity of the transaction and the level of uncertainty associated with it, the greater the likelihood of being bound to an inappropriate action, and hence the greater the implicit costs of contractual arrangements. This inflexibility tends to constrict the time span of contractual arrangements—as the confidence that any given state of the world (covering both market and technological domains) will occur decreases the more distant the relevant horizon. Committing a company to a particular activity becomes less desirable the more remote the specified date of performance. A trade-off exists between the opportunity costs of being bound to an inflexible agreement and the hazards of negotiating follow-on procurements in a condition of bilateral monopoly. Generally, the more idiosyncratic the investments associated with a particular transaction, the greater are the incentives to incur the costs of writing more detailed and longer-term contracts (see also Chapter 4 on this point). Greater uncertainty or complexity of a transaction, however, implies, on the one hand, an incentive to write more detailed agreements and, on the other, a disincentive to commit to long-term contractual relationships.

The feelings of those interviewed were mixed in regards to the best type of contract to draw. Some believed that a short contract where the intent of the alliance was described with provisions for management of the alliance was best while others felt that a more detailed contract was necessary. The shortest contract encountered was one page and dealt with a US$ 10 million deal. The longest was eight volumes (of about 100–200 pages each) that dealt with a US$ 18 million alliance. *Those happiest with their current outsourcing arrangements were those with a limited set of tightly defined contractual elements with a larger portion of the relationship handled through joint agreements consisting of broader performance objectives and appropriate governance mechanisms.* The nature of the

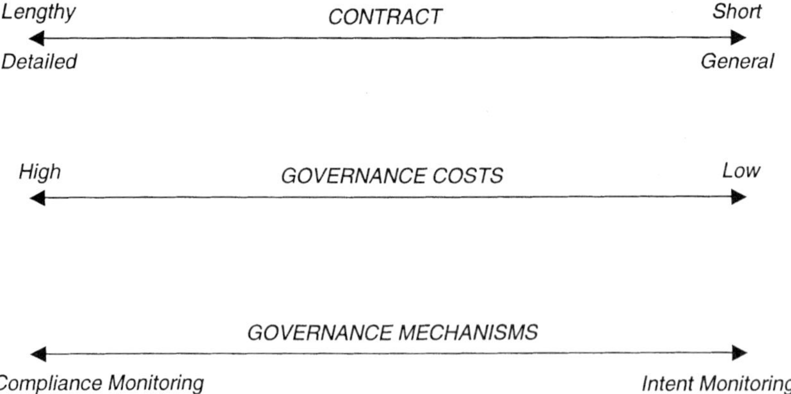

Figure 1.1 *Governance Structure*

specific contract to employ obviously is a situation-dependent decision resting on many factors, including the services involved, the nature of the organizations involved, the length of the arrangement and the views of both managements regarding governance. *One thing, however, can be said with virtual certainty—the truly critical success factors associated with successful outsourcing are those associated with vendor governance.*

Vendor governance mechanisms might best be viewed as a range of alternatives from a very tight and lengthy contract to no contract with a true partnership relationship. The types of tradeoffs inherent in the structure of the decision are shown in Figure 1.1. The ensuing discussion emphasizes the competing alternatives outlined in this Figure.

If a contract is to be the dominant form of vendor governance, then service requirements must be clearly understood and explicitly specified *in measurable form*. Similarly, the vendor's precise responsibilities must be agreed to and clearly articulated. Because a good bit is known about how to prepare such contracts, only issues of particular relevance to the outsourcing of information services will be addressed here. A contract should:

1. provide explicit provisions for maintaining data confidentiality and integrity as well as provisions for accessing, retrieving or transferring data if the vendor goes into bankruptcy;
2. provide explicit provisions to ensure that the vendor stocks critical items locally, requires a well-defined procedure and "continuous effort" (where a technician will work on a problem until it is fixed, no matter how long it takes) for problem resolution;

3. provide explicit provisions ensuring that the vendor will use up-to-date technologies and systems and ensuring the client's right to influence the vendor's technological directions;
4. provide explicit provisions ensuring that the vendor will employ knowledgeable and appropriately-skilled staff; and
5. provide explicit provisions for periodically renegotiating the contract during its life.

At the other end of the vendor governance continuum is the position that it is the nature of the *alliance relationship*, rather than a formal contract, which is the key to the successful governance of an outsourcing arrangement. While contracts that clearly state performance requirements can provide an easy "legal out" if a vendor performs poorly or does not respond to customer concerns, bringing an information services activity back in-house or moving to an alternative vendor requires far more than simply moving machines around. Systems and information services expertise are acquired and sharpened only over the long term.

The key to a successful vendor relationship is *flexibility*—both flexibility for the client to change service requirements and flexibility for the vendor to change the means by which service requirements are met. While most outsourcing pacts are signed to run over the course of many years, IS requirements and information technologies are going to change every year, every month, and every day. With today's competitive environment, neither clients nor vendors can afford to get locked into inflexible contractual arrangements or into any arrangement which stands the chance of ending up in the court system and thus becoming completely inflexible. Instead, *governance mechanisms based on mutual awareness and understanding* are preferred. Examples of such mechanisms include regular communication with vendors, internal staff who manage vendors, internal staff who interface between end-users or customers and vendors, and internal vendor oversight committees. Such mechanisms were summarized in Table 1.5.

The nature of the outsourcing relationship between Meritor Bank and EDS illustrates the previous point nicely (LaPlante, 1991). Prior to establishing the outsourcing arrangement, much of Meritor senior IS management's time was absorbed by the IS capital budgeting process or by justifying highly-paid technical personnel to executive management. Now, Meritor's IS management focuses on the strategic planning for the IS function and provides EDS with that statement of direction. EDS makes its own decisions on how to implement that strategic direction and the best way to allocate hardware and software resources to meet the bank's application development and operational needs.

Meritor's senior IS managers believe they have not given up important control to EDS—they do not care what computers are used, as long as performance is maintained. What they do care about is how the applications systems perform relative to business needs, and this they control entirely.

CONCLUSIONS AND IMPLICATIONS FOR PRACTICE

This re-emergence and explosive growth of a thriving information services industry has changed today's information services landscape dramatically and portends even more substantial changes in the future. It is difficult to imagine any firm in the future that will not attempt to leverage the resources of these vendors when defining its strategic posture. Such arrangements, *if not carefully designed and effectively governed*, will most surely prove disastrous. We thus conclude with a short list of guidelines which should enable a firm to more assuredly contemplate the decision to outsource one or more information services.

- *Understand your internal IS strengths and weaknesses*. How do you compare with others in your industry regarding (i) IS costs and productivity, (ii) your capability to apply IT for market success, (iii) the quality of your IS staff and IS management, and (iv) your ability to relate IS investments to business success? For which technologies, application domains and information services do you compare well with the "best of breed" in your industry? Which, if any, of these technologies, application domains and information services are crucial for the long-term success of your firm?

  Such an analysis must be done prior to any consideration of a major outsourcing deal. Not only does it focus on opportunities to leverage both the firm's and vendors' strengths, but it provides the core knowledge required to both negotiate with vendors and proactively influence the perspectives of a firm's senior executives regarding the strategic role of IT (and, thus, of the internal IS function) within the firm.
- *Become knowledgeable of the IS industry and, more specifically, of IS vendors specializing in your own industry*. What is the range of services available? Which vendors have already demonstrated competence within your industry and with those technologies, applications and services which you are considering outsourcing? Have any of your competitors outsourced portions of their IS activities? Why did they? How has it worked out? This really may be the key that

stimulates an executive to consider outsourcing and certainly to follow with a contract. The industry fit with a vendor is essential. Ask for extensive results-oriented references.

- *Gradually develop business relationships with one or more IS vendors.* What exactly is their competence? How trustworthy are they? What is their management style? How well do your managers and professionals interact with their management and staff? The key to the success of any outsourcing arrangement eventually comes down to the comfort and trust each partner has with the other. While this might seem less of a concern when an arrangement is to be governed primarily through a lengthy, detailed contract, you must remember that (i) your staff must first negotiate the contract with the vendor's staff, and (ii) the need will most certainly arise to renegotiate the initial contract. It is strongly advised to have already experienced a formal working relationship with any vendor prior to engaging the vendor in a large or critical outsourcing arrangement. In developing a relationship with a vendor, remember to develop the expertise internally to manage the relationship. Negotiating skills, conflict resolution skills, team leadership skills and skills to develop new and very different compensation and evaluation systems will all be required.
- *Clearly understand the business objectives to be attained through an outsourcing arrangement.* What is the primary intent of the relationship? To reduce costs? To ensure continued access to new technology? To undertake a radical change in your technological posture? To use technology to gain strategic flexibility? Not only will such an understanding enable you to deal more effectively in selecting and negotiating with a vendor, but different business objectives require distinct governance arrangements. If the intent is primarily to reduce costs, then a tightly defined contract, with appropriate contingency clauses, will most certainly play a dominant role in the governance of the relationship. On the other hand, if the intent is to gain access to new technology, then the relationship must be left in a principally undefined state to enable (i) your future strategic direction to dictate the nature of the desired new technology, and (ii) the vendor to have sufficient flexibility to restructure both the nature of the services being provided and the technical platform from which these services are provided. Your ability to formally measure the results you expect will contribute to your satisfaction with the partnership. Chapters 5 and 8 of this book seek to take debate about these issues further.
- *Recognize that change is the only thing you can confidently predict to occur in the future.* This, in fact, simultaneously represents the poten-

tial and limitation of the outsourcing alternative and is the dominant reason why outsourcing invariably adds to the complexity of a firm's information services activity. But, it is only by incorporating this final guideline into your thinking and decision making regarding outsourcing that you can act in an effective manner.

All of these points and our discussion of the examples and dimensions of outsourcing underscore the importance of focusing on the strategic, long-term aspects of a relationship. The short-term results will fade into unimportance when the implications of the long-term effects of partnerships become dominant. Often, the strategic elements occur much more quickly than one might initially anticipate. This is especially true in a time when the technological life cycle averages two and a half years and organizational social systems change very slowly. Preparation for shifts in technology management are challenging and difficult, but the social system in a business must be able to capitalize on the partnership for it to be effective.

REFERENCES

Anthes, G. (1991) Perot Wins 10-Year Outsourcing Deal, *Computerworld*, 8 April 1996. 30, 15.

Baird, I. and Thomas, H. (1985) Toward a Contingency Model of Strategic Risk Taking, *Academy of Management Review*, 10, 230–243.

Barreyre, P. (1988) The Concept of 'Impartition' Policies: A Different Approach to Vertical Integration Strategies, *Strategic Management Journal*, 9, 507–520.

Bettis, R. (1982) Risk Considerations in Modeling Corporate Strategy, *Academy of Management Proceedings*, 22–25.

Booker, E. (1990) Sun R&M Opts for Outsourcing, *Computerworld*, 6 August, 4.

Caldwell, B. and Krass, P. (1992) IBM Without the Shackles, *InformationWeek*, 4 May, 24–30.

Caldwell, B. (1992a) EDS Running Out of Gas at Enron, *InformationWeek*, 11 May, 13.

Caldwell, B. (1992b) Swapping Outsourcers, *InformationWeek*, 11 May, 12–13.

Carroll, P. and Wilke, J. (1989) Calculated Move. *Wall Street Journal*, 15 August, 1 and 4.

Clemons, E. and Knez M. (1988) Competition and Cooperation in Information Systems Innovation, *Information and Management*, 15, 25–35.

Computerworld (1990) Trends: outsourcing, 25 June, 30, 26, 122.

Due, R. (1992) The Real Costs of Outsourcing, *Information Systems Management*, 9, Winter, 78–81.

Eisenhardt, K. (1989) Agency Theory: An Assessment and Review, *Academy of Management Review*, 14, 57–74.

Gupta, U. and Gupta A. (1992) Outsourcing the IS Function: Is it Necessary for Your Organization? *Information Systems Management*, 9, Summer, 44–50.

Horwitt, E. (1992) J. P. Morgan on Outsource Bandwagon, *Computerworld*, 17 February, **26**, 39, 50.

Johnston, R. and Lawrence P. (1988) Beyond Vertical Integration—the Rise of the Value-Adding Partnership, *Harvard Business Review, 66*, July–August, 94–101.

Kelly, J. (1990) Outsourcing: Who Pulls the Strings? *Datamation*, 36, 15 September, 103–106.

Kirkpatrick, D. (1991) Why Not Farm Out Your Computing? *Fortune*, 23 September, 103, 104, 109 and 112.

Klein, B., Crawford, R. and Alchian, A. (1978) Vertical Integration, Appropriable Rents, and the Competitive Contracting Process, *The Journal of Law and Economics*, 21, 297–326.

Kogut, B. (1989) The Stability of Joint Ventures: Reciprocity and Competitive Rivalry, *The Journal of Industrial Economics*, 38, 183–198.

Kogut, B. and Zander, U. (1992) Knowledge of the Firm, Combinative Capabilities, and the Replication of Technology, *Organization Science*, 3, 383–397.

Lacity, M. and Hirschheim, R. (1993) *Information Systems Outsourcing: Myths, Metaphors and Realities*, Chichester: John Wiley and Sons.

Lacity, M., Hirschheim, R. and Willcocks, L. (1995) Realizing Outsourcing Expectations: Incredible Expectations, Credible Outcomes, *Journal of Information Systems Management*, 11, 7–18.

LaPlante, A. (1991) Taking a Second Look at the Concept of Outsourcing, *InfoWorld*, 13 May, 58 and 60.

Layne, R., Caldwell, B., Garvey, M. and Myers, K. (1989) IBM to Run Kodak Data Processing, *Information Week*, 31 July, 12–13.

Loh, L. and Venkatraman, N. (1992) Diffusion of Information Technology Outsourcing: Influence Sources and the Kodak Effect, *Information Systems Research*, 3, 334–358.

Lyons, T., Krachenberg, A. and Henke, J. (1990) Mixed Motive Marriages: What's Next for Buyer-Supplier Relations? *Sloan Management Review*, 31, 3, Spring, 29–36.

McMullen, J. (1990) New Allies: IS and Service Suppliers, *Datamation*, 36, 1 March, 42–46 and 51.

Montverde, K. and Teece, D. (1982) Supplier Switching Costs and Vertical Integration in the Automobile Industry, *Bell Journal of Economics*, 13, 206–213.

Ouchi, W. (1980) Markets, Bureaucracies, and Clans, *Administrative Science Quarterly*, 25, 129–141.

Pfeffer, J. (1981) *Power in Organizations*, Marshfield, Mass: Pitman.

Quinn, J. Doorley, T., and Paquette, P. (1990) Technology in Services: Rethinking Strategic Focus, *Sloan Management Review*, Winter, 79–87.

Rosenthal, S. and Salzman H. (1990) Hard Choices about Software: The Pitfalls of Procurement, *Sloan Management Review*, **31**, 4, Summer, 81–91.

Steiner, T. and Teixeira, D. (1990) *Technology in Banking: Creating Value and Destroying Profits*, Irwin, Homewood. Ill: Dow Jones.

Walker, G. and Weber, D. (1984) A Transaction Cost Approach to Make-or-Buy Decisions, *Administrative Science Quarterly*, 29, 373–391.

Walker, G. and Weber, D. (1987) Supplier Competition, Uncertainty, and Make-Or-Buy Decisions, *Academy of Management Journal*, 30, 589–596.

Wall Street Journal (1991). Changed Industry: Computers Become a Kind of Commodity, *Wall Street Journal*, 5 September, a1 and a4.

Wilder, C. (1989) Bank Hands Keys to IBM, *Computerworld*, 6 November, 8.

Wilder, C. (1991) Banking Giant Buys into Outsourcing, *Computerworld*, 11 November, 1 and 108.

Williamson, O. (1975) *Markets and Hierarchies*, Free Press: New York.
Williamson, O. (1979) Transaction-Cost Economics: The Governance of Contractual Relations, *The Journal of Law and Economics*, 22, 233–261.
Williamson, O. (1981) The Economics of Organization: The Transaction Cost Approach, *American Journal of Sociology*, 87, 548–577.
Willcocks, L. and Fitzgerald, G. (1994) *A Business Guide To IT Outsourcing IT: A Study of European Best Practice in the Selection, Management and Use of External IT Services*, Business Intelligence, London.
Willcocks, L., Fitzgerald, G. and Lacity, M. (1996) To Outsource IT Or Not? Recent Research On Economic And Evaluation Practice, *European Journal of Information Systems*, 5, 143–160.

2
Towards a Theoretically-based Contingency Model of Information Systems Outsourcing

VARUN GROVER, JAMES T. C. TENG AND MYUN J. CHEON

INTRODUCTION

In recent years there has been an increasing amount of attention paid to outsourcing of information systems (IS) functions in organizations. By 1992 a survey of IS senior executives could highlight outside services management as one of the six strategic management issues confronting organizations in their management of corporate systems (Clark, 1992). Another study by the Yankee Group in that year predicted that by 1994 every Fortune 500 company would have considered IS outsourcing. Subsequently, the changing and more strategic role of outsourcing in business firms has been given much coverage in trade publications like *Computerworld, Datamation, Network World,* and *MIS Week.*

This area of study has produced a number of conceptual and practitioner-oriented articles proposing the particular outsourcing practices that would be associated with various business strategies. In addition, recent research has begun to examine the determinants of outsourcing practices from a strategic perspective (see Introduction and Chapter 7). However, there has been little in the way of strong theoretical models to aid in understanding both the role of outsourcing in organizations and

Strategic Sourcing of Information Systems.
Edited by L. P. Willcocks and M. C. Lacity.

the determinants of various outsourcing practices. This deficiency in the literature needs to be addressed before significant progress can be made. The purpose of this chapter is to provide a foundation to guide future outsourcing research and practice by reviewing alternative theoretical models that have and can be applied to explain the role of outsourcing in an organization's IS management. In order to accomplish this task, we will first review the general background of outsourcing and offer a definition of outsourcing. In the context of outsourcing, we review the components of theory construction and its importance to the outsourcing research process. We will then present four specific theoretical perspectives and evaluate them for their potential in enhancing our prescriptive understanding of the determinants of outsourcing practices. Finally, these perspectives are put together toward a contingency model of outsourcing that can be used to guide future empirical studies.

OUTSOURCING: GENERAL BACKGROUND

In this chapter we define outsourcing of IS functions as: *the organizational decision to turn over part or all of an organization's IS functions to external service provider(s) in order for an organization to be able to achieve its goals*. This definition includes the following external services:

- applications development and maintenance
- systems operation
- networks/telecommunications management
- end-user computing support
- systems planning and management
- purchase of application software.

It excludes business consulting services, after-sale vendor services and the lease of telephone lines. An organization can obtain these services through complete outsourcing, facilities management, systems integration, time-sharing and other contracts (including rental, installation and procurement, and maintenance and programming).

The IS functions involve technological resources of the entire infrastructure including hardware, software, and communications systems deployed, and human resources with managers, programmers, systems administrators, maintenance and related personnel involved in the design, maintenance and operation of the overall IT infrastructure (Loh and Venkatraman, 1992). A rational perspective of outsourcing presumes that organizations attempt to make these decisions in their best interests.

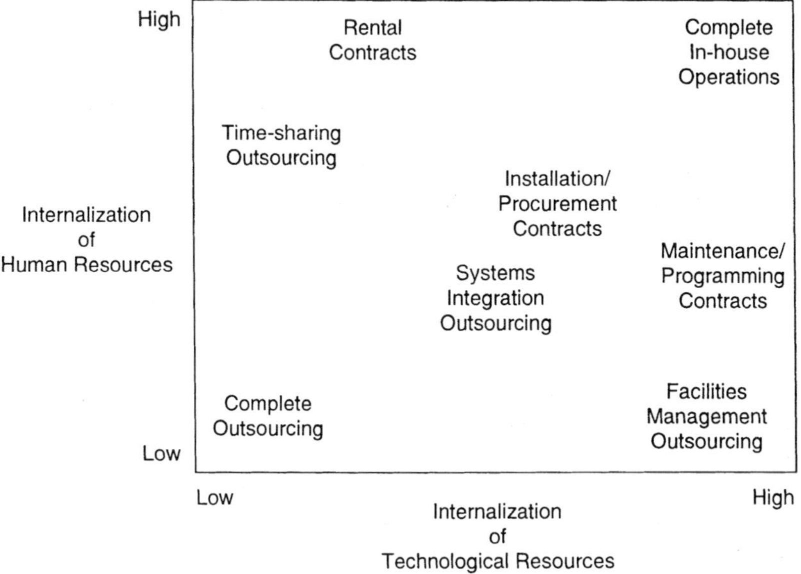

Source: Adapted from Loh and Venkatraman (1991).

Figure 2.1 *Alternative Types of IS Outsourcing*

It is important to note, however, that IS outsourcing is neither a new phenomenon nor is it homogeneous. There are various kinds of outsourcing arrangements, some of which are depicted in Figure 2.1. Facilities management, which involves high externalization (or low internalization) of human resources, and time sharing, which involves externalization of technical resources, have been around for decades. However, the *nature* of outsourcing has evolved. Compared with the 1970s, current outsourcing practices differ in the following key ways (Aucoin, 1991; Schiffman and Loftin, 1991):

1. Larger companies are outsourcing although there is evidence that in the current environment size does not affect the outsourcing decision (Grover, *et al.*, 1994b).
2. A greater range and depth of services are being outsourced.
3. Service providers are accepting more responsibility and risk.
4. The nature of the relationship with the service provider is evolving and in many cases is a partnership.
5. Information technology intensity and complexity is higher, giving

more companies the option of outsourcing in a competitive provider market.

The rapid changes in the technological base and the increasingly competitive environment have caused some companies to shift the focus of their outsourcing strategy from technology focus to information utilization and management. From this perspective, organizations can spend less time and resources building an internal computing infrastructure while concentrating its efforts on the effective use of information and the creation of new analytical data with which they can improve management's responsiveness to organizational needs (Grover and Teng, 1993). Others can choose their outsourcing strategy based on their current deficiencies and the nature of the outsourcing marketplace. Such flexibility offered to corporations in todays outsourcing environment provides the impetus for the need to develop a contingent model that facilitates evaluation and eventually prescriptions on IT outsourcing. Guidance for such a model can be obtained through theoretical perspectives in other fields.

THE ROLE OF THEORY IN OUTSOURCING RESEARCH AND PRACTICE

Rudner (1966) defines a theory as "a systematically related set of statements, including some law like generalizations, that is empirically testable" (p. 10). The purpose of theory is to increase scientific understanding through a systematized structure capable of both explaining and predicting phenomena (Rudner, 1966). In more detailed terms, Bacharach (1989) views a theory as "a system of constructs and variables in which the constructs are related to each other by propositions and variables are related to each other by hypotheses" (p. 498). The whole system, presented in Figure 2.2, is bounded by the theorist's assumptions. Dubin (1969) maintains that the notion of specific critical bounding assumptions is important because it sets the limitations in applying the theory.

The function of a theory, then, fulfils the objectives of prediction (knowledge of the outcome) and understanding (knowledge of the process) regarding the relationships among the variables of interest (Dubin, 1976). Thus, a good theory enables one to both predict what will happen given a set of values for certain variables, and to understand why this predicted value should result. Further, a good theory enables one to determine whether the theory is constructed such that empirical refutation is possible (Bacharach, 1989).

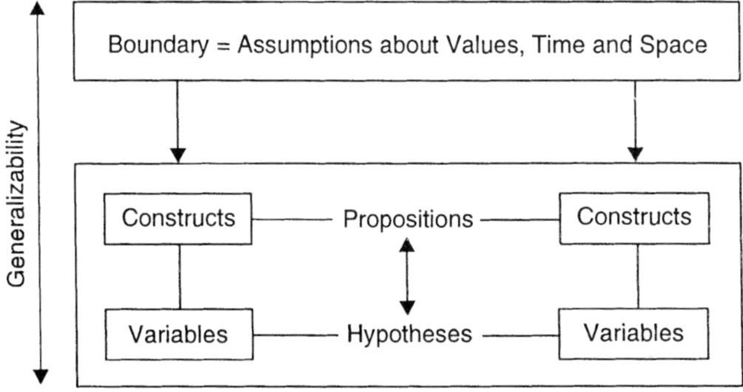

Source: Adapted from Bacharach (1989).

Figure 2.2 *Components of a Theory*

Although the primary goals between theorist-researchers and practitioners may differ (Dubin, 1976), a strong theoretical model has great value to both. Practitioners are concerned primarily with the accuracy of prediction of a theoretical model in order to guide their decision making of outsourcing; thus, an accurate theoretical model is "practical precisely because it advances knowledge in a scientific discipline, guides research toward critical questions, and enlightens the profession of management" (Van de Ven, 1989, p. 486). On the other hand, theorist researchers have greater concern for understanding the "why" behind the prediction. For them, a well-developed theoretical model allows for testing of the model and, based on these tests, revision of the model to increase its accuracy.

Outsourcing research and practice can benefit from various theoretical notions developed in the fields of strategic management and economics. Indeed, in later chapters in this section we will see explicit use of game theory and transaction cost theory, for example, each developed outside the information systems studies field. The next section will discuss the basic theoretical models we have selected, in order to describe each approach and its implications for outsourcing research and practice.

THEORETICAL MODELS OF OUTSOURCING

Strategic management as a discipline is concerned with how firms formulate and implement strategies in order to accomplish a desired performance goal (Schendel and Hofer, 1979). Economic theories examine the co-ordination and governance of economic agents in their transactions with one another. In the context of this chapter, resource-based theory (RBT), resource-dependence theory (RDT) from strategic management, and transaction cost theory (TCT) and agent cost theory (ACT) from economics are reviewed in order to understand the growing trend toward outsourcing of IS functions. We then attempt to develop from coordinating these theoretical approaches a contingency framework for analysing IS outsourcing phenomena.

Resource-based Theory (RBT)

Resource-based theory views a firm as a collection of productive resources. The growth of the firm depends upon a desire to utilize slack resources (Penrose, 1959). Rubin (1973) further defines a resource as a "fixed input which enables a firm to perform a particular task" (p. 937). A variety of authors have generated a list of firm resources which may enable a firm to conceive of and implement strategies that improve its efficiency and effectiveness (Barney, 1991; Hitt and Ireland, 1986; Thompson and Strickland, 1983). These possible firm resources can be conveniently classified into three categories: physical capital resources, human capital resources, and organizational capital resources (Barney, 1991).

According to the resource-based theory, competitive advantage can only occur in situations of firm resource heterogeneity and firm resource immobility. Firm resource heterogeneity refers to the resources of a firm (i.e., physical capital, human capital and organizational capital) and how different these resources are across firms. Firm resource immobility refers to the inability of competing firms to obtain resources from other firms (Barney, 1991; Williams, 1992).

In order for a firm's resource to provide sustained competitive advantage, four criteria must be attributable to the resources:

1. value: the resource must be valuable to the firm;
2. rareness: the resource must be unique or rare among a firm's current and potential competition;
3. imperfect immutability: the resource must be imperfectly imitable; and
4. nonsubstitutability: the resource can not be substituted with another resource by competing firms (Barney, 1991).

Thus, the essence of the resource-based theory is that given resource heterogeneity and resource immobility and satisfaction of the requirement of value, rareness, imperfect immutability, and non-substitutability, firm's resources can be a source of sustained competitive advantage. The role of resources in firm growth and (sustained) competitive advantage has been developed by Barney (1991), Grant (1991), Rumelt (1974), and Wernerfelt (1984). In other words, according to the resource-based approach to strategic management, a firm's competitive position (above-normal returns) depends on its ability to gain and defend advantageous positions concerning resources important to production and distribution (Barney, 1986; Conner, 1991; Rumelt, 1974; Wernerfelt, 1984).

Thus, the critical problem faced by the firm is how to maintain the distinctiveness of its product—or, for identical products, its low cost position—while not investing so much in obtaining this difference as to destroy above-normal returns. Distinctiveness in the product offering or low costs are tied directly to distinctiveness in the inputs (resources) used to produce the product (Conner, 1991). Grant (1991) provides in his five-stage procedure a practical framework for a resource-based approach to strategy formulation:

1. analyzing the firm's resource base;
2. appraising the firm's capabilities;
3. analyzing the profit-earning potential of the firm's resources and capabilities;
4. selecting a strategy; and
5. extending and upgrading the firm's pool of resources and capabilities.

Further, Grant (1991) argues that a resource-based approach to strategy is concerned not only with the deployment of existing resources and capabilities, but also with the development of the firm's resources and capabilities. In order both to fully exploit a firm's existing stock of resources and capabilities, and to develop competitive advantage, the external acquisition of complementary resources and capabilities may be necessary (Grant, 1991). This external acquisition (i.e., outsourcing) is known as filling gaps of resources and capabilities in the strategic management (Stevensen, 1976).

Filling gaps of resources and capabilities through outsourcing strategy not only maintains the firm's stock of resources and capabilities, but also augments resources and capabilities in order to buttress and extend positions of competitive advantage as well as broaden the firm's strategic opportunity set (Grant, 1991). Figure 2.3 indicates the relationships among firm's strategy, organizational resources, IS resources, IS capabilities and outsourcing. This resource-based perspective for outsourcing provides a framework for examining the pool of IS resources

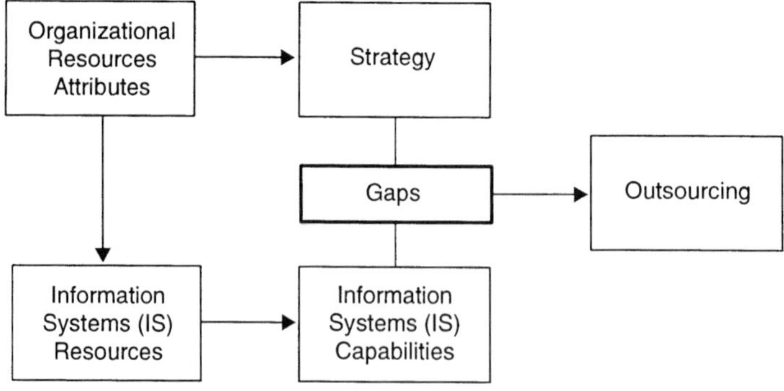

Figure 2.3 *A Resource-based Perspective of Outsourcing*

and capabilities (i.e., financial condition, people, machinery, facilities) that may or may not be able to carry out a given strategy during the formulation phase. Thus, the resource-based theory may demonstrate the fact that strategies are not universally implementable, but are contingent on having the necessary IS resource and capability base.

According to the resource-based perspective, outsourcing is a strategic decision which can be used to fill gaps (i.e., difference between desired capabilities and actual capabilities) in the firm's IS resources and capabilities (e.g., information quality, IS support quality, staff quality, cost effectiveness, and financial condition). The firm's IS resources and capabilities may vary depending both upon the firm's resource attributes (value, rareness, imperfect imitability and non-substitutability) and upon the proportion of the firm's resource allocated for IS. Thus, the outsourcing decision can be formulated as the following linear relationship:

Outsourcing = f (Gaps in IS capabilities)
Gaps = f (Resource attributes, Resource allocation).

Resource-dependence Theory (RDT)

While a resource-based approach to strategic management focuses on an internal analysis of a firm in terms of resources and capabilities, a resource-dependence theory focuses on an external environment of a firm and argues that all organizations find themselves dependent, in varying degrees, on some elements in their external environments (Aldrich, 1976; Aldrich and Pfeffer, 1976; Pfeffer and Salancik, 1978; and Thompson, 1967). This external dependence is usually based on the external elements' control of some resources which an organization needs, such as land, labor, capital, information, or a specific product or service (Kotter, 1979). Aldrich (1979) states that "environments affect organizations through the process of making available or withholding resources, and organizational forms can be ranked in terms of their efficacy in obtaining resources". Thus, a resource-dependence theory stresses the organizational necessity of adapting to environmental uncertainty, coping with problematic interdependence, and actively managing or controlling resource flows (Pfeffer and Salancik, 1978).

According to the source and nature of the interdependence between the environment and the organization, Emery and Trist (1965) describe four types of environments:

1. Placid-randomized, in which the necessary resources are randomly distributed, with a constant probability of uncovering them.
2. Placid-clustered, in which the pattern of resources are sequentially predictable.
3. Disturbed-reactive, in which the distributions and probabilities of resources are created by the actions of the organizations themselves.
4. Turbulent, in which there is the connection of group of organizations to other groups of organizations. They are immediately interconnected and interdependent. Based upon this work, Pfeffer and Salancik (1978) provide three dimensions of organizational task environments: concentration, munificence, and interconnectedness. Each dimension differs according to "the nature and the distribution of resources in environments, with different values on each dimension implying differences in appropriate structures and activities" (Aldrich, 1976, p. 54). Concentration refers to the extent to which power and authority in the environment is widely dispersed. Munificence refers to the availability or scarcity of critical resources. Interconnectedness refers to the number and pattern of linkages among organizations.

In the context of these dimensions of organizational task environments, a resource-dependence approach to strategic management argues that organizations adopt strategies to secure access to critical resources, to stabilize relations with the environment, and to enable survival (Pfeffer and Salancik, 1978; Zeithaml and Zeithaml, 1984). These strategies depend on the task environment and might involve alignment with powerful units in the environment, outsourcing or control of weaker units. Yuchtman and Seashore (1967) have defined organizational effectiveness in terms of the organization's success in obtaining scarce and valued resources from the environment. That is, resource dependence theory maintains that organizational survival is dependent on the acquisition of necessary resources from the environment.

To obtain resources externally that cannot be generated internally organizations might enter into exchange relationships with other organizations in the environment. That is, organizations alter their structures and behaviours to acquire and maintain needed resources (Ulrich and Barney, 1984). The organization is likely to attempt to form a mutually beneficial coalition. "For example, a firm can minimize its uncertainty in supply relationships by engaging in coalition activities such as forming links with influential individuals in supplier firms, becoming partners with such firms in joint ventures, or acquiring key supplier firms" (Ulrich and Barney, 1984, p. 472). Thus, resource dependence theory (Pfeffer and Salancik, 1978), which emphasizes the dependence of organizations on their external environment, provides a useful perspective from which to examine the relationship between an organization's decision to outsource IS functions and that organization's effectiveness.

Further, Pfeffer and Salancik (1978) argue that three factors are critical in determining the external dependence of one organization on another. First, there is the importance of the resource, the extent to which the organization requires it for continued operation and survival. The second is the extent to which the interest group has discretion over the resource allocation and use. And third, the extent to which there are few alternatives, or the extent of control over the resource by the interest group, is an important factor determining the dependence of the organization (pp. 45–46). Pfeffer and Salancik then define the term environmental dependence as "the product of the importance of a given input or output to the organization and the extent to which it is controlled by a relatively few organizations" (p. 51). Thus, the organization's dependence on any other organization (i.e., outsourcing) is determined by the importance of the resource to the organization, the number of potential suppliers, and the cost of switching suppliers.

Figure 2.4 shows the relationships among dimensions of organizational task environments, dimensions of resources, firm's strategy, and resource acquisition (i.e., outsourcing). The resource-dependence perspective for outsourcing provides a framework for examining those dimensions of task environments that may determine the firm's dimensions of resources. These dimensions of resources then determine an organization's decision to outsource IS functions. Further, a firm's strategy may affect the decision to outsource IS functions, since an organization may need to obtain critical resources from external sources in order to implement its strategy. Thus, outsourcing strategy is composed of different degrees of dependence of one organization on another in order to obtain critical resources which are not available

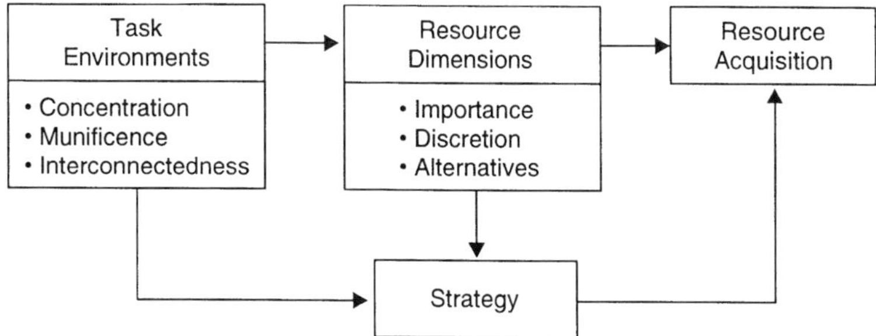

Figure 2.4 *A Resource Dependence Perspective of Outsourcing*

internally. Thus, outsourcing as a strategic option can be formulated as the following linear relationship:

Outsourcing = f (Dimensions of resources, Strategy)
Dimensions of resources = f (Task environments).

Transaction Cost Theory (TCT)

Transaction cost theory, introduced by Coase (1937) and developed principally by Williamson (1975, 1979, 1981, 1985), maintains that the organization of economic activity depends on balancing production economics, such as scale, against the cost of transacting. Transactions are here the exchanges of goods or services between economic actors, who are technologically separate units, inside and/or outside the organization (Williamson, 1981). The analysis of transactions focuses on achieving efficiency in their administration. In this perspective, organizational success depends on managing transactions efficiently. Organizations exist to mediate the economic transactions among members inside and/or outside the organization (Ulrich and Barney, 1984).

The transaction cost approach offers a method of evaluating the relative advantages of the different internal and external organization forms for handling transactions. This theory also provides an excellent framework for analysing the outsourcing option, since the essential choice here is between using an outsourcing service provider (a market mechanism) and providing in-house services (an organizational hierarchy) (Apte, 1990; Clemons and Row, 1989; Elam, 1988; Lacity and Hirschheim, 1993b). First, the theory seems to be very useful for investigating the outsourcing option as an economic reorganization of IS departments. Second, the theory appears to be useful for formulating an action plan that reduces transaction cost and thereby improves the benefit one can realize through outsourcing.

Transaction cost theory identifies two costs to be considered in determining whether the appropriate governance structure for a transaction is a market or a hierarchy: production costs and transaction costs. Outsourcing leads to smaller production cost (i.e., the cost of delivering IS functions) primarily due to the economies of scale that a service provider enjoys in providing IS functions such as data center and communication operations and systems development (Apte, 1990) and generally leads to higher transaction costs arising from negotiating, monitoring and enforcing contracts. Therefore, the outsourcing option can be evaluated with respect to the increase in transaction costs through framework that examines factors which influence the magnitude of transaction costs.

Transaction costs increase as a result of three factors: (i) asset specificity or the degree to which the transaction will produce an asset that is dedicated to a special purpose with poor alternative uses; (ii) the degree of uncertainty in the environment as it impacts the contract and its fulfillment; and (iii) infrequency of contracting, or the infrequency with which the two parties contract together (Williamson, 1985). Asset specificity, in the context of outsourcing, refers to the uniqueness of the firms hardware and/or software architectures and the skill set of IS employees. Such idiosyncratic investments would serve to increase the costs of any transactional relationship with a vendor. Uncertainty is another factor that influences transaction costs. Under conditions of high uncertainty in the relationship (due to unpredictable market, technological, economic trends, contractual complexity and quality of outputs), this might be mitigated through a complex control structure instigated by the firm or the adoption of standards. These mechanisms are used to reduce opportunism and increase costs of enforcing the transactional relationship. Also, the infrequency of contracting might increase associated transaction costs due to initial "relationship building" during contract negotiation. Consistency of goals between the contracting parties is critical to promote this relationship. It should be recognized, however, that certain IS functions tend to inherently be more "commoditized" and can benefit from market relationships (i.e., lower asset specificity, uncertainty and higher frequency of contracting) such as transaction processing while others such as specialized application development might benefit from hierarchical relationships.

Figure 2.5 indicates the relationships among transaction costs, their determinants, and outsourcing. Each of these factors raises the effort and cost of structuring an agreement between service receiver and provider that will assure the successful completion of the contract and its future enforcement. Based upon the factors determining the magnitude of transaction costs (or the relative tradeoff between transaction

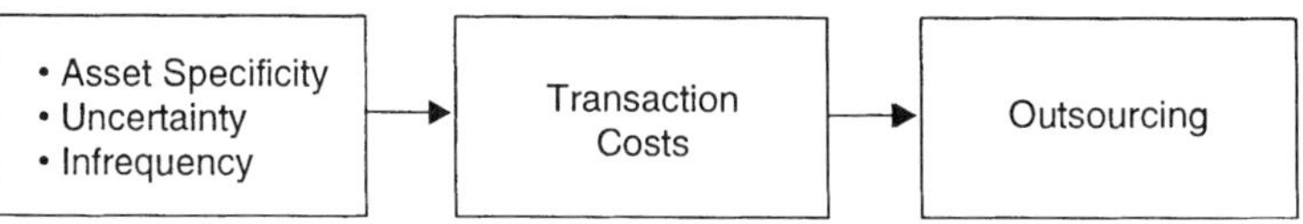

Figure 2.5 *A Transaction Costs Perspective of Outsourcing*

and production costs), the decision to outsource can be expressed as the following linear relationship:

Outsourcing = f (Transaction costs)
Transaction costs = f (Asset specificity, Uncertainty, Infrequency)

These concepts and issues are dealt with further in Chapter 4. The Introduction to this book also pointed to empirical studies revealing the strengths and limitations encountered when trying to operationalize transaction cost theory in the IS outsourcing field.

Agency Cost Theory (ACT)

Agency cost theory, developed by Jensen and Meckling (1976), Mitnick (1975, 1986), and Ross (1973), examines the reasons for principal-agent relationships and the problems inherent in them. Jensen and Meckling (1976) define an agency relationship as "a contract under which one or more persons (principal(s)) engage another person (the agent) to perform some service on their behalf which involves delegating some decision making authority to the agent".

The focus of agency theory is on determining the most efficient contract (behaviour-oriented versus outcome-oriented) that governs the relationship between a principal and an agent (Eisenhardt, 1988). The choice between a behaviour-based contract (e.g., hierarchy governance, insourcing) and outcome-based contract (e.g., market governance, outsourcing) depends on the agency costs, which are the costs incurred as a result of discrepancies between the objectives of the principal and those of agents. That is, the agency costs are the sum of (i) the monitoring costs by the principal; (ii) the bonding costs by the agent; and (iii) the residual loss of the principal. Monitoring costs are incurred by the principal in assessing the performance of the agent; bonding costs are incurred by the agent in assuring the principal of "his" commitment and the residual loss is the loss resulting from having an agent (with a parochial utility function) perform the task.

Agency cost theory provides a very usable framework for evaluating the relative advantage of the different internal and external organization forms for handling contracts between an outsourcing service

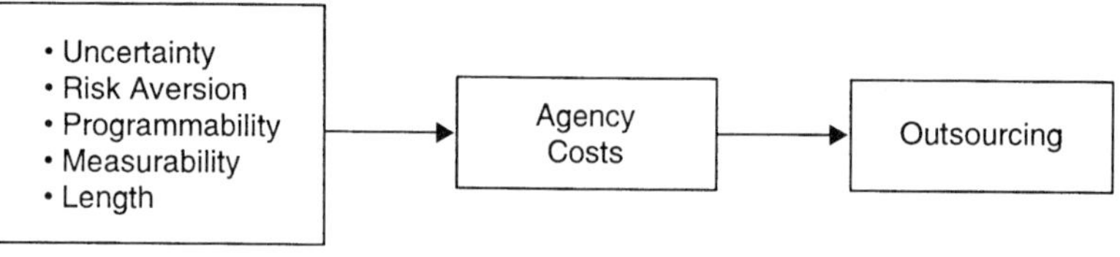

Figure 2.6 *An Agency Costs Perspective of Outsourcing*

receiver and a provider. An agency cost perspective of outsourcing offers a method of examining factors which influence the magnitude of agency costs. The presumption is that organizations will base their outsourcing decisions based on factors that influence agency costs. Agency costs are determined by (i) outcome uncertainty due to government policies, economic climate, technological change, competitor actions and so on; (ii) risk aversion of the outsourcing receiver (or provider); (iii) programmability or the degree to which appropriate behaviour by the outsourcing provider can be specified in advance; (iv) outcome measurability or the extent to which outcomes can be easily measured; and (v) length of agency relationship (Eisenhardt, 1989). Agency costs (monitoring, bonding and residual loss) increase in outsourcing relationships with high uncertainty, high risk aversion, low programmability, low outcome measurability and greater length of relationship.

Based upon the factors determining the magnitude of agency cost, the decision to outsource may be expressed as the following linear relationship (see Figure 2.6):

Outsourcing = f (Agency costs)
Agency costs = f (Uncertainty, Risk aversion, Programmability, Measurability, Length)

Chapter 3 also provides some discussion on agency theory. The following section integrates the theoretical perspectives discussed so far into a framework to guide empirical work in this area.

TOWARDS A CONTINGENCY MODEL FOR IS OUTSOURCING

Structural contingency theory has dominated the study of organizational design and performance during the past twenty years (Hofer, 1975; Miles and Snow, 1978; Miller and Friesen, 1978; Ginsberg and Venkatraman, 1985; Drazin and Van de Ven, 1985). It is the perspective underlying the prescribed dual approach to strategic analysis (Grant and King, 1982): environmental threats and opportunities analysis, and organizational strengths and weaknesses.

Contingency perspectives of business strategy indicate that the appropriateness of different strategies depends on the competitive setting of business (Hambrick and Lei, 1985). Further, the perspectives rest on the belief that "no universal set of strategic choices exists that is optimal for all businesses, irrespective of their resource positions and environmental context" (Ginsberg and Venkatraman, 1985, p. 421). Thus, effective strategies are those which achieve a fit or congruence between environmental conditions and organizational factors (Venkatraman and Camillus, 1985; Drazin and Van de Ven, 1985). Fahey and Cristensen (1986) present a strategy research paradigm which indicates that the central research question of strategy content is typically some variant of the following: What results arise from following strategies under different conditions? In the case of IS outsourcing, the question becomes: What results arise from following IS outsourcing strategies under different conditions? Therefore, the basic premise of contingency theory is that outsourcing strategy is only one of several types of economic restructuring by which an organization adapts to the environment (Child, 1987; Clemons and Row, 1989). Therefore, there are situations under which outsourcing may or may not be appropriate. These situations include discrepancies in IS factors, dimensions of IS resources, and firm's costs that are perceived by decision-makers as they seek to formulate the outsourcing strategy.

Figure 2.7 puts together the variety of contingency variables discussed earlier (in resource-based theory, resource-dependence theory, transaction costs theory and agency theory) into a conceptual model for studying outsourcing. We believe that such a framework can provide guidance in examining the various aspects of the outsourcing phenomenon in a consistent and cumulative manner.

Integrative Aspects of the Model

It should be emphasized that the various theoretical concepts depicted in the model are interrelated. For instance, based on perspectives of resource-based theory and transaction costs theory, Clemons and Row (1989) examine economic reorganization and the role IT plays in it. Economic restructuring is viewed in terms of changes in the allocation and integration of strategic resources. They suggest that change in competitive position comes from leveraging an advantage or mitigating a disadvantage in critical resources. Changes in economic structure are classified by the basic ways in which firms can alter or redeploy their resources:

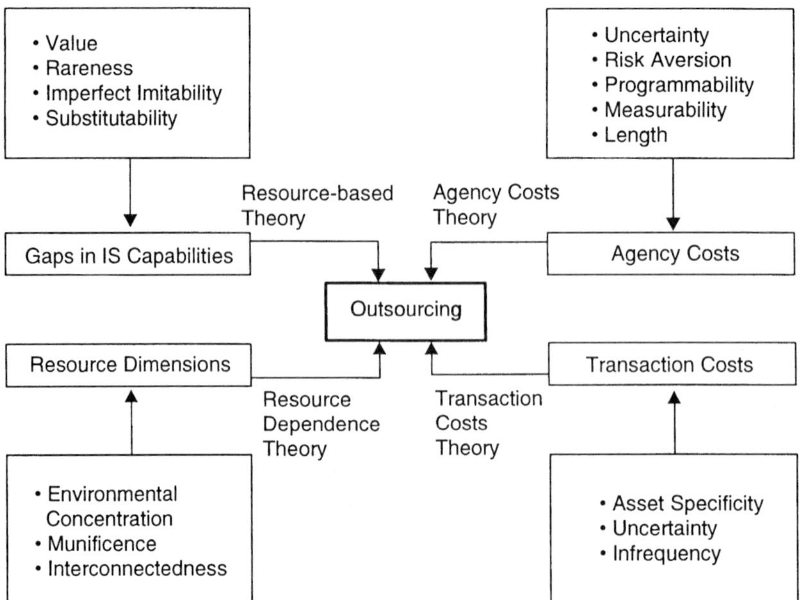

Figure 2.7 *A Conceptual Model for Studying Outsourcing*

1. *Horizontal integration of resources within a market*. Firms can expand or contract within a particular market, relative to the total market size. IT contributes to increasing scale economies both as a resource by itself and as a mechanism for coordinating other resources. Due to these scale economies, there could be pressure for increased concentration of the IT resource, depending on the importance of IT to the business and its cost relative to other costs. The form concentration takes—ownership consolidation, outsourcing and cooperative supply—depends on the potential economies of integration, the initial resource positions, and the transaction costs in transferring the services of the resource.

   Outsourcing strategy is adopted where the transaction costs of accessing the resources are low relative to the savings from scale economies, and where the risks of dependence are low. Smaller competitors may outsource the services of the resources from third parties who are larger players within the industry or from industries with significant overlap in the key resources.
2. *Horizontal integration of resources between markets*. Firms can expand into, or withdraw from, different markets and industries. Economic

benefits may be creating scale advantages in resources that are similar in multiple markets, reducing average unit costs. However, this type of economic restructuring can also create scope economies where the value of the integration is greater than the sum of the independent parts. This integration between markets can take on any form: ownership consolidation, outsourcing or co-operative agreement.

Outsourcing between markets is very common in financial services due to the high overlap in the resources required in the different markets.

3. *Vertical integration of resources*. Firms can expand into, or withdraw from, activities that are vertically related within a single value chain. Vertical resource integration refers to the transfer of goods and services along a single value chain. Unlike the horizontal integration case, vertical integration indicates that decreased transaction costs or increased production economies leads more to resource disintegration. IT can lead to vertical disintegration (outsourcing) in access to strategic resources when a firm (compared to larger competitors or other service providers) is at a scale disadvantage in operating those resources, and it is prohibitive to acquire the resources necessary to be competitive.

While resource dependence theory, though emphasizing that much organizational action is determined by environmental conditions, recognizes the possibility of intentional adaptation to environmental conditions through management actions, resource-based theory emphasizes the necessity of critical IS resources and capabilities. Thus, an organizational decision to outsource IS functions depends both on a firm's pool of IS resources and capabilities and on environmental conditions. Pfeffer and Salancik (1978) derive three roles for management—symbolic, responsive and discretionary—to explain how organizations may act upon the environment. The degree to which the organizations outsource their IS functions can be classified by the different roles for management actions:

- *Symbolic approach to outsourcing*. In the symbolic role, actions of an organization are unrelated to constraints. Organizational performance is determined primarily by existing firm's IS resources and capabilities. Thus, the outsourcing strategy involves low levels of dependence on external environment.
- *Responsive approach to outsourcing*. In the responsive role, organizational actions are developed in response to the demands of the environment. The organization acts according to the interdependencies it confronts. Here constraints and actions are directly re-

lated. It is expected here that the outsourcing option involves medium levels of dependence on external environment.

- *Discretionary approach to outsourcing*. In the discretionary role, constraints and environments are managed to suit the interests of the organization. Management's function is to direct the organization toward more favorable environments and to manage and establish negotiated environments favorable to the organization. Unlike other approaches, this approach to outsourcing involves high levels of dependence on environment.

Thus, the degree to outsource IS functions can be determined by the product of the organization's environmental conditions *and* the extent to which the organization needs to fill gaps in IS resources and capabilities.

Empirical Study Based on the Model

The model depicted provides insight, albeit preliminary, into the nature and structure of outsourcing concepts and variables. These can be used to direct inquiry into the phenomena. For instance, propositions based on resource-based theory would suggest that organizations that have deficiencies in their information resources would seek outsourcing alternatives. These propositions could relate to a homogeneous monolithic outsourcing or to discretionary introspection of specific IS functions (i.e., applications development may be retained in-house but operations and end-user computing outsourced). Similar introspection could facilitate assessment of the value, rareness, imitability and substitutability of IS resources. Based on resource-based theory, corporations that perceive these assessments in favor of their IS resource would tend to outsource. It could also be proposed that firms that follow aggressive strategies in fulfilling resource gaps tend to outsource more and have a higher risk profile of outsourcing arrangements.

Similarly, propositions based on resource-dependence theory seek to examine the nature of environmental resources (i.e., vendor market) and their ability to enter into contractual or partnership arrangements with powerful vendors. Propositions examining the vendor market, vendor versus firm power (concentration of resources) and uniqueness of IT skill desired (munificence) as related to degree and nature of outsourcing would facilitate understanding from this perspective. Integrated studies that look at both firm, environment and their interaction through strategy (e.g., symbolic, responsive and discretionary approaches) can provide greater explanatory power.

Transaction cost theory examines outsourcing from an economic perspective trading off transaction costs and production costs. Propositions based on this perspective would suggest that vendors possess inherent economies of scale due to production efficiency and labor specialization and moving IS functions with low asset specificity (e.g., network management, operations, transaction processing) would be "good" while unique products (applications, planning) should be insourced. There is preliminary evidence that supports and questions these notions (e.g., Lacity and Hirschheim, 1993a; McFarlan and Nolan, 1995). Also, transaction costs increase with asset specificity, uncertainty and infrequency in the didactic relationship, thereby making outsourcing difficult. Agency cost theory suggests that agency costs increase based on various factors. The costs of enforcing tight contracts based on uncertainty, measurability, length, programmability, and so on would inhibit outsourcing. These effects would be compounded if there was a lack of goal congruence between the contracting parties.

There has been some early empirical work on some of the factors suggested. For instance, Fitzgerald and Willcocks (1994) have examined the degree of uncertainty in contractual definition. Loh and Venkatraman (1992) have studied financial determinants of outsourcing. Grover, Cheon and Teng (1994a) and Teng, Cheon and Grover (1995) have evaluated the role of strategy in pursuing a resource gap model of the outsourcing of IS functions. Based on a market approach for meeting information processing requirements, Elam (1988) proposed the use of cooperative arrangements (e.g. outsourcing) for future IS organizations in the following areas:

- in developing back office and support applications, the IS organization will seek co-operative arrangements (external to the organization) that result in the divestment of skills, knowledge, and technology;
- in developing strategic applications, the IS organization will seek co-operative arrangements (external to the organization) that result in the acquisition of new skills, knowledge, and technology.

In later chapters others add to the debate on theoretical underpinnings, while in Part II on practices we will see several studies utilizing a variety of different theoretical approaches.

CONCLUSION

The increasing pervasiveness of IS outsourcing, the competitiveness and diversity of the vendor market and the growing interest among IS researchers to systematically examine this phenomena, provide the impetus for this chapter. The framework presented and the theoretical perspectives reviewed, both strategic and economic, provide insight into the complexity of variables that need to be studied. While making no pretensions of comprehensiveness, the framework, its concepts and interactions can guide future empirical research. While studies based on one theoretical perspective have been reported, opportunities exist to study the phenomenon in a more integrative manner, thereby facilitating a robust understanding. Future work should expand this model, identify specific and testable constructs, and propose and test hypotheses. Doing so, will contribute to understanding current research and to improving future research and practice while establishing a cumulative tradition for this work.

ACKNOWLEDGEMENT

This work was partially funded by a grant from the CIBER Center, College of Business Administration, University of South Carolina.

REFERENCES

Aldrich, H. (1976) Resource Dependence and Interorganizational Relations: Relations Between Local Employment Service Office and Social Services Sector Organizations, *Administration and Society*, **7**, 4, 419–455.

Aldrich, H. and Pfeffer, J. (1976) Environments of Organizations, *Annual Review of Sociology*, **2**, 79–105.

Apte, U. (1990) Global Outsourcing of Information Systems and Processing Services, *The Information Society*, **7**, 4, 287–303.

Aucoin, P. (1991) Internalizing The Vendor's Resources: Outsourcing in the 1990s, Critical Technology Report No. C-6-1, Chantico Publishing Co., Inc., Carrollton, Texas.

Bacharach, S. B. (1989) Organizational Theories: Some Criteria For Evaluation, *Academy of Management Review*, **14**, 4, 496–515.

Barney, J. (1986) Strategic Factor Markets: Expectations, Luck, and Business Strategy, *Management Science*, **32**, 10, 1231–1241.

Barney, J. (1991) Firm Resources and Sustained Competitive Advantage, *Journal of Management*, **17**, 1, 99–120.

Child, J. (1987) Information Technology, Organization, and the Response to Strategic Challenges, *California Management Review*, **30**, 1, 33–50.

Clark, Jr. T. D. (1992) Corporate Systems Management: An Overview And Research Perspective, *Communications of the ACM*, **35**, 2, 61–75.

Clemons, E. and Row, M. (1989) Information Technology and Economic Reorganization, in J. DeGross *et al.* (eds), Proceedings of the Tenth International Conference on Information Systems. Boston, Massachusetts, 341–351.

Coase, R. H. (1937) The Nature of the Firm, *Economica*, **4**, 13–16, 386-405.

Conner, K. R. (1991) A Historical Comparison of Resource-based Theory and Five Schools of Thought within Industrial Organization Economics: Do We Have a New Theory of the Firm? *Journal of Management*, **17**, 1, 121–154.

Drazin, R. and Van de Ven, A. H. (1985) Alternative Forms of Fit in Contingency Theory, *Administrative Science Quarterly*, **30**, 4, 514–539.

Dubin, R. (1969) *Theory Building*, New York: The Free Press.

Dubin, R. (1976) Theory Building in Applied Areas, in M. Dunnette (ed.), *Handbook of Industrial and Organizational Psychology*, Chicago: Rand McNally, 17–40.

Eisenhart, K. M. (1988) Agency- and Institutional-theory Explanations: The Case of Retail Sales Compensation, *Academy of Management Journal*, **31**, 3, 488–511.

Eisenhart, K. M. (1989) Agency Theory: An Assessment and Review, *Academy of Management Review*, **14**, 1, 57–74.

Elam, J. J. (1988) Establishing Cooperative External Relationships, in J. Elam *et al.* (eds), *Transforming the IS Organization*, Washington DC: ICIT Press, 83–98.

Emery, F. E. and Trist, E. L. (1965) The Causal Texture of Organizational Environments, *Human Relations*, **18**, 21–33.

Fahey, L. and Christensen, H. K. (1986) Evaluating the Research on Strategy Content, *Journal of Management*, **12**, 2, 167–183.

Fitzgerald, G. and Willcocks, L. (1994) Contacts and Partnerships in the Outsourcing of IT, Proceedings of the International Conference on Information Systems, Vancouver, British Columbia, 91–98.

Ginsberg, A. and Venkatraman, N. (1985) Contingency Perspectives of Organizational Strategy: A Critical Review of Empirical Research, *Academy of Management Review*, **10**, 3, 421–434.

Grant, J. and King, W. R. (1982) *The Logic of Strategic Planning*, Boston: Little, Brown and Company.

Grant, R. M. (1991) The Resource-based Theory of Competitive Advantage: Implications for Strategy Formulation, *California Management Review*, **33**, 3, 114–135.

Grover, V. and Teng, J. (1993) The Decision to Outsource Informtion Systems Functions, *Journal of Systems Management*, **44**, 11, 34–39.

Grover, V., Cheon, M. and Teng, J. (1994a) An Evaluation of the Impact of Corporate Strategy and Role of Information Technology on a Discrepancy Model of IS Functional Outsourcing, in *European Journal of Information Systems*, **3**, 3, 179–190.

Grover, V., Cheon, M. and Teng, J. (1994b) A Descriptive Study on the Outsourcing of IS Functions, *Information and Management*, **27**, 3–44.

Hambrick, D. and Lei, D. (1985) Toward an empirical priorization of contingency variables for business strategy, *Academy of Management Journal*, **28**, 4, 763–788.

Hitt, M. and Ireland, D. (1986) Relationships among Corporate Level Distinctive Competencies, Diversification Strategy, Corporate Strategy and Performance, *Journal of Management Studies*, **23**, 4, 401–416.

Hofer, C. W. (1975) Toward a Contingency Theory of Business Strategy, *Academy of Management Journal*, **18**, 4, 784–809.

Jensen, M. C. and Meckling, W. H. (1976) Theory of the Firm: Managerial Behavior, Agency Costs and Ownership Structure, *Journal of Financial Economics*, **3**, 4, 305–360.

Kotter, J. P. (1979) Managing External Dependence, *Academy of Management*

Review, **4**, 1, 87–92.

Lacity, M. C. and Hirschheim, R. (1993a) The Information Systems Outsourcing Bandwagon, *Sloan Management Review*, **34**, 4, 73–86.

Lacity, M. C. and Hirschheim, R. (1993b) *Information Systems Outsourcing: Myths, Metaphors, and Realities*, Chichester: John Wiley and Sons.

Loh, L. and Venkatraman, N. (1991) 'Outsourcing' as a Mechanism of Information Technology Governance: A Cross-sectional Analysis of its Determinants, Working Paper No. BPS 3272-91, Massachusetts Institute of Technology, Alfred P. Sloan School of Management, Cambridge.

Loh, L. and Venkatraman, N. (1992) Determinants of Information Technology Outsourcing, *Journal of Management Information Systems*, **9**, 1, 7–24.

McFarlan, F. W. and Nolan, R. L. (1995) How to Manage an IT Outsourcing Alliance, *Sloan Management Review*, **36**, Winter, 9–23.

Miles, R. and Snow, C. (1978) *Organizational Strategy, Structure and Process*, New York: McGraw-Hill.

Miller, D. and Freisen, P. H. (1978) Archetypes of Strategy Formulation, *Management Science*, **24**, 5, 921–933.

Mitnick, B. (1975) The Theory of Agency: the Policing "Paradox" and Regulatory Behavior, *Public Choice*, **24**, 27–42.

Mitnick, B. (1986) The Theory of Agency and Organizational Analysis, paper presented at annual meeting of American Political Science Association, Washington.

Penrose, E. T. (1959) *Theory of the Growth of the Firm*, Oxford: Blackwell.

Pfeffer, J. and Salancik, G. R. (1978) *The External Control of Organizations*, Boston: Pitman.

Ross, S. (1973) Economic Theory of Agency: the Principal Problem, *American Economic Review*, **63**, 2, 134–139.

Rubin, P. H. (1973) The Expansion of Firms, *Journal of Political Economy*, **81**, 4, 936–949.

Rudner, R. S. (1966) *Philosophy of Social Science*, Englewood Cliffs: Prentice Hall.

Rumelt, R. (1974) *Strategy, structure, and economic performance*, Cambridge, Mass: Harvard University Press.

Schendel, D. and Hofer, C. W. (eds) (1979) *Strategic Management: A New View of Business Policy and Planning*, Boston: Little, Brown & Company.

Schiffman, S. and Loftin, R. (1991) Outsourcing of Information Systems Services, in S.Melnyk (ed.), Proceedings of 1991 Decision Sciences Institute Annual Meeting, Miami Beach, Florida, 922–925.

Stevensen, H. H. (1976) Defining Corporate Strengths and Weaknesses, *Sloan Management Review*, **17**, 3, 51–68.

Teng, J., Cheon, M. and Grover, V. (1995) Decision to Outsource Information Systems Functions: Testing a Strategy-Theoretic Discrepancy Model. *Decision Sciences*, **26**, 1, 75–103.

Thompson, A. A. and Strickland, A. J. (1983) *Strategy Formulation and Implementation*, Dallas: Business Publications.

Thompson, J. D. (1967) *Organizations in Action*. New York: McGraw Hill.

Ulrich, D. and Barney, J. B. (1984) Perspectives in Organizations: Resource Dependence, Efficiency, and Population, *Academy of Management Review*, **9**, 3, 471–481.

Van de Ven, A. H. (1989) Nothing is Quite So Practical as a Good Theory, *Academy of Management Review*, **14**, 4, 486–489.

Venkatraman, N. and Camillus, J. C. (1985) Exploring the Concept of 'Fit' in

Strategy Management, *Academy of Management Review*, **9**, 3, 513–525.
Wernerfelt, B. (1984) A Resource-based View of the Firm, *Strategic Management Review*, **5**, 2, 171–180.
Williams, J. R. (1992) How Sustainable is Your Competitive Advantage? *California Management Review*, **34**, 3, 29–51.
Williamson, O. E. (1975) *Markets and Hierarchies: Analysis and Antitrust Implications*, New York: New Free Press.
Williamson, O. E. (1979) Transaction-cost Economics: the Governance of Contractual Relations, *Journal of Law and Economics*, **22**, 2, 233–261.
Williamson, O. E. (1981) The Economics of Organization: The Transaction Cost Approach, *American Journal of Sociology*, **87**, 3, 548–577.
Williamson, O. E. (1985) *The Economic Institutions of Capitalism*, New York: Free Press.
Yuchtman, E. and Seashore, S. E. (1967) A System Resource Approach to Organizational Effectiveness, *American Sociological Review*, **32**, 891–903.
Zeithaml, C. P. and Zeithaml, V. A. (1984) Environmental Management: Revising the Marketing Perspective, *Journal of Marketing*, **48**, 2, 46–53.

3

Can Game Theory Help Us To Understand Information Service Outsourcing Contracts?

RAMY ELITZUR AND ANTHONY WENSLEY

INTRODUCTION

In recent years game theory has provided valuable insights into many different types of interpersonal and intra- and inter-organizational events. In this chapter we investigate some of the ways in which game theory can help us understand the structure and function of information systems outsourcing arrangements. The aim here is to show the relevance of game theory to the interpretation of IS sourcing decisions and arrangements, and provide a comparative basis for assessing the other theoretical contributions in this section of the book. In the first part of the chapter we provide a brief review of two-person non-co-operative game theory. We discuss the basic concepts of dominance and Nash equilibria. In particular we stress the importance of the information structure of two-person games. In the second part of the chapter we provide a general game-theoretic interpretation of many key aspects of information systems outsourcing arrangements. In particular we investigate the rationales behind different ways of determining fees and the effects of the transfer of assets between the outsourcing company and the outsourcing vendor. In the third and final part of the chapter we discuss how one particular type of non-co-operative two-person game might be useful for modelling information systems out-

Strategic Sourcing of Information Systems.
Edited by L. P. Willcocks and M. C. Lacity.

sourcing arrangements. This model, the principal-agent model, has been extensively studied and in the hands of the authors has already provided some initial insights into information systems outsourcing arrangements.

GAME THEORY: A BRIEF SURVEY

Game theory involves the study of the *strategic interaction* between individuals or organizations. In this context the term strategic refers to the fact that the actions of players potentially influence the actions of other players. McMillan (1991) states that "game theory is the study of rational behaviour in situations involving interdependence". He further notes that:

> "[b]y interdependence, we mean that any player in the game is affected by what the others do; and in turn that player's actions affect the others. The outcome depends on everyones decisions; no one individual has full control over what happens."

Of course, there are many ways in which the actions of one individual may affect the actions of another individual or set of individuals. Aumann and Maschler (1995), in discussing the potential contribution of game theory state that:

> "One ... builds a simplified mathematical model, which is an abstraction that treats in highly simplified form just one or a few aspects of a complex situation. The analysis of such a highly simplified abstraction can very seldom lead to any specific recommendations in a specific situation. But it can lead to insights of a general nature. These insights can then be used by policy makers in making specific decisions or in formulating general policies."

This review will focus on two-person non-co-operative games. These are the most understood games and will provide powerful models for many situations found both in the managerial domain and ordinary life. Non-co-operative games do not exclude co-operation between the parties *per se*. To the extent that any individual or firm acts in co-operation with others involved in the game it is based on self-interest rather then the interests of any group or coalition.

The games that we shall investigate will be two player games where the actions of one player have an influence on the actions of the other player. A game is represented as a set of strategies for each player and a set of payoffs for each combination of strategies for each player. There

		Player C	
		Action 1	Action 2
Player R	Action 1	5,5	7,7
	Action 2	2,2	6,6

Figure 3.1 *The Normal Form of a Game*

are basically two ways of representing the structure of a game: *normal form* and *extensive form*. In the normal form representation, illustrated in Figure 3.1, one player's strategies are represented by the columns of a matrix and those of the other player by the rows of a matrix. In each of the cells of the matrix payoffs are represented with the payoff to the row player listed first.

In extensive form the game is represented by a directed graph or tree structure. The nodes of the graph represent decision points, the arrows or vertices of the graph represent possible decisions and the payoffs are represented by row vectors. If we were to represent the above game in extensive form it would look like Figure 3.2.

The first stage of applying game theory to any situation is to:

1. identify the players;
2. identify all the possible strategies available to all the players;
3. identify the payoffs associated with each possible combination of strategies.

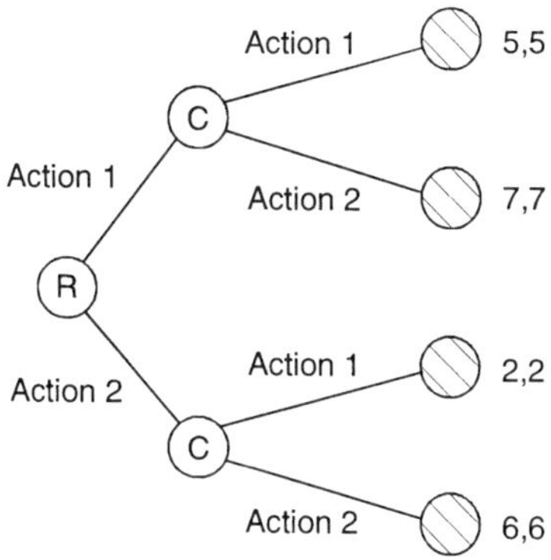

Figure 3.2 *The Extensive Form of a Game*

Lesson 1: Always Identify the Structure of the Game, the Players, the Strategies Available, and the Payoffs. This Alone May Help a Player to Plot Some Sort of Course Through the Minefield of Possible Strategies

Obviously a given strategy may involve any number of actions by a player. Initially we shall restrict ourselves to games involving single actions by each player. These actions may be taken simultaneously by each player or sequentially with one player moving first.

First let us consider the case where both players move simultaneously or players move sequentially but are not able to observe each other's moves. How can we make any prediction about what actions players are likely to take in this situation? There are two so-called solution concepts that can help us to suggest possible solution strategies for both players: *dominance* and *Nash equilibrium*.

The concept of dominance refers to the following situation:

Strategy S_i is *dominated by* strategy S_j if, for all possible strategies adopted by the other player, strategy S_j yields payoffs equal or greater than the payoffs associated with strategy S_i.

As a first step towards identifying a possible solution any dominated strategies for any player are eliminated iteratively. This leads to strategies that are referred to as *rationalizable strategies* by Hargreaves-Heap and Varoufakis (1995, p. 48) who define them as follows:

Rationalizable strategies are those strategies that are left in a two-person game after the process of successive elimination of dominated strategies is complete.

In the game represented in Figure 3.3 the successive elimination of dominated strategies leads to an unique equilibrium as discussed below.

As we have noted above, by convention the payoffs to the row player are given first and the payoffs to the column player second. If we investigate the game illustrated in Figure 3.3 from the perspective of Player C, she notes that whatever Player R does she will always be better off is she adopts a strategy of choosing Action 2. The analysis proceeds as follows.

If Player C chooses Action 1 then if Player R chooses Action 1 also she gets a payoff of 5. If Player R chooses Action 2 Player C gets a payoff of

		Player C	
		Action 1	Action 2
Player R	Action 1	5,5	7,7
	Action 2	2,2	6,6

Figure 3.3 *Game Leading to Equilibrium*

2. In contrast, if Player C chooses Action 2 and Player R chooses Action 1 Player C gets a payoff of 7 and if Player R chooses Action 2 she gets a payoff of 6. Thus, by choosing Action 2 Player C gets a higher payoff whatever Player R chooses to do compared to the payoffs she would have received had she chosen Action 1. In the parlance of game theory the strategy which corresponds to the choice of Action 2 by Player C is said to dominate the strategy that involves the choice of Action 1.

We may perform a similar analysis of the choices available to Player R. In this case we find that the strategy that involves the choice of Action 1 dominates the strategy involving the choice of Action 2. What do these observations tell us about what is likely to happen in this game? If we assume that both players act rationally and eliminate dominated strategies Player C will choose Action 2 and Player R will choose Action 1. Hence, each player will receive a payoff of 7.

Lesson 2: Always Look for Dominated Strategies. The Game May Be Much Simpler Than it Appears

This example demonstrates a number of the principles of game theory. In particular it demonstrates that games may have a solution, a best outcome for both participants that can be determined in advance of the game. In this case the players will select the solution provided that they are themselves rational. This solution is selected regardless of what they believe or do not believe about their counterpart. Hargreaves-Heap and Varoufakis (1995) refer to this situation as *zero-order common knowledge rationality*.

Situations where solutions can be identified making no assumptions about the beliefs or actions of others are unusual to say the least. Usually players have to make assumptions about how others will behave (*first-order common knowledge rationality*) or assumptions about how others will behave given the assumptions they make about the behaviour of other players (*second-order common knowledge rationality*). Clearly these analyses have to stop somewhere otherwise we are drawn into an infinite regression.

Lesson 3: The Strategies Chosen by Players Usually Depend on Their Assessment of the Beliefs of Other Players. It is Nearly Always in the Interest of Any Player to Gather As Much Information About Other Players, Their Preferences and Their Beliefs. As We Will See It Is Sometimes Appropriate for a Player to Reveal Private Information and Sometimes Appropriate to Conceal Private Information. Neither Strategy Necessarily Leads to an Optimal Solution

Clearly, different players may perceive the game in different ways and may thus have very different beliefs. It is essential that each player obtains as much information as possible about the perceptions and beliefs of the other players. These beliefs and perceptions may be revealed implicitly, through actions taken by the players or explicitly through statements. Of course neither of these two sources of information about other players are necessarily reliable and we must use some of the tools of game theory to assess their reliability and perhaps design mechanisms to improve the reliability of information we can obtain about other players.

Let us now modify the payoffs to the players in the game to develop a situation where at least one of the players must make assumptions about the behaviour of the other player. The modified game is represented in Figure 3.4.

In the case of the game in Figure 3.4 the situation for Player R has not changed—Action 1 still dominates Action 2. However, for Player C the situation is now more complicated. There is no dominant strategy. If

		Player C	
		Action 1	Action 2
Player R	Action 1	5,5	7,4
	Action 2	2,2	6,6

Figure 3.4 *Game Modified by Making Assumptions*

Player R chooses Action 1 Player C should choose Action 1. If, on the other hand, Player R chooses Action 2 Player C would be better off choosing Action 2. Thus the best strategy from the standpoint of Player C depends on the strategy adopted by Player R. Player C is likely to reason as follows: if Player R is rational he will choose the dominant strategy Action 1 and if he chooses this strategy my best response is to choose Action 2. The solution for the game is the same as before but in order to reach it Player C has made an assumption about how Player R will make a choice between strategies available to him.

At this stage it seems appropriate to introduce the notion of a *best response strategy* that may be defined (after Hargreaves-Heap and Varoufakis) as follows:

> A strategy for Player R is best response (or reply) to one of Player Cs, say strategy Ci, if it gives Player R the largest pay-off given that Player C has played Ci. Similarly for Player C.

We can see that the solutions proposed for the games presented to this point represent the best responses of one player assuming the other player makes his/her best response. In the case of both games the extent to which any player had to reason about the behaviour of the other player was limited. We will now consider a game in Figure 3.5 where both players have to reason about the behaviour of the other player in choosing their best response.

If Player R picks Action 1 then Player C will pick Action 2. If Player C picks Action 2 then Player R's best response is to pick Action 1. Thus we have a consistent set of best responses representing a *Nash equilibrium* solution to the game. In contrast, if Player R picks Action 2 then Player C will pick Action 2. If Player C picks Action 2 then Player R will pick Action 1. This is clearly not an equilibrium solution since it is inconsistent.

		Player C	
		Action 1	Action 2
Player R	Action 1	5,1	4,4
	Action 2	9, −1	0,0

Figure 3.5 *Game Involving Reasoning about Behaviour*

Lesson 4: Always Attempt to Look at a Game Through the Eyes of the Opposing Player Who Will Choose Her Best Response to Any Strategy You Invoke. Although This Lesson Seems Straightforward it Allows Us to Develop a Powerful Approach to Solving Games: for Each Strategy Available to You, Identify Your Payoff When the Other Player Chooses Her Best Response and Select the Strategy Providing the Maximum Payoff to You

Brandenburger and Nalebuff (1996, p. 61) argue that looking at a game through the eyes of the opposing player ''is perhaps the most profound insight of game theory.''

The concept of a Nash equilibrium is a very powerful concept in game theory. Hargreaves-Heap and Varoufakis define it in the following manner:

> ''A set of rationalisable strategies (one for each player) are in a Nash equilibrium if their implementation confirms the expectations of each player about the other's choice. Put differently, Nash strategies are the only rationalisable ones which, if implemented, confirm the expectations on which they were based. This is why they are often referred to as self-confirming strategies or why it can be said that this equilibrium concept requires that player beliefs are consistently aligned.'' (Hargreaves-Heap and Varoufakis, 1995, p. 53)

Another definition of a Nash equilibrium is provided by Rasmusen (1994, p. 23):

> ''A set of strategies of all players in a game is a Nash equilibrium if no player has incentive to deviate from his strategy given that the other players do not deviate.''

Every dominant-strategy equilibrium is a Nash equilibrium, but not every Nash equilibrium is a dominant-strategy equilibrium.

The game illustrated in Figure 3.6 has two Nash equilibria and is commonly referred to as the *Battle of the Sexes* game. To demonstrate the two equilibria consider the two lines of reasoning. If Player R chooses Action 1 then Player C's best response is to choose Action 1. If Player C chooses Action 1 then Player R's best response is Action 1. Conversely if Player R chooses Action 2 then Player C's best response is Action 2. If Player C chooses Action 2 then Player R's best response is to choose Action 2. Thus, there are two Nash equilibria: (1,1) and (2,2).

Both of the equilibria in the Battle of the Sexes are Pareto efficient. That is, no other combination of strategies can increase the payoff to one player without decreasing the payoff to the other player. The Battle of the Sexes is also interesting in that there is no guarantee that either of

		Player C	
		Action 1	Action 2
Player R	Action 1	4,2	0,0
	Action 2	0,0	2,4

Figure 3.6 *Game with Two Nash Equilibria*

the Nash equilibria will actually be achieved if both parties move simultaneously. What strategy each player adopts depends on their assumptions they make about how the other player will act. If play is sequential the first mover can force the selection of one of the equilibria by offering a credible pre-commitment to take a particular action. The player who makes the first move has a *first mover advantage*.

In a similar way to Figure 3.2, Figure 3.7 presents the other principal way of representing games, called *extensive form representation*. Representing a game in extensive form allows us to demonstrate the use of a technique called *backwards induction* in identifying optimal strategies for the parties. This is a process of reasoning that begins with outcomes and backs up the game tree to identify the best strategy to be followed by both parties. In the Battle of the Sexes game Player C moves last so we will consider her best responses first.

If Player R chooses Action 1 then Player C's best response is Action 1 giving a payoff of (4,2). On the other hand if Player R chooses Action 2 then Player C's best response is Action 2 giving a payoff of (2,4). Now,

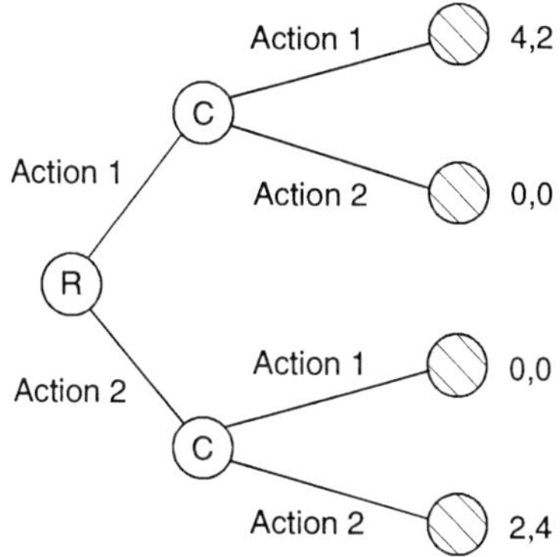

Figure 3.7 *Extensive Form Representation*

Player R has the choice of Action 1 or 2. Player C's best response to Action 1 leads to an outcome of (4,2) and her best response to Action 2 leads to a payoff of (2,4). Thus, the optimal action for Player R to take is Action 1 which results in an outcome of (4,2).

Aumann and Maschler (1995, p. 176) note that:

> "Traditionally, Game Theory has been concerned with games in which before the start of play, all players are informed of the rules of the game and the payoff function. They know, so to say, which game is being played; they have a complete description of the game . . . Such games are called games of complete information."

When the players in the *Battle of the Sexes* game are required to act simultaneously or act without knowing how the other part has acted the game is said to be one of *imperfect information*. Games of imperfect information involve at least one player not knowing exactly where they are at some point in the game. The extensive form representation of this version of the *Battle of the Sexes* is illustrated in Figure 3.8.

The dotted line enclosing the two decision nodes available to C represents that when C acts she does not know which action R has selected. In order to select an action C will attempt to identify which action R has taken based on her understanding of R's motivation, beliefs and assumptions.

Another important distinction is that between games of *complete* and *incomplete information*. Games of incomplete information occur when Nature moves first and is observed by at least one of the participants. In a sense we may think of Nature as being another participant in the game. An example of nature moving first is when we consider that

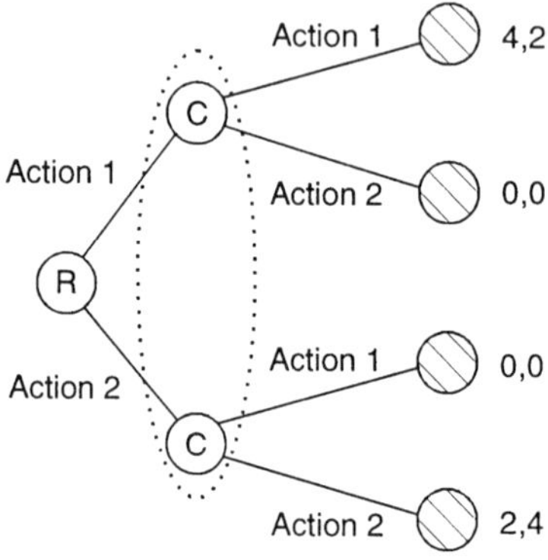

Figure 3.8 *Extensive Form Representation of a Game of Imperfect Information*

Nature selects the abilities of firms or individuals. Thus, Nature selects whether a firm is a high quality producer or a low quality producer. Such a selection is observed by the firm but not by other firms. In the game of bidding for a contract with customer firms the game is thus incomplete. It is also *imperfect* because at least one player has to make a move without knowing precisely what moves have been made by the other player prior to the move. A game of incomplete information also has imperfect information.

Lesson 5: Always Analyse the Information Structure of Any Game with Care. As in the Case of Richard Nixon, Who Knows What and When are Key Questions. The Answers Critically Affect the Strategies and Payoffs Available to the Players in Any Game

A further important distinction between games is that between games of *symmetric information* and *asymmetric information*. In the case of the former all players in the game are in possession of the same information at any stage of the game. In the case of the latter some player has useful *private information*. Private information is often present and one of the contributions of game theory is to provide insights into mechanisms that will induce players to reveal relevant private information since the lack of availability of such information may lead to the failure to reach an optimal solution or allow one party to exert power over another party. We will have much more to say about these mechanisms when we discuss the Principal Agent game later on in this chapter.

Lesson 6: Beware Asymmetric Information. Wherever Possible Investigate Whether it is Possible to Induce the Other Party to Reveal Relevant Private Information

If we consider the order in which actions are taken in a typical outsourcing deal, the outsourcing company asks for bids from outsourcing vendors. Subsequently, the outsourcing company and an outsourcing vendor may come to a detailed agreement. The outsourcing vendor then provides a service, or set of services. This is classically a game of incomplete information since some of the participants do not have full knowledge.

In their book on game theory Brandenburger and Nalebuff (1996) introduce the important notion of added value and in particular focus our attention on the fact that in analysing games we should be concerned with the size of the pie as well as the size of the slice any participant is able to obtain. What we mean by this is that most games of interest are not *zero-sum* where one player's gain is the others loss. They are what are referred to as *positive sum games*. In the outsourcing we assume that there is some potential for gains to be generated for both parties. Thus, there are gains to be had from co-operation. However, there are also risks associated with potential conflicts between the outsourcing company and the outsourcing vendor. One of the potential contributions of game theory is to clearly delineate the nature of these possible gains and losses and suggest ways in which gains may be enhanced and losses reduced.

We have said relatively little about the effects of power. Generally speaking the existence of power differentials between the two parties is likely to directly affect the ways in which any gains (or losses) arising from the game are divided up between the participants. The importance of power differentials in outsourcing arrangements has of course been widely recognized in research, theory and practice (for examples see Lacity and Hirschheim, 1993; Willcocks and Choi, 1995). Too great a power differential may also mean that some players are not prepared to even consider participating in the game from the outset. It is generally in the interest of any player to attempt to reduce the relative power of the other player.

Lesson 7: Evaluate the Relative Power of Yourself and the Other Player. Where Possible Take Actions to Increase Your Power Prior to Engaging in the Game. In Some Situations, However, You May Have to Act to Lessen Your Power Over the Other Player to Induce Him/Her to Enter the Game

Before proceeding to a more detailed analysis of the applicability of two-person games to information systems outsourcing arrangements we will investigate some of the more general insights that game theory can provide. In many cases these insights may prove to be just as valuable as the more precise insights that can sometimes be obtained from detailed mathematical analyses.

EMERGING ISSUES FOR INFORMATION SYSTEMS OUTSOURCING ARRANGEMENTS

Many characteristics of information systems outsourcing arrangements can be elucidated by viewing them through the lens of game theory. To illustrate the usefulness of game theory we will focus firstly on six typical issues arising in outsourcing situations: the transfer of information systems assets, risk sharing, technology upgrading, contract duration, relationship management and fee arrangements. We will consider each of these issues separately below.

Asset Transfer

One of the problems faced by an organization undertaking subcontracting for another organization is that the subcontractor may need to acquire assets in terms of machines, personnel, or software that really only have value when they are used to produce goods or services for the company engaging the subcontractor. In the context of a transactions cost approach to analysing organizational arrangements this problem is referred to generally as the problem of *asset specificity* (see Chapter 2). From a game-theoretic standpoint the existence of specific assets potentially alters the bargaining power of the parties involved.

When information systems are outsourced it is often the case that specific assets are actually transferred to the company providing the outsourcing services. This transfer provides benefits to both the outsourcing company and the outsourcing vendor and may also mitigate the potential dilution of the bargaining power of the outsourcing vendor. From the standpoint of the outsourcing company it is able to "sell" specific assets for significantly more than they would be worth on the open market. Hence the company is able to recapture some of the specific value of these information systems assets. The outsourcing vendor is able to obtain specific assets that would normally be difficult, if not impossible, to obtain otherwise. Finally, the threat of renegotiation by the outsourcing company is made less credible to the outsourcing vendor because it can be matched by a threat by the outsourcing vendor to withdraw services. By giving up its specific information systems assets the outsourcing company makes itself vulnerable to renegotiation threats from the outsourcing vendor since it may well not be able to obtain information services from any other vendor.

There may still be some disparity in the relative threats to renegotiate since the outsourcing vendor may be more concerned with reputation than the outsourcing company. After all, the outsourcing vendor may intend to enter into multiple outsourcing agreements with many companies. In contrast, the outsourcing company may intend to enter into a single outsourcing agreement that may last for several years.

Ignoring reputation, it would probably be in the interests of the outsourcing vendor to select just those companies that had information systems that were unique since they could renegotiate in the full and certain knowledge that no other information systems outsourcer could provide an equivalent service. However, although many companies recognize that their present information systems are unique this does not necessarily mean that they want to perpetuate this uniqueness. As we will discuss below, an outsourcing vendor may make its services more attractive by offering to develop standardized information systems for clients.

A different but related difficulty arises for the outsourcing company as the result of significant asset transfer when it comes time for contract renewal. In transferring assets the outsourcing company gives up specific assets and competencies. As a result of this transfer the outsourcing company weakens its bargaining position when it comes to the renewal of the outsourcing agreement. In order to address this concern there are a number of actions/commitments that the outsourcing vendor can make to assure the outsourcing company that it will not take advantage of its position.

One possible action is for the outsourcing vendor to ensure that a standard system is developed to replace the outsourcing company's present proprietary system. This ensures that there will be some competition with other outsourcing vendors at renewal time and in effect is similar to a component supplier with proprietary technology licencing its technology to other suppliers to reduce what is often termed the "hold-out" potential. Although such system standardization may or may not be requested by the outsourcing company it can clearly be used as a signal to the outsourcing company that the outsourcing vendor does not intend to take advantage of its knowledge and expertise advantage. Of course, if the outsourcing vendor is simply providing support services while the outsourcing company makes the transition to a new hardware and software platform this situation does not arise.

Another way of assuring the outsourcing company that it will not abuse its power at contract renewal time is for the outsourcing vendor to agree to retrain the necessary staff if the outsourcing company seeks to bring information systems back in-house at the end of the contract. It is not clear how credible such commitments are in situations where the outsourcing vendor has not previously demonstrated an ability to transfer assets and personnel back to an outsourcing company. It is also difficult to assess the efficacy of such transfers.

There is considerably more research to be done in this area to be able to understand the nature of provisions surrounding the transfer of assets between the outsourcing company and the outsourcing vendor. In addition, the signalling effect of systems standardization, the use of commonly accepted approaches to building systems, the training of staff in commonly accepted standards, the use of such quality standards as ISO 9002, are important to the outsourcing vendor and need further investigation. There are clearly in the interests of the outsourcing vendor and need to be better understood.

From the standpoint of our earlier review of game theory the major factor impacted by asset specificity is the distribution of power between the parties. The reduction of any power differential between outsourcing vendor and the outsourcing company may make the game more attractive by altering the payoffs for the parties, particularly the outsourcing vendor. In addition, by reducing the threat of renegotiation the transfer of assets increases the likelihood of any particular payoff materializing.

Risk Sharing

Many subcontracting agreements are structured to provide for a sharing of risk between the two parties. Indeed, whether planned or not, subcontracting arrangements will result in the apportionment of risk in some way between the parties. As we will discuss later, risk sharing is often reflected in the way in which fees are paid for the subcontractor's service.

The sharing of risk between the outsourcing company and the outsourcing vendor has a direct impact on the payoffs available to each party. By reducing the risk to which the outsourcing company is exposed the payoff for a particular alternative is increased from the outsourcing company's perspective. This may lead the outsourcing company to consider an alternative that it would not have considered in the absence of some type of risk sharing.

An interesting feature of outsourcing agreements is that it is not necessarily the case that the outsourcing company is larger than the outsourcing vendor. The reverse is often the case. One effect of this difference in size is that the outsourcing vendor may be more able to diversify its risks than the outsourcing company. This may well result in the outsourcing company being risk averse while the outsourcing vendor is risk neutral or at least relatively less risk averse. This provides opportunities for the outsourcing vendor to take on certain risks that the outsourcing company may not be prepared to take on—subject to an adjustment in the agreed fee structure, of course! Such risk sharing may induce the outsourcing company to enter into agreements that might otherwise not have appeared attractive to the outsourcing company. We will consider this topic in more detail later in the chapter when discussing different approaches to determining outsourcing fees.

Information systems are subject to a variety of different types of risk. The types of risk that will be relevant to an information systems outsourcing arrangement will vary depending on the nature of the products/services covered by the arrangement. For example, in cases where information systems development is outsourced the types of risk are often identified as *financial risk, business risk* and *technical risk.* Let us look into each of these risks in a little more detail.

- *Financial risk* refers to the possibility of financial loss. No information systems project yields certain returns or has costs that are known with certainty beforehand. Researchers in the field of finance have demonstrated that there are two key components of financial risk—systematic and unsystematic risk. Systematic risk is the risk associated with the project itself whereas the unsystematic risk is risk that can be diversified away. A small or medium-sized company may not be able to diversify away the unsystematic risk associated with a project. In this case the company may be motivated to employ an outsourcer because the reduction of overall risk associated with a project has the effect of increasing the value of the project. The relative power of the two parties entering into an outsourcing agreement will be an important factor in determining how the increased value is distributed between the parties.
- *Business risk* refers to the possibility that the business opportunity for which a particular application is being developed either fails to materialize or generates a far lower revenue stream than was expected. It is interesting to note that the likelihood that a system fails to deliver expected returns depends on many factors, not least of which are the effort and skill of the outsourcing vendor, the effort of the outsourcing company, and the extent to which the two communicate effectively with each other and many other stakeholders. It would make sense for the outsourcing vendor to be exposed to some of the business risk otherwise he/she has less incentive to produce and run a viable system. To this end it is suggested that the contract include performance characteristics broadly related to the business value of the system and the extent to which it provides value to the various stakeholders.

  The outsourcing vendor may have extensive knowledge relating to the development of business applications in the outsourcing company's area(s) of business. This may enable the outsourcing company to develop systems that are more likely to be successful hence reducing the risk of failure. In addition, specialist knowledge may enable the outsourcing vendor to develop systems that provide the customers of the outsourcing company with systems that are of greater value than those the outsourcing company could develop itself.
- *Technical risk* refers to the likelihood that it will not be possible to develop a system that will function technically. Engaging an out-

sourcing vendor may well result in a reduction of technical risk for a number of reasons. First, the outsourcing vendor may be able to retain personnel who are technically more skilled. Second, the outsourcing vendor is likely to have had more opportunity to develop technical skill. Third, if the outsourcing vendor has a portfolio of development projects it may be able to apply a variety of different technological solutions so that if one fails it has at least one other technological alternative to consider. Of course, the outsourcing vendor is likely to want to be compensated for reducing the outsourcing companys technical risk. Technical risk cannot be completely eliminated, especially when the outsourcing vendor is being asked to provide state-of-the-art technical solutions.

Another important risk faced by organizations that depend to a significant extent on information technology is *obsolescence risk*. Technologies that were state-of-the-art last year are passé this year. The risk of obsolescence can be reduced through thoughtful gathering of competitive intelligence, experimentation with a variety of technologies and partnering with organizations at the leading edge, technologically speaking.

Organizations also face the risk of losing key personnel. The information systems function is often considered to be a support function somewhat divorced from the primary value-adding processes of the organization. This makes it difficult for organizations to compensate individuals with significant technical expertise sufficiently. They are also unable to provide their technical staff with access to state-of-the-art problems or technologies. Employing an outsourcing vendor may counteract this risk by providing the information systems staff of outsourcing company with a superior employment environment. Of course, this is only beneficial to the outsourcing company if they are able to access their former employees.

From a game-theoretic perspective the opportunity to share risks may significantly alter payoffs and make investments more attractive to the outsourcing partners than they otherwise would have been.

Technology Upgrading

A concern that is common to many subcontracting agreements is how to structure such agreements to ensure that the subcontractor is motivated to use the most productive technology. In the case of information systems outsourcing the outsourcing company wants reassurance that the outsourcing vendor will upgrade its hardware, software and personnel as and when appropriate. A fixed-price contract may provide significant incentives for the outsourcing vendor to invest in technologies that improve its productivity. However, the benefits of any improvements in productivity will accrue only to the outsourcing vendor.

How do we ensure that the outsourcing vendor shares some of the benefits of investing in more productive technology? McMillan (1991) notes that one way to ensure that this takes place is to state explicitly in the contract an assumption about expected productivity improvements over the lifetime of the contract. This will induce the outsourcing vendor to at least match the productivity improvements that have been contracted for. It may also be appropriate to agree to share the benefits of any productivity improvements over and above those stipulated in the contract. This is an area that would benefit considerably from further research to determine the effects of the productivity clauses presently included in outsourcing contracts and investigate the potential effects of other possible clauses.

Another action that the outsourcing vendor can take is to demonstrate that it invests heavily in keeping its personnel up-to-date, that it replaces its hardware and software on a regular basis, and that it has alliances with major software and hardware vendors allowing it to have access to state-of-the-art technology. To the extent that the outsourcing vendor takes these actions before signing an outsourcing contract it is engaging in *signalling*.

If the outsourcing company requires that it take some, or all of these actions on assumption of the outsourcing contract the outsourcing company is engaging in what is termed *screening*. Screening occurs when the outsourcing company attempts to design a contract that will be significantly more attractive to the outsourcing vendor who intends to keep up-to-date compared to the outsourcing vendor who has no interest in keeping current. For screening to work efficiently it must be uneconomic for the outsourcing vendor who does not intend to keep up-to-date to enter into such agreements.

Technology upgrading is an interesting example of, first, investigating how the outsourcing vendor can be induced to create added value by investing in new technology, and second, of determining how the surplus will be divided between the parties. These two issues are clearly related.

Contract Duration

Generally speaking, the longer the duration of the contract the greater the danger that the outsourcing company will find itself "locked in." It is interesting to note that over the last decade the average duration of outsourcing contracts has decreased somewhat. One would expect that as the duration of an outsourcing contract increases, both parties will negotiate terms that reduce the likelihood of either party being "locked in". The principal rationale for this is that the existence of such a danger may undermine an agreement that may be valuable to both parties or result in an agreement that is less valuable as a result of the need to provide compensation for such a risk.

As we have noted earlier, there are a variety of ways by which the risk of either party being locked in can be reduced. The development of standardized systems, the use of commonly available technology, the use of generally accepted systems development techniques and clauses requiring the re-training of personnel when a particular outsourcing contract expires are just some examples. As we have noted previously in the section on asset specificity, the transfer of information systems assets from the outsourcing company to the outsourcing vendor may also reduce the likelihood of lock-in.

Another way of reducing the danger of lock-in is to provide for the possibility of contract renegotiation at intervals during the life of the contract. Such flexibility does incur costs. Contract renegotiation is itself costly and it may be difficult to restrict negotiations to a small subset of the terms of the contract.

Finally, the danger of lock-in may be reduced through the use of relatively vague contract language or flexible contract terms. Even if the contract language is not vague over the life of an outsourcing contract extending well into the future many unanticipated situations are likely to be encountered. Flexible or vague contracts require that the two parties establish close relationships to ensure the stability and predictability of the arrangement. Thus, relationship management, the topic of the next section, is critical to the success of long-term outsourcing arrangements.

Relationship Management

It is often a requirement of outsourcing contracts that a relatively intimate relationship be established between the outsourcing company and the outsourcing vendor. The existence of such a relationship may reduce the need for detailed monitoring of the performance of the outsourcing vendor by the outsourcing company. Ongoing relationships may lead to the establishment of trust and perceptions of common interest. The more the outsourcing vendor interacts with the outsourcing company the more comfortable they are likely to feel with each other.

Close relationships are likely to be enduring if they arise from genuine common interests. It is important to ensure that these common interests are established in the structure of the outsourcing arrangement and nurtured throughout the duration of the contract. In order to facilitate the establishment of common interests and understanding it is often argued that outsourcing companies should seek out outsourcing vendors with similar values and cultures.

However, an outsourcing company should be careful not to put too much faith in the effectiveness of close relationships in causing the outsourcing vendor to act in the best interest of the outsourcing company. The interests of the outsourcing company and the outsourcing vendor do not naturally coincide. The outsourcing company must find a way of designing a set of incentives that ensure that it is in the interest of the outsourcing vendor to act in the interest of the outsourcing company.

Close relationships allow each party to make inferences about the beliefs, perceptions and possible actions of the other party with more confidence than in situations where relationships are not close. Further, the trust that may arise in such relationships may lessen the perceived likelihood of demands for renegotiation.

Brandenburger and Nalebuff (1996) point up the interesting combination of co-operation and conflict that arises in many relationships. Co-operation arises with respect to establishing arrangements that create value that would not have existed otherwise. Conflict arises with respect to dividing up the resulting surplus value. The management of such hybrid relationships is difficult.

Fee Arrangements

One of the key elements of an outsourcing contract relates to how fees are structured and adjudicated. We will first consider how fees are typically calculated and examine the implications of a variety of different fee structures for both parties in an outsourcing arrangement.

How Are the Fees Calculated?

In cases where performance is easy to measure, fees may be relatively easy to determine. For example, in the case of facilities management CPU minutes, disk access times, tape mounts etc. may be relatively easy to verify. Even here, however, there may be problems since there may be a concern that the outsourcing vendor is not using the technology efficiently or not using state-of-the-art technology. For example, the outsourcing vendor may be using mainframe software and hardware when client/server network technology would be more efficient. Conversely, the outsourcing vendor may significantly upgrade its hardware/software but not pass on any of the savings resulting from improved productivity to the outsourcing company.

Problems of measurement are compounded when the outsourcing vendor has been contracted to provide information systems that are strategic. In these cases performance measures may have to be related to the business value of such systems rather than their technical performance.

One interesting set of issues with respect to the fees paid under outsourcing arrangements concerns whether fees are fixed or variable or some combination of fixed and variable. Let us examine these issues in a little more detail.

Minimum or Maximum Fees?

Outsourcing agreements may provide for minimum or maximum fees. We will look at the implications of each of these arrangements separately.

On the surface, minimum fees would seem to be of benefit to the outsourcing vendor since they guarantee that it receives a minimum level of payment regardless of demand from the outsourcing company. Why would the outsourcing company be prepared to offer such a guarantee? One answer relates to the magnitude of the specific assets that the outsourcing vendor has to acquire to provide the outsourcing company with information services. Clearly, the outsourcing vendor expects to earn a reasonable return on these assets—a minimum fee can guarantee a minimum acceptable return. The existence of this minimum level of return may guarantee that it is possible to reach an agreement and/or reduce any "risk premium" paid to the outsourcing vendor to compensate for the risk of being locked in.

From the standpoint of the outsourcing company a minimum fee represents the possibility of paying for a service when it is not required. Clearly it is in the interests of the outsourcing company to negotiate a minimum fee that represents a reasonable payment for the lowest level of services it expects to provide. If the outsourcing company feels that the outsourcing vendor is demanding too high a minimum fee there are at least two actions it might take to induce the outsourcing company to reduce its demands. It might indicate to the outsourcing vendor that it is prepared to accept a lower price for the specific assets being transferred to the outsourcing vendor and/or attempt to make an agreement not to renegotiate the contract more credible.

Establishing a maximum fee is of potential value to the outsourcing company since it establishes an upper limit on the potential costs associated with its acquisition of information services. Simultaneously with a maximum fee being a potential benefit to the outsourcing company it has the potential of requiring the outsourcing vendor to provide information services at a loss.

One rationale for the existence of a maximum fee is that it may provide an incentive for the outsourcing vendor to improve its productivity. The argument would be as follows. The outsourcing company has private information that its demands are likely to be very significantly above those envisaged in the maximum fee negotiated with the outsourcing vendor. In order to have any possibility of earning a reasonable return the outsourcing vendor is forced to either improve its productivity or reduce the quality of the services it provides.

The relative riskiness of maximum or minimum fee arrangements to either party to an outsourcing agreement depends on future demand patterns. Each party in the outsourcing agreement is in a different position with respect to their ability to forecast these demand patterns. It would seem that the outsourcing company is in a superior position with respect to forecasting the future level of business demand. In contrast the outsourcing vendor is in a superior position with respect to being able to forecast how business demands are translated into technical demand requirements. It is clearly in the interests of both parties to design mechanisms that encourage the disclosure of best estimates of demand patterns. By themselves minimum or maximum fees do not encourage such disclosure.

In establishing a maximum payment it is in the interests of the outsourcing company to underestimate expected demand while it is in the interests of the outsourcing vendor to overestimate the results of translating these business demands into technical demand requirements. The rationales for the establishment of minimum and maximum fees is clearly a fertile field for further analysis.

How Are Fee Adjustments Handled?

Many subcontracting agreements provide for the modification of fees/payments made under the agreement in certain circumstances. For instance, a car company may allow its parts suppliers to pass on raw materials price increases over which they have little control but may not allow any pass through of increases on labour costs. Adjustment mechanisms mitigate the risks of being locked in if unanticipated events occur. As we have noted earlier, such mechanisms bring with them both explicit costs (renegotiation costs) and implicit costs (some gains may be given up on renegotiation if the balance of power has changed).

Fixed Fees

Establishing fixed fees for certain information services is common practice in the industry and often relates to one-off project-based services rather than transaction-based services. For example, in systems development it is quite common for the outsourcing company to set fixed fees for specific projects. The establishment of fixed fees transfers any financial risks associated with a project to the outsourcing vendor. The outsourcing company will not have completely eliminated financial risk. The outsourcing vendor may still go bankrupt. In return for taking on financial risks the outsourcing vendor will expect to be compensated appropriately through a risk premium.

Usage Fees

In cases where it may be difficult to forecast demand and/or the costs faced by the outsourcing vendor do not have a very significant fixed component, a straight usage fee for services may be negotiated. Many outsourcing contracts provide for usage fees to remain constant within ranges of usage and be open to renegotiation, particularly if demand exceeds some maximum level.

Usage fees often seem particularly attractive to the outsourcing company as a means of switching fixed costs to variable costs. Such attractiveness may be illusory to the extent that often the variable costs will represent a blend of the outsourcing vendor's fixed and variable costs that at a certain level of demand may well exceed the previous level of fixed costs.

From a game-theoretic perspective it important that the outsourcing company has access to reliable and detailed information concerning the outsourcing vendor's cost structure. It is also vital that the outsourcing company has detailed knowledge of their own cost structure when it comes to information services—a state of affairs that is all too rare.

It is also worth pointing out that, as in the case of our discussion of the establishment of maximum and minimum fees, in negotiating levels of usage fees business demand and technical demand forecasts will be made by the outsourcing company and the outsourcing vendor respectively. As before, there is considerable scope for detailed further research into the interaction between these forecasts and actual levels of usage fees and the path of usage fees over time (both contracted for and actual).

Shared Savings

It has become popular to characterize the principal reason for outsourcing information services as a concern to reduce costs. For example, a workflow system may be implemented in an organization with the intention of reducing head count, increasing throughput, and reducing error. If the development of these systems is outsourced the outsourcing vendor may be provided with additional incentives in the contract through being able to share in the savings garnered through the implementation of the system.

One of the problems associated with fees determined in this manner is the credibility of the information concerning costs provided to each party. It is likely that both parties will have to develop sufficient trust in order to be able to open their books to each other. Another problem relates to the time period over which savings may accrue and the need for the outsourcing company to determine that the levels of service being provided by the new system are commensurate or better than the levels of service provided by the previous system.

Shared Revenue

The stimulus behind this approach to determining fees is similar to the cost savings approach except that it recognizes that systems should be developed ideally both to reduce the costs of business for the outsourcing company and increase revenues. Similar, though more extensive, problems arise with respect to the credibility of revenue information as with the cost savings approach. Revenue information is likely to be even more sensitive than cost information and therefore the outsourcing company will not be prepared to divulge it unless there is some assurance that the outsourcing vendor will not divulge it to a third party. Inevitably the use of this type of fee structure will require the development of a close trusting relationship between the outsourcing vendor and the outsourcing company.

Bottom Line Approaches

It would seem natural for the outsourcing company to negotiate fees based on realizable net profit from the implementation of new information systems/information services. This approach appears to be reasonable—it weeds out systems that decrease costs while at the same time reducing revenue-generating potential and conversely, systems that increase revenues while dramatically increasing present or future costs. The principal problem with this approach is that it is very difficult to make net profit figures credible to the outsourcing vendor. To fully satisfy the outsourcing vendor of the credibility of such figures the outsourcing company may have to disclose extremely sensitive information.

Combination Approaches

Many outsourcing contracts provide for a combination of approaches to determining fees. This allows for a tailoring of fee structures to match the information the parties are prepared to disclose to each other, the degree of exposure they are prepared to entertain, and so on. We are unable to investigate these combination approaches in detail here, but see Fitzgerald and Willcocks (1994) for a further discussion of fee types.

In the following section we return to analytic game theory and investigate in more detail than provided in Chapter 2 one approach to modelling information systems outsourcing arrangements. This is the *principal-agent model.*

MODELLING OUTSOURCING AGENTS AS PRINCIPAL—AGENT GAMES

Since outsourcing arrangements, in their simplest form, involve two organizations it seems natural to draw on a special-case game theoretic model called the principal-agent model, introduced in Chapter 2. In this model two agents (individuals or stylized individuals as in the case of organizations) enter into an arrangement in which one party (the agent) agrees to perform actions on behalf of another party (the principal) for some consideration. Typically the parties enter into some type of contact that governs their interaction and potentially could be enforced by the relevant legal system.

Let us look a little more closely at the principal-agent relationship. In its simplest form the principal contracts with the agent to perform some activity, say manage a company the principal owns. Over the course of the agreed period the agent exerts some effort in managing the company that is not directly observable by the principal and is costly to the agent. The principal can only observe the output of the organization that we can assume is some function of the effort expended by the agent and other variables corresponding to the economic environment faced by the firm. If the principal rewards the agent solely on outcome the risk is totally transferred to the agent whereas if the principal pays the agent regardless of outcome the principal assumes all the risk.

To reiterate, an outcome, observable by the principal and agent together, is a function of a number of factors that may include the agent's effort, information that is privately available to the agent, and actions that the agent may or may not take such as investing in new technologies. Although the outcome can be observed the principal is not able to judge whether the outcome is as beneficial to him as possible since he cannot observe the agent's effort and/or private information directly.

A further refinement of this situation occurs when the characteristics of the outcome are difficult to judge accurately. For instance, in the case of software development, issues with respect to reliability, robustness and maintainability, may be difficult to judge simply by inspection. Typically the software developer has private information that is relevant to the determination of the characteristics of the software. It may well be in the interests of the developer to make some of this information public. Examples of the types of information that may be relevant are testing procedures applied, qualifications of the software development staff, performance of staff on other software contracts, certification such as ISO 9002, and so on.

The principal-agent situation would not constitute a problem if the goals of the agent and the principal were congruent. Although we would still be faced with the problem that the principal could not directly observe the behaviour of the agent if we assume individual rationality then as the agent acts in his/her best interest they are also acting in the best interest of the principal. However, it is usually the case that the interests of the principal and the agent are not congruent. By acting in his own best interest the agent does not act in the best interest of the principal.

The key question for the principal is: can an incentive scheme, or a combination of incentives and punishments be developed that will ensure that the agent exerts an appropriate level of effort? It is worth noting at this juncture a distinction between a *first-best* solution and a *second-best* solution. A first-best solution represents what the principal would have achieved acting on his/her own behalf and the second-best solution represents the best that can be achieved through delegation to an agent. The difference between the wealth available to the principal in the case of a first-best solution and the second-best solution arises because of the lack of congruence between the interests of the two parties. The principal's welfare loss can be reduced through the creation of a detailed contract and monitoring activities carried out by the principal or other agents of the principal. These mechanisms are themselves costly. Thus optimal strategies for the principal will require detailed analysis.

In order to investigate principal/agent relationships more deeply it will be helpful to consider a number of prototypical types of situation that may be faced by the two parties. These situations can be modelled using two person games with *information asymmetry*. As we have noted earlier, the key aspect of the information asymmetries referred to above is that they are relevant—they relate to the assessment of key parameters of the service being provided. These parameters may relate to the effort expended in providing the service, the quality of the service, the true cost of the service, the extent to which the agent makes use of reliable and up-to-date information or technology in providing the service and so on.

In addition to information asymmetries, principal-agent games involve sequential actions that may or may not reveal some or all of the information that was hidden from one party at the outset of the game. In the introduction to this chapter we discussed two-person non-cooperative games in a very general way; it is now time to focus more specifically on principal-agent games. Rasmusen (1994) divides principal-agent asymmetric information games into four categories:

1. *Moral hazard with hidden actions*. The outsourcing company specifies a frequency of backup and audit of its data bases. To the extent that such activities cannot be observed directly by the outsourcing company the outsourcing vendor may not backup with the appropriate frequency. In order to ensure that the outsourcing vendor performs the backups the outsourcing company may design a contract with severe penalty clauses and a monitoring scheme.

   It is important to note that a penalty clause without monitoring will probably not be effective. Further, it is necessary that the penalties be legally enforceable otherwise they will carry little weight.
2. *Moral hazard with hidden knowledge (or hidden information)*. In this case the principal contracts with the agent who subsequently observes some external event that is not observed by the principal and is relevant to the interests of the principal. An example of this type of situation in the case of outsourcing occurs when there is a shift in technology that is either unobserved by the outsourcing company or observed but not fully comprehended by the outsourcing company.
3. *Adverse selection*. In this case agents come in two types unknown to the principal. In information systems outsourcing, an example of adverse selection occurs when a company contracts with a systems company to provide a systems solution. For simplicity software companies may be considered to comprise two different types—one providing high-quality systems, the other providing low-quality systems. Generally speaking, if it is not possible to distinguish between the two types of software companies the outsourcing company will assume that *all* companies are of lower quality. This assumption will result in high-quality companies failing to bid be-

cause they cannot earn sufficient returns to compensate for their higher quality. Thus, over time, the outsourcing company's assumption is borne out in practice.

In order to escape from the problem of adverse selection it may be in the interests of the software developer to indicate in some way that he/she is a high quality developer, by sending a signal to the outsourcing company. As we have noted previously it is important that the message, which will typically be some action, is uneconomic for the low-quality software developer to send and economically worthwhile for the high-quality software developer to send. We examine this type of principal/agent game in the next section.

4. *Signalling and screening*. In the case of signalling prior to contracting the agent engages in some costly activity with the intention of signalling superior skills or knowledge. Signalling may involve investment in costly assets prior to contracting. For instance, in the case of information systems outsourcing the agent may acquire personnel or systems that are relevant to the outsourcer. In contrast, screening involves the principal designing a contract that will differentiate between agents. Those agents who have the requisite skills/competencies will find the contract attractive while those lacking such skills/competencies will not.

As noted above, agency costs are an integral part of these games. There are a number of potential mechanisms for alleviating agency costs. We may attempt to reduce the likelihood that the agent will act opportunistically by (i) seeking to obtain enhanced information about his/her performance by establishing the reputation of the agent; (ii) developing risk-sharing contacts; (iii) active monitoring of the agent; and (iv) providing incentives. Each of these are discussed briefly below:

Reputation

Some of the mechanisms for ensuring that agents recognize the value of developing a reputation are as follows:

- Previous contract performance is used as a basis for deciding whether or not to renew outsourcing contracts.
- Industry associations share information about the performance of outsourcing vendors.
- Companies require that outsourcing contractors provide access to previous clients.
- Outsourcing contractors form alliances with other major firms that have well-established reputations.

- Outsourcing vendors form their own industry association with codes of ethical conduct.

All these mechanisms either establish a reputation or make it important that the outsourcing vendor maintains his/her reputation.

Risk-sharing Contracts

We have already seen this is the case in outsourcing contracts where part of the fee is contingent on the performance of the outsourcing company. Another example is provided by contracts that require the setting up of a joint company to provide outsourcing services. In outsourcing agreements that involve the development of systems the outsourcing vendor and the outsourcing company may agree to share in the potential benefits (or losses). For example, we have seen that some outsourcing contracts reward the outsourcing vendor with some percentage of the cost savings from a re-engineered business process.

Monitoring

The outsourcing company either monitors the performance of the outsourcing vendor on a regular basis or employs some third party to do the monitoring. As many auditors know, monitoring is never completely reliable. It is also costly and inevitably suffers from decreasing marginal returns. Still, however much an outsourcing company trusts its outsourcing vendor some form of monitoring is likely to be necessary. As Ronald Reagan was fond of reminding arms reduction negotiators: "trust but verify."

Incentives

As we have discussed above, provision of the appropriate incentives (and penalties) will reward the agent for appropriate behaviour and penalize him/her for inappropriate behaviour. Some of the incentives relate to risk sharing while others are more directly related to specific actions taken or not taken by the agent.

Analytic Approaches to Principal-Agent Games

One of the advantages of modelling outsourcing arrangements with principal-agent games is that these games are relatively well understood and their structure has been extensively analysed. We have chosen to spare the reader this detailed analysis since this would involve the use of rather daunting mathematics. However, to give a taste of the analysis the basic problem for the principal can be formulated as follows:

> The principal tries to identify an incentive scheme that will induce the agent to freely select an action, or set of actions, that will result in the maximization of the principal's utility. It is assumed that the agent will freely select the action or set of actions that maximize his/her utility.

The next step is to identify the structure of the game, the actions that can be taken by the parties and the order in which these actions will be taken. Often this stage of problem definition results in the creation of what is called a "time-line"—an indication of all the possible actions and the order in which they are taken.

In a simplified principal-agent game the "order of play" may be as follows:

1. The principal offers the agent some incentive scheme, penalty scheme and monitoring proposal.
2. The agent either accepts or rejects the contract.
3. If the agent accepts the contract he/she performs or fails to adequately perform the service as specified in the contract.
4. The principal may monitor the performance of the agent.
5. The principal pays the agent an appropriate fee or seeks to impose an appropriate penalty.

The next stage involves developing a mathematical function to describe the principals payoff as a function of the variables under his/her control—i.e. payment for service, monitoring regime and penalty scheme. Obviously it is in the interests of the principal to maximize his/her payoff. However, there are two constraints on this maximization. In the first place it must correspond to a state of the world where the agent maximizes his/her payoff—this constraint is called the *Incentive Compatibility Constraint* (ICC). Second, the agent must at least be rewarded enough to make him/her to take on the contract in the first place. This constraint is referred to as the *Participation Constraint* (PC).

Mathematically, the penultimate stage of the analysis involves maximizing the principals payoff subject to the two constraints. Whether we are able to derive a solution depends on the nature of the functions—the principal's payoff function and the two constraints. There are clearly a number of troubling issues here. First, what functions do we choose to represent the various payoff functions (of the principal and the agent)? Second, is it possible to derive a solution? In a recent paper Elitzur and Wensley (1995) have been able to provide a closed-form solution for one particular type of outsourcing arrangement.

Once a solution has been derived the final stage of the analysis typically involves what the economists term *comparative statics*. In comparative statics we investigate how the solution changes with changes in the variables that are relevant to the outsourcing decision. For example: How does the principal's payoff vary with the frequency of monitoring the performance of the agent?

Inevitably one of the problems of using a mathematical modelling approach to principal-agent games is that it may be difficult to decide what mathematical functions provide the best "fit" for the particular principal-agent game in question. Identifying suitable functions may be much less than half of the problem since it may transpire that it is not possible to derive a solution in terms of an incentive scheme. That is, in mathematical language, there may be no *closed form* solution. In these situations some researchers resort to simulation—that is, they investigate the payoffs to the principal and the agent for a range of different types of incentive scheme.

Although we have ourselves used mathematical modelling fairly extensively in our research into information services outsourcing arrangements we feel that the qualitative approach demonstrated in this chapter can yield interesting and useful insights without having to rely on nearly the same number of assumptions.

CONCLUSIONS

What, then, can game-theoretic analysis tell us? In the first place it can explain existing features of outsourcing relationships. For example, the fact that duration of outsourcing contracts has been dropping over time may be explained by increasing competition between outsourcing vendors. This increased competition in the outsourcing market has the effect of shifting power to outsourcing companies. We have also noted that features relating to technology upgrading, fee structures and asset transfer can be elucidated with the help of game theory.

Second, it may be able to provide recommendations as to how contracts can be structured more efficiently. These recommendations may arise in situations where contract terms have been absent in the past. For example, in a recent paper (Elitzur and Wensley, 1995) we suggest that the transfer of knowledge between the principal and the agent is an important issue. It may well represent the transfer of value between the two parties. We have noted that provision for the valuation of such knowledge is typically not provided for in outsourcing contracts. This does not necessarily mean that such knowledge should not be valued.

As much as anything it is our belief that game theoretic approaches to the analysis of outsourcing agreements provide a rich structure for modelling such complex arrangements. In providing such structure they provide both insightful explanations of existing agreements, some explanation concerning the evolution of outsourcing agreements, some suggestions about how agreements would be written and the weaknesses inherent in existing agreements, and a framework for further extending our understanding of such related issues as alliances and joint ventures.

A number of future directions for game-theoretic IS outsourcing research can be suggested. So far we have explored mainly the qualitative aspects of the game theoretic analysis of outsourcing contracts. There is considerably more work to be done in analysing the detailed structure of outsourcing agreements. It is also important to identify potential flaws or oversights in current outsourcing agreements.

Outsourcing games also often take place in the context of other games. Organizations engage in many strategic decisions that may impact outsourcing decisions and/or be impacted by outsourcing decisions. It may be appropriate to expand consideration of outsourcing games to recognize this broader context. Brandenburger and Nalebuff (1996, pp. 57–8) provide an excellent general discussion of this problem.

Descriptive approaches can only take us so far. In our own analytical work (Elitzur and Wensley, 1995) we have used the principal-agent paradigm and have been able to derive some limited results. The gold at the end of the rainbow of analytic game theory potentially provides the answer to two related questions:

1. To what extent are current information systems outsourcing agreements efficient?
2. How can efficient information systems outsourcing agreements be designed?

Insights into the answer to question 2 also allows us to identify situations where insourcing is likely to be preferred to outsourcing.

For our own part we doubt that analytic game theoretic analysis will lead to significant definitive answers. However, such analysis does result in our focusing on strategic and informational aspects of information systems outsourcing that, in our view, leads to a number of interesting and valuable insights.

We have been at pains to stress that information systems outsourcing is an example of subcontracting. Knowledge obtained from the analysis of traditional subcontracting arrangements can provide valuable insights for information systems outsourcing. We also suspect that the analysis of information systems outsourcing contracts will open up attractive new vistas for subcontracting research

REFERENCES

Aumann, R. and Maschler, M. (1995) *Repeated Games with Incomplete Information*, Cambridge, MA: The MIT Press.

Baiman, S. (1990) Agency Research in Managerial Accounting: A Second Look, *Accounting, Organizations and Society*, **15**, 4, 341–371.

Baird, D., Gertner, R. and Picker, R. (1994) *Game Theory and the Law*. Cambridge, MA: Harvard University Press.

Binmore, K. (1995) *Playing Fair*, Cambridge, MA: The MIT Press.

Brandenburger, A. and Nalebuff, B. (1996) *Co-opetition*, New York: Doubleday.

Dixit, A. and Nalebuff, B. (1991) *Thinking Strategically*, New York: W. W. Norton and Company.

Earl, M. (1996) The Risks of Outsourcing IT, *Sloan Management Review*, **37**, 3, 26–32.

Eggertsson, T. (1990) *Economic Behaviour and Institutions*, Cambridge, UK: Cambridge University Press.

Elitzur, R. and Wensley, A. (1995) *Modeling Information Systems Outsourcing Contracts: Some Analytic Approaches*, unpublished working paper, Faculty of Management, University of Toronto, Toronto.

Fitzgerald, G. and Willcocks, L. (1994) *Outsourcing Information Technology: Contracts and the Client/Vendor Relationship*, RDP 94/10, Oxford Institute of Information Management, Templeton College, Oxford.

Fudenberg, D. and Tirole, J. (1993) *Game Theory*, Cambridge, MA: The MIT Press.

Gibbons, R. (1992) *Game Theory for Applied Economists*, Princeton, NJ: Princeton University Press.

Hargreaves-Heap, S. and Varoufakis, Y. (1995) *Game Theory: A Critical Introduction*, New York: Routledge.

Hirshleifer, J. and Riley, J. (1992) *The Analytics of Uncertainty and Information*, Cambridge: Cambridge University Press.

Hurst, I. and Hanessian, B. (1995) Navigating IT channels: Integrate or outsource? *The McKinsey Quarterly*, 3, 102–111.

Kreps, D. (1992) *Game Theory and Economic Modelling*, Oxford: Clarendon Press.

Lacity, M. and Hirschheim, R. (1993) *Information Systems Outsourcing: Myths, Metaphors and Realities*, Chichester: John Wiley and Sons.

Lacity, M., Willcocks, L. and Feeny, D (1996) The Value of Selective IT Sourcing, *Sloan Management Review*, **37**, 3, 13–25.

McMillan, J. (1991) *Games, Strategies and Managers*, New York: Oxford University Press.

Rasmusen, E. (1994) *Games and Information*, 2nd ed., Oxford: Blackwell.

Willcocks, L. and Choi, C. (1995). Cooperative Partnership and Total IT Out-

sourcing: From Contractual Obligation To Strategic Alliance? *European Management Journal*, **13**, 1, 67–78.
Williamson, O. and Winter, S. (eds) (1993) *The Nature of the Firm*, Oxford: Oxford University Press.

4
The External Acquisition of Information Systems Knowledge

HARRY SCARBROUGH

INTRODUCTION

There are many different theoretical perspectives on IS outsourcing. The most common approaches, however, tend to focus on the way outsourcing decisions are taken and the criteria governing those decisions. A recurrent theme, for instance, is the contrast between rational and political decision processes (Lacity and Hirschheim, 1993; 1995). Similarly, many studies focus on relevant decision criteria, contrasting cost efficiency with core competencies as bases for calculating the pros and cons of outsourcing (Quinn and Hilmer, 1994).

In this chapter, however, I wish to propose a different theoretical perspective for understanding IS outsourcing. This involves viewing it not as the product of a decision process, but, more fundamentally, as a particular way of organizing knowledge. This is not to deny that managers do take decisions on outsourcing and that these decisions are important. However, such decision processes take place in a context which is defined primarily by the problems and implications of organizing knowledge. The perspective outlined here takes IS outsourcing issues out of the narrowly pragmatic arena in which they are normally viewed—will outsourcing in this or that context deliver costs or benefits to the firm?—and relocates them within a much wider

Strategic Sourcing of Information Systems.
Edited by L. P. Willcocks and M. C. Lacity.

debate on the way technological knowledge is formed, communicated and organized, thereby opening up parallels with cognate topics such as the management of R&D and the wider literature on technological innovation. It is surely significant, for instance (though strangely unremarked in the IS literature), that the IS outsourcing trend is directly paralleled by the "marketization" of other forms of expertise, including the subcontracting of R&D and the imposition of quasi-market disciplines on a range of professional groups (Scarbrough 1996).

The wider background to IS outsourcing reinforces my general argument which is that focusing exclusively on the motives and outcomes of IS outsourcing, or even on the decision processes themselves, fails to address critical questions to do with the way IS knowledge is communicated, organized and applied. The latter are an important influence on the initial outsourcing decisions and even more on the long-term effectiveness of the contractual arrangements that it produces. In this perspective, insourcing and outsourcing are neither good or bad in themselves but represent responses to the problems of organizing different kinds of knowledge.

This argument is developed through the analysis of an empirical study of IS projects in financial service firms in Scotland. This study was carried out by a research team drawn from the Universities of Edinburgh, Stirling and Warwick and was supported by a research grant from the Joint Committee of the ESRC and SERC. The study did not focus on formal IS outsourcing arrangements as such but on the external acquisition of IS knowledge. By focusing on the patchwork of contracting arrangements developed around specific IS projects, this study was able to address the external acquisition of knowledge in a more nuanced way than the more monolithic outcomes of formal outsourcing deals would typically allow. As a result we were able to examine the shifting threshhold between the internal and external acquisition of knowledge at the task rather than the contract level. (The study is comprehensively reported in Fincham *et al.*, 1994).

Clearly, the scope and methodology of this study did not follow the usual conventions of IS outsourcing research. However, its oblique approach does offer important advantages given the theoretical perspective outlined here. For example, the starting-point for major outsourcing decisions is defined by the existing in-house function. It follows that the initial decision is inevitably shaped by one-off factors of politics and perceptions which are not strictly relevant to the issue of long-term effectiveness. This is both an explanation for the problems of sustainability encountered by many such deals (Lacity, Hirschheim and Willcocks, 1994) and an argument for viewing outsourcing in terms of the organizational choices posed by IS knowledge. Innovative IS projects of the kind considered below offer a more controlled environment for examining such choices because in general the pros and cons of different organizational mechanisms are considered more even-handedly when no vital political interests are at stake. In fact, the needs of the innovation process itself tend to promote a rigorous appraisal of the optimal permutations of internal and external sources of knowledge. Equally, where classic outsourcing decisions tend to involve monotonic and undifferentiated organizational alternatives, the projects considered here drew on all the different forms in which IS knowledge can be traded (including, for instance, software packages as well as human knowledge) according to their relevance and utillity for specific tasks. Most importantly, instead of the polarized view adopted by some studies—insourcing *or* outsourcing—the study considers the much more common situation of firms having to manage both internal *and* external sources of IS knowledge, and the particular problems and advantages that such "multisourcing" poses (Wibbelsman and Maiero, 1994).

KNOWLEDGE FACTORS IN OUTSOURCING DECISIONS

A first step in developing the argument is simply to bring together the many different knowledge factors which are already cited by the existing literature on IS outsourcing and to relate these to the wider question of the organization of knowledge. For example, a number of studies cite the skills and technology of the existing IS function as an important factor in shaping decisions on outsourcing. Willcocks and Fitzgerald (1993) identify "in-house experience" as a critical determinant of successful outsourcing decisions. Taking a broader view of organizational knowledge, we might also see a knowledge constraint in comments on "the cultural fit between client and vendor, and the quality of the relationship between the relevant staff in both organizations" as influences on the sustainability of outsourcing arrangements (Willcocks, Lacity and Fitzgerald, 1995. See also Chapters 9, 10 and 11).

As for the strategic role of IS knowledge, much discussion has centred on the need to consider "core competencies" in the outsourcing decision. This is particularly stressed by Quinn and Hilmer who define such competencies as "skill or knowledge sets" embedded in the organization's systems. The strategic argument for protecting and cultivating core knowledge is that it provides a "long-term platform" for innovation and the creation of unique forms of customer value.

Thirdly, the distribution and communication of IS knowledge also appears as a factor in some studies. Sometimes, it operates conservatively to discourage outsourcing, as, for instance, in situations where the supplier market is underdeveloped. On the other hand, firms may see outsourcing as a means of gaining access to knowledge which is not available internally. A study by Lacity, Hirschheim and Willcocks (1994) found that "numerous companies consider outsourcing partly for the access to greater IT knowledge it would bring" (p.13). Similarly, Quinn and Hilmer (1994) cite Ford's management of its supplier networks: "by actively riding circuit on the best outside suppliers and experts, they obtain more stimulation and insights than any insider group could possibly offer" (p. 54).

These examples suggest that the influence of knowledge factors on outsourcing decisions can be either positive or negative depending on the circumstances of the firm. Consideration of core competencies, for example, may lead one firm to insource IS knowledge, while another carrying out the same calculation might come down in favour of outsourcing IS. In other words, actual organizational outcomes depend on the interaction or "fit" between the company context and the formation and distribution of IS knowledge.

The importance of contextual "fit" in shaping organizational outcomes is important here because it signals one of the important theoretical tools that can illuminate the organization of IS knowledge. For saying that organizational form should fit its context is actually restating the axiomatic principle of the contingency theory of organization. In organization studies (though not always in managerial practice), this approach long ago supplanted the idea that there is "one best way" of organizing business activities (see also Chapter 2).

Most variants of contingency theory are institutionally bounded in that they focus exclusively on choices within hierarchies; for example, the choice between functional versus product-market structures. The external acquisition of knowledge, however, as exemplified both by outsourcing decisions in general and by the IS projects detailed below, actually involves a choice between the much wider range of organizational designs encompassed by the institutional forms of markets and hierarchies. In this context, the work of Williamson (1975; 1981; 1985; 1986) and others in the field of the "New Institutional Economics" provides the most relevant version of contingency theory. Their account, which is based on "transaction cost analysis", therefore provides a benchmark for much of the discussion that follows. A detailed description of transaction cost economics appeared earlier in Chapter 2. However, it is worth rehearsing some of its tenets again for what follows.

Put simply, transaction costs are the costs of regulating a particular transaction, such as the acquisition of a standard software package (low transaction costs) or an outsourcing contract (much higher transaction costs because it includes the costs of both drawing up and monitoring the contract). Of course, Williamson does not argue that transaction costs on their own determine organizational choices. In part such choices are straightforwardly determined by the relative efficiencies of the firms involved (Kogut and Zander, 1992). Thus, in IS outsourcing the ability of vendor firms to achieve economies of scale and scope may be important factors in securing outsourcing contracts. However, transaction costs do become critical in the many cases where vendors do not possess gross efficiency advantages. Here Williamson argues that the costs of organizing a particular transaction will sway the final choice of "governance structure" applied to it .

Transaction cost analysis has been extensively applied to "make-buy" decisions in other contexts, and an increasing number of IS outsourcing studies have applied this approach systematically (for a critique see Lacity and Willcocks, 1996). Its relevance to outsourcing issues is undeniable. In particular, by defining the "transaction" as the basic building-block of such forms Williamson has defined a vantage point that explains the development of markets and hierarchies in the same conceptual terms. This is relevant to outsourcing decisions in general and innovative IS projects in particular because both these activities involve organizational choices *at the margin* where the multitude of individual decisions are exposed to the full force of prevailing technological and economic pressures.

The transactional framework is certainly relevant to understanding why different kinds of knowledge might be organized in different ways. Williamson highlights certain critical features of transactions features which will determine the cost efficiency of various organizational forms. At the risk of paraphrasing his analysis, as far as technological knowledge is concerned, these features include:

- asset-specificity: the organizational specificity of a certain body of knowledge;
- technological separability: the degree of interdependency between systems; and
- information impactedness: signals the relative difficulty of assessing the value of knowledge.

Three general transactional conditions which Williamson also highlights are, first, the frequency with which certain kinds of transaction take place—the more frequent the transaction the greater the incentive to develop a specialized governance structure or hierarchy. The second condition is the risk posed by a "small numbers bargaining condition", which effectively draws attention to the dangers of dependency on one or two suppliers. And third is the general condition of "opportunism", that is "interest-seeking with guile" which Williamson deems a universal fact of human nature. Being more opaque than others, knowledge-based transactions tend to especially prone to the depredations of opportunism, thereby acting as a spur to the hierarchical forms that are taken to dampen the more blatant varieties. To crudely summarize the implications of the transactional approach, company-specific knowledge would normally be organized within a hierarchy. Such knowledge is too specific to be profitably traded and hence has to be elicited through the employment relationships of the business hierarchy. On the other hand, where knowledge has general applicability and portability, it would normally be organized through the vendor-client relationships of the marketplace.

The relevance of this transactional analysis is amply underlined by a few examples from the IS literature. Quinn and Hilmer (1994, p. 49), for instance, invoke a kind of "information impactedness" to explain some of the early constraints on outsourcing:

> "Computing ... was largely kept in-house in its early years because the information available to a buyer of computing services and its ability to make judgements about such services were very different for the buying company (which knew very little) than for the supplier (which had excellent information)."

Again, where "technological separability" is low or non-existent, the transactional view would suggest hierarchical control rather than market relationships. This finds validation from the Willcocks and Fitzgerald (1993) comment that "systems interconnectedness and complexity" is a "critical determinant of successful outsourcing decisions." As they note (p. 227):

> "Some IT/IS activities may have simple interfaces with the rest of the organizations systems and with business users, and so be easy to isolate and contract out. Others may have complex and extensive interaction with a wide range of other systems, implying that there will be high switching costs involved."

Likewise, despite the cosy rhetoric of "partnership", a number of empirical studies cite vendor opportunism as a pervasive problem in market relationships. Lacity and Hirschheim (1995), for example, find that buyers who accept the notion of "strategic partnership" are often quickly disillusioned. As they note tartly, whatever language is used to describe an outsourcing contract, ultimately the buyer's costs are the vendor's profits. The possibility of firms exploiting their position is further enhanced where "a small numbers bargaining condition" exists; a situation neatly summarized by Quinn and Hilmers cautionary note (1994, p. 49): "If ... there is not sufficient depth in the market, overly powerful suppliers can hold the company to ransom."

Examples such as this illustrate the analytical power of the transactional approach. In contrast to the pragmatic checklists of much of the outsourcing literature, this perspective suggests that long-run organizational choice is something of a misnomer. Under the implacable pressures of transactional efficiency, organizational forms are determined by the fit between transaction and institution.

Yet, conceding the broad relevance of transactional issues to the organization of knowledge does not make it a complete answer to the questions posed by the external acquisition of IS knowledge, be that for IS outsourcing or innovation projects. In fact, there is plenty of evidence from the wider critical literature, and not least from the empirical study outlined below, to suggest serious flaws in the transactional approach to technological knowledge. In the following section I seek to address those shortcomings and suggest a series of revisions that make for a more complete and inclusive account of the organization of knowledge.

REVISING THE TRANSACTIONAL MODEL

Three major revisions to the Williamson approach will be suggested. First, redefining transactions to incorporate questions of social control alongside the material exchange. Second, incorporating knowledge and innovation as factors influencing the way such social control is exercised. Third, admitting the distinctive processes of knowledge communication into our understanding of knowledge-based transactions.

Redefining Transactions

Taking the first point, Williamson defines transactions as a discrete physical transfer "across a technologically separable interface." However, this economistic focus on material exchange does not seem to be an accurate definition of the generality of transactions, let alone those based on knowledge. Blau (1964), for example, sees exchange relationships in terms of trust. High trust "social exchange" is contrasted with low trust "economic exchange." In social exchange favours are given without expectation of immediate, specific or matching return. This creates "diffuse future obligations" and hence establishes relations of

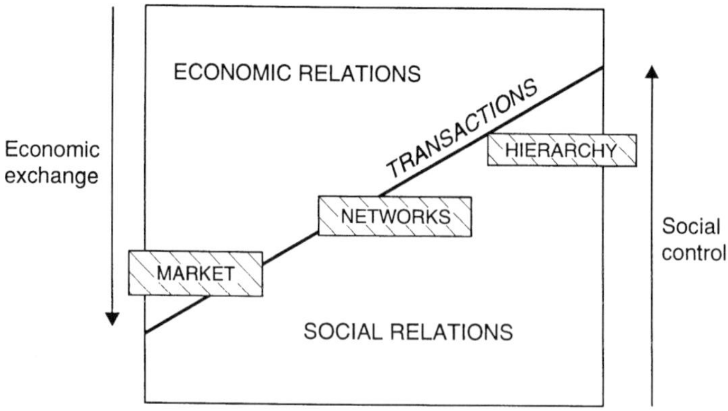

Figure 4.1 *Transactions as a Continuum*

trust between the parties. Arguably, even the simplest transactions imply some form of social control and certainly all transactions are embedded in a particular institutional context (Granovetter, 1985; Martin, 1993). Apart from the trust-based sanctions and incentives cited by Blau, the social influences on transactions range from diffuse social norms to elaborate occupational codes (Macauley, 1963) and the detailed controls exercised by hierarchical organizations .

The upshot of this analysis is to challenge Williamson's view that social control (in his terms, hierarchy) is extrinsic to transactions, and only emerges in the context of "market failure." Rather, to different degrees social control and material exchange seem to be closely intertwined in constituting the transaction itself. Instead of Williamson's institutional polarities of market or hierarchy, such interdependence suggests that transactions are better viewed as a continuum which cuts across these institutional forms (see Figure 4.1).

The importance of this continuum is underlined by the empirical studies confirming the existence of what Hennart (1993) terms the "swollen middle", which is the tendency for most transactions to cluster in the middle ground between the institutional poles of market and hierarchy. Hybrid varieties of organizational forms—"organizing methods" as Hennart puts it—regulate these transactions including networks, licences, joint ventures, trust-based partnerships and other instances of what Butler and Carney (1983) term "managed markets" (see Figure 4.2) .

These and other organizational arrangements manage the different admixtures of economic exchange and social control vested in particular transactions. Indeed, this transactional continuum even applies to specific organizational arrangements. Thus, IS outsourcing deals are

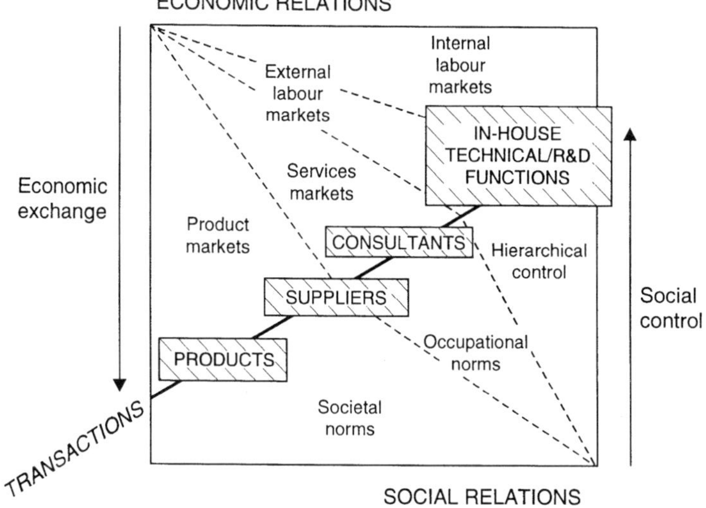

Figure 4.2 *Economic Exchange and Social Control*

not homogeneous but embody various gradations of what Quinn and Hilmer term "sourcing control."

The Role of Knowledge and Innovation

From the purely transactional point of view, the most critical aspects of knowledge are the constraints on its tradeability. Knowledge is difficult to evaluate and knowledge-based transactions suffer from "information impactedness'—in other words, the vendor has much greater information on the resource being traded than the potential buyer. But while these tradeability issues are certainly important, they are far from being the only features considered by potential buyers, nor are they necessarily the most important.

The reasons why other aspects of knowledge may be more important than its tradeability are usefully highlighted by the recent development of "resource-based theories" of the firm. These have demonstrated the limitations of the transactional approach and its emphasis on cost efficiency. Lazonick (1991) contrasts this approach with the narrow efficiency arguments of Williamson's transactional model. The latter, he says, implies an "adaptive" view of the firm in which "the key decisions are a series of adaptations to 'disturbances', taking as given those factors that constitute the prime elements of the organization's economic environment" (p. 214). Against this view, Lazonick counterposes the "innovative" model of the firm in which organizations actively utilize knowledge to create new sources of economic value through processes of innovation. In these contexts, the tradeability of knowledge may well be secondary to the contribution it makes to a firm's innovation capability.

To further confirm that "an approach based on the knowledge of the firm differs from a contracting perspective" (Kogut and Zander, 1992. p. 392), there is the widespread citing of one important strand of resource-based theory—the notion of core competencies—as one of the most important factors to be considered in outsourcing decisions (for example, Quinn and Hilmer, 1994). This kind of recognition demonstrates that knowledge and its distinctive characteristics are not a purely theoretical concern. The "skills or knowledge sets" that define core competencies challenge the transacational model by defining strategic criteria that are not reducible to a simple calculus of cost efficiency.

Knowledge Communication

A further important feature of knowledge-trading not addressed by the narrow transactional model is the importance attached to processes of communication. However great the economic incentives to trade, the transfer of knowledge is always potentially problematic—to use von Hippel's term, knowledge is "sticky data" (1990). Indeed, in contrast to the "physical exchanges" of Williamson's paradigm, studies of knowledge transfer generally make clear the vital role played by social and cultural processes of communication (Boisot, 1986). Wider studies of diffusion confirm the importance of the communicative aspects of knowledge transfer (Rogers, 1962).

The wider literature on knowledge transfer can be characterized in many different ways, but in this context three modal forms are particularly relevant:

1. *Professionalism*, that is the communication of knowledge through its embodiment in the learning and experience of individuals and groups. The occupational growth of the IS workforce is a powerful testimony of the continuing role of professionalism in communicating the more tacit or task specific forms of knowledge. Moreover, the professionalism of IS workers not only serves as a means of communicating knowledge within organizations, but also operates across them via occupational and sectoral networks of various kinds (Child and Smith, 1987).
2. *Objectification*, Here the communication process revolves around the pursuit of portability (Cooper, 1992), and universal applicability through standardization. The knowledge needed to use the technol-

ogy is kept to a bare minimum. IT hardware and software are classic examples of the objectification of knowledge.

3. *Organizational sedimentation*, where knowledge is communicated via methodologies, rules, standards, routines and structures (Argyris and Schon, 1978; Lyles and Schwenk 1992; Whipp and Clark 1986).

In broad terms, we can relate this point to the earlier discussion by mapping the communicability of knowledge as an extra dimension of the transactional continuum outlined earlier (see Figure 4.3). At one extreme, hierarchical control secures the communication of knowledge through rules and systems. At the other, processes of objectification and standardization serve the same function. And in-between stand varying degrees of professionalism whose role in a strictly functional sense involves communicating those residual tacit and local knowledges which elude the other processes.

Many writers see these means of knowledge transfer competing with each other. Professionalism, for instance, is seen as threatened by the de-skilling effects of technology and organizational control (Kraft, 1977). On the whole, though, the long-run evolution of the IS field suggests a more symbiotic relationship between these different processes of communication (Friedman and Cornford, 1989). Thus, the objectification of knowledge at one level often provides a platform for the development of new kinds of professional knowledge at another. Major breakthroughs in software such as the late 1960s break-up of IBM's stranglehold on software and later the development of the MS-DOS standard actually created new opportunities for the formation of specialist knowledge.

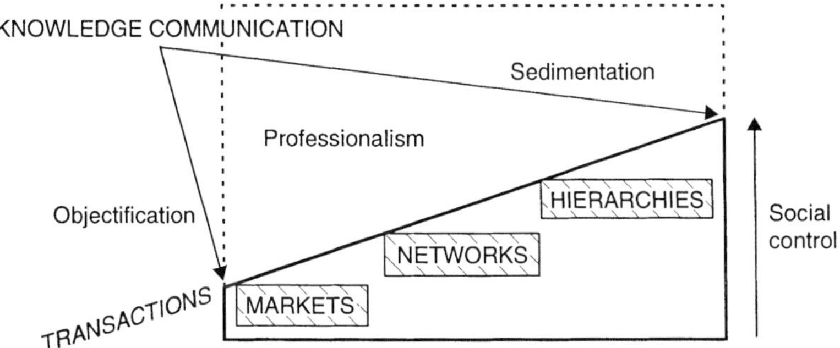

Figure 4.3 *Knowledge Communication and Tradeability*

Modelling the Organization of Knowledge

Revising the transactional model gives us a wider appreciation of the factors shaping the organization of knowledge. I have redefined the concept of the transaction to incorporate material, social and communicative exchange. This revised model suggests that the organization of knowledge-based transactions will be determined not simply by their tradeability, but also by their amenability to control and their communicability. Overall, the critical factors shaping knowledge organization can be summarized as follows:

1. The tradeability of a particular form of knowledge, including its specificity and the characteristics of vendor and buyer (including relative levels of knowledge about the resource being traded) influences the transactional efficiency of different organizational forms.
2. Innovation capability: the contribution which the knowledge in question makes to a firm's ability to innovate will influence the degree of social control applied to it and the importance which is attached to transactional efficiency.
3. Communicability: the relative effectiveness of different modes of communication for the particular body of knowledge will influence the way knowledge-based transactions are organized.

As per the contingency approach noted earlier, we would expect organizational outcomes (that is, the regulatory mix of social control and economic exchange) for knowledge-based transactions to reflect the interaction of these three factors with buyer/seller characteristics. The following case studies of the external acquisition of IS knowledge provide an opportunity to test the dynamics of this model and develop it further.

THE ORGANIZATION OF IS KNOWLEDGE: CASE STUDY EVIDENCE

The five case studies which are briefly outlined here are drawn from a larger study of IS projects in financial services that was carried out in Scotland between 1988 and 1991. Each case study involved interviews with top management, senior IS managers and IS developers, and tracked the development of an important IS project in which various forms and sources of IS knowledge were employed.

Each of the cases cited here illustrates a different way of organizing knowledge for a new IS project. However, I want to begin with a brief reference to the two case studies which defined the transactional extremities of the range. Unsurprisingly perhaps, these two cases tend to support the narrower form of the transactional model outlined earlier. In the first case, *Buildsoc*, one of the larger UK building societies, was carrying out the acquisition of an integrated software package to manage its product portfolio. This "Regan" package was described as an "all-singing, all-dancing package which will control all our lending portfolios, various products which we hope to put out such as a checking account, insurance services and so on." Regan was a customer-based system, as opposed to an account-based system. The aim was to maximize the cross-selling opportunities across Buildsoc's product portfolio: "For example, if a guy comes in for a mortgage, he may need a loan for a car or need insurance or a personal equity plan. And we know the total portfolio of that customer." (User Services Manager, Buildsoc).

The decision to buy the package rather than develop it internally was influenced by a number of factors. Timeliness was certainly a major issue: "We didn't have the time to develop that big system and so we bought Regan." Cost efficiency was also important, together with access to the latest technology. Not to put too fine a point on it, a case like this effectively underlines the major advantages of speed and cost produced by the marriage between market mechanisms and the objectification and standardization of knowledge.

At the opposite end of the transactional spectrum from Buildsoc's off-the-shelf package purchase was the development of the CABINET (Customer and Branch Information Network) system by the Bank of Scotland. CABINET involved the development of a customer information network linking all several hundred branches to the Bank's databases in Edinburgh. This network was designed to replace existing manual records and thereby both speed up responses to customer queries and assist the introduction of new financial services.

This project was both large scale and long term. The actual design stage of the project began in 1984 and even at that stage it was understood that implementation through various phases of development (each one adding some new element of functionality to the basic network) was likely to extend well into the 1990s. Although certain aspects of the project (notably office automation hardware and software) were subcontracted to external vendors, the core banking systems, including an integrated customer database, were developed by the Bank's in-house IS function.

Both the Buildsoc and the CABINET cases demonstrate the relevance of transactional considerations to the organization of knowledge. The Buildsoc project demonstrated certain of the classic characteristics that make transactions more amenable to market acquisition. Apart from the fact that this was a one-off transaction, other characteristics included the technological separability and low asset-specificity. Bespoke development was rejected because Buildsoc did not see firm-specific knowledge as particularly important to system success—indeed were happy to modify their own routines to the new system. Conversely, the CABINET project demonstrated a number of the opposite features. It involved a high level of systems interconnectedness, was highly asset-specific given the need for company-specific knowledge, and involved a long series of transactions and investments rather than a single exchange.

The support these cases give to the transactional model is not complete, however. Even in cases like this there are signs that knowledge is not an especially biddable resource. Thus in the Buildsoc case, the acquisition of the Regan package—superficially a model of transactional efficiency—proved to be a much more intractable proposition than management anticipated. In assessing the merits of a well-wrought, commercially tested package, firms often underestimate the knowledge implications of using it in their own, unique organizational environment. This is partly because such packages can never run themselves and typically need a degree of tacit, non-objectified knowledge to be effective. Package vendors seek to formalize this implementation knowledge through user manuals and help facilities, but as most computer users would testify, this is rarely completely successful. Then as well as the tacit knowledge needed to operate the package itself, there is generally the need for local knowledge to integrate the package into the host firm's own routines. These needs for tacit and asset-specific knowledge pose important constraints on the advantages of product standardization—they are the other side of the coin from the cost advantages produced by economies of scale.

Initially, managers at Buildsoc were unconcerned about these constraints because they saw the package as a fresh start in the development of their systems. But when the package was implemented, management soon realized that their confidence in this "technical fix" was badly misplaced. One of its champions had to admit:

> "Unfortunately, we have had some problems with it. It's an American-based system. There's some anglicisation required to be done and that's led to problems. We've had problems of sizing and unfortunately the whole thing has been beset with problems." (User Services Manager)

The need for "anglicization'—even for something as apparently trivial as the date format—shows how buying a package means buying the key assumptions buried within it; in this case, an assumption that the package would be implemented within a US "organizational environment."

Despite the support they lend to some aspects of the transactional model, even these cases showing the purest forms of hierarchical and market organization are not unequivocal. The Buildsoc case, in particular, suggests that knowledge is difficult to commodify because certain kinds of tacit and local knowledge resist objectification.

BANK OF SCOTLAND VISA

This case study reinforces the above points about the problems of commodifying knowledge, but in this project those problems are created not so much by the non-formal aspects of knowledge as by the learning effects associated with knowledge-based transactions.

Again, this is a case about the acquisition of a software package, and apart from the more favourable conclusion many of its features resonate with events at Buildsoc. The context for the package acquisition here was the strategic decision of the Bank of Scotland to develop its own credit-card processing facility—the Visa Centre. From the outset there was little doubt that the Bank would opt for a packaged solution to the processing needs of the new centre. Previous arguments about speed, separability and cost efficiency all operated here. As the Visa Centre would be a new greenfield development for the bank, the speed and cost advantages of a package were not compromised by the problems of customizing the package to an existing organization or systems. Indeed, the aim was to build the new Centre's organization and systems around the package. Even the choice of package was relatively uncontested; a choice made much easier by the knowledge of the managers who had been drafted into the credit card division from the Bank's in-house IS function.

As with the Buildsoc case, however, Visa Centre managers quickly found that the smooth process of package acquisition can also be a trap for the unwary. In the Visa Centre case, the potential trap was to do with the long-term implications of package acquisition. In outline, the nature of this trap is to do with the "lock-in" resulting from the path dependency of particular technologies. Packages are not static but evolve over time as vendors provide enhancements. As such enhancements are only available from one vendor, the initial purchase decision may be committing the buyer to long-term dependency on a single supplier (either that or refuse the enhancements and become locked in to a rapidly outdated package).

The Bank of Scotland only managed to spring this trap because the

Visa Centre's managers (good IS people all) decided to re-write the package to make it suit their own particular objectives. Had they been content merely to implement the standard package, they would quickly have confronted the dependency problems noted above. First, the package vendor established its own UK bureau in direct competition with other card processing centres, including VISA Centre. Subsequently, they refused to carry out maintenance on existing installations of the package in the UK. This meant that the only migration path for the package was through the vendor's own enhancements. The lock-in implications of this situation were spelled out by one of the Visa Centre managers: "the longer we go the more difficult that becomes because some of these enhancements depend on having previous enhancements. And if you haven't got that fixed in, you're not in a position to get the new thing."

This is not to say that all forms of package acquisition are pernicious to the buyer. Such problems exist only where package acquisition—or, to spell out its wider implications, the organization of knowledge through market relations—creates a short or long-term dependency on the supplier. In his transactional model, Williamson addresses such dependency in terms of the "small numbers bargaining situation" created by learning effects. However, in focusing exclusively on transactional efficiency his account glosses over the possible strategic inhibitions to the use of market mechanism for organizing and acquiring knowledge. This is well illustrated by the Visa Centre case. Crucially, the Bank of Scotland was unwilling to contemplate the potential dependencies created by a standardized package because it saw the Visa Centre as a major strategic commitment—this meant that IS decisions were viewed against a long-term strategic horizon, not the immediate pressures of cost efficiency .

The cases discussed so far demonstrate both the advantages and possible pitfalls of organizing and communicating knowledge through market mechanisms. Objectification and standardization confer important economic advantages but place severe limitations on dialogue with the system's developers. The local context cannot be properly reflected in the systems development process, and whatever organizational flexibility may exist to accommodate the standardized system there is a lively possibility of unforeseen design assumptions surfacing in the implementation process. Adding to the problems of a purely market-based approach are the issues of dependency and control raised by the Visa Centre case. However routine the technology—and card processing packages are a classic example of McFarlan's "Factory IT'—long-run learning effects create a possible "lock in" with a single vendor. Possible dependency of this sort turns calculations based on the immediate process of market exchange into more complicated equations balancing issues of control and cost efficiency.

CLYDESDALE TELEBANK

This case involved a joint development process between the in-house IS function of Clydesdale Bank and a software supplier—Software Partnership (SP). Together they developed a remote banking system—Telebank—which delivered screen-based banking services to Clydesdale customers' computer screeens via telephone-lines and modems.

Telebank was an important innovation for Clydesdale and its software partner. As such it raises important questions about the challenges which innovation processes pose for the organization of knowledge. From a transactional point of view, the problems of contracting for innovation are much greater than for routine forms of technology; the buyer is unable to specify their requirements in advance, and criteria on delivery, performance and cost are necessarily sketchy. Such problems suggest that the knowledge work deployed in the innovation process will either be managed within a hierarchy or will be tightly monitored through formal contractual means. Yet, to a significant degree the Telebank case confounded both of these expectations. Not only was a major part of the project subcontracted to the supplier firm, but the latter's work was monitored in only the most cursory way.

Thus, where previous cases merely exposed the limitations of the transactional model, this case has something to tell us about ways in which that model can be revised and extended. The reasoning behind this view rests on five critical factors which characterized systems development for the Telebank project: technological separability; mutual interest; mutual dependency; patterns of knowledge comunication; and strategic goals.

- *Technological separability* refers to the ability of the systems developers to separate the so-called "front end" of the new system from the banking elements that interfaced with secure databases and systems. This separability was important here in two senses. First, it meant that work on the front-end could be divorced in terms of both relevant knowledge and the wider security issues from the banking component. Second, it facilitated the creation of a robust division of labour between the respective IS groups; Software Partnership were minded to undertake the development of the front-end with a view to marketing it as a standard product to other banking organizations, while Clydesdale's own system developers maintained control over internal banking systems and data. In effect, the front-end served as a "gateway" or functional platform which acted as an "extra" buffer system between various end-user devices and the bank's secure databases. As the work on the front-end did not require organization-specific kowledge it was amenable to the kind of standardization envisaged by SP.

- *Mutual interest and mutual dependency*. On its own, though, technical feasibility was a necessary but not sufficient condition for collaborative development. The sufficiency only came with the emergence of a perceived mutual interest in successful innovation. Clydesdale management realized that the successful development of Telebank would provide an important addition to their product portfolio at significantly lower cost than developing it in-house. For Software Partnership it meant the creation of a marketable and potentially lucrative product. This mutual interest was cemented by a contract under which SP were given the right to re-sell the functional software platform as a generic package in return for agreeing a reduced fee for Telebank's development and guaranteeing future royalties to the Bank on the product's sales.
- *Patterns of knowledge communication*. Innovation processes, even collaboratively segmented ones like this, generally require an intensive "organic" pattern of knowledge communication (Burns and Stalker, 1961). Both developer teams placed great stress on creating the right environment for informal knowledge trading. On one hand, SP were keen to elicit knowledge about banking practices and systems. As the director of the software house reflected later:

  > "Unavoidably we've picked up a lot of knowledge and knowledge about what really matters to a bank. I would not for a moment suggest that we are the kind of organization that understands banking as a business to the same level of the people who are responsible in those areas. But what we do understand is what is important."

On the other hand, Clydesdale saw SP as a conduit to the kind of sectoral knowledge not available to in-house functions. As one of the Clydesdale managers put it:

> "There can be a danger sometimes in doing it in-house. You miss the proper understanding of the market . . . of the options and the technology because you tend then to tailor your cloth to suit your purse too much perhaps." (RR)

Mutual interest helps to explain the development of flexible and cooperative forms of work organization for the project. However, from the transactional viewpoint, this kind of work organization also increases the risk of opportunistic free-rider behaviour. In the transactional model, Clydesdale management would be expected to respond by seeking tight monitoring of SP's work inputs. In practice, however, Clydesdale management avowed themselves relaxed about the contribution made by SP's developers and made surprisingly little attempt to monitor their work.

Far from being irrational or merely complacent, such sang-froid has a lot to do with the possible sanctions on failure available to Clydesdale. Though less openly commented on, for obvious reasons, these were probably as important as the above-noted incentives for success. Nor were all of these sanctions contractual. One crucial sanction which was available Clydesdale management possessed—and indeed to other purchasers of IS services it seems (Willcocks, 1994)—was their ability to influence SP's reputation in their chosen marketplace. Thus both sides acknowledged that Telebank was a "high profile" project with an "enormous embarassment potential" if it failed. In a Scottish sector made up just of three major banks and indeed a British sector of only a handful more, it was not difficult for informal social and occupational networks to pick up and transmit the signs of "embarassment", or come to that of success, so the sanction was certainly real.

- *Strategic goals.* A final factor in the organization of the Telebank project was the strategic importance which Clydesdale Bank attached to the project. As Telebank had been identified from the outset as a strategic project, there was correspondingly more emphasis on product-market strategy and correspondingly less on cost efficiency. Of course, had Clydesdale's strategic interest lain in the competitive aspects of Telebank's technology this would have clashed with SP's interest in marketing the Telebank product. But, since Clydesdale's major competitors in Scotland had already developed their own remote banking systems, thereby downgrading the competitive qualities of the technology, strategic interests proved to be conveniently symmetrical rather than opposed.

Socio-technical Closure

By highlighting the importance of social control and communication these cases refute the axiomatic status that Williamson gives to transactional efficiency in the organization of knowledge. Cost efficiency is certainly important in shaping the way transactions are organized —hence the frequent recourse that firms have to external sources of IS knowledge. But privileging efficiency implies that transactions are simply moments of material exchange when most of the case-study evidence cited here suggests that they are better characterized as knowledge flows.

I have argued that a clearer understanding of the internal and external organization of IS knowledge alike depends crucially on moving away from Williamson's one-dimensional transactional model. However, in one important respect at least such a move creates more theoretical problems than it resolves. Rejecting the deterministic role of transactional efficiency may give us a better understanding of organizational *outcomes* but it still leaves us looking for alternative explanations of the process of organizational *choice*.

Even the cursory review of the above cases should squash any idea that such a process is determined by wider structural factors such as market forces or technology. A distinctive feature of every case is the way the pressures for control, exchange and communication create widely differing, sometimes contradictory, choice criteria. In the Buildsoc case, for example, the efficiency advantages of purchasing a standard package clashed with the need to communicate firm-specific knowledge on systems and practices. In the Visa case, the firm was confronted with an additional dilemma; how to balance the short-term efficiency advantages of package acquisition with the long-term problem of vendor dependency. And in the Clydesdale case, we saw both of these problems being supplemented by the uncertainty created by an innovation process.

One tentative conclusion to be drawn from all the cases is simply that we attach too much importance to formal organizational outcomes as against the social processes involved in achieving and sustaining them. Another way of putting this is to say that we neglect the creative role of social action in developing organizational forms—a role which is acutely stressed by the problems of managing the contradictory pressures of control, communication and exchange.

By and large, we do not see the invisible hand of cost efficiency operating unaided to shuffle transactions between market or hierarchy. This kind of institutional closure seems to be preempted by the contradictory qualities of such transactions. Instead, we see what I term "socio-technical closure'; groups and individuals acting concertedly to create finely balanced organizational arrangements capable of containing the contradictory impulses of their transactions. In such a process, "closure" involves fixing the critical organizational elements of the transaction; the terms of exchange, forms of control and the mechanisms for communicating knowledge. The Telebank case is an important case in point here. The relationship between Clysdesdale Bank and

Software Partnership was carefully designed not only to ensure an appropriate division of labour and economic spoils, but also to cultivate the required intensity of knowledge communications between the two groups.

The concept of social closure was originally associated with attempts by professional groups to place limits on social access to their expertise and privileges (Parkin, 1974). However, the term "socio-technical closure" refers to the more micro-level strategies of groups of IS managers and developers whose efforts are by definition more localized in their effects. The focus of those efforts is certainly in part the achievement of a social compact to delimit the transfer of a particular body of knowledge or expertise. This emphasis on social closure has particular importance in the organic knowledge flows required by innovation processes. However, there is also an element of "technical closure" here too—that is, arriving at a shared understanding and determination of the critical features and functions of a particular piece of technology (Pinch and Bijker, 1987). Obviously this is easier to achieve where that technology is routinized and standardized—a "technical fix" in other words—rather than innovative and unique. Our cases show, however, that aspects of both social and technical closure are important if knowledge-based transactions are to be managed effectively.

This view seems much closer to the new wisdom in, for instance, studies of firm-supplier relationships and corporate strategy than the ruthless pursuit of transactional efficiences which is the Williamson motif. The manifesto for "lean production" (Womack, Jones and Roos, 1990), for example, rejects the tyranny of cost as the basis for firm-supplier relations. Instead, it highlights the advantages of close relationships with suppliers as a means of sharing knowledge and developing mutually beneficial innovations.

CONCLUSIONS

At the beginning of this chapter I argued that outsourcing decisions could be usefully viewed in terms of the organization of knowledge. What this means in theoretical terms has been established both through a critique of the powerful transactional model of organization and through the analysis of a small sample of case studies. Taken together these have helped to revise and extend the transactional account by incorporating consideration of social control and knowledge communication into the model. The resulting account of the organization of IS knowledge is much less deterministic than Williamson's emphasis on institutional closure and transaction-organization fit. Transactional features such as tradeability and communicability are still seen as important, but being contradictory their effect is rather to create a space for social choice between different organizational forms (Hyman, 1987). In this perspective, the organization of knowledge is ultimately shaped by informal processes of socio-technical closure that are only partially embodied in formal legalistic arrangements.

But what do these theoretical points have to tell us about outsourcing practice? Reframing the outsourcing decision as one of organizational choice applied to IS knowledge has important implications for our sense of the most important influences and actors. It establishes, for instance, the critical influence of the intensity and quality of knowledge flows in the relationship between buyer and seller. Where an instrumental, arms-length relationship may be feasible with routinized, objectified technology, it probably precludes any meaningful kind of innovation, if only on grounds of greater user dependency. By the same token, though, in another context the potential for shared innovation gains may help to cement a longer lasting alliance between firms—not through the empty rhetoric of partnership, however, but because each party has complementary knowledges to contribute and a mutual interest in a successful outcome.

It should be clear by now that the usefulness of this knowledge-based view of outsourcing depends on the context. In simple terms, it becomes more relevant the more that the long-run development of the firm is based on specialized knowledge such as IT or R&D-inspired innovation. And it remains relevant to such firms whether management recognize it or not. Currently, many firms do acknowledge knowledge factors in taking their outsourcing decisions, but principally in terms of "core competencies." This analysis suggests that there may be many firms who have not adopted that framework explicitly who should still incorporate knowledge issues in their final organizational choice. This applies particularly to the path-dependent pattern of knowledge acquisition. The term "absorptive capacity" was coined by Cohen and Levinthal (1990) to describe the ease with which firms assimilate new technologies. They note that this is closely related to "prior knowledge" of that technology domain. In similar vein, Lacity and Hirschheim (1995) comment that many firms opt for outsourcing not realizing that it means foreclosing of future technological options in the IT area.

Finally, the analysis makes clear some of the limitations and contradictions of different institutional means of organizing knowledge. Applying market mechanisms to IS knowledge, for instance, may mean accepting some difficult tradeoffs between standardization and local adaptation. Nor does market acquisition necessarily release the firm from retaining some quantum of in-house IS knowledge. Circumventing the transactional problems of "information impactedness" is made easier by retaining some degree of technical expertise to be applied to the framing and monitoring of contracts (Quinn and Hilmer, 1994). For all of these reasons and more, we would be foolish to expect to see either outsourcing contracts or innovation projects being organized in the classical institutional mould of pure market or pure hierarchy. In the vast majority of cases, the heterogeneous nature of IS knowledge precludes any optimal organizational solution. Or rather, the optimal solution is the one constructed by buyers and sellers with reference to the particular needs of knowledge-based transactions. This will certainly reflect a hard-nosed view of their respective interests in the transaction, and the dangers of opportunism and dependency. It will also, however, reflect the strategic needs of the organizations concerned and the possible positive sum benefits to be derived from knowledge trading between them.

REFERENCES

Argyris, C. and Schon, D. (1978) *Organizational Learning: A Theory of Action Perspective*, Reading, Mass: Addison Wesley.

Blau, P. M. (1964) *Exchange and Power in Social Life*, New York: John Wiley & Sons.

Boisot, M. H. (1986) Markets and Hierarchies in a Cultural Perspective, *Organization Studies*, 7, 135–158.

Brady T. *et al.* (1991) The Objectification of IT Software, paper to the PICT National Network Conference, Wakefield Yorkshire, March.

Burns, T. and Stalker, G. M. (1961) *The Management of Innovation*, London: Tavistock Publications.

Butler, R. and Carney, M. G. (1983) Managing Markets: Implications for the Make-buy Decision, *Journal of Management Studies*, **20**, 2, 213–231.

Child, J. and Smith, C. (1987) The context and process of organizational transformation—Cadbury Limited in its sector, *Journal of Management Studies*, **24**, 6, 480–516.

Cohen, W. M. and Levinthal, D. A. (1990) Absorptive Capacity: A New Perspective on Learning and Innovation, *Administrative Science Quarterly*, 35, 128–152.

Cooper, R. (1992) Formal Organization as Representation: Remote Control, Displacement and Abbreviation, in M. Reed and M. Hughes (eds), *Rethinking Organization: New Directions in Organization Theory and Analysis*, London: Sage, 254–272.

Fincham, R. *et al.* (1994) *Expertise and Innovation: IT strategies in Financial Services*, Oxford: Oxford University Press.

Friedman, A. with Cornford, D. (1989) *Computer Systems Development: History Organisation and Implementation*, Chichester: John Wiley & Sons.

Granovetter, M (1985) Economic Action and Social Structure: The Problem of Embeddedness, *American Journal of Sociology*, **91**, 3, 481–510.

Hennart, J-F. (1993) Explaining the Swollen Middle: Why Most Transactions are a Mix of 'Market' and 'Hierarchy', *Organization Science*, **4**, 4, 529–547.

Hyman, R. (1987) Strategy Or Structure? Capital, Labour and Control, *Work, Employment and Society*, 1, 25–55.

Kogut, B. and Zander, U. (1992) Knowledge of the Firm, Combinative Capabilities and The Replication of Technology, *Organization Science*, **3**, 3, 383–397.

Kraft, P. (1977) *Programmers and Managers: The Routinization of Computer Programming in the United States*. New York: Springer-Verlag.

Lacity, M. and Hirschheim, R. (1993a) *Information Systems Outsourcing*, Chichester: John Wiley and Sons.

Lacity, M. and Hirschheim, R. (1993b) The Information Systems Outsourcing Bandwagon, *Sloan Management Review*, **35**, 1, Fall, 73–85.

Lacity, M. and Hirschheim R. (1995) *Beyond the Information Systems Outsourcing Bandwagon*, London: John Wiley and Sons.

Lacity, M., Hirschheim, R. and Willcocks, L. (1994) Realizing Outsourcing Expectations: Incredible Promise, Credible Outcomes, *Journal of Information Systems Management*, **11**, 4, Fall, 7–18.

Lacity, M. and Willcocks, L. (1996) Interpreting Information Technology Sourcing Decisions from a Transaction Cost Perspective: Findings and Critique, *Accounting Management and Information Technology*, **5**, 3/4, 203–244.

Lazonick, W. (1991) *Business Organization and the Myth of the Market Economy*, Cambridge: Cambridge University Press.

Lyles, M. A. and Schwenk, C. R. (1992) Top Management, Strategy and Organizational Knowledge Structures, *Journal of Management Studies*, **29**, 2, 155–174.

Macauley, S. (1963) Non Contractual Relations in Business: A Preliminary Study, *American Sociological Review*, 28, 55–67.

Martin, R. (1993) The New Behaviourism: A Critique of Economics and Organization, *Human Relations*, **46**, 9, 1085–1011.

Parkin, F. (1974) Strategies of Social Closure in Class Formation, in F. Parkin (ed.), *The Social Analysis of Class Structure*, London: Tavistock.

Pinch, T. and Bijker, W. (1987) The Social Construction of Facts and Artifacts: Or How the Sociology of Science and the Sociology of Technology Might Benefit Each Other, in W. E. Bijker, T. Hughes and T. J. Pinch (eds) (1987) *The Social Construction of Technological Systems*, London: MIT Press.

Quinn, J. B. and Hilmer, F. G. (1994) Strategic Outsourcing, *Sloan Management Review*, Summer 1994, 43–55.

Rogers, E. M. (1962) *Diffusion of Innovations*, New York: Free Press.

Scarbrough, H. (ed.) (1996) *The Management of Expertise*, London: Macmillan.

Tierney, M. and Wickham, J. (1989) Controlling Software Labour: Professional Ideologies and the Problem of Control, ESRC/PICT Workshop on Critical Perspectives on Software, Manchester, July.

Von Hippel, E. (1990) The Impact of "Sticky Data" on Innovation and Problem-solving, Sloan School of Management Working Paper, 3147-90-BPS, Cambridge, MA: MIT.

Whipp, R. and Clark, P. (1986) *Innovation and the Auto Industry: Production, Process and Work Organization*, London: Frances Pinter.

Wibbelsman, D. and Maiero, T. (1994) Co-sourcing, paper presented at the Outsourcing, Co-sourcing and Insourcing Conference, University of California, Berkeley.

Willcocks, L. (1994) Collaborating to Compete: Towards Strategic Partnerships in IT Outsourcing? Oxford Institute of Information Management, Research and Discussion Paper 94, 11, Templeton College, Oxford.

Willcocks, L. and Fitzgerald, G. (1993) Market As Opportunity? Case Studies in Outsourcing Information Technology and Services, *Journal of Strategic Information Systems*, **2**, 3, 223–242.

Willcocks, L., Lacity, M. and Fitzgerald, G. (1995) IT Outsourcing in Europe and the USA: Assessment Issues, *International Journal of Information Management*, **15**, 5, 333–351.

Williamson, O. E. (1975) *Markets and Hierarchies: Analysis and Antitrust Implications*, New York: The Free Press.

Williamson, O. (1981) The Economics of Organization: The Transaction Cost Approach, *American Journal of Sociology*, 87, 548–577.

Williamson, O. E. (1985) *The Economic Institutions of Capitalism*, New York: The Free Press.

Williamson, O. E. (1986) *Economic Organisation: Firms, Markets and Policy Control*, Brighton: Wheatsheaf Books.

Womack, J. P., Jones, D. T. and Roos, D. (1990) *The Machine that Changed the World*, Oxford: Maxwell Macmillan International.

5

A Framework for IS Outsourcing Strategy in Private and Public Sector Contexts

JONATHAN CRONK AND JOHN SHARP

INTRODUCTION

In Chapter 8, Leon de Looff presents a descriptional framework for assisting in information systems outsourcing decisions. Jurison, in Chapter 6, and others, for example Lacity, Willcocks and Feeny (1996) and McFarlan and Nolan (1995), have also produced useful frameworks for analysing sourcing decisions. The purpose of this chapter is to complement and extend this work. Specifically, the objectives are: (i) to examine the theory of outsourcing in general; (ii) to argue that there is a need to develop a strategic framework to make it possible which IT/IS activities should be outsourced and which should be obtained internally; (iii) to demonstrate how a classification due to Perry, Stott and Smallwood (1993) can be applied by private sector organizations to the sourcing decision in the IT/IS field; and, (iv) to examine how the Perry, Stott and Smallwood model can be applied within public sector organizations, using specific examples drawn from the United Kingdom.

The Development of the Outsourcing Concept

Earlier chapters have each presented their own preferred definitions of outsourcing. Here we rely on two working definitions to orientate our

Strategic Sourcing of Information Systems.
Edited by L. P. Willcocks and M. C. Lacity.

discussion. A thorough, if somewhat legalistic, definition of outsourcing is given by Gilbert (1993, p. 7):

> "Outsourcing is the process by which a corporation, a governmental agency or another business entity subcontracts to a third party—the 'outsourcer'—the performance of certain services or the operation of certain equipment required for its internal operations."

Quinn (1992, p. 32) although not providing an explicit definition of the term identifies the underlying notion of outsourcing:

> "Each activity within a firm's value chain and within its traditional staff groups must be considered a 'service', which can just as easily be purchased externally."

The trend has been for organizations to grow bigger and more complex, requiring elaborate administrative functions and rules to permit their control. These sorts of organizations are referred to by Mintzberg (1989) and Weber (1924) and others as "bureaucracies." The need for control, coupled with the pervasive growth motive, has led many large bureaucratic organizations to perform all manner of support services internally. To quote Henry Mintzberg (1989, p. 136):

> "The obsession with control helps to explain the frequent proliferation of support staff in these organizations. Many of the staff services could be purchased from outside suppliers."

Problems Associated with Large, Complex Organizations

There are a number of problems associated with large, complex organizations:

1. Managers within organizations often make decisions for personal reasons rather than to maximize profit (Argyris, 1985), e.g. by biasing justifications for long-term investments in areas they control.
2. Compensation systems can be influenced more by internal comparisons than by the external marketplace. A high technology company, for example, may have to offer a package of benefits to marketers and scientists in order to compete with other similar organizations for their scarce and valuable skills. It is extremely difficult to refuse such facilities to employees with less scarce skills, who can have a cost to the company that is 50 per cent above the "going rate" for such work.
3. In a large bureaucracy decisions have to be made by coalition and

consensus. Decision making in such an environment, however, may take too long to be commercially effective and be too far removed from the needs of the customer or the marketplace.

These and other similar problems have led management theorists to question the advisability of such complexity.

Theoretical Background to Outsourcing: Organizational Theory from the Late 1970s

It is necessary to revisit the core competence debate traced in earlier chapters in a little more detail, because this forms the essential backgound to the framework we wish to develop. In the late 1970s and early 1980s there was a growing realization that there were inefficiencies inherent in the large, complex organizational forms prevalent at that time. Peters and Waterman (1982) proposed eight characteristics common, they said, to America's best-run companies. One of these principles was "stick to the knitting." As a result of this and related thinking, many large corporations began to focus on a set of "core competences" (Prahalad and Hamel, 1990) that distinguished them from their competition. This led many corporations to think in terms of divesting themselves of divisions that did not fall within the core competence. The development of this line of thought, which crystallized during the late 1980s and early 1990s, is that many elements of an organization's activities are unrelated to its core competence and should be treated accordingly. This thinking was precipitated by analyses such as Porter's value chain (Porter, 1985) which helped managers focus on the way value was added by various organizational activities. This was amplified by Aaker (1992) and others who advocated concentrating energies on those activities that gave the enterprise strategic competitive advantage.

As mentioned in the Introduction and other chapters, Quinn (1992) and Quinn and Hilmer (1994) have taken this approach further. They advocate outsourcing activities that fall outside the core intellectual properties that distinguish the enterprise from others, since specialist intellect is the core resource of most organizations through which they deliver a superior service to the customer. Most activities in the value chain can be defined as services. Each service can be examined from a customer perspective to see if it is one which the organization knows how to perform better than anyone else in the world. If it is, it should be retained and the intellectual resources surrounding it should be protected by any possible means. Any services that the organization is unable to perform better than anyone else should be outsourced. The exceptions are those activities it must retain in order to build barriers to entry around its core competences. The basis of this argument is that the success of an organization is the product of all the elements of the value chain. The better each of these is, the better the whole:

> "To the extent that knowledge about the specific service activity is more important than knowledge about the end product itself, specialized suppliers can produce higher value-added at a lower cost for their service than almost any integrated company." (Quinn, 1992, p. 47).

This line of argument is extended by Perry, Stott and Smallwood (1993). They define a concept called the "Unit of Competitive Advantage" or UCA. The UCA is similar to Quinn's "core competence" in that it is that which distinguishes the organization from competitors but, whereas Quinn focuses on intellectual capability, Perry, Stott and Smallwood look at processes. According to their theory, the work done within a company should be analysed into four categories: *UCA work* (defined above), *value-added support work*, *essential support work* and *non-essential work*. The value-added support work is there because it enhances the UCA. It is not managed purely on a cost basis as it is part of the value chain. An example of this sort of work would be the logistics process in a large global television manufacturing company. Better logistics will not gain market share, but they may enhance profitability. The essential support work is that which adds no value to the UCA but is necessary for some reason. An example would be the site security department at a jam factory. The non-essential work is that which would have no effect on the cost or value of the product if it were not performed.

Perry, Stott and Smallwood propose a methodology for action based on this analysis. All non-essential work should be eliminated. Any non-UCA work that is putting the enterprise at a competitive disadvantage should be brought up to standard. An example of this would be a supermarket chain without good EPOS systems. Lastly, UCA processes should be improved as rapidly as possible.

In doing these things, the UCA processes should remain within the ownership and control of the enterprise. The value-added support processes should be grouped close to the UCA processes and the essential support processes should be separated from both in order to avoid resource conflict. An example of the application of this thinking would be the splitting of a traditional Personnel department. The value-added processes such as management development would be distributed within the business units they support, such as marketing. Salary administration, on the other hand, could be performed centrally.

In order to understand how to provide such processes, Perry, Stott

	Proprietary capability	Generic capability
Value-added support work	**Provide** (Develop best internal capability possible)	**Broker** (Develop ongoing access to the best capability possible)
Essential support work	**Maintain** (Manage internal capability to meet cost and quality standards)	**Contract out** (Monitor to secure compliance)

Source: Perry *et al.* (1993, p. 86) Reproduced by permission of John Wiley and Sons

Figure 5.1 *Options for Managing Non-UCA Work*

and Smallwood propose a matrix analysis. Having separated the work into value-added and essential support, it is further categorized by whether or not it contains secret or unique characteristics. Some processes are secret because they may reveal proprietary information, others may not be available on the open market. These are classified as "proprietary" and all others as "generic." The sourcing strategy is then developed according to the decision matrix shown in Figure 5.1.

In summary, the analysis allows resources to be focused internally on developing the processes that give competitive advantage and the proprietary processes that best support them whilst maintaining control over generic and essential processes with the appropriate level of resource at a minimal organizational burden.

When applied to IT services the Perry *et al.* model has much in common with the widely-used IS portfolio framework of McFarlan, McKenney and Pyburn (1983). However, it has two advantages over that model. Firstly, in a business sense, it provides a richer classification in that UCA work is identified and treated differently to support work; non-essential work is also considered; and finally a 2×2 matrix is applied to *support work only*. Secondly, it applies to business processes rather than information systems. Given the current concerns with Business Process Redesign (Davenport, 1993; Willcocks and Currie, 1997)—for instance the whole of the UK Engineering and Physical Sciences Research Council's Innovative Manufacturing Initiative relies on a Business Process framework—such an orientation is a fairly natural one in considering IT outsourcing. Equally, from the older perspective of Structured Analysis (DeMarco, 1978) a process orientation is also an appropriate one. For these reasons it forms the basis of a framework for the consideration of IT outsourcing, that is presented later.

An alternative perspective is that of Williamson (1975), who calls the "insource" decision the choice of *hierarchical governance* and the "outsource" decision *market governance.* Markets exhibit scale economies and therefore have lower *production costs* than hierarchies. Production costs will be further reduced according to their frequency; recurrent transactions costing less than occasional ones. Williamson postulates that these advantages are offset by higher *co-ordination costs* in dealing with markets. The basic building blocks of Williamson's version of transaction cost theory have been detailed earlier. (See in particular Chapters 2 and 4 for descriptions of the concepts of asset specificity, uncertainty, idiosyncratic assets, and threat of opportunism). As market co-ordination costs are difficult to measure and predict, managers in bureaucratic organizations, who are usually risk averse, generally favour in-house production and concentrate on minimizing production costs. Williamson argues that this tendency should be reversed and that it should be the norm to take advantage of the scale economies of the market and to try to minimize the effects of asset specificity, uncertainty and the threat of opportunism on co-ordination costs. Williamson (1979) advances a methodology for the market versus hierarchy decision (see also Chapter 4):

- *Occasional/recurrent, non-specific transactions* should be subject to market governance as they have low co-ordination costs and can attract high scale economies.
- *Occasional, mixed/idiosyncratic transactions* should also go to the market. The economies of scale in these cases are associated with the fact that the external source can make better use of scarce resources than the internal, by spreading their use over several customers. In these cases, strategies must be devised to reduce uncertainty and the possibility of opportunism. The key mechanism for this is the contract.
- *Recurrent, mixed transactions* will often be insourced as it appears easier to acquire or develop the specific asset than to control it in the market. The recurrent nature of such transactions means that the specific asset may be fully utilized in-house. Williamson asserts that this class of transaction should also be outsourced. Relationships should be long term in order that both parties can gain full advantage of the investment involved. Vendor and customer are protected contractually.
- *Recurrent, idiosyncratic transactions* will have similar costs of produc-

> tion in the market as in the hierarchy. Co-ordination costs will be higher externally, leading to an insource decision. This will be compounded if there is the possibility of opportunism in the market. Williamson points out, however, that it may be possible to take measures to reduce the specificity of the asset by internal standardization in cases where there is little uncertainty. It would then take on the characteristics of the recurrent mixed or recurrent non-specific transaction and should, with due attention to contractual protection, be outsourced.

Williamson's theoretical approach has been extended by Malone, Yates and Benjamin (1987). They note that recent advances in IT, particularly in electronic communications, deliver the potential to dramatically reduce co-ordination costs. IT can also, as in the case of Computer Aided Design (CAD), reduce asset specificity by reducing the degree of expertise required for a particular task. They argue that the effects of IT advances magnify and accelerate the trend towards more market governance, in other words favour the outsource decision.

Outsourcing in Information Technology

Outsourcing in Information Technology is not a new phenomenon. Reinforcing the point made in earlier chapters, Leonard (1992, p. 44) commented that: "Facilities management arrangements have been used ... since the 1960s and other types of outsourcing are very common." In fact, during that decade, the cost of computing was such that most small businesses obtained their computer services from central suppliers known as "Bureaux." Since then, several types of supplier organization have been formed to supply resources or to manage services. What *is* new is that the term "outsourcing" has been used as a generic term for all of these types of external procurement decisions and for the "sell the lot" type of total outsource.

Lacity and Hirschheim's study (1993a) of public outsourcing reviews concluded that historically most outsourcing decisions had been made to reduce cost. Much of the literature reviewed in their text treats IT as a utility. Most of the articles reported success in the main objective of cost reduction and a catalogue of additional benefits. A study of their bibliography reveals that the majority of their sources were published in 1989 and 1990. They were, therefore, mostly concerned with the large, less fragmented type of outsource contract that was prevalent up to that period.

Their case studies revealed that a large number of outsourcing decisions had, indeed, been made for wholly or partially political reasons.

Some were viewed as very successful, some very unsuccessful and the bulk as a mixture. The most telling insight was that most senior managers regarded IT as an overhead burden. This predisposed them to look upon outsourcing as a way to reduce cost. A number of reasons were given for looking at outsourcing but cost saving or cost avoidance was always the rationale given for a positive *decision* to outsource.

Lacity and Hirschheim point out that there is a tendency for the literature to report successes, rather than failures (Lacity and Hirschheim, 1993a). The same text draws attention to another point. Most articles are written during the early days of an outsource arrangement. Often, outsource arrangements are attractive to the customer in the short term and many of the problems only come to light later on. Moreover, it can be supposed that articles are more usually inspired by events rather than by their absence. Certainly, even as at 1997, there have been very few articles of the "why we didn't outsource" variety.

Lacity and Hirschheim (1993a/b; 1995) refute several "myths" regarding the economics of outsourcing. They report that the scale economies popularly believed to accrue to large datacentre operations have been eroded by the pricing policies of hardware and software vendors. Most reported cost savings, they argue, are made because an inefficient in-house operation is compared with an efficient outsource option. Therefore they build a compensating mechanism into their methodology aimed at redressing managerial bias towards outsourcing.

As Lacity and Hirschheim (1993a) point out, the economies of scale associated with facilities management some years ago have been eroded to the degree that they are no longer a deciding factor. The site specificity and human asset specificity of many installations has increased with the move towards client-server. This leads to the conclusion that datacentre and LAN management are by nature recurrent idiosyncratic transactions which may be performed as economically in the hierarchy as in the market. Lacity and Hirschheim conclude that the problems and risks inherent in outsourcing IT tend to outweigh the negligible cost advantages. They urge that the internal operation be encouraged to reach the same state of efficiency as the best outsource option, at which point the vendor's profit margin will probably outweigh its scale economies. Their recommended procedure for the evaluation of outsourcing is shown in Figure 5.2. Should there still be significant reasons for outsourcing, they emphasize that the contract is the only safeguard for the customer and vendor alike.

Fitzgerald and Willcocks (1994) extended this analysis by considering the types of outsourcing situations that can be regulated effectively by contractual means. They conclude that where the service applies to a situation of relative certainty and outcomes can be tightly defined, a

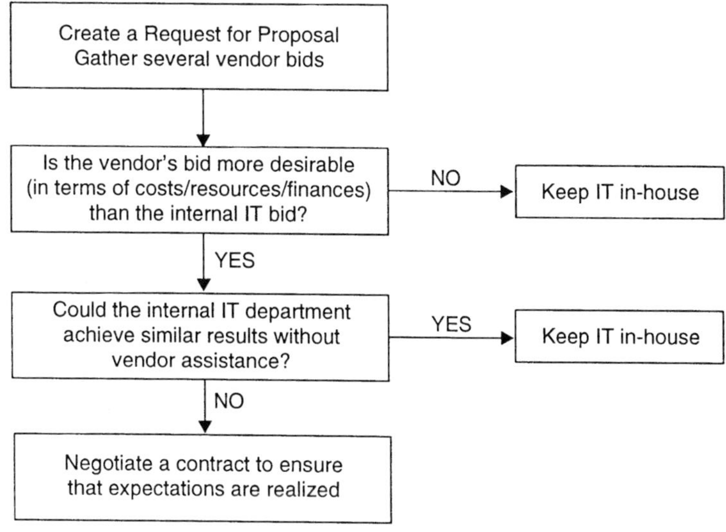

Source: Adapted from Lacity and Hirschheim (1993a). Reproduced by permission of John Wiley and Sons

Figure 5.2 *Proposed Outsourcing Evaluation Process*

fixed fee contract is appropriate. Conversely, where there is a high degree of uncertainty and tight definition of outputs is impossible, a Risk/Reward contract is appropriate. Other contingencies do not lend themselves to effective regulation by contract.

Willcocks, Lacity and Fitzgerald (1995) review a variety of studies and 43 case histories of outsourcing projects. Evaluation is seen to be particularly problematic with difficulties in surfacing hidden costs, comparing external and internal bids on an equal basis and the effort required to develop effective measurement systems. Their work might be construed as providing a justification of a competitive advantage/strategic approach to the outsourcing decision of the sort that typifies many information systems strategy methodologies (see, for example, Earl, 1989).

An alternative approach, also based on a "strategic" perspective, to dealing with the pitfalls of outsourcing is "hybrid-outsourcing" in which internal staff function as junior team members to external consultants (Buck-Lew, 1992). Other authors, for example McFarlan and Nolan (1995) have developed this idea further by looking at strategic alliances between outsourcers and their customers.

TOWARDS A STRATEGIC FRAMEWORK FOR OUTSOURCING DECISIONS

Most writers (for example Fitzgerald and Willcocks, 1993a; see also the Introduction and chapter 1) and recent market studies agree that the UK IT outsourcing market has been growing rapidly. None seem to believe the market to be contracting. The growth would appear to be due to a range of factors which include increased awareness of the benefits of outsourcing, trends toward Open Systems and Client-Server, the maturing market and increased buyer power. On the last point Nixon (1993, p. 7) puts it thus: "In data processing, vendors face a competitive environment that features a variety of solutions from which institutions can choose." The effect of this (Porter, 1980) is that the IT outsourcing market is becoming increasingly competitive. At the same time, it is becoming increasingly easy to procure services in smaller tranches. It therefore behoves organizations to establish ways of using IT outsourcing strategically.

The general outsourcing literature discussed above and the more specific IT outsourcing literature point to the need for a strategic framework for IT outsourcing. Willcocks, Lacity and Fitzgerald (1995) identify a number of key issues—relating to retained in-house capability—to be subsumed within such an approach:

1. strategic thinking on IT in relation to the business;
2. systems integration;
3. eliciting business demand for IT;
4. spotting business opportunities for the use of IT;
5. an "informed buyer" role;
6. contract monitoring; and
7. the ability to lever vendor relations to advantage.

Though Gable and Sharp (1992) present an econometric study of success factors in a certain type of outsourcing, most writers have contented themselves with deriving precepts from the literature. Thus, Lacity and Hirschheim (1993a) give a list of contractual guidelines derived from the literature and their case studies which has considerable overlap with similar lists given by other authors, for example Ketler and Walstrom (1993).

Our concern is to present a framework that supports the first five of the items in the above list (since the last two refer to managing a post-decision arrangement) and that attempts to answer the question: *How can the management of an organization decide which, if any, Information*

Technology processes to outsource? This framework has similarities with that of Fitzgerald and Willcocks (1993b) in that it attempts to base the decision on the strategic role of the processes concerned as either "core" or "commodity." Practitioners such as Wilder (1990) or Clermont (1991) have proposed similar divisions of IT systems into "commodity" or "value added."

Before discussing our framework, a conceptual shift is proposed. Williamson (1975; 1979) regards the market as the best form of governance, all other things being equal, and strives to find ways to make economic arguments for outsourcing. Lacity and Hirschheim (1993a) take the opposite approach. They start from the basis that, wherever possible, IT should be insourced. In order to get over the adversarial nature of any decision where a stance has been taken, it is proposed that the term "outsourcing" be used more specifically and the term "sourcing" be used generically. This is defined as follows:

> Sourcing in IT is the process of deciding which elements of the IT skills mix should be procured from outside the organization and which from within. If from outside, sourcing includes the identification of the best potential vendor and the formation and management of a business relationship. If from inside, sourcing includes the process of ensuring the same level of business commitment from the internal resources as would be sought externally.

The approach has similarities with that of Lacity, Willcocks and Feeny (1996).

Core Competence Analysis and the Segmentation of the IT Function

There are certain key capabilities that distinguish an organization from its competitors. The basic assumption is that IT is not one seamless whole. It is vital to understand the relative strategic importance of the processes supported by IT components in order to make sourcing decisions for those components. In finding the core competences, it is helpful to concentrate on the intellectual capabilities of the organization (Quinn, 1992). If elements of IT are found to *be* core competences, then the sourcing activity for them is over in so far as they must be performed within the organization to protect its competitive position.

We follow a variety of authors (for example Scott Morton, 1991) in dividing the IT function into Infrastructure and Services. The first principle underlying this division is founded on the need for organizational continuity and the opinion of authors such as Willcocks, Lacity and Fitzgerald (1995) and many practitioners (Laabs, 1993; Nixon, 1993; Withington, 1993). The customer must maintain enough expertise in-house to manage the outsourced services. Withington (1993, p. 124) calls this maintaining a "cadre of competence." The management of IT is not confined to one individual, but to a core of employees that perform this function on behalf of the organization. Most businesses cannot exist for more than a few days without IT so any strategy must minimize the threat of non-continuity. Therefore, there will be a small core of employees that are responsible for maintaining business continuity. In a small company, this might be as few as two (never less, in case of unforeseen illness or other causes of absence). In a larger company, this could be a much larger number.

The second principle is that this group must have within it, or have access to sufficient skills and knowledge to make informed sourcing decisions on behalf of the organization. *If an organization accepts outsourcing as a significant option for supporting its value chain, then the quality of sourcing decisions will affect its success*, that is sourcing of IT is a "Value Adding" activity (see also Lacity, Willcocks and Feeny, 1996).

The third principle comes from the need for a technology strategy for IT. That the field is changing rapidly is demonstrated by the change in attitudes to Open Systems in the course of the last five years. If Open Systems were to become a reality, an IT strategy might not be necessary in that IT components would be interchangeable. Today's reality, however, is far from such a utopian concept. At the moment, the technology life cycle in IT is still shortening. Ten years ago, networks of personal computers were in their infancy. Now, they are a fact of life and form the basic infrastructure of information delivery. Personal computers that were "leading edge" at that time are barely adequate to process the software mix required on today's desktop. Conversely, mainframes and minicomputers purchased then are still well within their investment life and the systems developed on them are expected to last for years.

Furthermore, the richness of the software market means it is easily possible for different users and user groups in an organization to use different software products to do the same job. The shifting pattern and growing pervasiveness of IT in work, coupled with the dramatic increase in the pace of organizational change, means that the interchange of documents, files and even processes between these individuals must be planned for, even if it does not currently take place (Lambert and Peppard, 1993). To cope with this, standards have to be set and constantly reviewed. Most network based infrastructures today are almost organic in nature, evolving as each new component and user is added. Investment decisions are a constant compromise between the requirements of the individual to optimally utilize the latest available technology and the constraints placed upon that individual by his/her role in the organization.

The IT infrastructure, then, includes the cables and network components, the network operating systems, the computers themselves and their operating and management systems and some of the technical activities that surround them such as performance management and capacity planning.

Aside from technology, the other main IT infrastructure component is data. Galliers (1992) suggests that management of corporate data is seen as a problem area by IS and non-IS managers alike. In historical, monolithic computer environments, the computer systems largely prescribed the way people worked. Networked personal computers, on the other hand, enable knowledge workers to find new ways to work. In such an environment, information can be needed anywhere and can be generated by anyone. In the future, document images and "multimedia" elements will follow the same pattern. To leave this pattern to develop unchecked will result in, at best, duplication of effort and, at worse, chaos. Common cataloguing and management systems must be used to avoid this (Sprague, 1995). The management of data is therefore a key infrastructural component and the choice of data management tools is a key decision in IT strategy.

The internal IT management group needs to maintain enough knowledge about the current state of technology and the needs of the organization to manage the transitional process. It must understand the current technology mix well enough to facilitate informed purchasing decisions. For these reasons we believe that infrastructural decisions should be technology-led with a strong business influence.

All the other elements of IT can be regarded as "services." All of them support business processes or the processes that support business processes. They include business applications, user support, central operations and hardware maintenance. Systems development can be regarded either as a service to business applications or, conceptually, as the procurement function for those applications.

By contrast with Infrastucture decisions we believe that Service decisions should be business-led but should take account of and influence the infrastructure.

The infrastructure/service split is modelled in Figure 5.3. It will be noted that one service can support more than one process and one process can be supported by more than one service. The infrastructure, however, for reasons we shall argue in the next section, must be considered as an indivisible whole.

Business Processes	P1		P2	P3
IT Services	S1	S2	S3	
IT Infrastructure	*Indivisible Whole*			

Figure 5.3 *The IT Service/Infrastructure Model*

There are, of course, grey areas. Is an electronic mail system infrastructure or service? It would probably be categorized as infrastructure as it needs to be organization-wide, but what about Word Processing software, for example? The answer to this may depend on a number of factors such as the nature of the business and the current state of its IT infrastructure. Either way, a formal decision should be made about each element of IT. The reasons for this will become evident in the next two sections.

Segmentation of Services: Essential and Value Adding vs Proprietary and Generic

Having divided IT into services and infrastructure we now classify services into "Value Adding" and "Essential" in the manner of the Perry, Stott and Smallwood model (1993), explained earlier. This analysis needs careful thought. Is an IT service that supports a process in the same category as that process? What about an IT service that supports an IT service? Is an IT service the same as an application system? If we think in terms of *work*, as do Perry *et al.* then the problem is simplified. The IT work is either so integrated with the process that it is part of the process or it is not integrated and is, therefore, a support service. An application system is not work, it is the specification, construction and maintenance of that system that is work. An IT service that supports an IT service follows the same rules. A service that is integral with the process it supports takes on the same classification as that process. A service that is not integrated with the process will take on the classification of the "next level" except in the case of a UCA support service which may either be value adding or essential support. This Service Analysis Matrix is represented in Figure 5.4.

The same logic can be followed for IT services supporting other support services, until a picture is built up of the classification of each service by each process it supports, as exemplified in Figure 5.5. It will be noted that each service may be value adding or essential support

IT SERVICE:	UCAP	VAP	ESP
Integrated with process	UCA	VA	ES
Not integrated with process	VA/ES	ES	ES

Key:
- UCA Unit of Competitive Advantage IT Service
- VA Value Adding IT Service
- ES Essential IT Service
- UCAP Unit of Competitive Advantage Business Process
- VAP Value Adding Business Process
- ESP Essential Support Business Process

Figure 5.4 *IT Service Analysis Matrix*

depending upon the process or service it supports. As noted earlier, each service may support several processes, e.g. system specification, which supports all three processes listed, and each process may be supported by several services, e.g. Process 2, which is supported by system specification, construction and testing and help desk support.

Having broken the IT service segment down into component services and classified these services as value adding or essential support, it is now possible to analyse each in the manner of the "Options for managing non-UCA work" shown in Figure 5.1. This analysis generates four possible courses of action: "Provide, Maintain, Broker and Contract Out." In practice, these would have to be translated into meaningful approaches for the particular service. The generic, essential support category "Contract Out" might translate to "find the cheapest, reliable package" when applied to system construction, for example. Again, "Broker" might mean "engage best consulting systems house in class."

	Process 1 (UCA)	Process 2 (VA)	Process 3 (ES)
System specification	VA	VA	ES
Construction and testing	VA	ES	
System maintenance	VA		ES
Help desk support	ES	ES	ES

Figure 5.5 *IT Service Support Matrix*

Obviously some services, by their nature, will be indivisible for the organization. If they are needed at different "standards" by different business processes, they would need to be kept at the higher standard and the additional overhead carried by the organization.

Segmentation of Infrastructure: Managing the Technology Life Cycle

A similar process to that taken with services can be applied to the infrastructure. Infrastructure planning and management is work that requires skill and expertise. The difference between the analytical requirement for the infrastructure and for services is that the infrastructure is indivisible and that it is subject to the technology life cycle. Both of these statements need explanation.

The Infrastructure is Indivisible

Network-based infrastructures are organic in nature in that they evolve as individual parts are replaced or changed (Joosten, Ploeger and Brinkkempner, 1995). Each change affects, potentially, many other components. The specialist worker in each technology present in the infrastructure needs, therefore, to work in a team with the other such specialists. They need to make decisions as a group.

The Technology Life Cycle

Technology life cycles are shortening. New technologies arrive with increasing rapidity. Some will be relevant to the organization and some will not. Some of these will have niche uses and others will eventually pervade the whole organization. Some will replace current technologies; others will be optional. The group that manages the infrastructure must also advise the business on the technical aspects of IT Service procurement. It is essential that this group has within it the technical knowledge to understand and manage the core technologies present in the infrastructure.

One approach to the outsourcing decision for IT infrastructure would be for the organization routinely to outsource the work of supporting the technologies at the beginning and end of the technology life cycle. Emergent technologies could be supported, if required, by consultants who can obtain the scale economies to support the costs of learning. Mature technologies would be well understood and established in the market and would take on the attributes of commodities. In this way internal staff, who are tried and trusted and used to working in the team, can be released from managing the mature technologies in order to retrain on those technologies that are moving into the growth phase in the organization's infrastructure. Any component of the infrastructure that is to be outsourced should now be reclassified as a service and treated in the manner of the previous section. Any generic, pervasive, essential support service should be examined to see if it now forms part of the infrastructure. All infrastructural components should have service levels set in response to the needs of the services or business processes they support or to the needs imposed by interaction with other infrastructural components.

APPLYING THE PERRY, STOTT AND SMALLWOOD MODEL TO PUBLIC SECTOR CONTEXTS

The primary focus of the Perry *et al.* model is clearly on the private sector enterprise operating within a competitive market. In the United Kingdom (UK) in the 1990s, however, the public sector has made much of the running in the outsourcing of IT and, therefore, desirably, any framework to support the outsourcing decision in IT should be capable of application in the public sector also. We shall argue that the Perry *et al.* model can be extended to the public sector with suitable adaptations. Rather than range over the whole public sector we confine our discussions to the examples of UK local government and local police authorities. The latter, until the 1990s, were part of the local government apparatus and have, inevitably, been affected by pressures for outsourcing in local government.

Although local government had probably always purchased infrequently used services from outside, the benefits of so doing began first to be urged by commentators in the 1970s. Arguments were usually based on comparison with other countries in Europe and elsewhere in the world where services such as refuse collection had always been let by local government under contract. Some commentators, following Williamson (1975), argued that local authorities that had hitherto carried out their operations internally could benefit considerably by purchasing certain frequently used services, e.g. highways maintenance, from commercial suppliers. Competition from other similar suppliers would result in a market price for the service substantially lower than that obtainable internally.

With the advent of the Conservative government in 1979 in the UK, these ideas began to be applied in earnest in local government through a Central Government series of initiatives designed to ensure that services such as refuse collection were put out to competitive tender. The Local Government Planning and Land Act (1980) required local authorities in England and Wales to put out certain maintenance work on buildings and highways to compulsory competitive tendering (CCT) (Greenwood and Wilson, 1994). These moves were encouraged by the extension of CCT in the 1988 Local Government Act (Vincent-Jones, 1994), to refuse collection, grounds and vehicle maintenance, school and welfare catering, sports and leisure management and so on. The majority of the original contracts were won by "Direct Service Organizations" set up by local councils through redesignating previous internal providers of the services concerned. This led to a purchaser/provider split within many activities in local government. By 1996 CCT was being scheduled to be extended to a variety of other more "white collar" local government services, for example IT services and engineering services by 1998. In fact, however, many local authorities had already voluntarily begun to contract out such services especially in IT, with a number of authorities having opted to purchase all their IT support from outside suppliers.

A number of commentators, for example The Audit Commission (1993), have identified problems with the general post-1988 round of CCT in areas of contract specification, contract monitoring and in the enforcement of contract provisions in cases of poor performance. These observations parallel those of Fitzgerald and Willcocks (1994) noted earlier.

CCT had been a mechanism for bringing about outsourcing of local government services. Clearly the problems with outsourcing in the private sector were likely to arise also in a local government context. Moreover, with the extension of CCT to professional services, in particular to IT, it is conceivable that the difficulties could grow further and that pressures could lead to the retention of insourcing. As at 1997, even if CCT were to be abolished, however, the attractions of workforce flexibility and low-cost supply by external providers specializing in the type of service being sought would remain. Local government would still need to consider under what circumstances outsourcing of IT is appropriate, where it should be used, and how it is best managed. The attractions of extending the Perry *et al.* model to this sector are, therefore, obvious.

Special Features of IT Outsourcing in Local Authorities

The context of IT outsourcing in local government differs from the private sector in a number of ways. As the above discussion shows, the need to outsource was imposed by Central Government; many contracts under CCT were won by internal "provider" units; and a great number of external suppliers have actually arisen through the transfer of internal staff to consultancy firms (as at early 1997 recent private sector agreements had also exhibited this characteristic).

It is arguable also that local authorities have a wider repertoire of outsourcing opportunities open to them than is commonly the case in the private sector. In particular, one possibility is to obtain software from another local authority with acknowledged expertise in developing it. A longstanding route to development is via a consortium of local authorities or police authorities. A refinement on this favoured in the mid-1990s, for example by UK police forces, is for such a consortium to designate a "lead authority" for any particular information system. This lead authority then takes the responsibility for developing the system on behalf of the consortium. A fourth approach is for a strategic alliance, along the lines of Quinn and Hilmer (1994) with a major supplier, e.g. ICL, McDonnell Douglas, to develop a software package that can be adopted by other authorities. In the UK local government context, council tax and library systems have been widespread examples of this type of development.

Adapting the Perry, Scott and Smallwood Model

Although it might be argued that the emergence of competition under CCT between internal and external providers made the notion of competitive advantage applicable also in Local Authorities, we prefer to replace Perry *et al*'s UCA with the notion of *Leading Competence Advantage* (LCA). By this, we mean that a particular authority can clearly identify itself as the leader in the IT process concerned amongst UK local authorities and that *there are no potential external suppliers with greater competence*. As at 1996 it was probable that for many areas of IT no external supplier did have comparable competence to the leading local authorities, and that there was a reasonable national consensus about who those authorities were. In other areas, an authority needed to make a realistic appraisal of its special competences. The notion of Value Adding Processes are, in this context, to be understood as processes supporting LCA ones. The definition of Essential Support Processes remains as before.

With these modifications we can identify the following strategies for outsourcing as being appropriate:

1. LCA-related systems should not be sourced from an external supplier but should be developed by the authority itself. The authority may consider, however, entering into a strategic alliance with an external supplier to develop a system from which the authority will derive royalty income.

2. Value Added systems, if local authority related (the equivalent of proprietary), can either be sourced via: another authority; some form of consortium arrangement; or by a package developed through an alliance between a local authority and an external supplier.
3. Generic Value Added systems, e.g. Word Processing software, are sourced as in the private sector.
4. Generic Essential Support systems, e.g. a system to support debt recovery through the courts, will also be sourced as in the private sector.
5. Local authority related Essential Support Systems, e.g. provision of statistics to Central Government, can be sourced in a similar way to local authority specific Value Added Systems.

What Should Local Authorities Not Outsource?

Some local authorities have already outsourced their entire IT activity. The implication of this is, in terms of the arguments above, that they do not consider themselves as having an LCA in any area of IT. However, our earlier arguments about the need to preserve a "cadre of competence" both to manage the outsourcing processes and to manage the infrastructure still apply. As far as the latter point is concerned, integration of hitherto distinct local authority functional areas, e.g. highways and planning, has been increasingly important in the mid-1990s.

As in the private sector, the cadre of competence needs to be within a central group. The purchaser/provider split, however, has tended to make it more difficult to maintain such central groups. A further problem is that the high level of expertise required of members of this central group makes them attractive to consulting firms wishing to develop a presence in the local government field and it is difficult for local authorities to match the salary levels offered outside. Notwithstanding these difficulties, we feel that our earlier arguments apply at least as strongly in the local authority context. Cadre of competence-related activities should not be outsourced and should be supplied from a central resource. It is our belief that these considerations form the basis for a similar analysis to be applied to organizations considering outsourcing in other public sector contexts, whether in the UK or elsewhere.

CONCLUSION

Early interest in outsourcing, especially in the IT field, was predominantly from the standpoint of cost reduction through the application of market pressures to the organization. This was particularly the case in the UK public sector as exemplified by local authorities. The UK Central Government imposed policy of Compulsory Competitive Tendering was an attempt to achieve such benefits in local government operations.

This position was changing by 1995–7 in the private sector, through the evolution of a "strategic" view of outsourcing as a preferred option where the organization did not possess unique intellectual property (see for example Quinn and Hilmer, 1994; also the Introduction). Within IT, authors such as Lacity and Hirschheim (1993) and Willcocks, Lacity and Fitzgerald (1995) have argued that cost savings from outsourcing are often nugatory and initially might be better achieved through attempting to improve the efficiency of the organization's own IT function. Taken together these two sets of arguments suggest that there is a need for a framework that would enable decisions to be taken about how to *source* IT services within private sector organizations, whether from inside or outside the organization. Clearly, similar issues also arise in local authorities and it is plausible that some of the rigidities of CCT will eventually be relaxed to the extent that local authorities will also have much greater flexibility about how to source IT services.

The classification of Perry, Stott and Smallwood (1993) into UCA work and non-UCA work and their associated value adding and essential support services, appears to provide such a framework for the private sector. With appropriate modifications it can also be applied as a decision framework for public sector organizations considering outsourcing IT.

REFERENCES

Aaker, D. A. (1992) *Strategic Market Management*, New York: John Wiley and Sons.

Argyris, C. (1985) *Strategy, Change and Defensive Routines*, New York: Addison-Wesley.

Audit Commission (1993) Realising the Benefits of Competition: The Client Role for Contracted Services, Audit Commission, London.

Buck-Lew, M. (1992) To Outsource Or Not? *International Journal Of Information Management*, **12** ,1, 3–20.

Clermont, P. (1991) Outsourcing Without Guilt, *Computerworld*, **25**, 29, 67.

Davenport, H. (1993) *Process Innovation: Reengineering Work Through Information Technology*, Boston: Harvard Business School Press.

DeMarco, T. (1978) *Structured Analysis and System Specification*, New York: Yourdon.

Earl, M. J. (1989) *Management Strategies for Information Technology*, London: Prentice Hall.

Fitzgerald, G. and Willcocks, L. (1993) *Information Technology Outsourcing Practice: A Survey*, London: Business Intelligence.

Fitzgerald, G. and Willcocks, L. (1994) Contracts and Partnerships in the Outsourcing of IT, Proceedings of the Fifteenth International Conference on Information Systems, Vancouver, 14–17 December, 91–98.

Gable, G. and Sharp, J. (1992) Outsourcing Assistance With Computer System Selection: A Success Factors Approach, Hawaii International Conference on System Sciences, 7–10 January, 566–577.

Galliers, R. (1992) Key Information Systems Management Issues for the 1990s, *Journal of Strategic Information Systems*, **1**, 4, 178–180.

Gilbert, F. (1993) Issues to Consider Before Outsourcing, *The National Law Journal*, 16, 15 November, s7.

Greenwood, J. and Wilson, D. (1994) Towards the Contract State: CCT in Local Government, *Parliamentary Affairs*, **47**, 3, 405–419.

Joosten, S., Ploeger, E. and Brinkkempner, S. (1995) The Contribution of Groupware to Corporate Communication: Towards the Horizontal Organization, Proceedings of the Third European Conference on Information Systems, Athens, 1–3 June, 649–661.

Ketler, K. and Walstrom, J. (1993) The Outsourcing Decision, *International Journal of Information Management*, **13**, 6, 449–460.

Laabs, J. (1993) Why HR is Turning to Outsourcing, *Personnel Journal*, **62**, 9, 92.

Lacity, M. and Hirschheim, R. (1993a) *Information Systems Outsourcing*, Chichester: John Wiley and Sons.

Lacity, M. and Hirschheim, R. (1993b) The Information Systems Outsourcing Bandwagon, *Sloan Management Review*, **35**, 1, 73–86.

Lacity, M. and Hirschheim, R. (1995) *Beyond The Information Systems Outsourcing Bandwagon: The Insourcing Response*, Chichester: John Wiley and Sons.

Lacity, M., Willcocks, L. and Feeny, D. (1996) The Value of Selective IT Sourcing. *Sloan Management Review*, **37**, 3, 13–25.

Lambert, R. and Peppard, J. (1993) Information Technology and New Organizational Forms: Destination But No Road Map? *Journal of Strategic Information Systems*, **2**, 3, 180–205.

Leonard, W. (1992) Outsourcing: Radical Surgery or Banking Cure-all? *Bankers Monthly*, October, 44.

Malone, T. Yates, J. and Benjamin, R. (1987) Electronic Markets and Electronic Hierarchies, *Communications of the ACM*, **30**, 6, 484–497.

McFarlan, F., McKenney, J. and Pyburn, P. (1983) The Information Archipelago—Plotting A Course, *Harvard Business Review*, **56**, 1, 145–160.

McFarlan, F. and Nolan, R. (1995) How to Manage an IT Outsourcing Alliance, *Sloan Management Review*, **36**, 2, 9–23.

Mintzberg, H. (1989) *Mintzberg on Management*, New York: Macmillan.

Nixon, B. (1993) Is Outsourcing Still In? The Simple Answer Is, Yes, *Savings and Community Banker*, 7 July.

Perry, L., Stott, R. and Smallwood, W. (1993) *Real Time Strategy: Improvising Team Based Planning for a Fast-Changing World*, New York: John Wiley and Sons.

Peters, T. and Waterman, R., (1982) *In Search of Excellence*, New York: Harper and Row.

Porter, M. (1980) *Competitive Strategy*, New York: Free Press.

Porter, M. (1985) *Competitive Advantage*, New York: Free Press.
Prahalad, C. and Hamel, G. (1990) The Core Competence of the Corporation. *Harvard Business Review*, **63**, 3, 79–91.
Quinn, J. (1992) *Intelligent Enterprise*, New York: Free Press.
Quinn, J. and Hilmer, F. (1994) Strategic Outsourcing, *Sloan Management Review*, **35**, 4, 43–55.
Scott Morton, M. (ed.) (1991) *The Corporation of the 1990s: Information Technology and Organizational Transformation*, New York: Oxford.
Sprague, R. (1995) Electronic Document Management, *MIS Quarterly*, **19**, 1, 29–49.
Vincent-Jones, P. (1994) The Limits of Near-contractual Governance: Local Authority Internal Trading Under CCT, *Journal of Law and Society*, **21**, 2, 214–237.
Weber, M. (1924) The Theory of Social and Economic Organization (translation 1947, Henderson, A. M. and Parsons, T.) New York: Free Press.
Wilder, C. (1990) Outsourcing: From Fad to Respectability, *Computerworld*, 24, 1.
Willcocks, L. and Currie, W. (1997) Does Radical Reengineering Really Work? Recent Case Evidence, in Willcocks, L., Feeny, D. and Islei, G. (eds), *Managing Information Technology as a Strategic Resource*, Maidenhead: McGraw Hill.
Willcocks, L. and Fitzgerald, G. (1993) Market As Opportunity? Case Studies in Outsourcing Information Technology and Services, *Journal of Strategic Information Systems*, **2**, 3, 223–242.
Willcocks, L., Lacity, M. and Fitzgerald, G. (1995) IT Outsourcing in Europe and the USA: Assessment Issues, Proceedings of the Third European Conference on Information Systems, Athens, 1–3 June, 247–260.
Williamson, O. (1975) *Markets and Hierarchies*, New York: Free Press.
Williamson, O. (1979) Transaction Cost Economics: The Governance of Contractual Relations, *Journal of Law and Economics*, **22**, 2, 233–261.
Withington F. (1993) Outsourcing: Flower or Weed? *Datamation*, **39**, 21, 124.

6
A Risk-Return Model for Information Technology Outsourcing Decisions

JAAK JURISON

INTRODUCTION

Information technology (IT) outsourcing is a major issue facing managers in today's rapidly changing business environment. IT outsourcing, the process of subcontracting some or all of a firm's IT functions to another firm, is not a new phenomenon. It has been around for many years under such names as service bureaux, timesharing or facilities management. But, as earlier chapters have made clear, in recent years IT outsourcing has received renewed interest among managers and researchers. This surge of interest can be attributed to the expanded size and scope of outsourcing activities. Outsourcing has grown and evolved to a point where it includes a wide spectrum of IT functions, including long-term contracts for managing the core of a firm's IT operations, often accompanied by a transfer of IT assets to the vendor. Examples of high visibility large-scale outsourcing contracts abound: Eastman Kodak, General Dynamics, McDonnell Douglas, Delta Airlines and Xerox Corporation in the US; British Aerospace and Inland Revenue Service in the UK. As argued earlier, these "mega-deals" reflect the notion that the best way a firm can create value is to focus its management attention and skills on its core functions and outsource all other activities (Quinn, 1992; Quinn, Dooley and Paquettte, 1990; Quinn

Strategic Sourcing of Information Systems.
Edited by L. P. Willcocks and M. C. Lacity.

and Hilmer, 1994). Many firms have come to regard IT as a support function that can be left to vendors who are experts in managing technology (Huber, 1993).

While the large-scale outsourcing contracts continue to capture media attention, empirical data provide evidence that they are actually an exception rather than the rule. Surveys of outsourcing practices in the US indicate that only a small percentage of firms outsource the core of their IS operations (Venkatraman and Loh, 1993; Jurison, Patane and Tan, 1993; Lacity and Willcocks, 1996; Willcocks and Fitzgerald, 1994). Most companies are outsourcing well under 40 per cent of their IT functions and the contracts are significantly smaller in size and scope than the large-scale contracts reported in the business press. The majority of companies are outsourcing selectively, outsourcing only those functions in which the vendors offer clear business advantages and managing the remaining functions internally. Applications development is the most widely outsourced function, followed by training, data centre management, network management, systems analysis, and end-user computing (Patane and Jurison, 1994). These studies indicate that outsourcing is not a one-shot decision of whether to outsource or insource the firms total IT operations, but an ongoing series of decisions regarding the governance of IT. In effect, these decisions are an integral part of the process by which management maximizes the value of IT. For this reason they are among the most important and consequential decisions managers can make.

The fundamental question in all outsourcing decisions is, why should a particular function or activity be outsourced? There are many reasons for considering outsourcing—Table 6.1 lists a set of expected benefits of outsourcing compiled from a variety of publications (Benko, 1992; Dué, 1992; Jurison, Patane and Tan, 1993; Khosrowpour, Subramanian and Gunterman, 1995; Lacity and Hirschheim, 1993a; Venkatraman and Loh, 1993; Lacity, Hirschheim and Willcocks, 1994). The predominant reason for outsourcing is to cut operating costs and improve efficiency. Often a vendor can achieve economies of scale that may not be achievable internally and pass back some of the savings to the client. Two other reasons frequently cited are (i) access to IT expertise and competence, and (ii) flexibility in managing IT resources. Some firms may find it difficult, time consuming, or expensive to hire new personnel, especially if special technical expertise is needed. For these firms, outsourcing can provide ready access to skilled labour. But this can also be interpreted as a way to avoid recruiting and training expenses—a variant of the economic motive to reduce cost. The motivation to achieve more flexibility in managing IT resources can also be viewed as a variant of the economic imperative. The objective in this

Table 6.1 *Potential Benefits of Outsourcing*

- Cost savings through economies of scale
- Cash infusion
- Reduced capital spending
- Faster applications development
- Improved service and quality
- Access to IT expertise and competence
- Access to new technologies
- Flexibility in managing IT resources
- Elimination of a troublesome function

Table 6.2 *Outsourcing Risks*

- Irreversibility of the outsourcing decision
- Breach of contract by the vendor
- Loss of autonomy and control over IT decisions
- Vendor's inability to deliver
- Loss of control over vendor
- Uncontrollable contract growth
- Loss of critical skills
- Biased portrayal by vendors
- Vendor lock-in
- Loss of control over data
- Loss of employee morale and productivity
- Lack of trust
- Hidden costs

case is to be able to cope more easily with increasing volatility in business volume and let the vendor absorb the fluctuations in the IT workload. In effect, the outsourcer is converting from a headcount-based fixed cost to a variable cost structure, hoping to achieve cost savings in the long run. In summary, the accumulated evidence from literature appears to indicate that economic considerations, in one form or another, have the primary role in IT outsourcing decisions.

In contrast to the optimistic media coverage of outsourcing, there is growing evidence that outsourcing entails a significant amount of risk (Quinn and Hilmer, 1994; McFarlan and Nolan, 1995). In their in-depth multi-case studies of IT outsourcing practices, Lacity and Hirschheim (1993a/b) found several failures as well as successes. High risk, whether perceived or real, is the primary reason why many managers are against outsourcing. Table 6.2 is a compilation of outsourcing risks frequently cited in literature (Benko, 1992; Dué, 1992; Jurison, Patane and Tan, 1993; Khosrowpour, Subramanian and Gunterman, 1995; Lacity and Hirschheim, 1993a; Venkatraman and Loh, 1993). The dominant risk is the irreversibility of the decision. This is of particular concern for those executives who are considering outsourcing the core of their IT operations. Once outsourced, it is very costly and difficult to bring the work back into the firm if the outsourcing arrangement turns out to be unsatisfactory. Other frequently cited concerns about outsourcing are the loss of control over IT resources and the possibility of being taken advantage of by the vendor. All these concerns reflect managements perception that, although outsourcing can have potential economic benefits, it can expose a company to significant business risk.

Based on a study of outsourcing practices in 209 *Fortune 500* corporations, Venkatraman and Loh (1993) conclude that outsourcing should be viewed as the process of balancing benefits and risks through a portfolio of relationships. Quinn and Hilmer (1994) reach a similar conclusion. According to their research, outsourcing decisions involve finding a balance between the potential for obtaining competitive advantage and the degree of strategic vulnerability.

The principal contribution of this chapter is the development of a model for describing the relationship between outsourcing benefits and risks. It uses Williamson's transaction cost theory as a theoretical foundation for explaining outsourcing decisions. The relationship between risk and economic benefits has its roots in classical financial theory. By drawing on these two theories, the paper develops a model for integrating risk into outsourcing decisions in a systematic fashion. The aim of this chapter is to show that almost all outsourcing decisions can be considered as a tradeoff between financial benefits and risk. The model has implications for managers who make outsourcing decisions and for researchers who are looking for improved insights into the role of outsourcing in organizations.

THEORETICAL FOUNDATIONS

Transaction Cost Theory

In essence, an IT outsourcing decision is analogous to a classical make-or-buy decision. It involves seeking answers to two key questions:

- Should the firm outsource certain IT functions or provide these services internally?
- In case the decision is to outsource, which vendor and what type of contractual arrangement should be selected?

Outsourcing decisions can be analysed from several perspectives. They can be viewed either as rational decisions, driven by economic motives, or political decisions, driven by power and political tactics (Lacity and Hirschheim, 1993a). Although both views have merit for analysing outsourcing decisions, the analysis in this chapter follows the rational decision-making perspective based on Williamsons transaction cost theory. This approach was selected because of the widely adopted view that most outsourcing decisions are economically motivated and that transaction cost theory provides a clear focus on the issues that distinguish between internal and market-based solutions to IT functions.

Transaction cost theory regards the transaction as the basic unit of analysis in the study of organizations and holds that the central goal of organizations is economic efficiency (Williamson, 1975). A major part of transaction theory is focused on the governance structure of transactions. Its primary concern is which activities should be performed within the firm, which outside the firm, and why? According to Williamson (1981), "a transaction occurs when a good or service is transferred across a technologically separable interface." For any given good or service, a firm has two alternatives: to provide it internally (vertical integration through the firm's hierarchy) or purchase it from a vendor (through a transaction in the marketplace). In either case there are two types of costs: production and co-ordination. Production costs are the costs of producing the goods or services and include the costs of labour, capital and materials. Co-ordination costs are the costs of controlling and monitoring workers if the task is performed internally. If the task is performed outside the firm by a vendor, co-ordination costs take the form of transaction costs. These costs arise from the need to define, negotiate and enforce contracts, and to monitor and co-ordinate activities across organizational boundaries. Williamson argues that markets offer lower production costs than hierarchies through economies of scale. However, markets have high transaction costs because vendors tend to behave opportunistically and therefore require monitoring of their activities. Hierarchies, on the other hand, tend to have higher production costs because of their inability to achieve economies of scale. But hierarchies should have lower co-ordination costs because employees have less opportunity for opportunistic behaviour. Therefore, the most economic choice must take place within the context of a trade-off that includes both the production and co-ordination costs.

Although cost economies are central to the transaction cost theory, Williamson recognizes the existence of other variables that influence the costs and the choice of governance. These are asset specificity, uncertainty, and frequency of transactions (Williamson, 1985). Only the first two dimensions are of interest for the purpose of this chapter.

Asset specificity is defined as the degree of customization of the transaction. High asset specific transactions require specialized physical or human assets that cannot be used for transactions with other firms. Asset specificity generally tends to increase production cost because specific assets have limited utility in other markets. Transactions with high asset specificity tend to be designed for long-term continuous relationships between the buyer and the vendor. Transactions involve some degree of uncertainty because it is prohibitively costly or impossible to have perfect information necessary to make an informed decision. Therefore as uncertainty increases, the tendency to shift from markets to hierarchies increases.

Transaction cost theory relies on two key assumptions about human behaviour. The first assumption is that humans are subject to bounded rationality. This means that humans are unable to foresee the complexities and contingencies in contractual relationships and consequently can only achieve incomplete contracts. The second assumption is that agents, acting in their own self-interest, are subject to opportunistic behaviour. Opportunistic behaviour is exhibited when a vendor takes advantage of the client to advance its own interest. These two behaviours give rise to significant risk for the outsourcer.

Decision Making Under Risk

Risk, defined most generally, refers to the chance or probability that some unfavorable event or outcome will occur. It has different meanings in different contexts. In business decisions, risk is typically defined as the chance of loss associated with a given managerial decision. Management theorists frequently define risk as a condition under which the outcomes of a decision and the probabilities associated with the outcomes are known. However, in many business decisions, all the possible outcomes and the probabilities of their occurrence are not fully known. Some scientists refer to this condition as uncertainty. The distinction between risk and uncertainty is not always clear in management literature and there is considerable overlap in the usage of these terms (Baird and Thomas, 1985). Financial theorists define risk as variance or dispersion of outcomes, because it implies incomplete information and inability to predict outcomes. For the purposes of this paper, risk is broadly defined to include uncertainty and the results of uncertainty because this definition appears to reflect the way managers consider risk in decisions regarding cost and benefit issues.

The theoretical foundation for understanding managerial decision making under risk comes from the modern theory of investments and finance. This theory treats a firm as a set of potential investments from which the most profitable ones are chosen. Profitability is determined by the rate of return on the proposed investment. The rate of return has to be high enough to be attractive to the financial market, that is, investors who provide the funds for the firm. The investors demand returns that are commensurate with the perceived risk level of the investment. The higher the risk, the higher the required or expected return. This relationship is defined as follows:

Expected return = Risk-free return + Risk premium

The risk premium is the reward that an investor expects to receive from assuming the risk and it increases linearly as function of increased risk. A detailed mathematical treatment of this relationship is provided by the Capital Asset Pricing Model (CAPM), put forth by Lintner (1965) and Sharpe (1964). The CAPM expresses the risk and return relation by the following equation:

$$R_i = R_f + \beta_i (R_m - R_f)$$

where

R_i = *expected return on an investment*
R_f = the risk-free interest rate
R_m = expected return on the stock market as a whole
β_i = the measure of the investment's risk.

In essence, the expected return on an investment is the risk-free interest plus the market risk premium ($R_m - R_f$) weighted by the measure of the specific investment's risk β_i. This linear relation between expected return and risk is called the *security market line* (SML). Although developed in the context of the securities market, CAPM provides the theoretical foundation for dealing with risk in managerial decision making, particularly in capital investment decisions. It provides a methodology for quantifying risk and translating that risk into estimates of expected return.

Underlying Assumptions

Before attempting to integrate the two theories for outsourcing decision making, it is useful to review the nature of the assumptions underlying the two theories. The transaction cost theory assumes that decision makers are rational people who adopt organizational forms that best economize on transaction costs. It also makes additional assumptions about human behaviour. It assumes that humans are subject to bounded rationality and that some agents are subject to opportunism. The latter two assumptions add realism to the theory and distinguish it from neoclassical economics. The theory is useful for studying various organizational forms, but it is particularly relevant for explaining the trade-offs between internal and market-based approaches for providing products and services. The broad concepts of transaction cost theory have been empirically validated in a variety of sourcing and vertical integration situations (Walker, 1988; Walker and Weber, 1984; Monteverde and Teece, 1982). Empirical support to the applicability of the theory to IT outsourcing decisions comes from the research by Lacity and Hirschheim (1993a/b). Their study of outsourcing decisions in 13 firms indicates that practically all outsourcing decisions can be explained by the transaction cost theory. In their research they also tested the applicability of a rival organization theory to IT outsourcing decisions. This theory, based on Pfeffers (1981) power model, holds that decision outcomes are primarily influenced by power and politics, not by rational cost-economizing motives. Lacity and Hirschheim conclude that while the power model can not explain all outsourcing decisions, it offers useful insight to complement the transaction cost perspective. Bakos and Kemerer (1992), in their review of the application of economic theories in IT research, confirm that the transaction cost theory provides a solid theoretical base for launching investigations into the area of IT outsourcing.

The conceptual framework for risk and return also assumes that decision makers are rational. In addition, several simplifying assumptions are made in the mathematical derivation of the Capital Asset Pricing Model. By defining risk as the variance of the investment return, the model assumes that (i) investors dislike risk and like high expected returns, (ii) the capital markets are perfect, and (iii) there exists a risk-free asset paying a safe return. While these assumptions do not entirely conform to reality, the relaxation of these assumptions leaves the model reasonably unchanged. Although the model has not been perfectly validated by empirical tests, its main implications have been upheld (Copeland and Weston, 1983). The two most relevant implications for this paper are the existence of a (i) linear and (ii) positive relationship between risk and return.

The CAPM provides a useful and practical conceptual framework for managerial decision making, particularly for capital budgeting and cost of capital determination (Mullins, 1982). The cost of capital is used by corporate managers as a hurdle rate in evaluating investments. The CAPM allows managers to adjust hurdle rates for individual projects depending on their levels of risk. Its primary application to information systems is in the role of determining risk-adjusted hurdle rates for IT investments (Yan Tam, 1992). A major criticism of the risk-adjusted hurdle rates is that they tend to have a discouraging effect on IT investments, particularly on strategic information systems (Clemons and Weber, 1990).

RISK AND RETURN MODEL

By applying the risk-return model from the financial theory to transaction cost economics, we can develop a conceptual model for analysing outsourcing decisions. The basic variables in the model are cost and risk. The relationship between the two variables is shown graphically in Figure 6.1 by defining the economic benefits from outsourcing (ΔC) on the vertical axis and the added risk from outsourcing (ΔR) on the horizontal axis. ΔC is defined as the net difference between the cost of performing the task internally (C_I) and the cost of outsourcing (C_O), taking into account both the production costs and co-ordination costs. ΔR represents the difference between the level of outsourcing risk (R_O) and the level of risk in performing the function internally (R_I).

The diagonal straight line represents the boundary between outsourcing and insourcing. (Lacity and Hirschheim (1995) define insourcing as "an outsourcing evaluation outcome which results in the selection of the internal IS department's bid over external vendor bids.") The area above and to the left of the line defines IT functions that should be outsourced, while the functions below and to the right of the line can be performed better internally.

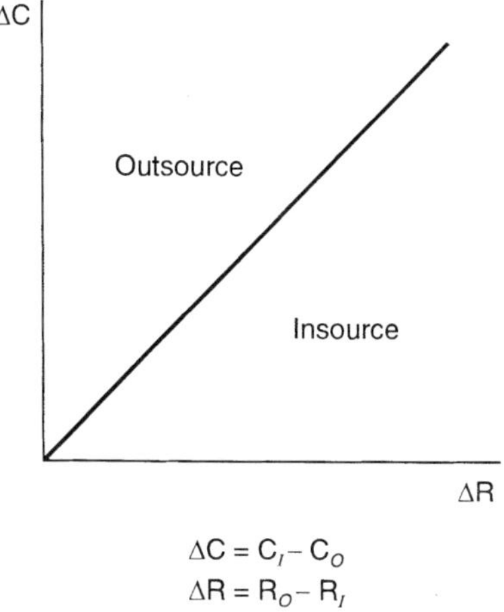

$$\Delta C = C_I - C_O$$
$$\Delta R = R_O - R_I$$

Figure 6.1 *Risk and Return Model for IT Outsourcing Decisions*

It is important to note that the model is not limited only to cases where ΔR is positive (i.e. outsourcing increases risk). It can also describe circumstances where the impetus for outsourcing is to reduce risk. For example, Quinn (1992) argues that outsourcing can reduce risk for firms that need to invest in order to expand their facilities, acquire new technology, or develop new capabilities. In cases where outsourcing is expected to reduce risk, ΔR is negative. By extending the boundary line in Figure 6.1 to the region of negative ΔR and ΔC, we can see that if outsourcing is driven by a desire to reduce risk, then it can be justified even if it leads to higher cost.

While the expected economic benefits can be determined in a relatively straightforward manner from vendor proposals and internal benchmarks, risk is more difficult to identify and measure. One of the difficulties lies in the fact that risk is multidimensional and has many components, some of which are controllable and some are uncontrollable. Another complication is that risk is subjective—not all managers perceive risk in the same way. Managers who seek to avoid or minimize risks are generally considered risk averse. Given a choice between risky and less risky alternatives with identical economic outcomes, they tend to select the less risky alternative. But the degree of risk aversion varies among managers. Given the same alternatives, some managers might accept more risk than others. Therefore it is more realistic to consider the line in Figure 6.1 not as a distinct dividing line but as a grey area between outsourcing and insourcing regions, that accommodates a spread in decision-makers' attitudes toward risk.

Risk Analysis

In the classical risk analysis process, risk determination consists of a logical sequence of three activities: risk identification, risk measurement, and risk evaluation (Hertz and Thomas, 1983). In the risk identification phase managers develop an understanding of the nature and potential impact of risk. In the risk measurement phase, an attempt is made to assess risk quantitatively by estimating probabilities of outcomes or by classifying risk into various categories of risk (e.g. low, medium, high). In the evaluation phase managers evaluate the underlying assumptions about risk elements, test the sensitivities of outcomes to the assumptions and take into consideration the influence of other intangible factors. At this point management must consider various tradeoffs and decide how much risk it is willing to accept.

If the possible outcomes can be defined in financial terms and their probabilities can be estimated, then risk can be calculated as the expected value of the outcomes. In this case, both cost and risk can be defined in monetary terms and the problem becomes a straightforward cost tradeoff. But in many decisions, particularly in outsourcing situations, it is unlikely that the outcomes and their probabilities are known, thus making it difficult to deal with risk quantitatively. One approach, frequently used in business organizations, is to classify risk by the type and the level of severity. This is also a commonly-used method of treating risk in IT literature. Categories of IT risks have been defined by Parker *et al.* (1990), Keen (1991), Clemons and Weber (1990), Willcocks and Margetts (1994), and Sherer (1993). The practical value of categorization is that it allows managers to adopt a contingency approach by selecting a set of management tools appropriate for a particular type of risk (McFarlan, 1981).

Example

The use of the proposed risk-return model is now illustrated with a case of outsourcing decision making. Although the case is theoretical, it blends a variety of real-world situations, which are based on published case studies and interviews with key decision-makers in outsourcing evaluations.

Company X is experiencing a problem that is common throughout most business firms today. Its IT costs are growing steadily and the CEO feels that they are out of control. Faced with increasing competitive pressures, he concludes that something needs to be done to get IT costs back in line. He has read numerous trade journals describing how several *Fortune 100* firms have outsourced their IS departments in order to lower their IT costs. He asks a group of senior business managers and IT leaders to consider the possibility of outsourcing. After discussions with several IT vendors and attending outsourcing seminars, the management team concludes that outsourcing can be a potential solution to their IT budget problem. However, the team considers outsourcing all of the firm's IT functions with a single vendor too risky, but feels that outsourcing selected IT functions with a small number of vendors warrants further consideration. A task force, consisting of senior managers from IS and business units, is formed to explore outsourcing options in more detail and make recommendations.

The task force identifies the following IT functions as candidates for outsourcing: data processing (DP) operations, telecommunications, applications development and hardware maintenance. Requests for Proposal (RFPs) are prepared and sent to qualified vendors for competitive bids. The internal IS department is also asked to bid to determine the lowest cost of performing these functions in-house. The task force, after evaluating all proposals, estimates the costs and risks for each option.

To determine the cost savings (ΔC), they subtract total outsourcing costs (vendor bid plus the internal cost of managing the vendor) from the cost of performing the function internally. Because the savings do not accrue uniformly over time, net present value is used to take into account the time value of money.

Risk is estimated in two steps. First, all risks are identified, including the risk of performing a particular function in-house. Then a consensus is formed on the level of risk of each option (very low, low, medium, high, very high) relative to the risk of doing the work in-house. By placing all outsourcing options on the risk-reward diagram (Figure 6.2), the task force can now systematically analyse the relative merits and risks of all options, individually as well as in the aggregate. For the sake of clarity, only the best option for each function under consideration is shown in Figure 6.2. Hardware maintenance and telecommunications offer savings at low risk and are therefore obvious candidates for outsourcing. However, the choices for applications development and DP operations are less obvious and require more detailed analysis. Although both these functions offer potentially large savings, they also expose the firm to high levels of risk.

After carefully examining the risks in outsourcing DP operations, the task force concludes that the major risk factors are the loss of control

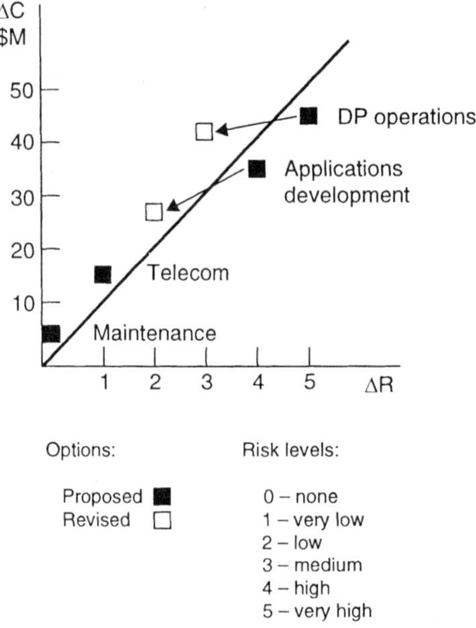

Figure 6.2 *Company X Risk and Return Analysis*

over DP service, hidden costs, inability to manage changes in service levels, and the potential for vendor opportunism. The task force then considers various ways to reduce these risks. By rejecting the vendor's proposed contract and negotiating a well-defined contract where service levels, cost structures, penalties for non-performance, and termination clauses are clearly spelled out, the risk can be reduced from very high to medium. But in order to do that, the firm needs to hire an outsourcing consultant to help draft and negotiate the contract. Furthermore, to enforce the contract, the firm must establish an oversight group to manage the interface with the vendor. Both of these actions increase the transaction cost, resulting in a relatively small reduction in the expected benefits. What initially appeared to be an unacceptably risky option, is now one that looks quite favourable from the cost-risk perspective and makes a compelling case for outsourcing.

The sources of risk in applications development are loss of control over critical strategic applications and inability to control vendor's cost, schedule and technical quality. By examining these risks in more detail, the task team realizes that by retaining critical strategic software in-house and outsourcing only conventional operational support, the firm can reduce its risk and is still able to achieve significant, albeit smaller, cost savings. The risk in outsourced software development can be reduced further by imposing strong project management and configuration controls on the vendor. In this fashion the firm is still able to achieve significant cost savings in applications development, but at a greatly reduced risk level.

The systematic analysis of benefits and risks demonstrates how management can explore outsourcing options and arrive at solutions that are likely to be successful in the long run. In this case the firm is expected to achieve $95 million in cost savings without exposing the firm to excessive levels of risk. Although the case oversimplifies the complexities of outsourcing decisions, it serves as an example to illustrate the practical application of the model.

Risk Reduction Methods

As the example illustrates, there are many different ways to reduce or control outsourcing risk. It is important to recognize components of risk that are controllable from those that are beyond the control of the firm. By focusing on the controllable components of risk, managers can define risk reduction options and evaluate their potential effectiveness and cost impacts.

A range of options is available for managing controllable risk. One option is to increase vendor oversight through project management, frequent vendor reporting, on-site representatives or a combination of management techniques. Another approach is to make the vendor share the risks. Fixed fee contracts, penalty clauses, special arrangements for handling changes, and early termination clauses are contractual mechanisms designed to shift a significant part of the risk to the vendor. These risk-sharing arrangements are gaining popularity as IT managers are becoming more experienced with outsourcing.

It is also important to note that risk containment measures are contingent on the type of activity to be outsourced. For example, a fixed fee contract is effective for a well-defined development program, but not for a long-term data centre management contract. Fitzgerald and Willcocks (1994) have developed a framework for selecting various contractual arrangements based on the degree of uncertainty in defining and specifying the requirements and the degree of contractual definition. This framework is useful for understanding outsourcing risks that arise from different types of contracts and provides guidance for selecting contractual arrangements for minimizing risk.

Regardless of which approach is used, all risk reduction measures tend to increase co-ordination costs. Eventually the co-ordination costs may reach a level where it becomes more attractive to perform the whole task internally. Some firms, unable to find adequate contractual protection from risk, have chosen to treat the vendor as a strategic partner, hoping that effective relationship management will minimize risk. But partnerships are not easy to manage and require a great deal of management attention (McFarlan and Nolan, 1995). All the above-described approaches serve to illustrate that the key to successful outsourcing lies in finding innovative ways to reduce risk without creating excessive transaction costs. In other words, successful outsourcers find ways to operate as far to the left from the boundary line in Figure 6.1 as possible.

The conceptual model can be generalized to a wide range of outsourcing decisions and can be used to explain the preference for in-house solutions for strategic IT functions. For these activities, outsourcing exposes the firm to an extremely high level of risk that cannot be offset by any amount of cost savings. It is believed that practically all issues surrounding outsourcing can be expressed in terms of cost and risk, making them analysable within the framework of the proposed model.

Although the model in the preceding discussion has been used to explain the outsourcer's decision-making process, it can also be used to describe the vendor's evaluation of new business opportunities. For a vendor the issue is, under what condition should we bid or accept a contract? Instead of cost savings, the vendor must evaluate the expected profit with respect to the risk of not realizing the profit. If the vendor perceives the contract as too risky, it may decline to bid, include a risk premium in the bid price, or propose an alternate contractual arrangement to lower its risk.

IMPLICATIONS FOR PRACTICE AND RESEARCH

The proposed model has significant implications for both practitioners and researchers. For practitioners, it offers a framework for considering outsourcing risk in a systematic way. In too many evaluations risk is given inadequate attention (Willcocks, Lacity and Fitzgerald, 1995), and even when it is considered, it is often done implicitly. The proposed model makes risk an explicit component of the decision-making process and helps managers to conduct risk assessment in a more rational way.

The value of the model is by no means limited to the decision of whether to outsource or insource. It can be an effective tool for evaluating and comparing several vendor proposals for outsourcing. It is important to note that the model provides only a framework for assisting management in making outsourcing decisions. Its purpose is not to replace management judgment and experience—they are and will always be essential in any decision-making process under uncertainty.

The model has several implications for researchers. First, it adds an important dimension to the transaction cost perspective. It also provides a framework for analysing and understanding outsourcing decisions, helping to explain why some firms find it more advantageous to outsource certain IT functions while others prefer internal solutions.

As a preliminary conceptual model, it is intended to stimulate future research. More studies are necessary to test and validate the model with empirical data. There is also a need to systematically classify outsourcing risks and develop measures for describing risk in quantitative terms. This is perhaps the most important and challenging research area. One of the main reasons why risk has been ignored in many management and IT studies is the difficulty of understanding, defining, and measuring it. There are many opportunities for investigating risk and its role in outsourcing decisions and in the management of the client/vendor interface. The contractual and relationship framework of Fitzgerald and Willcocks (1994) offers much promise in this area.

As noted earlier, outsourcing decisions can be analysed and interpreted from either economic or political perspectives. Although the proposed risk/return model treats outsourcing from the economic perspective, it can also provide a rich framework for analysing decisions from the political perspective. For example, political motives exhibit themselves in self-serving and biased assumptions about the problem. Risk, being subjective, can be easily defined, interpreted and manipulated by political actors to influence a decision outcome. Another interesting area is to view outsourcing from the agency theory perspective. This perspective can be promising for exploring situations where the client and vendor goals differ or are in conflict.

CONCLUSIONS

The goal of this chapter has been to integrate the major elements from transaction cost theory and financial theory into a conceptual model for systematic analysis of outsourcing decisions. It shows that almost all outsourcing decisions can be considered as a tradeoff between financial benefits and risk (Loh and Venkatraman, 1995). This conclusion is supported by previous research findings which indicate that cost and risk are the primary variables affecting outsourcing decisions. The conceptual model is consistent with managerial decision-making practices as characterized by Conrad and Plotkin (1968): "And in considering capital and other investments, managers in the industrial sector of the economy as a matter of course weigh risk and return together."

The model is intended to help managers make more informed outsourcing decisions and find better ways of managing risk. It is hoped that the model will also be a stimulant for future research on IT governance issues.

REFERENCES

Baird, I. S. and Thomas, H. (1985) Toward A Contingency Model of Strategic Risk Taking, *Academy of Management Review*, **10**,, 2, 230–245.

Bakos J. Y. and C. F. Kemerer (1992) Recent Applications of Economic Theory in Information Technology Research, *Decision Support Systems*, **8**, 5, 365–386.

Benko, C. (1992) Outsourcing Evaluation: A Profitable Process, *Information Systems Management*, **10**, 2, 45–50.

Clemons, E. K and Weber, B. W. (1990) Strategic Information Technology Investments: Guidelines for Decision Making. *Journal of Management Information Systems*, **7**, 2, 9–28.

Conrad, G. R. and Plotkin, I. H. (1968) Risk/Return: U.S. Industry Pattern, *Harvard Business Review*, **46**, 3, 90–99.

Copeland, T. E. and Weston, J. F. (1983) Financial Theory and Corporate Policy, 3rd ed., Reading, MA: Addison-Wesley.

Dué, R. T. (1992) The Real Costs Of Outsourcing, *Information Systems Management*, **9**, 1, 78–81.

Fitzgerald, G. and Willcocks L. (1994) Contracts and Partnerships in the Outsourcing of IT, Proceedings of the Fifteenth International Conference of Information Systems, Vancouver, BC, Canada, 14–17 December, 91–98.

Hertz, D. B. and Thomas H. (1983) *Risk Analysis and its Applications*, Chichester: John Wiley and Sons.

Huber, R. (1993) How Continental Outsourced its ''Crown Jewels', *Harvard Business Review*, **71**, 1, 121–129.

Khosrowpour, M., Subramanian, G. H. and Gunterman, J. (1995) Outsourcing: Organizational Benefits and Potential Problems, in Khosrowpour, M. (ed.), *Managing Information Technology Investments with Outsourcing*, Idea Group Publishing, Harrisburg. Pennsylvania, 244–268.

Jurison, J., Patane, J. and Tan M. (1993) An Examination of Information Systems Outsourcing Practices in Large US Firms: Implications for Global Service Providers, Proceeding of the 1993 Pan Pacific Conference on Information Systems, Kaohsiung, Taiwan, 18–21.

Keen, P. G. W. (1991) *Shaping the Future: Business Design through Information Technology*, Boston, MA: Harvard Business School Press.

Lacity, M. C. and Hirschheim R. (1993a) *Information Systems Outsourcing: Myths, Metaphors and Realities*. Chichester: John Wiley and Sons.

Lacity, M. C. and Hirschhem R. (1993b) The Information Systems Outsourcing Bandwagon, *Sloan Management Review*, **35**, 1, 73–86.

Lacity, M. C. and Hirschheim R. (1995) *Beyond the Information Systems Outsourcing Bandwagon: The Insourcing Response*, Chichester: John Wiley and Sons.

Lacity, M. C., Hirschheim, R. and Willcocks, L. P. (1994) Realizing Outsourcing Expectations, *Information Systems Management*, **11**, 4, 7–18.

Lacity, M. C., Willcocks, L. P. and Feeny, D. F. (1995) IT Outsourcing: Maximize Flexibility and Control, *Harvard Business Review*, **73**, 3, 84–93.

Lacity, M. and Willcocks, L. (1996). Best Practices in Information Technology Sourcing, Oxford Executive Research Briefing, Templeton College, Oxford.

Lintner, J. (1965) Security Prices, Risk, and Maximum Gains from Diversification, *Review of Economics and Statistics*, **47**, 1, 13–37.

Loh, L. and Venkatraman (1995) An Empirical Study of Information Technology Outsourcing: Benefits, Risks, and Performance Implications, Proceedings of the Sixteenth International Conference on Information Systems, Amsterdam, Netherlands, 10–13 December, 277–288.

McFarlan, W. F. (1981) Portfolio Approach to Information Systems, *Harvard Business Review*, **59**, 5, 142–150.

McFarlan, W. F. and Nolan, R. L. (1995) How to Manage IT Outsourcing Alliance, *Sloan Management Review*, **36**, 2, 9–23.

Monteverde, K. and Teece, D. J. (1982) Supplier Switching Costs in Vertical Integration in the Automobile Industry, *Bell Journal of Economics*, **13**, 1, 206–213.

Mullins, D. W. Jr. (1982) Does The Capital Asset Pricing Model Work? *Harvard Business Review*, **60**, 1, 105–114.

Parker, M. M., Trainor, H. E. and Benson, R. J. (1990) *Information Strategy and Economics*, Englewood Cliffs, N.J: Prentice Hall, Inc.

Patane, J. and Jurison, J. (1994) Is Global Outsourcing Diminishing the Prospects for American Programmers? *Journal of Systems Management*, **45**, 3, 6–10.

Pfeffer, J. (1981) *Power in Organizations*, Marshfield, MA: Pitman.

Quinn, J. B. (1992) *Intelligent Enterprise*, New York: Free Press.

Quinn, J. B., Dooley T. L. and Paquette P. C. (1990) Beyond Products: Service-based Strategy, *Harvard Business Review*, **68**, 2, 58–67.

Quinn, J. B. and Hilmer, F. G. (1994) Strategic Outsourcing, *Sloan Management Review*, **35**, 4, 43–55.

Sharpe, W. F. (1964) Capital Asset Prices: A Theory of Market Equilibrium under Conditions of Risk, *Journal of Finance*, **19**, 3, 425–442.

Sherer, S. (1993) Purchasing Software Systems: Managing the Risk, *Information and Management*, **24**, 5, 257–266.

Walker, G. (1988) Strategic Sourcing, Vertical Integration, and Transaction Costs, *Interfaces*, **18**, 3, 62–73.

Walker, G. and Weber, D. (1984) A Transaction Cost Approach to Make-Or-Buy Decisions, *Administrative Science Quarterly*, **29**, 373–391.

Venkatraman, N. and Loh, L. (1993) Strategic Issues in Information Technology Sourcing: Patterns, Perspectives, and Prescriptions, MIT Sloan School of Management Working Paper No. 3535–93, Cambridge, MA.

Willcocks, L. and Fitzgerald, G. (1994) *A Business Guide to Outsourcing IT. A Study of European Best Practice in the Selection, Management and Use of External IT Services*, London: Business Intelligence.

Willcocks, L. and Margetts, H. (1994) Risk and Information Systems: Developing the Analysis, in Willcocks, L. (ed.), *Information Management: The Evaluation of Information Systems Investments*, London: Chapman and Hall.

Willcocks, L., Lacity, M. and Fitzgerald, G. (1995) IT Outsourcing in Europe and the USA: Assessment Issues, Oxford Institute of Information Management Working Paper RDP95/2, Templeton College, Oxford.

Williamson, O. (1975) *Markets and Hierarchies*, New York: Free Press.

Williamson, O. (1985) *The Economic Institutions of Capitalism*, New York: Free Press.

Williamson, O. (1981) The Economics of Organization: The Transaction Cost Approach, *American Journal of Sociology*, **87**, 3, 548–577

Yan Tam, K. (1992). Capital Budgeting in Information Systems Development, *Information and Management*, **23**, 5, 345–357.

PART II

Practices

7
Financial and Strategic Motivations Behind IS Outsourcing

KERRY McLELLAN, BARBARA L. MARCOLIN AND PAUL W. BEAMISH

INTRODUCTION

Information Systems (IS) have become central to many companies and industries to the point that systems support, if not drive, the business strategy (Blanton, Watson and Moody, 1992; *CIO Journal*, 1993; McFarlan, 1984). For instance, the airline industry has been transformed by technological reservation systems and as a result has tried to forge new alliances with related industries such as credit cards, hotels and car rental agencies (Brown, 1990; Halper 1992a/b). With the rise in dominance of IT for many industries, IS departments and functions have become a core competency (Prahalad and Hamel, 1990; Burch, 1990) or a fundamental business activity for competitive advantage in these new business environments.

Under these circumstances, when technology becomes so central to a business's success, theories posit that a core competency should be tightly controlled and maintained within the boundaries of the business so that competitive advantage is not lost or leaked to competitors.

Game theory (Parkhe, 1993b) suggests that mutual co-operation will only occur if negative outcomes, such as leakage of core competencies,

Strategic Sourcing of Information Systems.
Edited by L. P. Willcocks and M. C. Lacity.

are avoided (see Chapter 3). The transaction cost paradigm holds opportunism central to its foundation implying that self-enforcing agreements are created to control this underlying opportunistic behaviour inherent in managers (Parkhe, 1993b). As Jurison points out in Chapter 6, any alliance would hence be focused on minimizing or avoiding the harmful effects of opportunism, and each partner would protect a core competency closely.

Yet, given these perspectives, the banking industry in the late 1980s and early 1990s was rife with announcements of companies outsourcing their IS departments, which had long been viewed as core competencies (Huff and Beattie, 1985; Tuman, 1988; Burch, 1990). Banks' traditional, hierarchically-structured, in-house IS departments were being handed over to third party vendors who would deliver these tasks for the firms. Some examples included Bank of New England (Wilder, 1991), California Republic Bank (Cummings, 1992a), First American Bank Shares Corp., and Meritor Financial Services (LaPlante, 1991), although many others could also be found, and many outsourcing vendors were focusing on the banking sector and introducing new services quickly (Betts, 1991). It appears that Information Technology (IT) outsourcing was now occurring in long-term contracts for a department that had been considered core to the business. This study tries to resolve the observed contradictions and answer the question: Why would banks outsource the IS department or major IS functions when they had been considered core to the banking industry and theories predicted they would be retained in-house?

The present research offers evidence from seven case studies of IT outsourcing arrangements to suggest that companies are forming IT outsourcing alliances with vendors for several financial and strategic reasons. These motivations offer one plausible explantation of the communication factors and rationale which might be driving the imitation behaviours found by Venkatraman, Loh and Koh (1994) to be so influential. Even though the financial reasons are fairly straightforward, the strategic reasons explain the contradictory stance of releasing a "core" competency, which has been observed in the banking industry, and justify the term "alliance" for these ventures.

BACKGROUND LITERATURE

IT outsourcing activities have grown rapidly in the past few years to support an industry worth $29 billion in 1990 that is predicted to be worth over $50 billion by the late 1990s (Teresko, 1990; Safer, 1992). In its recent form, by 1997 outsourcing has been having a very substantial impact on IS departments within organizations. From contracting out a few IS functions to outsourcing the entire IS operations, companies are handing over IS to third party vendors who deliver these tasks for the organization. In fact, many large and well-known companies, such as Eastman Kodak and McDonnell Douglas, have been using outsourcing in attempts to transform their IS organizations (Cummings, 1992b; Pantages *et al.*, 1992). These dramatic shifts can mean upheaval and new opportunities. For IS management, outsourcing can be a traumatic experience, but for the company it can mean substantial savings and new strategic initiatives (Teresko, 1990; Henderson, 1990).

This new trend mirrored discussions that researchers from Business Policy, International Business and Organizational Theory had been having on an emerging organizational form, the strategic network created by non-equity alliances (Porter, 1985; Jarillo, 1988; MacMillan and Farmer, 1979; Van de Ven, 1976; Powell, 1987). Although strategic networks have come to be viewed as an organizational form distinct from the traditional dichotomous view of "market versus hierarchical" forms of organization, there are many different perspectives in this literature.

Jarillo (1988, p. 32) synthesized existing strategic network theory and developed a definition for this inter-organizational relationship. He describes strategic networks as:

> "long-term, purposeful arrangements among distinct but related for-profit organizations that allow those firms in them to gain or sustain competitive advantage *vis-a-vis* their competitors outside the network."

Jarillo (1988, p. 35) also brought Porter's concept of a value chain (1985) into the analysis to explain why organizations set up strategic networks and yet remained "independent" from each other. He concludes:

> "The strategic implications of a network arrangement are important. It allows a firm to specialize in those activities of the value chain that are essential to its competitive advantage, reaping all the benefits of specialization, focus, and possible size."

Other researchers have identified and described an emerging "intermediate" form of organization which complemented the strategic network perspective. MacMillan and Farmer (1979; Farmer and MacMillan, 1976) identified an intermediate form and discussed managing systems outside the traditional boundaries of the organization. Van de Ven (1976) and Van de Ven and Ferry (1980) provided early insights into network relationships between not-for-profit organizations which suggested that alternative network forms of inter-organization existed and were the appropriate relationship in some contexts. Thorelli (1986) extended this work into for-profit organizations and identified a broad range of inter-organizational relationships which exist between traditional views of the hierarchial organizational structures and market transactions. These early works formed the groundwork for the emerging intermediate forms of organization.

Miles and Snow (1986) referred to "dynamic networks" as a new organizational form that would come as a result of large scale vertical disaggregation, internal and external brokering, full disclosure information systems, and market substitutes for administrative mechanisms. They saw networks developing within and between organizational entities in intra-firm structures as well as inter-organizational relations.

Powell (1987) observed the upheavals in traditional organizational structures and described an emerging hybrid form between markets and hierarchies. He noted that internal structural changes, including the increased use of profit centres and transfer pricing, were shifting away from the traditional hierarchical structures. Furthermore, he observed that these changes extended to inter-firm relationships which now emphasized long-term focus and more formal ties. Powell discussed the decreased reliance on pure market transactions, yet saw many similarities between this new hybrid arrangement and traditional hierarchical structures that offered the strengths of both markets and hierarchies.

Johanson and Mattsson (1987) suggested that network perspectives and transactional cost approaches to inter-organizational relations were different. They noted that the assumption of co-operation in networks elicited very different "expected" behaviours than would be elicited with the assumption of opportunism in transaction cost theory. Co-operation fosters productive, committed behaviours and opportunism creates doubt, restraint, protectivism and short-term focus. It is best summed up as outward looking versus defensive.

Other researchers offered evidence of the two most important factors in sustaining inter-organizational networks, trust and a long-term outlook (Thorelli, 1986; Jarillo and Ricart, 1987; Parkhe, 1993), while still others explained how firms could use this new form. Jarillo (1988) provided a comprehensive review of the roles that strategic networks could play as an organization form, the economic justification for networks, and the implications for management. Barreyre (1988) and Johnston and Lawrence (1988) offered good examples for understanding the impartation and disaggregation policies of firms looking at networks as an alternative to vertical integration. Many other researchers have concentrated on the numerous similarities between inter- and intra-organizational networks to explore the plenitude of network variations observed in the field (Teece, 1981; Boudette, 1989; Sharder, Lincoln and Hoffman, 1989; Quinn and Paquette, 1990). All of these different perspectives and research avenues can help managers to understand the potential value of strategic networks as they consider whether their present organizational form fits with today's turbulent environment.

Overall, the concept of organizational boundaries is in a state of flux. Researchers are actively trying to investigate non-equity alliances and strategic networks, and are devoting considerable attention to developing theory. However, as the preceding discussion demonstrated, the work has a broad range of perspectives but no clearly accepted dominant theoretical paradigm. Nevertheless, in the midst of the diverse views, a few common findings can be discerned:

- Networks are viewed as distinct and intermediate forms between the dichotomous forms of hierarchies and markets.
- Inter-organizational relationships are recognized, stable, formalized, non-equity based alliances.
- Networks have the potential to create value for the members, a widely accepted premise suggested by Jarillo's research.

The strategic network concept captures the essence of many observed characteristics in recent IT outsourcing activities occurring within the banking industry. The same concepts discussed in the alliance literature were being repeated by many firms which were undertaking IT outsourcing. The discussions emphasized the firms' (i) new partnership, (ii) long-term contracts, (iii) co-operation and trust while pursuing mutual, purposeful, business goals, (iv) independent organizations focusing on their primary tasks yet sharing resources, and (v) added value from the strategic perspectives of the partners (Clemons and Row, 1992; Krpan, 1993; Van Brussel, 1992). These discussions suggest that IS outsourcing contracts had evolved from the buyer/supplier perspectives of service bureau and facilities management contracts to the partnership perspective of system integration outsourcing. A new outsourcing form was emerging which mirrored the strategic networks discussed at the business and corporate levels of strategy. Yet, outsourcing the IS function which had been considered a core competency sharply contrasted with the advice suggested by prevailing theories.

Much of the past evidence on IT outsourcing has described experiences of different companies involved in outsourcing arrangements. The literature usually involved anecdotal evidence and spanned many industries such as banking, health care, petroleum, chemical, governments, food processing, insurance and retail (Pantages *et al.*, 1992;

Juneau, 1992; Margolis, 1992). Some of the recent outsourcing literature also offers company-specific examples of the financial and strategic motivations behind the outsourcing decision (Sinensky and Wasch, 1992; Schwartz, 1992; McFarlan and Nolan, 1995). The literature also presents the application of various models to the outsourcing activities, such as economies of scale (Barron, 1992), and transaction cost and agency theory (Clemons and Row, 1992; Bakos and Kemerer, 1992). The opportunistic focus of this work channels the research into situations where the relationship is focused on buyer and seller type transactions (Clemons and Kleindorfer, 1992; Richmond *et al.*, 1992).

A notable piece of work by Loh and Venkatraman (1992a) begins to offer a framework for understanding the co-operation seen in several recent outsourcing ventures. They presented an outsourcing research model that described the factors which determine an organization's motivation to outsource IS activities. They suggested that lower IT and business competence lead to more IT outsourcing activities. Specifically, they found more IS outsourcing was taking place in organizations that had higher business costs, higher IT costs, and lower IT performance. Although they posited that business performance and financial leverage might also prompt companies to undertake IT outsourcing, they did not find that these two factors were significantly related to more outsourcing activities. However, they identified the first three factors—business costs, IT costs and IT performance—as the prime determinants of IT outsourcing activities in 55 major United States (US) corporations.

In another study, Venkatraman, Loh and Koh (1994) investigated the diffusion of IT outsourcing at an organizational level by studying the patterns of diffusion among recent outsourcing announcements. They found support for the internal-influence model or imitation behaviour within a social system, but this influence only emerged since the Kodak announcement to outsource. Hence, the communication topics within the social system of the industry and the mimicking behaviours appeared to be increasing the rate and level of adoption of IT outsourcing.

Several propositions emerged from the literature review and initial interviews which suggested that IT outsourcing was motivated by complex rationale. These propositions were used to guide the remaining research steps.

METHODOLOGY

In-depth case studies were required to capture the motivations and rationales behind the emerging IT outsourcing decisions. Case studies facilitated a rich, detailed and thorough investigation into the phenomenon of interest, and avoided the removed, transaction focus of surveys or econometrical analysis (Parkhe, 1993a, pp. 234–235; Yin, 1984, 1989; Glaser and Strauss, 1967). Quantitatively oriented research designs have failed to capture fully the range of motivations behind the IS outsourcing decisions, and lack the detail required for understanding the inner workings and the strategic perspectives that drive many of these decisions (Earl, 1993; Hamel, 1991; Prahalad, 1975).

An *embedded case design* as suggested by Yin (1989) and others (Parkhe, 1993a; Bourgeois and Eisenhardt, 1988; Eisenhardt, 1989) was employed. This design dictates a methodical, systematic sequence of steps while investigating multiple sites. As shown in Figure 7.1, the methodology encompassed a series of steps including framework development, data collection protocol design, initial case study, and several replications. Yin (1989) suggests that *replication* facilitates the test-

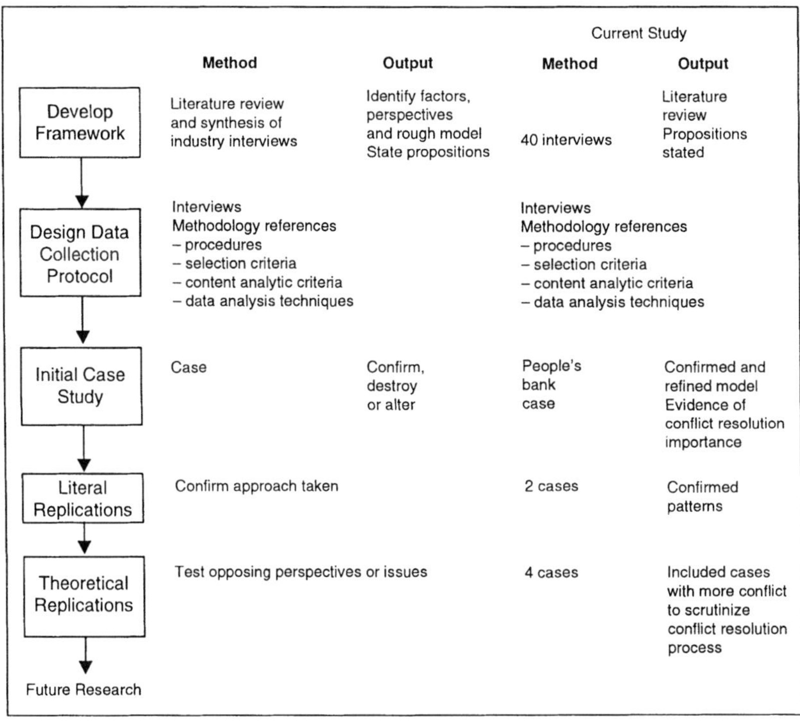

Source: Yin (1984), Parkhe (1993a).

Figure 7.1 *Embedded Case Design*

ing of the patterns and findings of each preceding case. In this study, *literal replications* were undertaken to confirm the findings of the initial case study, and *theoretical replications* were undertaken to explore suggested deviations raised by the conflict resolution issue which was discovered to be very critical. Multiple case studies create more reliable and valid results since they are retested in each new setting. Systematic reviews and interviews ensured the data were gathered consistently, and triangulation of data sources facilitated an extensive review of the evidence surrounding the IT outsourcing relationship (see data collection below for a complete explanation).

The unit of analysis was on the IT outsourcing relationship between the companies and vendors (Yin, 1989). Each party discussed their perspective of the outsourcing relationship and was focused by the interviewer on two organizational issues: the strategic decision-making process and the outsourcing relationship characteristics. Obviously, the senior company management were more knowledgeable about the strategic rationale behind the decisions, but the vendors' account managers were surprisingly informed and aware of their clients' rationale. Both parties talked directly about the outsourcing relationship. These views provided a richer, deeper and sharper review of the chosen outsourcing activities.

Sample

Seven outsourcing alliances were chosen based on the researcher's judgement and were companies in the banking industry who had formed an outsourcing alliance with either Electronic Data Systems (EDS) or Systematics. The support and assistance of these vendors were important for arranging the firms' interviews. Five banks had aligned with Systematics and two banks had aligned with EDS. Two other EDS sites had been arranged but business events eventually led to their withdrawal from the study. Hence, the study is somewhat oriented towards Systematics' experiences, but it is still improved by the two EDS sites that were included. Multiple sites with single vendors foster a stronger research design since vendor effects can be considered in the evaluation process. The vendors were also two of the leading IT outsourcing vendors lending credibility to the eventual results.

Firms varied in size from medium to large regional US banks with \$2–\$30 billion in assets. Banks with less than \$1 billion of assets were not considered because the outsourcing relationships were not as rich or as complex. Their systems were simpler, business scopes were narrower, and outsourcing relationships were straightforward. Because this study hoped to explore complex inter-organizational linkages, these small financial institutions did not fit this criteria. Table 7.1 shows the breakdown by company. It contains the institutions, the chosen vendor, contract date, contract length, activities outsourced, percentage of IS budget outsourced and past outsourcing experience. In general, the outsourcing contracts had been signed in the late 1980s for a five to ten year period. In all cases, at least 75 per cent of the IS budget was outsourced, representing a major organizational change for these firms. Few, but not all banks, had some limited experience with functional outsourcing, but not necessarily with IT outsourcing. Full case descriptions are included in Appendix A to augment this overview with the banks' details about their business focus, predominant outsourcing rationale, and activities outsourced.

Reliability and Validity

To maximize the psychometric quality of the data, case researchers should follow several guidelines when establishing construct validity, internal validity, external validity and reliability (Yin, 1989; Parkhe, 1993a; Eisenhardt, 1989) as shown in Table 7.2. Our study followed these steps exactly.

Construct validity

This was built by triangulating on multiple data sources, establishing a chain of evidence and having the respondents review the transcripts. Data were collected through open-ended interviews with top company and vendor account management, in sessions which lasted between two and six hours, with the average being four hours long. People interviewed in the companies included four CEOs or Presidents, eight executive or senior vice-presidents, and one bank's system development manager. People interviewed in the vendors included seven account managers and nine assistant account managers, those usually responsible for major areas such as software or program development. In addition to the interview data, two-day long orientations with the vendors' top management were conducted. The president, vice-president marketing, VP human resources, and VP operations and district managers from Systematics discussed their business and challenges with the researcher. A similar orientation was undertaken with EDS and included the president of EDS Canada and several industry group vice-presidents in one session, and the vice-presidents of vertical US markets, such as financial industry, in another session. Furthermore, archival records and company documents were perused. The researcher reviewed the financial statements, budgets, organizational

Table 7.1 *Description of Outsourcing Activities*

Institution/Vendor/ Contract Date	Current Contract Length	Activities Outsourced	Activities Retained In-house	Est. % of IS Budget Outsourced	Previous Outsourcing Experience
People's Heritage Bank/ Sytematics/Feb 1988	7	All mainframe IS functions— Hardware, software, personnel and transaction processing Teller Networking, Development	A Couple of Network (LAN) systems	90	Previous IS joint venture with four other banks
Meritor Bank/EDS/April 1989	10	All IS functions— Hardware, software, personnel, transaction processing, system development and IS management	Nothing	100	Loan and mortgage processing
First Fidelity Bancorporation/EDS/August 1990	10	All transaction processing, network management, system development (the latter only for first two years), and System Integration	Major IS business planning and Application Development	75	None but several since
Republic Bank/ Systematics/1982	7	Operations, systems programming and some applications development	Very Unique IS Business product systems	85	None but several since
Brenton Bank/ Systematics/August 1987	5	All IS functions except shared responsibility for branch automation platform	Branch automation platform	95	None but several since
Gainer Bank/ Systematics/September 1987	5	All IS functions	Nothing	100	Credit card and student loan processing
Integra Bank/ Systematics/1977	7	All mainframe IS functions	Internal LANs for office automation and PCs.	85	None but several since

charts, outsourcing contracts or agreements (in most cases), and outsourcing requests for proposals in each case. From these multiple data sources, both qualitative and quantitative data were collected over the period from the summer of 1990 until May 1992.

The chain of evidence was established through systematic interviewing and analytic methods. A structured interview guide was developed in the preliminary work and was used to probe questions extensively, to ask for explanations, to cross-check answers, and to discuss discrepancies and inconsistencies. The rigorous interviewing method ensured the issues were captured as accurately as possible representing the facts and timing of the issues. Interviews were transcribed within 48 hours, and then re-read by *all* participants. Additional comments were provided to clarify any incomplete or inaccurate issues, and sometimes comprised up to ten pages of additional information. Sensitive data were highlighted. In the analysis process when conclusions were drawn, they were always compared back to the data. This explicit link between the data and conclusions ensured accurate statements were being drawn.

Not only did the respondents re-read the interview notes, but many reviewed the conclusions. Results were discussed with four banks over the telephone and three banks face to face until the company members were confident they were accurate. The conclusions did not present any *surprises* to the company management, but provided them with a wider picture encompassing a broader corporate-wide perspective and better understanding of industry practice. The results, findings, suggestions and implications for the companies were presented to three banks and the two vendors in a day-long seminar. Once again senior vendor management attended these sessions. In EDS Canada, there were five people from the executive vice-president, to senior VPs and the financial officer. In Systematics, there was the executive committee chaired by the president and attended by eight vice-presidents. The vendors received copies of the written results and working papers.

Reliability was maintained by compiling databases of the qualitative and quantitative data, and by following a systematic case study protocol. Formal assembly of the data into binders provided a concrete reference point. A summary binder of the transcripts, evidence and qualitative conclusions was created and served to maintain findings with references to the data sources as the issues emerged. The numerical data were compiled into a statistical data base for further analysis. Links between the two ensured that cross references could be maintained and checked as broader generalizations were being made. Procedures were followed to ensure similar items were located across all sites. "Check-off" lists were maintained.

Table 7.2 *Scientific Rigour and Case Study Research*

To maximize this criterion of research quality	This strategy is advantgeous	During this phase of research	Comments
Construct Validity	Triangulate multiple sources of evidence to test for convergence	Data collection	Open-ended interviews with top management officials and board members, attendance at executive meetings, archival records documentation
	Establish Chain of Evidence	Data Collection	Explicit links among the questions asked, data collected and conclusions drawn
	Have key informant's review drafts	Composition	From both partners in IJV
Internal Validity	Do within-case analysis, then cross-case pattern matching	Data Analysis	Systematically match patterns obtained in initial case study (Phase 1), with literal replications (Phase 2), with theoretical replications (Phase 3)
	Do explanation building: shaping hypotheses by searching evidence for "why" behind relationships	Data Analysis	Linking data to emergent theory, while ruling out alternative explanations and rival hypotheses
	Do Time Series analysis	Data Analysis	Using simple time series, complex time series or chronologies, array events on a time axis to determine causal events (ruling out compelling rival causal sequences). The logic behind that basic sequence of a cause and its effect cannot be temporally inverted

External	Theoretical (not random) sampling of IJVs from specified population to constrain extraneous variation and focus on theoretically useful categories	Research Design	Systematically match patterns obtained in initial case study (Phase 1), with literal replications (Phase 2), and with theoretical replications (Phase 3)
	Use replication (not sampling) logic in multiple-case studies	Research Design	Analytic (not Statistical) generalizations through induction
	Comparison of evidence with extant literature	Data Analysis	Uncover commonalities and conflicts, then push to generalize across cases
Reliability	Develop case study database	Data Collection	Formally assembled qualitative and quantitative evidentiary materials
	Use case study protocol	Data Collection	Thorough and systematic documentation to enhance external reviewer's confidence

Source: Developed from Yin (1984), Eisenhardt (1989), and Parkhe (1993). Reproduced by permission from Academy of Management.

Internal Validity

As described above the phenomenon was studied and evaluated through a series of steps to ensure the conclusions had internal validity (See Table 7.2). Forty interviews with vendors, bankers and insurance executives, both involved in and avoiding IT outsourcing relationships, helped to establish the propositions and to frame the subsequent study. Phase 1 represented the initial case study at People's Heritage Bank which refined the ideas and issues through systematic pattern matching. Phase 2 represented the literal replication of two case studies to confirm the patterns found in the initial case study, and Phase 3 represented the theoretical replication of four case studies to consider suspected deviations because of conflict resolution issues.

Each case was analysed separately to provide a succinct description of the known dimensions and issues. Descriptions of the cases are provided in Appendix A. Subsequently, cross-case pattern matching was undertaken to discern the rationales and motivations for the IT outsourcing decision (Berelson, 1971). The analysis brought forth the major financial and strategic motivations behind the banks' decisions. Pattern matching which produced the results followed a systematic process by two researchers. Each researcher reviewed independently the collective data set segmented by bank, vendor, and conflict versus relatively-little conflict situations. Patterns were listed across these divisions, and macro conclusions were noted. Implications within an area or issue were noted at the end of the data. These patterns, conclusions and implications were then compared between the two researchers for consistency and aggregation. The conclusions were critiqued at each stage and alternative explanations were probed with the involved parties to dispel or clarify the issue. After two months of discussing the patterns, the researchers agreed upon a final version and then reviewed the overall findings.

External Validity

Generalizability was enhanced through the use of multiple case studies. The seven cases encompassed firms which contracted with two leading IT outsourcing vendors, thus making the findings relevant to an important and large group of existing and aspiring IT outsourcing vendors. The replication of factors within and across vendors facilitates a stronger statement of findings. The outcomes are not likely situation or vendor specific, but apply to a broader group in an enduring way. Reinforcing evidence for this statement is found in the consistency of the results with many early findings of past works. However, the outcomes also suggest compelling deviations from past research, and offer explanations for them.

RESULTS AND DISCUSSION

The results discussed here focus on the motivations and rationale behind IS outsourcing from a corporate level and hence are not directly comparable to some past literature (Lacity, Hirschheim and Willcocks, 1994; Willcocks and Fitzgerald, 1994). This past work has discussed problems encountered in contract negotiation and relationship management stages of IS outsourcing and brings up conflicts in service level determination, monitoring, negotiation processes and daily interactions of clients and vendors. Although similar conflicts occurred in the banks studied here, the partners were able to resolve the issues satisfactorily such that trust was maintained and a positive, overall outcome was achieved.

Nevertheless, other literature suggests that outsourcing occurs when firms have: (i) financial motivations; (ii) unresponsive IS departments; (iii) little need to control IS; and (iv) non-core IS activities (Huff, 1991; Loh and Venkatraman, 1992; Teresko, 1990). The summary of the overall rationale and motivations behind the banks' IT outsourcing decisions is given in Table 7.3 and provides solid support for the first belief that financial concerns were a strong motivation for outsourcing activities. Even though the firms had financial motivations, they had been financially strong and were not threatened by impending failure. Most of the institutions studied (five out of seven) had histories of strong management as demonstrated by their consistently high financial performance. In addition, the firms reviewed for the preliminary work conducted prior to this study revealed a pattern of financial stability. The financial motivations expressed by the companies involved in outsourcing were seen as preventative measures to avoid potential cost problems, or as mechanisms to enhance performance further.

Two institutions had disappointing financial performance. FFB had suffered from lacklustre performance prior to its outsourcing relationship, however, it was not in immediate financial difficulty. The bank had to make changes or potentially it would be in financial trouble within the next few years. This situation was by no means evidence of a weak organization, and in fact FFB was still ranked in the top 50 US banks. Only one bank in this research, Meritor Bank, was experiencing clear financial difficulties. The Meritor executives were also the only ones that listed financial cost control as their predominant motivation for entering into an outsourcing relationship. However, even in this

Table 7.3 *Case Study Characteristics of Outsourcing Relationships*

FACTOR	PEOPLES 1	INTEGRA 2	GAINER 3	BRENTON 4	REPUBLIC 5	MERITOR 6	FFB 7
Financial performance	Excellent	Good	Excellent	Good	Excellent	Financial Difficulty	Lacklustre
Year/History of OS relationship	88/2 yrs	77/15 yrs w/SI	87/5 yrs	87/4 yrs	82/10 yrs with SI	89/2 yrs	91/6 mo.
Financial Motivation	High	Initially 20 yrs	Medium	High	High	High	Med–High
Hardware	High	ago–High	Medium	Low	High	High	Med–High
–Discounts							
–Purchasing savvy		Current–					
–Utilization		Medium					
Software	High		Low	High (dev)	High	High	Med–High
–Discounts							
–Proprietary solutions		Wanted costs					
–Ability to bundle		more variable					
IS personnel	High		High (Manage personnel risk) (small town)	High	High	High	Med–High
–Staff size							
–Expertise							
Business operating costs	Emerging		Very Low	High	High	High	High
Responsiveness of Internal IS Dept	Medium	Had been eliminated		Medium	Out of control costs	N/A	Low
—out of control costs	—High	—improve quality in the IS Dept	—High	—High	—High		—High
—flexible systems	—Moderate				—Low		—Low
—politics (reacting to management's preferred directions)	—N/A		—N/A		—Low, break the political cycle		—Low

Driving Forces for OS	Financial Manage Tech for new business growth	Financial improve quality of IS Dept—get standard IS product	Financial— IS Staff Improve IS Mgmt and IS personnel Get good quality centrally supported systems	Financial Internal Restructure Link a better IS Dept to business strategy	Financial Get IT operational expertise	Financial Downsize Restructure cost base to survive	Financial Restructure integrate business for growth
Strategic motivation							
Change Organizations Boundaries	Emerged–very important for merger and acquisitions	Emerged later as a benefit	Initially no, but high after being acquired by National Bank of Detroit	Very Important Integrate existing banks	No	Very important, –downsize –major reason	Very, important, –merger
Restructure	Emerging	Long history where this important. Current motive was other things	No	High–Move high costs to unitary	Moderate, link business and technology strategy for a tight fit	High–had to have complete variable costs to fit the dramatic downsize	High
Mitigrate Technological Risk and Uncertainty	High, expanding into new business areas	No	High	Low	Moderate	No	No
Access New Technology	High, new business	No	Medium	Med	No	No	No
Improve IS Management	Medium	Currently High. Maintain high standards	High	High	High	No	High
Link IT and Business Strategy	Emerged	No – only in the past	Emerged	*A priori* – align them	*A priori*	No	Emerged

alliance, management had other goals. The firm needed to convert a large fixed expense into a variable one that would be more flexible and would support the bank's new strategic direction which involved restructuring and retrenchment into certain business areas. Outsourcing was viewed as an essential ingredient in this initiative.

Hence, the financial motivations which are now described are a key part of the IT outsourcing decision, but, as we will explain below, are not the only dominant ones.

Financial Motivations: Outsourcing Affects IT Cost, IT Performance and Business Cost

Financial motivations definitely exist for firms which explored IT outsourcing. A financial motivation was expressed very strongly by all parties involved in the case studies (See Table 7.3). In fact, 75 per cent of the bank executives (9 out of 12 people) expected cost savings from the outsourcing relationships, and 83 per cent (10 out of 12 people) actually believed they received these financial benefits. In the discussions, four areas were suggested where IT and business costs could be decreased by the outsourcing activity. These included hardware costs, software costs, IS personnel costs and business operations costs. The executives believed that more benefits could have been realized in these areas if their firms had considered a broader range of outsourcing activities when initially defining the relationship. For most firms in the sample, it was their first outsourcing relationship and they were proceeding cautiously. Current management theory had provided few guidelines for identifying and optimizing the economic benefits possible, but had executives attained more prior knowledge of outsourcing's potential benefits they believe it would have led to greater organizational gains.

These savings in hardware, software, IS personnel and business operating costs were directly related to efficiency and effectiveness improvements. Efficiency was dramatically improved for hardware activities, software purchasing and IS staff size. Effectiveness, the perspective that the firms were able to do much better with many business aspects, was realized in terms of more appropriate and tailored software, greater range of and flexibility in task assignment for IS expertise, and better business operational integration and consolidation (for non-interest expenses).

The financial saving in an outsourcing relationship represented a dramatic decrease in costs for the clients. On average, there was a 19 per cent reduction in IT costs in the first year. The savings on computer hardware, software, and IT personnel were considered to be significant by 92 per cent of the executives interviewed (26 people). In addition, given the relatively fixed nature of the outsourcing contract price, the savings in subsequent years were anticipated by bank executives to be even greater. Not only is IT an important skill for financial sector firms, but it is also a very significant expenditure, representing more than 8 per cent of the sample firms' non-interest costs. When related organizational cost savings are also considered, the average savings realized from the outsourcing arrangements resulted in an average profitability increase of more than 10 per cent.

Overall, Gainer believed "in-house costs would have been 18 per cent higher", and hence outsourcing was managing this area much better. Most banks (six out of seven) found that "it would be impractical to bring IS back in-house" after outsourcing. They estimated that the costs of re-establishing the IS department and the linkages equivalent to the vendor's structure and disciplined management would be too high. The banks could not meet their outsourcing vendor's cost structure through internalization, and thought that an alternative vendor would be sought if their current relationship floundered.

The most significant contribution of this research on IT outsourcing's economic benefits is the actual estimate and examples of cost savings, which are more specific than most previous studies (but see also Lacity and Willcocks, 1995). Another important observation is the complex and multi-faceted nature of these savings. It is important to consider the full spectrum of potential advantages in order to best structure an outsourcing relationship that maximizes the economic benefits to the institution.

Unresponsive IS Departments

The second belief found in the literature—that firms outsourced because their IS departments did not respond to organizational needs—was also supported by this research (see Table 7.3). The widely-accepted view in both the managerial and academic spheres is that weak IS organizations, lacking the management resources to operate IS effectively in-house, may be forced to enter into outsourcing arrangements (Huff, 1991). The senior executives frequently mentioned the lack of strategically-thinking managers (e.g., IS and general managers) and turned to outsourcing to provide the managers with more time for this activity and not weigh them down with day-to-day operations or unnecessary details. In particular, this factor was emphasized by executives from both Republic Bank and Brenton Bank.

Likewise, the firms wanted to create a more flexible IS organization to react to the changing company. A more responsive IS organization was a key motivation for outsourcing. A good example of this was seen in the People's Heritage Bank, where a senior executive noted the increased capability of the firm's IT to support the bank's entry into new business areas.

However, the remaining two beliefs found in the literature were not upheld by the seven banks studied in this research project. Outsourcing was occurring in firms that required tight IS control and that had core IS activities. The executives revealed that there had been a much more complex perspective on the factors underlying the outsourcing trend. Their views indicated that the contracts were becoming much broader in scope, reflecting the formation of complex inter-organizational relationships which could not be defined as simple buyer-supplier arrangements that are motivated predominately by cost considerations. In fact, strong strategic motivations were suggested for outsourcing IS activities that were considered core to the business, in firms that required tight IS control.

Strategic Motivations: Core IS Activities and Tight Control

The belief that outsourcing was only appropriate when IS was not considered a core function of the firm's industry was not held by the executives interviewed in the case studies. Core activities were defined by a firm's management as those that provide the competitive capabilities that lead to competitive advantage (McLellan, 1993; Prahalad, 1975; Prahalad and Hamel, 1990). This definition implies that a core activity is central to the competitive nature of the industry.

The executives involved in outsourcing relationships clearly viewed the IS function as central to their competitiveness within the banking industry, yet the firms still chose to outsource much, if not all, of the IS activities. This decision is in direct contrast to the conventional outsourcing wisdom.

Bank information systems consist of both commodity-like and unique applications. Commodity applications are those that process transactions usually in very high volumes, and include such things as customer file management and transaction processing. It is difficult to achieve competitive advantage through differentiation in commodity-like IT activities. Unique applications are those that make a significant contribution to a firm-specific "product" such as mortgage and investment. Both types of applications are intricately linked to "back-office" operations throughout the bank, making it somewhat difficult to clearly delineate what is IT and what is operations.

As shown in Table 7.4, 11 of 12 of the bank executives considered the overall IS function, including both commodity and unique applications, to be one of the three most important competitive activities within their

Table 7.4 *Ranking the IS Function*

	Within the Banking Industry		Within their Firm	
	n=12	n=17	n=12	n=17
	Banks	Vendors	Banks	Vendors
IS is the primary competitive resource	22%	20%	38%	6%
IS is second or third most important	70%	80%	50%	75%
IS is lower than third	8%	–	12%	19%

Note: In the firms where another function was considered to be a greater competitive capability than IS, the most frequently cited functions were Marketing, Service, Human Resource Service and Training.
In firms where IS was considered an equal competitive capability, the most frequently cited alternative functions were Lending and Credit Management.

banks. Out of the seven different functions cited by the executives as critical to the firm, the clear indication was that IS ranked as a primary means by which firms within the banking industry achieved competitive advantage. Only one bank executive failed to rank IS in the top three core functions for the firm. Clearly, the executives considered IS to be a core activity both for their firms and for the financial sector. This evidence contradicts the widely-held belief that core IS activities are not being outsourced. At the organizational level, executives considered IS to be core, but recognized that at a micro- or individual IT-activity level, some different aspects may not be core.

The question remains as to why core IS activities were outsourced when conventional wisdom suggested these activities should be tightly controlled? The rationale drawn from the executives' discussions is as follows. An activity that contributes to the competitive capabilities of a company is considered to be core. In the banking industry, the executives clearly view IS as one of these activities. Outsourcing offers an opportunity to use resources beyond those contained in the bank to increase competitive capabilities within the IS function. Table 7.5 offers examples of how the banks used technology for just this purpose. The descriptions highlight the unique ways that vendor and bank capabilities were combined to create competitive advantage. The unique advantage came from combining the vendor's resources with the bank's at a time when no other competitor was doing the same. The combination may not be sustainable in the long term, but it gave competitive advantage to the bank *at the time*. Long-term advantage will depend on the ability to identify the next unique combination no one else is exploiting in the marketplace. However, sustainable competitive advantage is

Table 7.5 *Applications for Competitive Advantage*

Bank	Description
People's Heritage Bank	Created an IS consolidation and integration engine. The bank could selectively access specialized IS skills not available (or retainable) in their market and compile a team for integrating the systems from new, smaller acquisitions. At the time, the IS integration engine was a unique competitive advantage because the bank combined resources (speed, combination and scale of resources) in unique ways to outperform their competitors, although the advantage may not be sustainable in the long term. The central IS integration knowledge remained with the bank.
Meritor Bank	Used technology and systems to support the disaggregation of several bank business units and maximize their sales value. EDS provided the data centre resources and applications in the desired combination for each sale while maintaining an independent set of core applications for the firm. The bank was then able to develop a process of extracting a business unit or asset. Competitive advantage was achieved by reacting quickly to market demands through the timely creation of independent systems which allowed the bank to survive the dramatic market realignment at a time when competitors went out of business or were bought out.
First Fidelity Bancorporation	Developed a system integration process to perform quick and easy system consolidations by using EDS resources and bank processes. Facilitated growth strategy as the bank was able to buy and integrate the systems from one new bank per month. Bank felt this was key to their competitive advantage.
Republic Bank	No immediate competitive advantage system as the bank was currently fighting out of control IS costs.
Brenton Bank	System for integrated account statements combining fragmented services into one-stop customer shopping. Provided customer lock-in six months before competitors. Unique combination of Systematics and bank skills for a service which, at the time, no other compeitor was providing.
Gainer Bank	Drew upon the functionality of Systematics' systems to provide wider range of customer services in combinations suitable to the bank's markets. Systems became a competitive equalizer which enabled the bank to compete against larger firms and overcome the problems of size.
Integra Bank	Used their role with Systematics (the firm's size, long history and beta test experience) to drive system development at the vendor to their advantage. New software functionality was available to them before competitors in their markets and the bank could stay ahead of the wave. In addition, customer-based market niches were giving Integra some sustainable advantages.

strongest if tied to firm-specific capabilities (Clemons and Row, 1987). These banks, as seen by the examples, created competitive advantage by exploiting their own strengths and market situations while drawing upon the IS resources of the vendor.

Nonetheless, effective utilization of these vendor resources is only possible if there is a governance structure in place that allows the bank sufficient leverage and control over the resources. The contracts, the trust, the working relationship with account executives, and the alliance nature of outsourcing relationships found in this research provide such a governance structure for the observed outsourcing arrangements.

These executives clearly felt that as long as "an entity" within senior management's "control" could deliver the IT services as needed, the organizational linkages could be in-house or outsourced across the firm's boundary. The question then became, which entity could provide the best IS service and product? The senior bank executives emphasized the importance of trust as a precursor to outsourcing their IT function. Their views confirm previous research by Beamish and Banks (1987) that trust is important to the success of alliances. Such findings should highlight to vendors the importance of maintaining or enhancing their reputation for trustworthiness. Opportunistic behaviour in one relationship has the potential to cause much greater damage in other relationships and future potential business.

In summary, contrary to conventional wisdom, outsourcing was occurring in firms that considered IS to be a core function and that required tight IS control. Not only did the senior managers claim that IT was strategic, they also offered examples of how technology was being used to create a competitive advantage at the time. The executives suggested that this was occurring because their firms had strong strategic motivations, and could create the necessary IS controls. These strategic motivations seemed to be aimed at improving a firm's capabilities and business performance. It is interesting to read these findings into the frameworks suggested in Chapters 5 and 8.

Improve Business Performance

Loh and Venkatraman (1992) proposed business performance as one of the determinants of IS outsourcing activities, but this conclusion was not supported by their analysis. This research suggests that the nature of business performance may be long term and would only be detected after a period of time, a feature which would not be detected in a cross-sectional study like the one undertaken by Loh and Venkatraman. Therefore, although business performance was not supported in their multiple regression analysis, the executives from our research indicated that they had many strategic initiatives which they hoped would improve long-term business performance.

The executives suggested several motivations behind their IS outsourcing decisions that centred around facilitating strategic change. These reasons included changing the organizational boundaries, restructuring the organizations, mitigating technological risk and uncertainty, accessing new technology, and improving the management of IS operations. These objectives were aimed at repositioning and improving competitive performance of their bank within their competitive environment, a task which would eventually affect business performance. The sites which were chosen as literal replications of the outsourcing phenomena observed (they were those sites with outsourcing relationships very similar to the pilot site), produced patterns which confirmed the important motivational influences. The sites which were chosen as theoretical replications to investigate the influence of conflict management extended the results to a wider population. Although the outsourcing relationship was more turbulent in these theoretical replications (with greater conflicts and resolutions), the results indicated that the financial and strategic motivations were similar across the low- and high-conflict situations. No discernable difference could be found in the summary results presented in Table 7.3. It appears that as long as conflicts are resolved, companies are able to accomplish a broad range of goals with their outsourcing arrangements. The strategic outcomes of these outsourcing relationships are now explained.

Changing Organizational Boundaries

For many firms, altering their boundaries was a predominant motivation. This change involved expanding or contracting the business activities, either through mergers and acquisitions, or through downsizing the core business. Outsourcing facilitated these processes. Significant change in organizational boundaries occurred in six out of seven of the banks studied (all except Gainer).

Growth through Mergers and Acquisitions

Outsourcing facilitated the banks' desire to create a shared, integrated system platform to support and link new business activities into the existing organization (Lacity, Hirschheim and Willcocks, 1994). US banking organizations tended to have highly developed hierarchical organizations surrounding their core activities, which included the IS functions. These complex structures presented obstacles to growth through acquisition or consolidation because they usually contained unique and not easily integrated system platforms. The system integration process, if not impossible, had been lengthy and arduous, in part because there usually was not an overarching perspective of the bank's activities. The business, and hence IS activities, had often organized into independent geographic or business areas. To facilitate growth most banks adopted a holding company structure. In addition, the regulatory environment within the US had encouraged the holding company approach to growth. These factors had created organizations with a multitude of independent, duplicated, operational structures which limited the economies that could be achieved in a traditional US banking strategy.

However, the banks were better able to integrate common activities with outsourcing. The outsourcing vendor not only brought an external perspective, but also contributed the necessary resources for this process. Once a company-wide, integrated system platform was installed, the bank could expand much more easily with the ability to achieve cost efficiencies. New mergers or acquisitions could be linked into this common application platform very easily.

First Fidelity Bancorporation (FFB) provides a clear example of using outsourcing to support an integrative growth strategy. The bank effectively used its outsourcing relationship to facilitate the consolidation process and then to integrate ten recently-acquired banks. The bank's structure had been similar to that of many mid-sized US banks, where the subsidiary banks had been operated autonomously under the holding company. The shift from the original eight to 18 banks would have been impossible under the former holding company structure. When the senior executives decided in March 1990 to grow the bank, they recognized that the existing systems were incompatible and would hamper the achievement of the required cost efficiencies available from consolidation. They estimated that the process of using internal IS resources to transform the organization in preparation for growth would take at least three years, if the change were possible at all. The bank had recognized that it needed more than resources to bring about the dramatic change. A senior executive from FFB commented on the decision:

> "This [integration] was an activity the bank definitely could not have pulled off internally. Although EDS brought some resources, its biggest role was as a catalyst, an agent of change."

The outsourcing arrangement not only facilitated the consolidation of the original eight banks, but eased the integration of ten additional banks. FFB eventually developed the capability to acquire and integrate banks at the pace of one per month. Despite the increased size, outsourcing has cut more than $20 million dollars (or 20 per cent) from FFB's 1990 IS costs, and held them at a reasonable level. In addition, the operations consolidation saved $50 million per annum, as well as creating the infrastructure necessary to achieve significant efficiencies when integrating future acquisitions.

Another bank had also used outsourcing successfully to facilitate a merger. Integra Bank had been the product of a merger between two financial institutions that shared a common outsourcing vendor. This common vendor enabled the merger to proceed more smoothly and produced an institution that was truly integrated with common systems across the organization. The vendor's scope of software products also facilitated the expansion of the clients' business boundary by reducing the learning curve for support technology and by enabling inter-organizational mergers through rapid technology integration. Clearly, outsourcing can have a profound impact on a bank's growth strategy by simplifying mergers and acquisitions.

Downsizing the Core Business

Outsourcing was also used by one bank to downsize its organizational structure. Meritor Bank decided to downsize from an asset base of $21 billion to one of $6 billion. Outsourcing provided the flexible infrastructure that had been required to quickly restructure the bank and trim off business units which were no longer viable within the newly-focused company strategy. In the process, the IS activities, assets and personnel were shifted to the vendor's central data centre as required. Essentially, a large fixed cost became variable and flexible, thereby facilitating the de-integration of the business units. A Meritor executive believed that "one result has been the freeing up of substantial management time. For example, the [senior vice president] has been able to take on additional responsibilities." Outsourcing was a central part of a restructuring strategy that helped the bank remain viable when it appeared that Meritor would not survive.

Outsourcing has helped to change organizational boundaries through expansion or contraction, by providing the slack resources required (Penrose, 1968) and by providing a flexible IS organization. Outsourcing has facilitated this strategic initiative.

Restructuring the Organization

A desire to restructure their organizations was a prime motivation for employing outsourcing activities in four banks (e.g., FFB, People's,

Brenton, Meritor), a moderate motivation for Republic, and a past motivation for Integra. All but one firm found it necessary to unlock the organizational structure that had been firmly entrenched in the firm's management system, corporate culture, bureaucracy, and employees' resistance to massive organizational change. Many banks reported having tried previously to reorganize their company, but found the process impossible because of these barriers, and eventually had given up in frustration and exhaustion.

Outsourcing provided the catalyst required to sustain the organizational transitions that had to take place. Banking firms had developed complex organizational structures based upon product, geographic or international contingencies. Although core skills, such as the IS function, had sometimes cut across functional groupings, generally they were conceived of as being based upon functional activities, and thus hard to separate or restructure. Outsourcing provided the means of accessing, highlighting and integrating core functional activities into structures with strategic business units ordered along other contingent dimensions.

Prior to outsourcing, the old structures exhibited difficulties that took on many forms. In some cases, users and IT service providers complained about the convoluted internal communications, and the difficult response processes required to handle requests in a timely, organized manner. In other firms, the executives found it difficult to balance the dilemma of a centralized versus decentralized IT structure. A centralized structure offered higher cost savings, but the decentralized structure appeared to be more responsive to the needs of the various business units.

Outsourcing decreased many of these organizational tensions. Essentially it lifted IT out from under the hierarchy and placed it *beside* the organization, removing or greatly reducing the communications and structural problems. In most sites, this new structure simplified communications for users so that requests were not delayed in bureaucratic committees and complex hierarchies. It also provided a better mechanism for costing back user requests, prioritizing technology initiatives, and controlling expenditures. In effect, many of the organizations were able to enjoy the benefits of both centralized and decentralized IT structures for many parts of their businesses. Theoretically, this restructuring should have been possible without outsourcing but, as illustrated by these sites, the massive change required a strong catalyst. Outsourcing provided this boost.

Mitigating Technological Risk and Uncertainty

Outsourcing with a specialized, experienced vendor through a well-defined contract may reduce the technological uncertainty and risk inherent in today's business environment. IS contains a large component of technological uncertainty with its rapidly changing foundation. When IT is expected to support a strategic thrust, then one of the management goals is to reduce this technological uncertainty. Past experience with internal IT efforts, and executives' recognition that their internal department may have limited experience with the required technology, drives up the risk factor. Thus, the executives are constantly looking for ways to mitigate the technological risk.

One bank executive related the decision process underlying his assessment of IS technological risk to the business attractiveness of mutual fund and investment product offerings. He used a process that developed a conservative estimate on the time and expense factors surrounding the implementation of the IT components. He had asked for and received information on an IT implementation time frame and cost estimates from the internal IS department. He then expanded or "bracketed" the time and expenditure estimate by 100 per cent, because of previous experience with other major IT projects. Obviously, this process of assigning technological risk has a serious impact on decisions regarding the attractiveness of new business initiatives.

Similar stories about this "bracketing process" were heard from several other institutions and all were related to the assignment of technological risk. As a result, the technological risk perceived by executives was undoubtedly having a very significant impact upon which business opportunities were pursued. The executives saw outsourcing as a way to significantly reduce or remove this risk, so that decisions could then be made based upon an evaluation of the business fundamentals. The technological risk would be managed by the outsourcing vendor, while the organization concentrated on the strategic business rationale. Obviously, the senior executives had to trust that the vendor could deliver the technology that had been promised.

Transferring technological risk and uncertainty to the outsourcing vendor does not abdicate management's responsibility to consider that risk. The risk still exists, but the vendor's organization is expected to provide many skills and resources to lessen this risk and concern. If the right outsourcing vendor is chosen, clients buy expertise and access to organizational learning, which they would have seen demonstrated through the vendor's expertise and capabilities in the targeted business area. In essence, this purchased IT expertise, proven through demonstrated results, reduces the technological risk for the organization.

Accordingly, technology within the firm is treated the same as other functional areas—it is a resource that must be managed. It just happens that some of the resources are being purchased from an external party, and the firm must manage these risk profiles.

Accessing New Technology

Outsourcing can also support a firm's strategic initiatives by providing early and cost-effective access to emerging hardware and software technology. The vendors provide clients with access to specialized resources that can scan and evaluate relevant technologies. When potentially valuable technologies had been identified, the vendor, with its particular skill set and knowledge base, could effectively implement this technology into the day-to-day operations. Many of these emerging technologies have the potential to fundamentally change the firm's business environment.

For example, Brenton Bank was reoriented by several suggestions from its outsourcing vendor, Systematics. A senior Systematics executive recounts his firm's technology contributions to the bank:

> "In the case of the optical disk storage, this is the first [Systematics] site to try this technology. We brought them the idea of trying it. I view this technology as the beginning of the way to image processing. The other [new] technologies also came as a result of suggestions we made."

Generally, as a result of being hooked into the large network of relationships established by the outsourcing vendor, the companies gained access to new technologies. For some banks, the result was the development of more advanced Customer Information File systems that were impossible for an individual bank to develop. The larger scale and broader market scope of the major outsourcing vendors offered clients a window on expensive revolutionary technologies. For example, many clients were now seriously considering image processing and integrated client-server networks that they had hesitated to undertake previously. The outsourcing vendor was able to accelerate a firm's access to these technologies at a more reasonable cost. The banks could then concentrate on banking issues but become more "technologically aware", and potentially achieve a technological advantage over non-outsourcing competitors.

Improving the Management of IS Operations

The desire to manage daily IS operations better motivated many banks to outsource. Essentially, the outsourcing vendor brought a business orientation, rather than a cost orientation, to the daily IS operations. The account managers installed by the vendors were often more broadly skilled and experienced at operations management. IS operations took on a profit orientation that was reflected in an increased view of the rest of the bank's organization as customers who, if given better, reasonably priced service, might purchase additional products.

This new orientation brought many benefits to the banks. Outsourcing provided better IT planning, better IT support resources, and better IS career opportunities. The market-oriented, cost-conscious discipline imposed by the outsourcing vendor helped to improve the IT planning systems that had been used prior to the outsourcing arrangements. The improved IT planning would support the business strategy formulation and foster greater competitive advantages for the banks. Several banks commented on how IT planning had improved. An executive from Integra Bank cited the need to replace the bank's software as the primary motivation underlying the decision to outsource IS. He recognized that the previous IT planning process would have hindered this process:

> "There were extensive [IT] plans that bore no relation to reality. First in terms of our company's financial resource capabilities, and second in terms of the ability of our people to absorb change."

After outsourcing, the IT planning system at Integra improved dramatically, and according to the same executive: 'The [IT] planning is more comprehensive and is attainable within resource and time constraints." An executive at Republic Bank summed up the impact of its vendor on IT planning: "Systematics brought management discipline, focus and scope to technology [planning] decisions that had been previously lacking in the bank."

Another benefit for managing IS better was the improved IT support resources available to the firms after outsourcing. The specialized central software support resources offered by the vendors played a key role in the effective maintenance of new systems at many banks. Integra Bank thought its system support was much better. Likewise, a senior executive at Republic noted: "I envision a permanent relationship. There are very significant benefits from the central maintenance of the software. It provides the management discipline that is lacking in the in-house IS operations."

Furthermore, the management of IS personnel improved since better IS career opportunities were created by the outsourcing arrangements. In traditional IS organizations, the limited career paths and relatively few challenging assignments, resulted in many good people leaving the firms, and a high turnover cost. Since the outsourcing vendors were growing rapidly, they could offer improved career opportunities and retain skilled employees thereby lowering the turnover costs. For instance, when Meritor Bank outsourced their IS operations to EDS, 260 employees were transferred to the vendor. Although the transition undoubtedly caused upheaval for some of the IS staff, EDS provided them with a greater variety of career opportunities. A transferred executive from Meritor commented on the transition: "For myself, I now view the experience positively in terms of career opportunities and training. I believe that most of the staff would now prefer to stay with EDS."

From the bank's perspective, the final benefit of improved IS management was the removal of the IS salary sub-unit, an organizational irritant that had existed for many years. Historically, the IS salaries were much higher than the bank's salary structure, because of the difficulty of acquiring and retaining systems personnel. This discrepancy displaced an upward pressure on the salaries of other functional units which the bank could not afford. The more consistent organization-wide salary structure was much easier to manage and the costs were easier to control.

In summary, the executives involved in the outsourcing relationships expressed many strategic motivations for using IS outsourcing. These strategic initiatives expanded organizational boundaries, restructured the business and IT units, mitigated technological risk and uncertainty, accessed new technology, and provided better daily IS operations. Eventually, the executives thought these steps would improve business performance, but some of the impacts were not expected for many years down the road.

Link IT and Business Strategy

A serendipitous benefit of outsourcing that became an *ex post* rationalization for the activities was the strong linkage forged between IT and business strategies. Tighter linkages between IS resources and the business strategy formulation process was expressed as a key outcome for many firms in this research. Before outsourcing, knowledge of organizational IT resources had been buried within most firms. Many senior executives involved in strategic planning were unaware of IT implications, risks or opportunities, but recognized that IT was an important function within their business. After outsourcing, the firms were able to achieve a much tighter linkage between technological capabilities and opportunities, and the business strategy formulation process.

This tight linkage between technology and strategy occurred with outsourcing for two reasons. First, in the past, the hands-off approach towards IS functions and the inability to stay current on all of the diverse IT implications had kept many senior executives in the dark about the IS function. Many financial sector organizations managed IT through steering committees which filtered and stopped the flow of information to and from senior executives. Few top executives were interested in, committed to or participated in these steering committees and hence could be isolated from many technology issues. However, with the outsourcing relationship the IS function developed a much higher profile, because of the opportunities and risks it demonstrated to the executives. Many senior bank executives were paying attention to IS for the first time, as they viewed the IS-business "alliance" as having a much higher profile than it had been in the past. A primary reason for this newly-discovered interest in IT was the large financial risk involved in the contracts. Typically, the price represented 8–10 per cent of the banks's non-interest expenditures and therefore attracted senior management attention.

Second, the new outsourcing arrangement between the two organizations raised the IS relationship to a peer-to-peer association. This new stature propelled executives to take a more active interest in IT. In fact, the outsourcing vendors helped draw the executives into this more active IT role by insisting that their relationship include a more formalized executive technology committee to direct policy setting. The formalized, frequent and more direct communication helped to strengthen the linkage between IT and strategy formulation.

These new "elevated" IT-business strategy committees improved the IT communications within the banks. Many committees were now viewed as "brainstorming groups", and skirting the mundane IT management issues which senior executives neither had the time nor inclination to review (these topics were previously the focus of technology steering committees). One CEO, who was initially pressured into committee participation by the outsourcing arrangement, began to learn more about IT and its possibilities. For him, there were now two additional strategic advantages that outsourcing provided. One, he received information much more quickly than he had received it through the previous hierarchical communication system. Two, he now had access to virtually unlimited IT resources to support business strategies. Organizational barriers had been removed. If he wanted information on the technology necessary to support a new product idea, he could now go beyond the limits of the internal organizational knowledge, and tap into the vendor's much larger and broader resources.

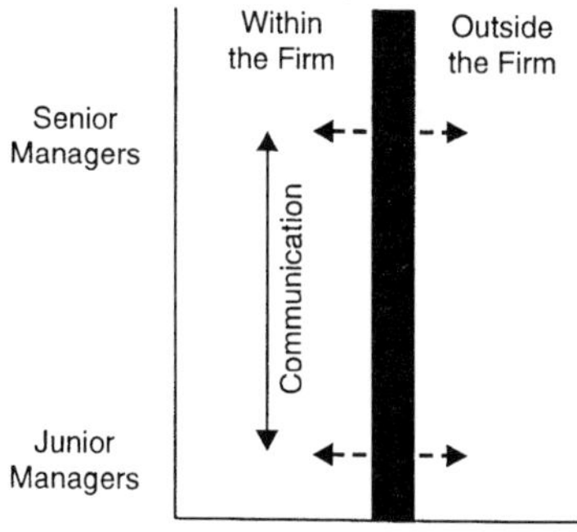

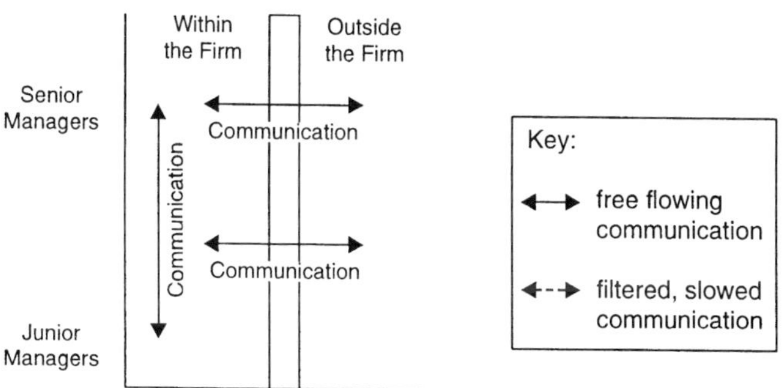

Figure 7.2 *Communication Flows*

Figure 7.2 illustrates the change in communications flows after an outsourcing arrangement is undertaken. In one organization, the change in communication flows was quite dramatic and provides a good example of this process. Basically, before outsourcing, communication had passed sluggishly through many levels to reach upper management. After outsourcing, it tended also to flow in a horizontal manner, with easier access to both outside knowledge and to senior executives (as suggested by the hollow bar). Two layers of management were usually bypassed under the outsourcing arrangement. The CEO of one large regional US bank had not initially considered IT to be a core competence, but rather perceived it as an overhead item whose cost should be minimized. His primary motivation for outsourcing had been to reduce this cost. However, after forming the alliance, he concluded that IT was an important organizational competence. He attributed this change in attitude to the ability under the outsourcing arrangement to link business strategies and organizational IT capabilities more tightly. CEOs had become more involved in IT strategy and increasingly aware of its potential contribution to new business opportunities. The non-performing or unknown IS service that had been perceived in the past was viewed increasingly as an accessible resource and a potentially valuable competitive tool.

This tighter linkage also created more innovative and resourceful organizations that were quick to exploit market opportunities. For example, People's Heritage Bank used the vendor's experience in the commercial banking business to facilitate a quick entry into commercial fee-based services. This activity has been a successful growth area for the bank. Other banks have expanded into cash management, factoring, brokeraging, mutual funds, and correspondent mortgage processing. The flexibility created by the streamlined organization, rapid communications flows, and improved knowledge and skills base, had given the banks a competitive advantage that enabled them to differentiate themselves. It also decreased the costs associated with organizational learning within new business areas.

Executives at both Republic and Brenton Banks pointed out that most initiatives to date have been for providing enhanced products for existing markets. Increased system flexibility allowed FFB to grow into contiguous geographic areas and to expand its market. Overall, banks were able to focus on developing new business areas or products and ensuring a firmer grip on their markets as a result of the improved linkages between required business strategies and IT capabilities.

Although linking IT and business strategies had not really been an *a priori* motivation for the outsourcing that occurred in the firms studied, it was definitely recognized as an outsourcing benefit by the executives involved. These linkages are likely to be motivations for other firms which follow in the outsourcing arena once this potential benefit is recognized.

CONCLUSIONS

Much of the prevailing wisdom about IS outsourcing seems to have been confirmed by these case studies. Financial motivations underlie many IS outsourcing decisions, and unresponsive IS departments are accelerating the pace of the outsourcing process. However, contrary to conventional wisdom, IS outsourcing is taking place within firms and industries which utilize IS activities that are considered core competencies. Several strategic motivations were presented that may explain this management decision.

Knowledge of these strategic motivations may improve the understanding of the role of business performance in an outsourcing decision. Business performance had not been found to be related to IS outsourcing activities in a comprehensive study conducted previously (Loh and Venkatraman, 1992). It appears that many strategic initiatives behind outsourcing may not have an impact on the organization for several years. Hence, it may take five years before the implications of business performance on IS outsourcing are fully realized. It may also be the case that some negative impacts may emerge over such a time period, as reported in several cases in Lacity and Willcocks (1995).

Within this research, IS outsourcing was found to have profound effects on the expenses for the banks. These large financial savings were being realized for both IT costs and business costs, and more specifically, in terms of hardware, software, IS personnel and business operational costs. Overall, the firms realized a 19 per cent reduction in the IT costs within the first year, with the potential for much larger savings in rationalized and consolidated operations. Savings in subsequent years were anticipated to be even higher.

The research helps to give more detail on the reasons for outsourcing discussed earlier in Chapter 1. While the financial motivations were very strong for the participating firms, unresponsive IS departments also contributed to top management's decision to outsource. Furthermore, outsourcing was occurring in firms where IS had been considered a core skill. This was happening while maintaining tight management control of the IS function. The arrangement was possible because of the alliance governance structure that evolved as the basis of most comprehensive IT outsourcing relationships. The trust built up in these alliances had allowed the banks to concentrate on their strategic initiatives while believing the best IS resources would be available in the right quantity and quality. This renewed business emphasis has improved the firm's business performance in many ways. The banks claimed they were better able to change their organizational boundaries, restructure their organization, mitigate technological risk and uncertainty, access new technology, and improve the management of their IS operations.

Part of the reason the prevailing outsourcing wisdom did not hold for these firms is that outsourcing has changed from past practices. Outsourcing knowledge predominantly had been forged on service bureau and facilities management capabilities and not on the more complex and dedicated private-label outsourcing that is occurring today. Since some outsourcing has taken on a new shape, more as a strategic alliance, it appears to work differently and firms must re-evaluate this option through a new lens. The new outsourcing would seem to offer many benefits and strategic advantages for the partners. However, as argued in the Introduction of this book, good in-house management is a *sine qua non* that should not be ignored. From a gestalt, corporate perspective these firms are achieving many positive results from IT outsourcing, but none would argue that the process is not without conflict. The conflict arises in the specification of contract details and the daily work interactions of the parties, and needs to be resolved. If the majority of conflicts are resolved positively, the overall feeling is that IT outsourcing is good for the firm. This does not mean there are no contentious issues from time-to-time, but overall the benefits outweigh the problems from the senior manager's perspective. Most managers involved in outsourcing activities would advise others to use outsourcing wisely, and to create the necessary organizational linkages and controls to ensure it works for their firm.

An important part of this research was to determine why firms would outsource a core skill, and whether this was a sound strategic decision or one motivated primarily by immediate economic gain. The research findings revealed that, although the financial motivations for outsourcing are an important part of the decision, the strategic motivations appear to be increasingly more important. Outsourcing can play both a central and a support role in many strategic initiatives. Essentially, it offers access to additional capabilities that can have a profound effect on expanding the set of strategic options available to a firm. A vendor's economies of scale and scope allow the firms to undertake dramatic financial and strategic changes. Outsourcing facilitates these changes.

REFERENCES

Bakos, J. Y. , and Kemerer C. F. (1992) Recent Applications of Economic Theory in Information Technology Research, *Decision Support Systems*, 8, 365–386.

Barreyre, P. Y. (1988) The Concept of "Impartation" Policies: A Different Approach to Vertical Integration Strategies, *Strategic Management Journal*, 9, 507–520.

Barron, T. (1992) Some New Results in Testing for Economies of Scale in Computing, *Decision Support Systems*, 8, 405–429.

Beamish, P. and Banks, J. C. (1987) Equity Joint Ventures and the Theory of the Multinational Enterprise, *Journal of International Business Studies*, Summer, 1–16.

Berelson, B. (1971) Content Analysis in Communication Research, New York: Hafner Publishing Company.

Betts, M. (1991) Study: Outsourcing Big in Bank's Future, *Computerworld*, **25**, 40, 8.

Blanton J. E. , Watson H. J. and Moody J. (1992) Toward a Better Understanding of Information Technology Organization: A Comparative Case Study, *MIS Quarterly*, December, 531–555.

Boudette, N. (1989) Networked to Dismantle Old Structures, *Industry Week*, 16 January, 27–31.

Bourgeois, L. J. III and Eisenhardt, K. M. (1988) Strategic Decision Processes in High Velocity Environments: Four Cases in the Microcomputer Industry, *Management Science*, **34**, 7, 816–835.

Brown, B. (1990) Hyatt Chain Cuts Over New Global Reservation Network, *Network World*, **7**, 41, 2 and 86.

Burch, J. G. (1990) Planning and Building Strategic Information Systems, *Journal of Systems Management*, 41, 21–27.

CIO Journal (1993) Chief Information Officer Journal's first Annual Survey, CIO Journal, **5**, 3, 5–64.

Clemons, E. K. and Kleindorfer, P. R. (1992) An Economic Analysis of Interorganizational Information Technology, *Decision Support Systems*, 8, 431–446.

Clemons, E. K. and Row, M. (1987) Structural Differences among Firms: a Potential Source of Competitive Advantage in the Application of Information Technology, Proceedings of the Eighth International Conference on Information Systems, December, 6–9.

Clemons, E. K. and Row, M. C. (1992) Information Technology and Industrial Cooperation: the Changing Economies of Coordination and Ownership, *Journal of Management Information Systems*, **9**, 2, 9–28.

Cummings, J. (1992a) Banks Off-loads Data Center, Network Upgrade to Unisys, *Network World*, **9**, 41, 51 and 59.

Cummings, J. (1992b) IBM unit, EDS Announce 10-year Outsourcing Deals, *Network World*, **10**, 1, 2–51.

Earl, M. J. (1993) Experiences in Strategic Information Planning, *MIS Quarterly*, March, 1–24.

Eisenhardt, K. M. (1989) Making Fast Strategic Decisions in High-velocity Environments, *Academy of Management Journal*, **32**, 3, 543–576.

Farmer, D. H. and MacMillan, K. (1976) Voluntary Collaboration vs Disloyalty to Suppliers, *Journal of Purchasing in Materials Management*, **12**, 4, 3–8.

Glaser, B. G. and Strauss, A. L. (1967) The Discovery of Grounded Theory, Chicago: Aldine Publishing.

Halper, M. (1992a) Hertz Revamp eyes HP Minis, Outsourcing, *Computerworld*, **26**, 40, 1 and 16.

Halper, M. (1992b) Marriott Suit Damns AMR Role in Confirm, *Computerworld*, **26**, 41, 1 and 8.

Hamel, G. P. (1991) Competition for Competence and Inter-partner Learning within International Strategic Alliances, *Strategic Management Journal*, 12, 83–103.

Henderson, J. C. (1990) Plugging Into Strategic Partnerships: the Critical IS Connection, *Sloan Management Review*, 31, 7–18.

Huff, S. L. (1991) Outsourcing of Information Services, *Business Quarterly*, 54, 4, 62–65.

Huff, S. L. and Beattie, S. E. (1985) Strategic Versus Competitive Information Systems, *Business Quarterly*, 50, 97–102.

Jarillo, J. C. (1988) On Strategic Networks, *Strategic Management Journal*, 9, 31–41.

Jarillo, J. C. and Ricart, J. E. (1987) Sustaining Networks, *Interfaces*, 17, 82–91.

Johanson, J. and Mattsson, L. G. (1987) Interorganizational Relations in Industrial Systems: a Network Approach Compared with the Transaction-cost Approach, *International Studies of Management and Organization*, 1, 34–38.

Johnston, R. and Lawrence, P. (1988) Beyond Vertical Integration—the Rise of Value-adding Partnership, *Harvard Business Review*, July–August, 94–101.

Juneau, L. (1992) Big Outsourcers Not Always Better, *Network World*, **9**, 7, 36.

Krpan, J. (1993) The Dollars and Sense of Outsourcing, *CMA Magazine*, **66**, 10, 10 and 12.

Lacity, M. , Hirschheim, R. and Willcocks, L. (1994) Realizing Outsourcing Expectations, *Information Systems Management*, **11**, 4, 7–18.

Lacity, M. and Willcocks, L. (1995) Interpreting Information Technology Sourcing Decisions from a Transaction Cost Perspective: Findings and Critique, *Accounting, Management And Information Technology*, **5**, 3/4, 203–244.

LaPlante, A. (1991) Taking a Second Look at the Concept of Outsourcing, *Infoworld*, **13**, 19, s8–s9.

Loh, L. and Venkatraman, N. (1992a) Determinants of Information Technology Outsourcing: A Cross-sectional Analysis, *Journal of Management Information Systems*, **9**, 1, 7–24.

MacMillan, K. and Farmer, D. (1979) Redefining the Boundaries of the Firm, *Journal of Industrial Economics*, **2**, 3, 277–285.

Margolis, N. (1992) Revlon Makes Over IS Unit, *Computerworld*, **26**, 6, 1–24.

McFarlan, F. W. (1984) Information Technology Changes the Way You Compete, *Harvard Business Review*, **62**, 3, 98–103.

McFarlan, W. and Nolan, R. (1995) How to Manage an IT Outsourcing Alliance, *Sloan Management Review*, **36**, 2, 9–24.

McLellan, K. (1993) Outsourcing Core Skills into Non-equity Alliance Networks, Unpublished Dissertation, Western Business School, The University of Western Ontario, London, Ontario.

Miles, R. and Snow, C. (1986) Organizations: New Concepts for New Forms, *California Management Review*, 3, 62–73.

Pantages, A. *et al.* (1992) The Datamation 100: Shared Medical Systems Corp; Mentor Graphics corp. ; ASK Computer Systems inc. , Eastman Kodak Co. ; Systematics Information Services inc, *Datamation*, **38**, 13, 134–138.

Parkhe, A. (1993a) ''Messy'' Research, Methodological Predispositions, and Theory Development in International Joint Ventures, *Academy of Management Review*, **18**, 2, 227–268.

Parkhe, A. (1993b) Strategic Alliance Structuring: A Game Theoretic and Transaction Cost Examination of Interfirm Cooperation, *Academy of Management Journal*, **36**, 4, 794–829.

Penrose, E. T. (1968) *The Theory of the Growth of the Firm*, Oxford: Basil Blackwell.

Porter, M. (1985) *Competitive Advantage*, New York: The Free Press.

Powell, W. (1987) Hybrid Organizational Arrangements: New Form or Transitional Development? *California Management Review*, Fall, 67–87.

Prahalad C. K. (1975) The Strategic Process in a Multinational Corporation, Doctoral Dissertation, Harvard Business School.

Prahalad, C. K. and Hamel, G. (1990) The Core Competence of the Corporation, *Harvard Business Review*, May–June, 79–91.

Quinn, J. and Paquette, P. (1990) Technology in Services: Creating Organiza-

tional Revolutions, *Sloan Management Review*, Winter, 67–68.
Richmond, W. B. , Seidmann, A. and Whinston, A. B. (1992) Incomplete Contracting Issues in Information Systems Development Outsourcing, *Decision Support Systems*, 8, 459–477.
Safer, A. (1992) Revenge of the Nerds, *Canadian Business*, **65**, 10, 137–142.
Schwartz, J. (1992) Ordering Out for IS, *CIO*, **5**, 7, 18.
Sharder, C. B. , Lincoln, J. R. and Hoffman, A. N. (1989) The Network Structures of Organizations: Effects of Task Contingencies and Distribution Form, *Human Relations*, 42, 43–66.
Sinensky, A. and Wasch, R. S. (1992) Understanding Outsourcing: A Strategy for Insurance Companies, *Journal of Systems Management*, **43**, 1, 32–33, 36.
Teece, D. J. (1981) Internal Organization and Economic Performance: An Empirical Analysis of the Profitability of Principal Firms, *The Journal of Industrial Economics*, December, 173–199.
Teresko, J. (1990) Make or Buy? Now It's a Data-processing Question, Too, *Industry Week*, 16 July, 54–55.
Thorelli, H. (1986) Networks: Between Markets and Hierarchies, *Strategic Management Journal*, 7, 37–51.
Tuman, J. (1988) Shaping Corporate Strategy with Information Technology, *Project Management Journal*, 19, 35–42.
Van Brussel, C. (1992) Canada Post Executive Defends Outsourcing, *Computing Canada*, **18**, 26, 1 and 6.
Van de Ven, A. H. (1976) On the Nature, Formation and Maintenance of Relations Among Organizations, *Academy of Management Review*, 1, 24–36.
Van de Ven, A. H. and Ferry, D. L. (1980) *Measuring and Assessing Organizations*, New York: John Wiley and Sons.
Venkatraman, N. , Loh, L. and Koh, J. (1994) The Adoption of Corporate Governance Mechanisms: A Test of Competing Diffusion Models, *Management Science*, **40**, 4, 496–507.
Wilder, C. (1991) Bank's IS Awaits FCIC Actions, *Computerworld*, **25**, 2, 8.
Willcocks, L. and Fitzgerald, G. (1994) IT Outsourcing and the Changing Shape of the Information Systems Function: Recent Research Findings, Oxford Institute of Information Management, Templeton College, Oxford.
Yin, R. K. (1984 and 1989) *Case Study Research: Design and Methods*, Beverley Hills, CA: Sage Publications.

APPENDIX A
CASE DESCRIPTIONS

People's Heritage Bank

Located in the New England area, People's serves a retail and middle market customer in both retail and commercial banking. They have a good reputation and have had excellent financial performance over the years. The senior management group's current motives for change were driven by the desire to control financial costs and to manage technology better as the firm undertook new business growth. The long-term outsourcing contract with Systematics moved a large portion (90 per cent) of the IS activities to the vendor. Except for a few network LAN systems, all other IS activities were shifted. This included all mainframe functions and developmental activities. The outsourcing contract was a substantial shift for this firm, even though they had limited experience with joint ventures in the IS area in the past. The bank viewed outsourcing as providing a cost effective means to improve technology. People's location in Lewiston, Maine had made specialized personnel recruitment and retention difficult. Outsourcing was viewed as a means for promoting a broad range of management objectives, including the personnel challenge.

Meritor Bank

Located in the Philadelphia area, Meritor was in severe financial distress and had to downsize drastically to survive. Their financial position drove the decision to outsource 100 per cent of the IS activities to EDS. Management's prime objective was to create a flexible and variable cost structure to facilitate the shrinking organization, but to poise itself for survival with as strong a technology capability as possible. The bank did not want to get entrenched into a position from which it could not recover.

First Fidelity Bancorporation

FFB was a medium-sized US bank which wanted to grow beyond its New Jersey and Pennsylvania boundaries. Streamlining costs, integrating systems, and restructuring the banking network in the restructuring US banking environment were prime motivations for senior management's consideration of IS outsourcing. Senior management had plans to radically grow the bank in the customer-oriented marketplace which was emerging. The president and the senior executive vice-president for Operations and Systems made the decision to outsource 75 per cent of the IS activities to EDS after extensive discussions with the internal IS management and IS consultants. The motivations focused on accommodating the bank's financial, integrative and growth objectives. Several major IS activities were transferred to EDS, some permanently and some temporarily. All transaction processing and network management were transferred permanently to EDS's care. Associated hardware, staff and procedures were taken over by the vendor. System integration of corporate-wide banking applications were undertaken by both the bank and the vendor. System development activities were temporarily transferred to the vendor for an initial two-year term, after which it would resort back to the bank's control.

At the same time, several major IS activities were maintained under FFB's control. Major IS planning and some application development stayed within the bank. This arrangement was made because FFB management was uncomfortable about relinquishing its organizational technology capability completely.

Republic Bank

In the New York area, Republic served commercial and conservative retail customers. The bank had an excellent track record of financial performance and was currently driven to consider outsourcing to improve cost structures and to access IS operational expertise that was lacking within the organization. The outsourcing contract with Systematics saw 85 per cent of the IS activities move over to the vendor. All activities except some very unique systems used to support industry-specific applications (such as precious metals trading) were outsourced. This included operations, systems programming and some application development. Republic had previously spun off its IS group into an independent subsidiary and the president of this subsidiary had made the decision to seek a technology partner.

Brenton Bank

Brenton was a medium-sized US bank in the Iowa area. The bank was experiencing fairly good financial performance, but was currently seeking to streamline costs, to restructure internally, and to establish closer links between business strategy and the IS department. These objectives stemmed from a desire to stay competitive as inter-state banking spread and larger competitors entered their markets. The outsourcing contract to Systematics saw 95 per cent of the IS activities being taken over by the vendor. Except for a unique branch automation platform (kept primarily for internal political reasons), all IS activities were transferred to Systematics. This included transaction processing and system development.

Gainer Bank

Serving the Indiana area, Gainer had grown into a medium-sized bank. The current challenges facing the bank stemmed from a desire to manage the risk associated with its IS personnel. Located in a small US town, the firm had a difficult time attracting and retaining competent IS staff with the right skills. Senior corporate management's financial concerns related to improving IS management and personnel, while trying to get good quality, centrally supported, systems. This decision was made by senior management who were also interested in making their institution a more attractive and easily integrated acquisition target. In this effort, Gainers outsourced 100 per cent of their IS activities to Systematics. Only a co-ordinating management team remained within the bank to integrate IS functions with the business activities.

Integra Bank

Integra Bank was a rapidly growing Pittsburg bank. Twenty years ago Integra began outsourcing IS activities to Systematics, but was currently trying to put additional pressure on Systematics to make further improvements on the quality of its IS products and services. The recent contract extension to outsource even more IS services saw 85 per cent of the activities fall under the vendor's control, with only internal LANs for office automation and personal computer support remaining within the firm's control. This decision to extend the scope of the relationship was made because Integra's senior management believed they were going to have more input into Systematics product development and service levels.

8
Information Systems Outsourcing: Theories, Case Evidence and a Decision Framework

LEON A. DE LOOFF

INTRODUCTION

One of the decisions that needs to be made by management in every organization, when (re)organizing the IS function, is the decision as to what part of the IS function is to be performed internally and what part could be better outsourced to external suppliers. IS suppliers often predict large cost reductions and improvements in quality and responsiveness if organizations hand over their IS function to them. Some client organizations, however, find themselves locked into unfavourable contracts or, with reorganization, internalize previously outsourced IS activities (Douglass, 1993; see also Chapter 11). As earlier chapters have indicated, public outsourcing reports are, nevertheless, often overly optimistic (Lacity and Willcocks, 1996) and currently, many organizations are still not that clear as to whether they can expect benefits from outsourcing. The objective of the research presented below is to provide support for the management of those organizations wishing to make IS sourcing decisions. The objective is achieved by analysing what effects can be expected from outsourcing part or all of an organization's IS function.

Strategic Sourcing of Information Systems.
Edited by L. P. Willcocks and M. C. Lacity.

Pilot Study

Before starting the research reported on here, a pilot study was made to determine whether the subject justified further research and to identify areas that needed additional investigation. This pilot study consisted of 30 interviews of personnel from client and supplier organizations involved in recent outsourcing decisions (Van der Vlis, 1993; Van der Vlis, Berghout and De Looff, 1993). The questions put during the interviews focused on the steps in the decision process, the functionaries involved in the decision process and the arguments they used. The following conclusions were drawn:

- Terminology in IS outsourcing is far from clear. Authors and practitioners use different terms for different concepts. This leads to non-comparable research results and to disagreements between clients and suppliers.
- Formal methods and a theoretical foundation for IS outsourcing decisions are largely lacking. Most authors merely state pro's and con's, without stating to which situations these effects apply and under which conditions the pro's outweigh the con's, or vice versa. Practitioners make decisions based on ideology, fashion and personal expectations instead of systematic analysis of actual consequences in comparable situations.
- Outsourcing can have numerous different effects, and organizations differ in the emphasis they put on the effects. For example, some organizations only considered cost reduction, while others emphasized improvements in quality of service or a reduction in staffing levels.
- Different arguments tend to apply to different types of outsourcing and to different types of information systems, IS components and IS activities.
- Arguments were also found to depend on the specific situation: the characteristics of the organization and responsible persons, the information systems in use, the competitive environment, the availability of appropriate suppliers, and a variety of other contingent factors.

Outline of the Study

The conclusions drawn in the pilot study justified further research, especially with regard to terminology, theoretical foundation and empirical research into actual consequences of IS outsourcing. A descriptional framework was developed to describe different types of outsourcing in a structured way. This was used for the case study research, and can be used by decision makers to describe alternatives in IS outsourcing decisions. Several organizational theories were applied to the IS outsourcing decision, to establish relationships between situational factors, types of outsourcing and the effects of outsourcing.

In-depth empirical research, aimed at testing the descriptional framework and validating the findings from the organizational theories, was conducted in a further six organizations. Each of these research directions is elaborated in the following sections.

IS OUTSOURCING FRAMEWORK

Outsourcing is what Williamson (1985) calls the "market versus hierarchy" decision. Rands (1992) calls it the "make-or-buy" decision, while Gurbaxani and Whang (1991) and Porter (1980) label it "vertical integration". In this study, IS outsourcing was defined as the situation in which part or all of the IS activities an organization needs are performed by one or more external suppliers. Changing from internal provision to outsourcing may involve the transfer of the IS staff or other resources needed to perform these activities, to the supplier's organization. The aggregate of IS activities an organization needs is referred to as the organization's IS function.

The definition used here is very broad and includes all sorts of external relationships, for example: hiring an external consultant to select a database management system; having a new order system developed, maintained and operated by an IS provider; selling the entire IS department including hardware and software and transferring IS personnel to an external supplier. Many terms have been introduced in the literature and in practice for these different types of outsourcing. Lacity and Hirschheim (1993) distinguish Body Shop (contracting personnel to meet short-term demand), Project Management (outsourcing a specific portion of IS work) and Total Outsourcing (putting the vendor in total charge of a significant piece of IS work). They differentiate between outsourcing Data Processing, Telecommunications, Planning, Strategic Systems or the entire IS department. Other terms include *pure versus hybrid outsourcing* (Buck-Lew, 1992), *systems integration, facilities management, data center privatization, service bureau* and *third party maintenance*. As is clear from other chapters, there is no consensus about the meaning of these terms, and many classifications are neither complete nor mutually exclusive (Ang, 1994). This makes analysis of theory and practice difficult and impedes rational decision making.

In this research, instead of choosing or redefining terms, the types of

I Dimensions of the IS function

Information systems	☐ Production IS	☐ Personnel IS	☒ Land Registry IS	☐ Fleet Management IS	and so on
IS components	☒ Hardware	☒ Software	☐ Data	☐ IS personnel	☒ Procedures
IS activities	☐ Planning	☒ Development	☒ Implementation	☒ Maintenance	☒ Operation

II Provider

Owned by client	☒ no	☐ partially	☐ totally
Dependent on client	☐ no	☒ partially	☐ totally

III Relationship between client and provider

Clients choice of provider	☒ free	☐ limited	☐ none		
Provider's choice of client	☒ free	☐ limited	☐ none		
Spanning multiple transactions	☐ no	☒ preferred position	☐ fixed conditions	☒ guaranteed spending	
Payment based on	☐ time and materials	☒ fixed free	☒ work load	☐ benefits to client	
Co-ordination mechanisms	☒ mutual adjustment	☐ direct supervision	☐ work process	☒ output	☐ skills
Resolving disputes	☐ litigation	☐ third party arbitration	☒ escalation procedures	☐ common authorities	

IV Arrangement — IS components

		Hardware	Software	Data	IS personnel	Procedures
Location	Client	☐	☐	☐	☐	n/a
	Supplier	☒	☒	☒	☒	
Ownership/ employment	Client	☐	☐	☒	☐	☐
	Supplier	☒	☒	☐	☒	☒
Exclusiveness	Dedicated	☐	☐	☒	☐	☐
	Dedicated	☒	☒	☐	☒	☒
Control	Client	☐	☐	☒	☐	☐
	Supplier	☒	☒	☐	☒	☒

Key: ☒ = present ☐ = absent

Figure 8.1 *Descriptional Framework for IS Outsourcing*

outsourcing will be described using the framework summarized in Figure 8.1. The variables in this figure can be filled in for each part of the IS function. Any combination is possible and any combination may be appropriate in particular circumstances. One of the cases of this research is filled in as an example, to demonstrate the use of the framework. Each of the variables is discussed below.

Dimensions of the IS Function

Outsourcing may involve all of an organization's IS function or part of it. Information systems can, as can all dynamic open systems, be described in analytical, functional and temporal terms (Brussard, 1988). The parts of the IS function can thus be described in terms of three dimensions: the functional *information systems*, the analytical *components* and the temporal *IS activities* (see Figure 8.2).

Information systems can be distinguished by the business process they support or control, i.e. the order scheduling IS, the financial IS, the IS for processing insurance claims and so on. An information system can be seen as consisting of five components: hardware, software, personnel and the procedures by which they work, and data. IS activities comprise the planning, development, implementation, maintenance and operation of information systems.

The three dimensions can be used to describe what part of an organization's IS function is outsourced, by determining what IS activities are

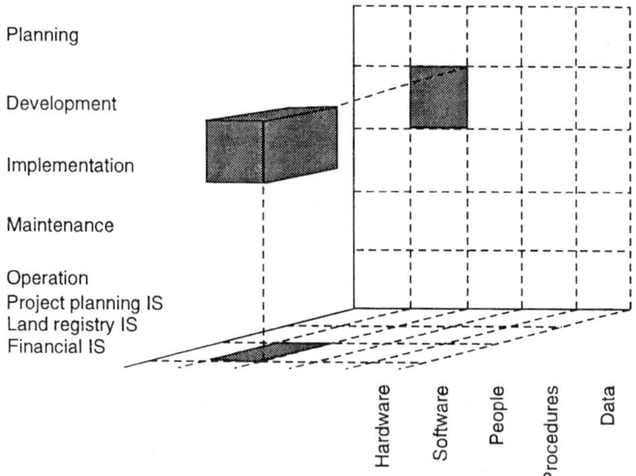

Figure 8.2 *Dimensions of the IS Function*

accomplished with regard to which components of what information system. An organization can, for example, decide to outsource the *development* of the *software* for the *financial IS*. This example is indicated by the grey cube in Figure 8.2.

The distinction between analytical and functional views is necessary because each of the analytical components can be used for more than one functional information system and vice versa (Brussard, 1988). For example, a database of the inventory of finished products can be used by both the inventory management system and the sales system. When outsourcing the sales system, provision must be made for this interconnectedness, to make sure both systems can use the database. The same holds for information systems using several kinds of hardware, or hardware used by several information systems, and for components used by more than one organization, such as inter-organizational information systems and IS joint ventures between organizations in the same industry.

Provider

A gradation can be seen in the distinction between internal and external providers. The provider can be:

- a business unit's IS department;
- a central IS department at the parent company;
- a separate IS company that is jointly owned by the client and:
  —several other organizations in the same industry
  —an independent supplier;
- an IS supplier with which the client has a relationship spanning multiple transactions, concerning for example, guaranteed spending, fixed tariffs or a preferred position
- an IS supplier who is heavily dependent upon the client for most of his business;
- an independent IS supplier with no connection to the client.

This list is neither complete nor disjunctive, and combinations can occur (Michell and Fitzgerald, 1997). The supplier may or may not be the client's former internal IS department (see Chapter 11 for examples of this form). In the framework, the gradation is indicated by the degree to which the provider is owned by the client, and whether the provider is dependent on the client for most of his business.

Relationship

The dichotomy of internal provision versus outsourcing is also not sharp: organizational arrangements exist between the extremes of pure *market* and pure *hierarchy* relationships. Williamson (1985) mentions three contracting modes and four corresponding governance modes (see Table 8.1; also Chapter 4). Ang and Beath (1993) note hierarchical elements in market relations regarding IS development (Table 8.2). Fitzgerald and Willcocks (1994) distinguish six types of contracts, some of which have hierarchical elements (Table 8.3). Conversely, Mantelaers (1995) found that market elements are applied in some hierarchical settings (Table 8.4).

The authors mentioned above stress different aspects of contracts and relationships. The taxonomy given in the framework in Figure 8.1 encompasses these aspects. The first two variables indicate whether the client and the supplier are free to choose their business partners. The relationship between client and supplier can be restricted to individual transactions or span multiple transactions. Payment can be based on different grounds, and several co-ordination mechanisms and mechanisms for resolving disputes are distinguished.

Outsourcing Arrangement

Ang (1994) describes outsourcing using three conceptualizations of organizational boundaries:

1. geographical (an activity is performed or located at or away from the premises of the business unit);
2. legal (property rights of physical assets and employment of personnel are maintained or relinquished by the client); and
3. control (behavioural control is maintained or relinquished by the client).

I make a further distinction between dedicated versus shared use of resources, leading to four variables for describing outsourcing arrangements: location, ownership and employment, dedicated or shared use, and control.

Hardware can be placed and personnel can work at the supplier's or the customer's site. Placing hardware and personnel at the supplier's site can lead to lower costs if office space at the customer's site is scarce or expensive, and to savings made because it is possible for the supplier to use hardware and personnel for multiple clients. However, customers may choose to keep hardware and personnel at their site, to

Table 8.1 *Contracting and Governance Modes*

Contracting mode		Corresponding governance mode(s)	
Classical contracting	Entails comprehensive contracting whereby all relevant future contingencies pertaining to the supply of a good or service are described and discounted	Market governance	Products are standardized. The relationship is not valued independently
Neoclassical contracting	Introduces flexibility, goodwill is often more important than the letter of the contract	Trilateral governance	Third party assistance is preferred over litigation
Relational contracting	Relational approach where the reference point is the entire relationship as it has developed through time	Bilateral governance	The autonomy of the parties is maintained
		Unified governance	The transaction is organized within the firm

Source: Williamson (1985). Reproduced by permission of Free Press.

Table 8.2. *Hierarchical Elements in IS Development Outsourcing Contracts*

Hierarchical element	Examples
Command structures and authority systems	One or both parties are authorized to make discretionary decisions, issue orders, or demand performance, such as the right to audit work-in-progress, to choose and to change personnel from contractor, or to cancel the project at pre-specified points
Ruled-based incentive systems	Penalties for delay in delivery
Standard operating procedures	Progress reports and meetings
Non-market based pricing systems	Cost-recovery pricing based on the value of the inputs, instead of market prices based on the value of the output
Informal dispute resolution mechanisms	Procedures for conflict resolution before parties take legal action. This usually involves escalation procedures in which the higher management of both parties or a third party try to resolve the dispute

Source: Ang and Beath (1993). Reproduced by permission of S. Ang.

have (a feeling of) more control over the resources (Ang, 1994). Hardware and software can be owned by the customer or the supplier, and personnel can have an employment relationship with the customer or with the supplier. In the latter case, the supplier's personnel work for the customer in a contractor relationship instead of an employment relationship (Ang, 1994). Supplier ownership of hardware and software allows for shared use of resources and can generate cash infusions if client resources are sold to the supplier. Ownership of resources and employment of personnel by the customer may increase control (Ang,

Table 8.3 *Types of Outsourcing Contracts*

Contract	Payment based on
Time and materials	the actual use of personnel and materials
Fixed fee	a lump sum for a defined work load or service
Fixed fee plus variable element	predicted changes in, for example, workloads or business circumstances
Cost plus management fee	the real costs incurred by the vendor plus a percentage
Fee plus incentive scheme	some benefits that accrue to the client company or performance over and above an agreed baseline
Share of risk and reward	how well the client company or a joint venture performs

Source: Fitzgerald and Willcocks, (1994). Reproduced by permission of International Conference on Information System.

Table 8.4 *Market Elements in Hierarchical Relationships*

Market element	Description
Internal transfer pricing	The IS department charges the business units for the services delivered
Free choice of provider	Business units are not obliged to take services from the internal IS department. The internal IS department has to compete with external IS suppliers on the internal "market"
External service provision	The internal IS department offers services to external organizations and competes with external IS suppliers on the external market.
Internal contracts	The middle managers agree with the top management to deliver certain output or meet certain targets using no more than an agreed amount of resources

Source: Mantelaers (1995). Reproduced by permission of P. Mantelaers.

1994) but will increase fixed costs and decrease flexibility in the IS activities portfolio.

If hardware or software is owned and personnel is employed by the supplier, the customer can choose to have dedicated, exclusive use of these resources, or let the supplier share these resources between multiple customers. Dedicated use may be chosen for security reasons, to keep intellectual rights or to maintain competitive use of software. Shared use will increase the possibility of economies of scale. Information systems activities can be controlled by the supplier or by the client. Willcocks and Fitzgerald (1993) distinguish "commissioning of a third party ... to manage a client organization's [Information Technology] assets, people and/or activities", which they call outsourcing, and "contracts which call for the market to provide resources to be deployed under the buyer's management and control", which Lacity, Willcocks and Feeney (1995) call insourcing.

Using the Framework

The framework can be used by management in organizations to describe different outsourcing options in a decision process, or to evaluate actual IS outsourcing situations. An IS outsourcing situation or option can be described by marking the appropriate boxes. The example in Figure 8.1 is case number 4 of the Appendix, and comprised the outsourcing of the development, implementation, maintenance and operation of the hardware, software and procedures for the public land registry. The supplier was not owned by the client, but the client represented about a quarter of the supplier's business volume. The client and the provider were both free to choose their business partners, but the supplier had a preferred position and the client had guaranteed to spend a certain amount with the supplier. The system was developed for a fixed fee, while operation was charged based on the workload. The client co-operated with the supplier by specifying the required output, and, during the development, by mutual adjustment between the IS personnel and the future users of the system. Disputes were resolved by higher management, following escalation procedures. All components were located at the supplier's site. The supplier owned and controlled all components except the client's data, and shared the components among multiple clients. The client owned and controlled the data.

THEORETICAL FOUNDATIONS

Several organizational theories were applied to establish a theoretical foundation for IS outsourcing decisions. Table 8.5 summarizes these theories by describing the assumptions and major constructs, and the way the theories can be applied to IS outsourcing. The table also gives the major author(s) on each theory and the authors who apply the theory to the IS outsourcing decision.

CASE STUDIES

The objective of the case study research was to test the descriptional framework and to examine the implications derived from the organizational theories. In-depth longitudinal case study research was conducted into the actual effects of outsourcing. Most of the empirical studies available currently are based upon opinions and expectations of stakeholders, before or shortly after signing a contract for IS outsourcing. The pilot study indicated, however, that the positive and negative consequences of outsourcing only become apparent after one or more years, for example at the time of contract renewal or when the customer is switching to another supplier or internalizes the IS activities (see also Chapters 4 and 11). The case studies therefore encompassed the outsourcing decision process as well as implementation of the IS outsourcing and an evaluation of the decision, after one or two years. Cases were selected for:

- Retrospective research into terminated outsourcing processes (up to ten years back);
- Longitudinal research into current outsourcing processes, during two succeeding years following a decision on IS outsourcing.

Table 8.5 *Organizational Theories applied to IS Outsourcing*

Theory and Major Authors	Assumptions	Major Constructs	Implications for IS Outsourcing
Division of Labour (Adam Smith, in Douma and Schreuder, 1992)	Efficiency increases when activities are performed on a larger scale	Scale	If a supplier performs certain activities on a larger scale as the client, outsourcing increases efficiency
Micro economics Douma and Schreuder (1992)	In a perfect market, only suppliers that produce a certain good in the most efficient way will eventually survive	Conditions for a perfect market: —many independent buyers and sellers —free market entry and exit —standardized products —perfect information on price and products	Outsourcing is advisable only if the corresponding market largely complies to conditions for a perfect market
Co-ordination Theory (Mintzberg, 1979; Ang, 1994)	Organizing consists of division of labour and creating co-ordination. Co-ordination is easier within a group than between groups	Co-ordination mechanisms: —mutual adjustment —direct supervision —standardization of work process —standardization of output —standardization of skills	Internally: all mechanisms applicable Outsourcing: standardization of skills (selection of supplier) and output (requirements in contract)
Transaction Cost Theory (Williamson, 1975, 1985; Aubert 1993, 1994; Lacity and Hirschheim 1993, 1994; Loh, 1994; Loh and Venkatraman, 1992)	Most markets are imperfect. Transactions are governed by market or hierarchy depending on which mechanism is most efficient for that transaction	Characteristics of transactions: —uncertainty —bounded rationality —number of suppliers (ex ante or ex post) —frequency —asset specificity	Outsourcing is not recommended for IS activities if: —uncertainty is high —client has insufficient knowledge of IS (market) —number of suppliers (ex ante or ex post) is small —frequency is high —asset specificity is high

Agency Theory (Jensen and Meckling, 1976; Eisenhardt, 1989; Gurbaxani and Kemerer, 1989)	Principal and agent may have inconsistent goals Principal can not perfectly and costlessly monitor the actions of the agent	Good incongruence Information asymmetries Measurability Uncertainty Incentive schemes Monitoring mechanisms	Goal incongruence and information asymmetries are larger in outsourcing Outsourcing is not recommended when measurability is low and uncertainty is high In outsourcing, incentive schemes and monitoring mechanisms reduce goal incongruence and information asymmetries
Power (Pfeffer, 1981; Lacity and Hirschheim, 1993)	Stakeholders promote their position by using power	Sources of power: authority, creating dependencies, providing resources, absorbing uncertainty and being irreplaceable Political tactics: selective use of decision criteria and information, use of outside experts, building coalitions and co-operation	—Power and political tactics are present in outsourcing decision processes —Distribution of power will be changed by outsourcing —Outsourcing is not recommended if supplier is expected to be more powerful
Competitive Strategy (Porter, 1980, 1985)	Competitive position of an organization is determined by five competitive threats	competitive threats: —rivalry among existing firms —bargaining power of suppliers —bargaining power of buyers —threat of new entrants —threat of substitute goods	—Outsourcing may influence an organization's competitive use of information technology —Integration of the IS function raises barriers for potential entrants —If the bargaining power of IS suppliers is large, then outsourcing is dangerous

The questions in this case study research focused on the actual changes and improvements due to outsourcing, instead of the opinions and the personal expectations of interested parties.

Research Design

Case study research is defined as research in which a small number of entities is examined with regard to a large number of variables, and no experimental control is used (Nissen, Klein and Hirschheim, 1991). It is a useful strategy for contemporary phenomena, closely related in their context, where no control of independent variables is possible (which makes experiments untenable) (Benbasat, Goldstein and Mead, 1987; Yin, 1984). Case study research is also needed when consistent terminology is not available and the measuring of relevant variables is complex and labour intensive, making large-scale surveys unfeasible (De Looff and Berghout, 1994). IS outsourcing complies with these criteria (De Looff, 1994).

Yin (1984) proposes several tactics for increasing the quality of a research design, aimed at improving construct validity, internal and external validity and reliability. To improve construct validity, multiple sources of evidence should be used. The following case studies used interviews with well-informed personnel from client organizations and documentation on the outsourcing decisions and on the outsourced IS activities. A chain of evidence was established by asking explicitly whether certain positive or negative consequences of outsourcing were caused by certain circumstances and the specific type of outsourcing. Interviewees were asked to clarify these presumed relationships.

Internal validity was improved by comparing cases to see if similar decisions in different situations or different decisions in similar situations led to different consequences, in the way the theories predicted. Each situation was also investigated before and immediately after the implementation of an outsourcing decision and at the time the consequences of the decision became clear. To maximize external validity, the cases were selected deliberately to obtain variety in all the relevant variables, especially in type of organization, type of outsourcing arrangement and whether the outsourcing succeeded or not.

To increase reliability, all procedures were written down in a case study protocol. The protocol covered selection of cases and interviewees, the preparation for the interviews, and data collection and analysis. All data was kept in a case study database. For each case, the following items were stored:

- name of the organization
- name and position of interviewee(s)

- interview report(s)
- references to documents
- summaries of documents
- case study report.

Data Collection

The information needed for the research was obtained from the IS management and the general management of the participating client organizations, at both the top and the user department level. Table 8.6 summarizes the positions of the interviewees, most of whom were staff of the central IS department or IS manager of a user department. These functionaries were well informed and available for interviewing.

The interviews were semi-structured using a list of subjects. Each of the variables in the study was operationalized in specific questions. Each subject was discussed in each interview, although not necessarily in same order. Interviewees were free to elaborate on each subject within time constraints. Additional questions were asked, if necessary, to complete the required information per subject. No tape recorder was used but notes were taken in the interviews, which took between one and two hours. The data gathered from interviews was compared to documentation provided by the interviewees. Interviewees suggested both formal and informal documents, relating to all phases of the outsourcing decision and the implementation. Documents included:

- internal memoranda from parties involved in the outsourcing decisions: top management, IS staff, unions, external advisors and IS suppliers;
- external assessments of internal IS services and IS suppliers;
- project documentation, (requests for) proposals, contracts, bills and correspondence.

Table 8.6 *Positions of Interviewees*

Position	Number of Interviewees
Top	
General manager (CEO/CFO)	3
IS manager (CIO)	5
IS staff	19
User departments	
General Manager	3
IS manager	27
IS staff	4

Data analysis

The notes of each interview were transcribed into an interview report, and each document was summarized. A case study report was compiled for each case, based on data obtained from the interview(s) and documents. Each case study report was given a standardized structure, in which all relevant variables were grouped chronologically, and the value of all the variables was determined for each case. If interviewees expanded on a subject, their explanation was added to the report. In cases where interviewees and/or documents disagreed, the interviewees were requested to clarify the situation.

Both quantitative and qualitative analysis was performed. The quantitative analysis consisted of counting how many cases fell into each of the categories and how many confirmed or rejected the propositions, while the qualitative analysis consisted of looking at the explanations of the interviewees, the causal structures and the exceptions and adjustments made to the implications derived from the organizational theories.

Description Of Cases

A total of 23 IS outsourcing arrangements within six organizations was investigated in this research project for a period of two years. The organizations that participated are presented in Table 8.7, while the case studies are described briefly in the Appendix. Cases and interviewees are not presented with the corresponding organization, to preserve the anonymity and confidentiality of the interviewees and their organizations.

Presentation of the results of the case studies is restricted to the cross-case analysis; confidentiality and space constraints impede describing individual cases, except as typical examples of, or exceptions to the findings. Qualitative data, explanations and background information are added, if applicable. The numbers in the following tables do not always add up to the total number of cases or interviewees. Some questions did not apply to all of the cases and some cases fell into more than one category. Full details of the case study results can be found in De Looff (1996b).

Decision Process

Table 8.8 summarizes the positions of the functionaries officially involved in the IS outsourcing decisions, and their attitude towards the

Table 8.7 *Organizations Participating in the Case Study Research*

	RWS	Ministry of Social Affairs	Dutch Railways	Central Bureau of Statistics	Municipality of Eindhoven	DSM
Expenditure (million Dfl*)	2900	35 000	4200	300	1200	8000
Number of employees	10 000	2400	29 000	2500	2100	21 000
Industry	Government	Government	Transport	Research	Local government	Manufacturing
Primary process	Public works and water management	Social security, employment and labour conditions	Transport of passengers and freight	Providing social and economic statistics	Maintaining the local infrastructure	Producing chemicals for the global market

*1 Dfl (Dutch guilder) is approximately £0.40 or US$ 0.65

Table 8.8 *Functionaries Involved in Decision Process and Attitude Towards Outsourcing Decision*

	For	Against
Top		
General manager (CEO/CFO)	9	0
IS manager (CIO)	2	6
IS staff	0	4
User departments		
General manager	5	2
IS manager	13	2
IS staff	1	0

outsourcing decision. All outsourcing decisions that involved the transfer of people were taken by general top management.

A formal method for IS outsourcing decisions was not used in any of the cases. Interviewees indicated that such methods were not available, and that they believed IS outsourcing decisions were too strategic or political to be captured by formal analysis. Decisions were based mainly on ideology ("markets are inherently more efficient") or staff level reduction programmes. Little analysis was made of the current situation and possibility for internal improvements. The lead time of the decision process was on average 13 per cent of the length of the resulting contract. In some cases, outsourcing was seen as mandatory, and internal provision was not considered.

In most cases involving the transfer of people or resources to a supplier, the decision process took significantly more time. In one extreme case, it took three years to outsource the IS department, with a subsequent contract for three years. The actual decision to outsource, however, was often made at a very early stage and by very few people, usually top or financial management, at a level where no detailed knowledge of the IS function and the IS market was present.

The criteria the decision makers used in their decisions are provided in Table 8.9, together with the importance the general management and the IS management attached to each of the criteria. Top management today puts a strong and one-sided emphasis on cost reduction or a reduction in staffing levels, almost irrespective of the consequences. Other criteria, such as quality, flexibility and competitive use of IT, are hardly ever valued as important by general management. This confirms one conclusion of Lacity and Hirschheim (1994) that in many cases "outsourcing appears to be a symptom of the problem of demonstrating the value of IS".

Many outsourcing decisions were forced by constraints from higher

Table 8.9 *Importance of Criteria for Outsourcing as Perceived by General and IS Management*

	General management			IS management		
	low	med	high	low	med	high
Costs	2	3	18	4	8	11
Lead time	4	12	7	3	14	6
Efficiency	4	5	14	4	11	8
Staffing levels	3	2	18	4	7	12
Quality	9	6	8	3	4	16
Flexibility	7	11	5	5	11	7
Controllability	5	12	6	3	13	7
Continuity	10	10	3	5	13	5
Competitiveness	18	3	2	13	8	5

authorities (Table 8.10). After most of the large-scale outsourcing operation, subsequent IS activities had to be outsourced, often to the same supplier, because of a shortage of staff and other resources, or because of contractual obligations, even when interviewees believed a particular activity would be performed better internally or by another supplier.

As can be seen from Table 8.11, maintaining internal provision, possibly with internal improvements, was seldom considered in the decision process. Even if internal provision *was* considered, the comparison was often inadequate and not based on systematic analysis. Co-operation with other organizations in the same industry was considered in seven cases, but actually chosen in no more than two cases. In the remaining five cases, co-operation was rejected or had failed because the pertinent organizations could not agree on the requirements or the strategy.

Type of Outsourcing

Tables 8.12 and 8.13 summarize the IS activities, IS components and information systems involved in the cases of this research.

Table 8.10 *Constraints in the Decision Process*

Contraints	No. of cases
Shortage of staff and not allowed to hire personnel	13
Outsourcing is company policy	4
Obliged to take services from internal provider	1

Table 8.11 *Alternatives for Outsourcing Considered in the Decision Process*

Alternatives	Number of Cases
Internal provision	3
Internal provision with improvements:	
consolidation	3
internal transfer pricing	4
free choice of provider	1
internal contracts	1
external service provision	2
Co-operation with other organizations in same industry	7

Table 8.12 *Number of Cases of Outsourcing IS Activities with Regard to IS Components*

	IS Components				
IS activities	Software	Hardware	Data	People	Procedures
Planning	2	2	2	2	2
Development	17	13	12	12	15
Implementation	15	12	10	11	13
Maintenance	16	13	10	11	13
Operation	11	11	9	8	8

Table 8.13 *Number of Cases of Outsourcing IS Activities with Regard to Informtion Systems*

	Information systems		
IS activities	office automation	support systems	primary systems
Planning	2	2	2
Development	4	7	15
Implementation	4	8	12
Maintenance	5	9	13
Operation	6	9	11

Table 8.14 *Number of Cases in each Type of Outsourcing*

II Provider					
Owned by client	no 20	partially 0	totally 3		
Dependent on client	no 10	partially 5	totally 8		
III Relationship between client and provider					
Client's choice of provider	free 12	limited 4	none 7		
Provider's choice of client	free 21	limited 2	none 0		
Spanning multiple transactions	no 9	preferred position 12	fixed conditions 11	guaranteed spending 12	
Payment based on	time and materials 18	fixed fee 8	workload 9	benefits to client 0	
Co-ordination mechanisms	mutual adjustment 13	direct supervision 8	work process 5	output 20	skills 15
Resolving disputes	litigation 14	third party arbitration 2	escalation procedures 10	common authorities 4	

IV Arrangement		IS components				
		Hardware	Software	Data	IS Personnel	Procedures
Location	Client	15	15	15	5	n/a
	Supplier	8	8	8	18	
Ownership/ employment	Client	15	16	23	0	17
	Supplier	8	7	0	23	6
Exclusiveness	Dedicted	16	17	23	2	18
	Shared	7	6	0	21	5
Control	Client	15	16	23	4	17
	Supplier	8	7	0	19	6

Table 8.14 summarizes how many cases fell in each of the categories of the other variables that describe the type of outsourcing.

The client owned the supplier in no more than three cases, but the supplier was partially or totally dependent upon the client for their business volume in 13 cases. For most of these 13 cases, this was explained by the fact that the supplier was the former internal IS department of the client, and the outsourced department had not (yet) managed to engage a significant number of other clients.

Relationships spanning multiple transactions were found in half the number of cases, again mainly between clients and their former internal IS departments. Payment based on time and materials was used mostly for planning and for development of innovative information systems, because specifying requirements for these activities is difficult. Contracts in which payment was based on some benefits that accrued to the client company were not found in this research. This type of contract is perhaps not yet accepted widely, at least in the Netherlands. Some interviewees replied that it would be very difficult to use this type of payment, because many other factors besides the performance of the supplier influence the benefits.

Co-ordination by mutual adjustment was found in the cases of former internal IS departments, between employees that used to be colleagues before the IS department was outsourced. In these cases, the relationship was not that businesslike, contracts were not relied on, and most contracts were too informal to do so. Resolving disputes by third party arbitration appeared just twice. In none of the 14 cases that involved litigation were disagreements actually brought to court. Escalation procedures appeared to be quite common, especially between parties with a long-term relationship.

Hardware, software and procedures were located, owned and controlled by, the supplier and shared among multiple clients in one-third of the cases. Data was located at the supplier's site in the same cases, but never owned or controlled by the supplier or shared among clients. In almost all cases, the IS personnel was located at, and employed and controlled by, the supplier and used by multiple clients. Some clients preferred to have the IS personnel at their own site and under their control.

Selection of Supplier

Selecting a supplier comprises determining which suppliers might be appropriate for certain IS activities, requesting a proposal, and evaluating the proposals. Table 8.15 lists the functionaries involved in the selection process.

Table 8.15 *Functionaries Involved in Selection Process*

	Number of cases
Top	
General manager (CEO)	5
IS manager (CIO)	4
IS staff	2
User departments	
General manager	5
IS manager	9
IS staff	3

Formal criteria for the selection of a supplier were found in no more than nine out of 23 cases. In the other 14 cases, selection was based on general impressions of the appropriateness of the supplier. A formal method to evaluate suppliers was used in no more than three out of the nine cases in which formal criteria were used. The methods that were used included assessment of the value of the criteria by more than one functionary, using objective measures to assess the value, and deriving the choice of the supplier from the scores in a formalized way. In other cases, criteria were assessed by one functionary, based on personal impressions or data provided by the suppliers.

Even in the cases where formal criteria or evaluation methods were used, the actual choice was sometimes determined by personal impressions and preferences, the method being used mainly to rationalize and justify the choice.

The criteria for selection included characteristics of the suppliers and of their proposals (see Table 8.16). The six clients that bought ready-made software packages hardly analysed the characteristics of the supplier, even though this was found to be important for the continuity of the support and the release of new versions. Whether the client valued the supplier's experience in the client's business process and industry, or in the pertinent technology, activity and type of outsourcing, depended upon the specificness of the outsourced activity. For the outsourcing of firm-specific systems, it is more important that the supplier knows the business process and industry, than for outsourcing non-specific systems or infrastructural components such as the client's network, and vice versa.

The consequences for the IS personnel were valued as very important in all of the five cases that involved the transfer of personnel to the supplier.

A criterion that was remarkable for its absence was the power of the

Table 8.16 *Importance of Criteria for Selection of Supplier*

Criteria	Importance		
	Low	Medium	High
Supplier size			
—people	4	5	2
—revenue	4	5	2
Financial position	5	3	2
Specialism			
—pertinent technology	1	3	12
—pertinent activity	3	5	10
—pertinent business process	3	3	8
—pertinent type of outsourcing	6	5	4
—industry of client	4	5	5
Proposal			
—costs	3	7	8
—lead time	1	11	6
—quality	0	3	16
—consequences for personnel	11	1	5

supplier with respect to the client, measured by, for example, the relative size of the supplier and the percentage of the workload the client represented.

Implementation

The lead time for the implementation of the outsourcing decision was on average 23 per cent of the length of the contract. Lead time included preparing the requests for proposals, evaluating the proposals, negotiating the contract(s), and the actual transition time to the new situation. The costs of the implementation were, on average, 12 per cent of the total costs of the outsourced activities. These costs included the initial costs of moving people and hardware, and the cost of productivity loss during the transition period. The initial costs and the lead time were significantly higher if the outsourcing included the transfer of people and hardware (21 per cent versus 7 per cent) and were almost always higher than expected by the interviewees.

Consequences

The consequences of the IS outsourcing decisions in the cases investigated are categorized in Table 8.17. Low controllability was not always caused by the supplier. Sometimes the client's budget and

Table 8.17 *Number of Cases in each Category of Consequence of IS Outsourcing*

Consequence	Category			
Costs (million of Dfl*)	<1 mDfl	1–5 mDfl	5–50 mDfl	>50 mDfl
	3	7	8	4
Lead time (years)	<1 year	1–2 years	2-3 years	>3 years
	5	7	7	4
Efficiency (% of optimum)	<80%	80–90%	90–95%	>95%
	5	4	6	8
Staffing levels (reduction in full time equivalents)	0 fte	1–200 fte	>200 fte	
	17	3	3	
Quality (meeting requirements)	low	medium	high	
	4	13	6	
Flexibility (% extra time and costs of changes)	>20%	10–20%	5–10%	<5%
	2	4	4	13
Controllability of:	>150	120–150	105–120	<105
—costs (actual compared to budget)	3	4	9	7
—lead time (actual compared to planning)	4	5	9	5
Continuity	low	medium	high	
	6	12	5	
Competiveness	low	medium	high	n/a
	1	3	2	17

* 1 Dfl (Dutch guilder) is approximately £0.40 or US$ 0.65.

Table 8.18 *Number of Cases in each Category of Circumstances*

Circumstances	Category			
Scale (scale of supplier compared to scale of client for	same scale	2–3 times	4–5 times	>5 times
pertinent activity)	8	2	4	9
Interconnectedness with:	0	1–2	3–4	>4
—number of other information systems	10	4	2	7
—number of other IS components	9	6	0	8
—number of other IS activities	0	17	3	3
Number of suppliers (number of acceptable proposals	1	2–3	4–5	>5
received)	9	11	2	1
Number of separate transactions	1	2–3	4–5	>5
	6	8	3	6
Specifiability	low	medium	high	
	10	7	6	
Measurability	low	medium	high	
	10	10	3	
Uncertainty	low	medium	high	
	4	10	9	
Specificness	client	industry	all firms	
	14	7	2	
Innovativeness (new to both client and supplier, one of them,	both	one	neither	
or neither of them)	14	5	4	
Power of provider	<20%	20–50%	50–80%	>80%
—importance of client to provider (% of sales)	12	3	4	4
—importance of provider to client (% of spending)	4	13	5	1
	<10%	10–20%	>20%	
—costs and time to change provider (% of total)	10	7	6	

planning were unrealistic, or clients changed or added to the requirements, after the activities had started. The cases with low or medium continuity included suppliers that went bankrupt, but also cases where the supplier was taken over. In other cases, the supplier stopped releasing new versions of software packages or no longer supported old versions. The turnover of IS personnel provided by some suppliers was very high.

Circumstances

A number of the circumstances that organizational theories predict to be of influence to IS outsourcing are presented in Table 8.18.

The supplier performed the outsourced activities at the same scale as the client in eight cases. Economies of scale were not achieved in these cases, even though that was often cited as an advantage of outsourcing. The highly interconnected cases included outsourcing of the client's network or other parts of the technical infrastructure. If the quality of service in these cases was low, disagreements often arose as to who was responsible for solving the problem: the provider of the network services, or the provider of the systems using the network.

It is remarkable that in 20 out of the 23 cases three or fewer adequate proposals were received, and that in nine of those cases just a single proposal was adequate. Separate transactions with separate contracts were endorsed for consecutive IS activities or for different subsystems. This improved controllability, because estimates of costs and lead time were more accurate after the previous activities were finished, and because the client had the option to switch to another supplier for other transactions. The separate transactions led, however, to some coordination problems, if separate transactions were outsourced to different suppliers.

The distribution of power between client and supplier, measured by the percentage of spending and business volume, was more or less equal. The client was more powerful in seven cases, while the supplier depended more upon the client in 12 cases. The costs and time to change to another supplier, or to internalize the outsourced activities, was over 20 per cent of total costs and time in six cases, which gave these suppliers additional power to "lock in" the client.

CONCLUSIONS

A descriptional framework for IS outsourcing was used to describe different types of outsourcing, in terms of the part of the IS function involved, the outsourcing relationship and provider and the variables location, ownership/employment, dedicated versus shared use and control. The framework was very useful for structuring the findings from the organizational theories, as well as for describing the individual cases systematically.

A theoretical foundation for the IS outsourcing decision was derived from established organizational theories. Theories found to be applicable included theories on division of labour, standard economic theory, co-ordination theory, transaction cost economics, agency theory and theories on power in organizations and competitive strategy. This supports and complements the contents of the chapters in Part One of this book.

The descriptional framework and the findings from the organizational theories were investigated by longitudinal in-depth case study research into 23 IS outsourcing arrangements. The case research focused on actual improvements instead of opinions and expectations of stakeholders, and comprised retrospective research going back for up to ten years and longitudinal research over a period of two years. This covered long-term consequences, thus revealing impacts of outsourcing that may be significant but not apparent on shorter time horizons. Large outsourcing decisions tend to be taken mainly by top or financial management and involve different stakeholders with different interests and perceptions with regard to the IS function (see Introduction).

The research has a number of implications for the management of sourcing decisions and arrangements. Thus the case studies show that outsourcing is advisable only in situations where the advantages of scale can be ascertained, sufficient suppliers are available, the requirements for services can be specified in advance and measured afterwards, and activities are not highly interconnected. Organizations choosing outsourcing should be aware of the fact that potential improvements are not established automatically. An effort has to be made to enforce improvements, and to make sure that the advantages of these improvements benefit, at least partly, their organization. As argued by Lacity, Willcocks and Feeny, (1995), arrangements that minimize dependency, such as multiple suppliers and different suppliers for consecutive phases, appear to give the best results.

A lack of systematic analysis was observed in the early stages of most outsourcing decisions. Information systems outsourcing decisions should start with analysing the current situation thoroughly, by examining the problems that gave rise to considering outsourcing and evaluating all available internal and external alternatives. Outsourcing decisions have long-term impacts and must be based on a long-term IS strategy. This strategy should include analysis of the IS activities to be performed, evaluation of the internal IS services, the possibility for internal improvement and the evaluation of all expected effects of IS outsourcing.

A decision model was developed (De Looff, 1996a, 1996b), that can then be used by the management of organizations that are (re)organizing their IS function, or are considering measures to improve the quality and efficiency of the IS activities. The framework and the results of the case study research were incorporated in the model, together with recommendations with regard to the decision process.

REFERENCES

Ang, S. (1994) Towards Conceptual Clarity of Outsourcing, in Glasson, B. *et al.* (eds), Proceedings of the IFIP TC8 Open Conference on Business Process Re-engineering, Gold Coast Queensland, Australia, 8–11 May, 131–141.

Ang, S. and Beath, C. M. (1993) Hierarchical Elements in Software Contracts, *Journal of Organizational Computing*, **3**, 3, 329–361.

Aubert, B., Rivard, S. and Patry, M. (1993) A Transaction Costs Approach to Outsourcing: Some Empirical Evidence, in Gallupe, B. and Todd, P. (eds), Proceedings of the ASAC IS Division, 14, Lake Louise, 164–175.

Aubert, B., Rivard, S. and Patry, M. (1994) Development of Measures to Assess Dimensions of IS Operation Transactions, in DeGross, J., Huff, S., and Munro, M. (eds), Proceedings of the Fifteenth International Conference on Information Systems, Vancouver, Canada, 13–26.

Benbasat, I., Goldstein, D. and Mead, M. (1987) The Case Research Strategy in Studies of Information Systems, *MIS Quarterly*, **11**, 3, 369–386.

Brussard, B. K. (1988) Information Resource Management in the Public Sector. *Information and Management*, 15, 85–92.

Buck-Lew, M. (1992) To Outsource or Not? *International Journal of Information Management*, 12, 3–20.

Douma, S. and Schreuder, H. (1992) *Economic Approaches to Organizations*, Englewood Cliffs, New Jersey: Prentice Hall.

Douglass, D. (ed.) (1993) New Wrinkles in IS Outsourcing, *I/S Analyzer*, 31, 9.

Eisenhardt, K. (1989) Agency Theory: An Assessment and Review, *Academy of Management Review*, **14**, 1, 57–74.

Fitzgerald, G. and Willcocks, L. (1994) Contracts and Partnerships in the Outsourcing of IT, in DeGross, J. I., Huff, S. L. and Munro, M. C. (eds), Proceedings of the Fifteenth International Conference on Information Systems, Vancouver, Canada, 91–98.

Gurbaxani, V. and Kemerer, C. F. (1989) An Agent-theoretic Perspective on the Management of Information Systems, in Proceedings of the 22nd Hawaii International Conference on System Sciences, 141–150.

Gurbaxani, V. and Whang, S. (1991) The Impact of Information Systems on Organizations and Markets, *Communications of the ACM*, **34**, 1, 59–73.

Jensen, M. C. and Meckling, W. H. (1976) Theory of the Firm: Managerial Behaviour, Agency Costs and Ownership Structure, *Journal of Financial*

Economics, 3, 305–360.
Lacity, M. C. and Hirschheim, R. (1993) *Information Systems Outsourcing; Myths, Metaphors and Realities*, Chichester: John Wiley and Sons.
Lacity, M. and Hirschheim, R. (1994) IS Outsourcing Evaluations: Lessons from the Field, in Glasson, B. C. *et al.* (eds), Proceedings of the IFIP TC8 Open Conference on Business Process Re-engineering, Gold Coast Queensland, Australia, 8–11 May, 363–373.
Lacity, M. and Willcocks, L. (1996) Best Practices in Information Technology Sourcing, Oxford Executive Research Briefings No. 2, Templeton College, Oxford.
Lacity, M., Willcocks, L. and Feeny, D. (1996) The Value of Selective IT Sourcing, *Sloan Management Review*, **37**, 3, 13–25.
Lacity, M., Willcocks, L. and Feeny, D. (1995) IT Outsourcing: Maximize Flexibility and Control, *Harvard Business Review*, May–June, 84–93.
Loh, L. (1994) An Organizational-Economic Blueprint for Information Technology Outsourcing: Concepts and Evidence, in DeGross, J., Huff, S., and Munro, M. (eds), Proceedings of the Fifteenth International Conference on Information Systems, Vancouver, Canada, 73–90.
Loh, L. and Venkatraman, N. (1992) Determinants of Information Technology Outsourcing: A Cross-Sectional Analysis, *Journal of Management Information Systems*, **9**, 1, 7–24.
Looff, L. A. de (1994) Decision Support for Outsourcing the IS function, Proceedings of the Ernst and Young/ICIS Doctoral Consortium of the Fifteenth Annual International Conference on Information Systems, Vancouver, Canada.
Looff, L. A. de (1996a) Information Systems Outsourcing: Innovative Concept for Leaner Information Systems Management? Proceedings of the 1996 IRMA International Conference, Washington, 22–25 May.
Looff, L. A. de (1996b) A Model for Information Systems Outsourcing Decision Making, PhD Thesis, Delft University of Technology, The Netherlands.
Looff, L. A. de, and Berghout, E. W. (1994) Research Strategies in IS (in Dutch), Research Report TWI 94–17, Delft University of Technology, Delft, The Netherlands.
Mantelaers, P. (1995) Information Capacity Engineering (in Dutch), PhD Thesis, Delft University of Technology, Delft, The Netherlands.
Michell, V. and Fitzgerald, G. (1997) The IT Outsourcing Marketplace: Vendors and Their Selection, *Journal of Information Technology*, **12**, 3, 130–148.
Mintzberg, H. (1979) *The Structuring of Organizations*, Englewood Cliffs, New Jersey: Prentice Hall.
Nissen, H. -E., Klein, H. and Hirschheim, R. (eds) (1991) Information Systems Research: Contemporary Approaches and Emergent Traditions, in Proceedings of the IFIP TC8/WG 8. 2 Working Conference, Copenhagen, Denmark.
Pfeffer, J. (1981) *Power in Organizations*, Marshfield, Massachusetts: Pitman.
Porter, M. E. (1980) *Competitive Strategy: Techniques for Analyzing Industries and Competitors*, New York: The Free Press.
Porter, M. E. and V. E. Millar (1985) How Information Gives You Competitive Advantage, *Harvard Business Review*, **63**, 4, 59–81.
Rands, T. (1992) The Key Role of Applications Software Make-or-Buy Decisions, *Journal of Strategic Information System*, **1**, 4, 215–223.
Vlis, P. K. van der, (1993) Outsourcing the IS Function (in Dutch), Master Thesis, Delft University of Technology, The Netherlands.

Vlis, P. van der, Looff, L. de and Berghout, E. (1993) Mutual Trust is Essential; Research into Outsourcing Decisions (in Dutch), *Computable*, 5 November, 17–21.
Willcocks, L. and Fitzgerald, G. (1993) Market as Opportunity? Case Studies in Outsourcing Information Technology and Services, *Journal of Strategic Information Systems*, **2**, 3, 223–242.
Williamson, O. E. (1975) *Markets and Hierarchies*, New York: MacMillan.
Williamson, O. E. (1985) *The Economic Institutions of Capitalism*, Sage: Free Press.
Yin, R. (1984) *Case Study Research: Design and Methods*, Newbury Park: Sage.

ACKNOWLEDGEMENTS

I would like to thank all the organizations and interviewees involved in this study for their co-operation. The research is supported by a grant of the Dutch Ministry of Home Affairs. I thank Bas Brussaard, Egon Berghout and Miranda Aldham-Breary for their comments on earlier drafts.

APPENDIX A : LIST OF CASES

1. Development of a system to predict air pollution by road traffic on proposed routes of motorways. It was intended to be performed in co-operation with the Ministry of the Environment.
2. Development, implementation, maintenance and operation of a system for planning and managing maintenance of buildings and installations. During the development, another database management system was prescribed.
3. Selection, implementation and operation of a software package for calculating and paying social security benefits. One of the first software packages available for this complicated and fast-changing area.
4. Development, implementation, maintenance and operation of a system for the public land registry. The system was highly connected with the system for taxes on real estate, and the new system speeded the collection of taxes considerably.
5. Privatization of an IS department, involving the transfer of 200 employees and 25 million Dfl worth of mainframes and other resources. The department was sold to a consortium of IS suppliers and spending was guaranteed for a period of five years. After these five years, the consortium sold the company to one of the world's largest outsourcing companies.
6. Development of a system for managing the maintenance of railways. The system was not implemented, because the maintenance process was reorganized.
7. Privatization of an internal IS department. The department was sold to a supplier that consisted of outsourced departments of other organizations.

8. Operation of network hardware and software for over 1000 workstations. Internalized two years later, because of unsatisfactory performance and the tariffs of the supplier.
9. Development of a system for storage and retrieval of all collective labour agreements in The Netherlands. Publishers were interested in co-operation, but the client did not agree with selling the database commercially.
10. Operation of a large network. A contract with a network supplier to provide personnel if the workload was high or one of the four internal network specialists was not available. After a year, the specialists were trained to be able to replace one another and the contract was terminated.
11. Information planning for an information-intensive user department. A consultant was hired to take interviews and write the information plan.
12. Development, implementation and maintenance of a system for storing and processing huge amounts of measurements of water levels, water quality, and so on.
13. Development, implementation and maintenance of a system for the granting and monitoring of licences for discharging effluent water.
14. Selection and lease of a human resources information system. Very few packages were available for human resources at a ministry.
15. Development, implementation and maintenance of a system for managing the flow of large ships passing through locks and weirs, under bridges, and past traffic posts.
16. Transforming a central IS department into an independent subsidiary, but maintaining full ownership. Even after many years, the subsidiary is still dependent upon the parent company for most of the business volume.
17. Implementation of two software packages for the management and retrieval of all documentation of a ministry. The packages were selected by a team with members from several ministries.
18. Development of a system for planning and recording inspections of manufacturing installations under pressure.
19. Outsourcing of the data gathering process for social and economic statistics was considered, but rejected, among other reasons because of the importance of the process and the interconnectedness with the data processing. Instead, some internal improvements were made.
20. Outsourcing of the IS department to a large organization with an IS department that offered services to external clients. The fact that this organization had little experience with providing IS services to external clients led to some problems.
21. Co-operation between several municipalities in a region, to provide all IS activities the municipalities needed. The joint venture was owned by two municipalities, and served over 100 other municipalities. The joint venture was privatized and sold to a holding. Two years later the holding went bankrupt, and the joint venture was sold to another IS supplier.
22. Information planning for a user department with a very large budget (over 800 million Dfl). The result was unsatisfactory, because the level of aggregation was too high, and practical implications were missing.

23. Development, implementation, maintenance and operation of a financial information system comprising all financial aspects of the organization. Co-operation with other similar organizations was abandoned, because of differences in requirements.

9
Outsourcing Practices and Views of America's Most Effective IS Users

MARION G. SOBOL AND UDAY APTE

INTRODUCTION

As detailed already in this book, outsourcing of information systems (IS) functions received a major impetus with Kodak's 1989 landmark decision to outsource its entire IS function (Loh and Venkatraman, 1992a). Tracing its roots to the traditional timesharing and professional services of the 1960s, outsourcing (i.e., selectively turning over some or all of a function to a third party contractor) has become a valid option today for all IS functions, ranging from simple data entry to contract programming, facilities management and full system integration. The information systems trade literature of the past few years is replete with reports and anecdotal information on new outsourcing arrangements between large and small, well-known and obscure companies. However, as has been made clear in earlier chapters, research into the phenomenon has been limited, but recently has begun to show a growth rate on a par with that of the phenomenon itself. In addition to the material in this book we have already seen applications of a transaction cost economics framework (Williamson, 1986; Walker, 1985), analytical approaches such as game theory (Richmond, Seidmann and Whinston, 1993) and mixed integer programming techniques (Chaudhury and Rao, 1992) to prescribe managerial actions. Meanwhile others

Strategic Sourcing of Information Systems.
Edited by L. P. Willcocks and M. C. Lacity. © 1998 John Wiley & Sons Ltd

have applied empirical approaches to uncover determinants of outsourcing (see, for example, Lacity, Hirschheim and Willcocks (1994), Ang (1993), Arnett and Jones (1994), and Grover, Cheon and Teng (1994)). More recent work has focused on outsourcing to maximize flexibility and control, and to provide for strategic alliances (Lacity, Willcocks and Feeney, 1995; McFarlan and Nolan, 1995).

Even so, some fundamental issues concerning outsourcing—reasons for outsourcing, the pros and cons of outsourcing, the activities that are best to outsource, comparison of domestic versus global outsourcing, and the implications of all of the above for companies with different characteristics—remain far from settled. Providing answers to some of these issues, by studying the practices and views of the most effective users of MIS, is the focus of the research presented in this chapter. We ask four research questions, the answers to which can benefit both MIS researchers and practitioners:

1. *Company Type*: What type of companies are more likely to outsource information system functions? The company classifications we consider include manufacturing versus service, small versus large, those that spend a large part of MIS budget on strategic uses versus those that spend only a small part, and those with centralized MIS functions versus those with decentralized MIS functions.
2. *Outsourced Functions*: What information system functions are being outsourced? Do different types of companies as listed above tend to outsource different types of functions? The functions we considered included software development and maintenance, data communications network, support operations, disaster recovery, data center operations, integrated system development, training, and back-office clerical tasks including data entry.
3. *Outsourcing Decision*: What are the reasons for and against outsourcing of MIS functions? What monetary rewards (i.e., cost savings) are needed for outsourcing? Who usually initiates the efforts to outsource? Who makes the final decision? Again, how do these considerations correlate to the company type or the functions being outsourced?
4. *Comparison of Global Versus Domestic Outsourcing*: This research throws further light on the issues discussed in Chapter 13 of this book. Our findings will suggest that while companies may readily outsource domestically (i.e., within the United States), they are not as eager to outsource globally (i.e., outside the United States) due to some of the inherent difficulties and risks. Therefore, it has been important to study the views of MIS executives on global outsourcing and to compare these views to their views on domestic outsourc-

ing. We carry out this comparison in terms of the first three questions: company types, IS function being outsourced, and reasons for and against outsourcing.

The scope of this research was limited to the study of practices and attitudes of the most effective users of IS toward domestic and global outsourcing of IS functions. Testing the validity of transaction cost economics as it applies to IS outsourcing was not the objective of this study, neither was the goal to measure the perceived success or failure of outsourcing decisions. Both issues are, of course, covered in detail in earlier chapters (see Chapters 2, 4 and 5). As we discuss later, the sample of our study consisted of companies rated to be the most effective users of IS by *Computerworld*. We assumed that the outsourcing views, practices and decisions of these companies were also effective and that much could be learned from their detailed study.

DOMESTIC AND GLOBAL OUTSOURCING: AN OVERVIEW

The growth of outsourcing as an important strategy can be attributed to a number of factors. IS departments are no longer experiencing the generous budget increases that occurred in the 1970s and 1980s. In fact, cost reduction pressures often trigger companies to consider outsourcing of information systems (Lacity and Hirschheim, 1993; Lacity and Willcocks, 1996). Other important reasons include the difficulty of finding suitable systems professionals, the need for access to leading-edge information technology, and the increased availability of outsourcing services in the marketplace (Apte, 1992; see also Chapters 1 and 7).

The risks and costs of outsourcing are sometimes lost amid the rhetoric about outsourcing's benefits (Meyer, 1994). Loss of control over the quality of the software and the project's timetable (Foxman, 1994), reduced flexibility, and loss of strategic alignment (Walker, 1985) are amongst the commonly expressed drawbacks of outsourcing. As earlier chapters indicate, the costs of negotiating and monitoring the outsourcing contract with the vendor, and the cost of reverting to the in-house option should outsourcing fail, can also be substantial. Information system executives can see outsourcing as a clear threat to their own, and to their subordinates', long-term career prospects. Also, the outsourcer can lose touch with the advances in information technology and thereby may lose the ability to plan and implement strategic application of information technology.

In the 1994–7 period there has been a dramatic increase in the size of the market for outsourcing and the number of outsourcing vendors. In all this it is clear that, aside from traditional vendors such as Andersen Consulting, EDS, and the other big six accounting firms, the outsourcing market has also attracted traditional computing vendors including IBM, and Unisys. As estimated by The Yankee Group, a consulting firm, the value of the IS outsourcing market was about $26 billion in 1989. The market was expected to grow annually at about 15 per cent to reach $50 billion by 1994. In the same frame, the global outsourcing market was expected to grow from $101 billion in 1989 to $240 billion in 1994 (McMullen, 1990). Studies mentioned in the Introduction of this volume suggest a continuing expansion of the market since 1994.

The significant disparity of salary levels of personnel between developed and underdeveloped countries (Apte, 1992) has made *global outsourcing* a small but rapidly growing segment of the overall outsourcing market. Not all information systems activities are suitable for global outsourcing. For example, facilities management would suffer from the geographic limitations inherent in a global setting. On the other hand, the data entry and contract programming, and to some extent the systems integration and support activities, are arenas where vendors from underdeveloped countries can certainly compete (see Chapter 13). Data entry was one of the earliest tasks to be globally outsourced. It requires the lowest level of computer literacy and needs very little interaction between the customer and the vendor. The customer can mail data forms to the vendor and the vendor in turn can send the computerized data back via telecommunication lines or by mailing magnetic tapes. Outsourcing has not been limited to simple data entry. A small, yet growing trend is also observed in outsourcing of software development activities. For example, GE Appliances has outsourced some of its programming projects to Infosys, a small software house in India (Apte and Mason, 1995a). Several well-known American companies, including Hewlett-Packard, Texas Instruments, Digital Equipment Corporation and more recently IBM, have set up operation in the cities of Bangalore and Bombay in India.

Patane and Jurison (1994) surveyed IS executives of firms with an IT base of larger than $25 million to determine future global outsourcing trends and their impact on US programmers. They found that most innovative, leading edge, and strategic applications are not outsourced presently and are not likely to be outsourced to foreign countries in the future in spite of attractive labour rate differentials. It is expected that the future approaches to application development will be a judicious mix of outsourcing and in-house development.

There are many problems involved in managing the global outsourcing relationship which are not found in in-house software development or in dealing with a US-based outsourcing vendor. Global outsourcing can lead to substantial benefits: significant cost savings and capital market gains, faster cycle time, help in developing and operating global information systems, and access to foreign markets and skilled labour pools. These benefits have encouraged many companies to begin use of, or investigation into, the global outsourcing option. However, with advantages come certain pitfalls which await the unwary. Some of the main drawbacks are problems of communication and co-ordination, lack of control over quality and timetable, possible violation of intellectual property rights, unclear government attitudes towards transborder data flow and trade in services, and inadequate infrastructure within the vendor's home country (see also Chapter 13). The outsourcer should, therefore, approach the global outsourcing option with care (Apte and Mason, 1995b). Additionally, Lei and Slocum (1992) show how outsourcing in general can lead to takeover of a company's strategic business as the company to whom the work is outsourced becomes more closely aligned with the outsourcing company.

THE EMPIRICAL STUDY: METHODOLOGY, QUESTIONNAIRE AND SAMPLE

The research methodology of a questionnaire-based mail survey was used for this study. In the 1991 and 1992 issues of *Computerworld*, the 100 companies who made the most effective use of MIS were chosen. With the objective of studying the outsourcing practices and views of these efficient users and learning from it, the sample for the study was obtained in late 1993 by mailing questionnaires to the chief information officers (CIOs) of companies listed in 1991 and/or 1992 *Computerworld Premier 100* issues. Since there was some overlap in the two years, a total of 149 companies were contained in this sample frame. Typically, these were large companies with median annual revenues of $3500 million and median annual MIS budget of $65 million. The median MIS department employed 350 workers while the mean number of MIS employees was 872.

The CIOs of these companies were surveyed to determine (i) to what extent they outsourced their IS functions both domestically and globally; and (ii) what their views on outsourcing were. Forty-eight companies out of 149 responded to the survey. This response rate of 32 per cent is quite high for a mail questionnaire. Indeed, given that about one-third of the companies had responded and that the data was to be used to get overall percentages and was to be generally divided into no more than two categories, the sample size was considered to be adequate for tests of statistical significance.

The sizes and the industry sector composition of companies responding to the survey were representative of the companies in the sample frame. A comparison study of late and early responders indicated that on almost every question there was no significant difference in the response rates of earlier or later respondents. This measure has been used to study the effects of non-response, assuming that late respondents are more like non-responders. It appears that there is little non-response bias in our survey.

Computerworld had used seven criteria to identify 100 companies that made the most effective use of information systems among the *Fortune 500* industrial and service companies. In both the 1991 and 1992 studies, a combined total of 600 companies were evaluated. The most important evaluation criterion was the peer assessment of a company. Executives from peer companies were asked to select and rank five companies in their industry that in their opinion were the most effective users of information systems. The total peer score was computed based on the combination of all rankings a company received. The second criterion was how committed a company was to the use of information systems. The IS budget as a percentage of revenue was used for this ranking. Next, a non-IS measure, company's profit growth over the past five years, was used. The remaining measures were all related to IS: market value of major hardware as a percentage of total revenue, IS staff expenditures, and IS training expenditures as a percentage of combined corporate budget. The final measure was the percentage of employees having access to PCs and terminals.

In 1994, the criteria for choosing *Premier 100* companies were significantly changed by *Computerworld* to a new one based on "Information Productivity Index" developed by Strassman (1994). It is interesting to note that only 13 companies that made the *Computerworld Premier 100* lists in 1991 and/or 1992 also made the 1994 list.

The four-page questionnaire used in our study was divided in six sections containing both closed-ended and open-ended questions. The first section asked whether the firm was engaged in outsourcing, what cost saving it desired for outsourcing, and the type of IS function/s that it outsourced, if any. The next two sections investigated the reasons for and against outsourcing. Respondents were asked to rate each statement, in a series of statements capturing the generally accepted advantages and disadvantages of outsourcing, on a nine-point, Likert-type scale representing the statement's importance as they perceived it.

The fourth and the fifth sections of the questionnaire dealt with global outsourcing. These sections included questions similar to the ones asked earlier in the context of domestic outsourcing. The sixth and the final section gathered information concerning the MIS department, such as size of the budget, number of IS professionals, and the extent of centralization of IS functions. Information concerning the executive/s (CEO, CIO or user department head) who initiated the investigation into the outsourcing option, and the executive/s who made the final decision, was also elicited in the final section of the questionnaire.

RESULTS

The extent to which information system functions were being outsourced, domestically and globally, was one of the most basic questions we investigated in the study. Our survey showed that a large percentge (77.1 per cent) of companies outsourced domestically at least one of their MIS functions, while only 16.7 per cent outsourced globally. However, the percentage of companies engaged in global outsourcing of IS functions is likely to go up in the future, since 67 per cent of companies indicated that they were willing to consider global outsourcing as a valid option. The extent of IS outsourcing found in our study compares well with findings of the research reported by McFarlan and Nolan (1995), who report that "more than half of midsize to large firms have outsourced or are considering some type of outsourcing of their IT activities".

Outsourced Functions

As shown in Table 9.1, the two most important functions outsourced domestically were support operations (i.e., equipment maintenance/services) and training and education. Almost one in two companies outsourced these functions. The next important functions outsourced were disaster recovery (two out of five companies) and software development (one-third of companies).

Next in order were functions such as data entry, development of a fully integrated system (hardware, software and networking), and data communication networks, which were outsourced at a frequency of roughly one in five. The remaining functions (telephone support of customers, transaction processing and back office clerical tasks) were outsourced by 10 per cent or less of the companies studied.

Advantages and Disadvantages

We now come to the important reasons for and against outsourcing. These reasons were investigated by first using open-ended questions

Table 9.1 *MIS Functions Outsourced Domestically and Globally*

Function	*Percentage*	*Outsourcing*
	Domestically*	Globally*
Support operations (Equipment maintenance/service)	47.9	6.3
Training and education	47.9	6.3
Disaster recovery	39.6	6.3
Data entry	22.9	2.1
Development of fully integrated system (hardware, software, networking)	20.8	6.3
Data communication networks	18.8	4.2
Software maintenance	14.6	0
Data center (computer) operation	12.5	2.1
Telephone support of customers	10.4	0
Bank office clerical tasks	6.3	0
Transaction processing	4.2	2.1
Other	6.3	0
Outsourced at least one function	77.1	16.7

*Domestically is defined as within the USA and Globally is defined as outside the USA.

and then following up with closed-ended questions. In closed-ended questions, respondents were asked to rate the importance of each of the seven advantages and seven disadvantages of domestic outsourcing using a nine-point rating scale that spanned values from 1 (unimportant) to 9 (very important). In Table 9.2, the answers to the closed-ended questions about advantages and disadvantages of domestic outsourcing have been ranked in order of their median scores on the importance scale.

The principal advantages of domestic outsourcing are cost containment, and the reduced need to hire IS professionals. These advantages received median importance scores of eight and seven points respectively. In secondary position are improved cost predictability, improved ability to focus on strategic use of IS, and increased accessibility of vendors; all receiving a median score of six points. At the bottom of the list are technology-related issues such as increased access to leading-edge technology, or reduced need for capital investment in new technology.

As far as the disadvantages are concerned, the primary problems, receiving a median importance score of seven points each, are difficulty in monitoring vendor performance, and the loss of control over timeliness and quality of IS functions. In secondary position are the difficulties in explaining the business needs to vendors, and the potential for loss of secrets and intellectual property. The final two disadvantages of

Table 9.2 *Importance Ratings for Advantages and Disadvantages of Domestic Outsourcing**

Advantages	Median Importance Classification	Disadvantages	Median Importance Classification
1. Allows cost containment	8.0	Monitoring outsourcing vendors is difficult	7.0
2. Reduces need to hire IS professionals	7.0	Loss of quality and time control	7.0
3. Improves cost predictability	6.0	Difficult to explain business needs to vendor	6.5
4. Leaves more time to focus on strategic IS use	6.0	Leads to potential loss of secrets and intellectual property	6.0
5. More accessible now—more vendors available	6.0	Limits long-term career prospects of IS staff	5.0
6. Gives access to leading edge technology	5.0	Outsourcing controls are high cost	5.0
7. Reduces need for capital investment in new technology	5.0	Decreases size of IS department	3.0

*Domestic means within the USA

outsourcing, receiving a score of five points each, were the limits placed by outsourcing on the long-term career prospects of IS staff, and the high cost of outsourcing contracts. Interestingly, the downsizing of MIS departments resulting from outsourcing was not consider to be a critical drawback by the responding executives, as this factor received a score of only three points on the nine-point scale.

The two main advantages of global outsourcing (see Table 9.3), both receiving a score of six points each, are the low salaries in foreign countries and the access to a larger group of trained professionals. Reduced cycle time for system development and improved access to global markets are next in importance.

The strongest disadvantage of global outsourcing, that received a score of seven points, is the uncertainty about host government's attitudes toward transborder data flows (TDF) and trade in IS services. TDF laws originated in the 1970s from concerns about the integrity and confidentiality of personal data. These were later extended to protect associations and corporations. Jarvenpaa and Ives (1991) report the findings of a study in 1985—of 370 service companies studied, 63 per cent considered TDF regulations to be serious potential problem,

Table 9.3 *Importance Ratings for Added Advantages and Disadvantages of Global Outsourcing**

	Advantages	Median Importance Classification	Disadvantages	Median Importance Classification
1.	Low salaries abroad allow cost reduction	6.0	Unclear government attitudes toward transborder data flow and trade in IS services	7.0
2.	Global outsourcing gives access to larger group of highly schooled professionals	6.0	Data communications difficulty with foreign vendors	6.5
3.	Reduced cycle time for system development	5.0	Difficulty in verbal communication with foreign vendors	6.0
4.	Improves access to global markets	5.0	Can lead to serious violation of intellectual property rights	5.0
5.	—		Time difference in working hours	4.0
6.	—		Cultural differences with a foreign vendor	4.0

*Global means outside the USA. Based on previous studies (Apte, 1992) total of ten added advantages and disadvantages of global outsourcing, over and above those of domestic outsourcing, were presented in the closed-end questions. Four are considered advantages and six are considered disadvantages.

although only 31% per cent reported problems with TDF at the time. Perhaps, in reality, TDF laws did not deter the development of global information systems because foreign officials didn't know how to interpret or enforce TDF laws. As Jarvenpaa and Ives further report (p. 43), "although TDF laws and regulations were not perceived to be a major obstacle to global IT, worldwide data management and data standardization within firms were perceived to present significant barriers for international data sharing".

Difficulty in communicating with the foreign vendor—both in data communication and in verbal communication—is another important disadvantage of global outsourcing. These factors received scores of six and a half and six respectively. The potential for violation of intellectual property rights, which received a rating of six points for domestic outsourcing, was rated only five points for global outsourcing. Considering the well-publicized cases of piracy of patents and software in many countries including China, it was reasonable to expect that the violation of intellectual property rights would have received at least equal, if not higher, score for global outsourcing than that for domestic outsourcing. Perhaps the companies responding to the survey felt that the unique nature of their businesses, or various controls such as data encryption that they may have instituted, had reduced the risk of intellectual property violation. Finally, the difficulty in dealing with differences in working hours and with cultural differences are considered the least important disadvantages of global outsourcing.

Outsourcing Decision

Outsourcing of IS functions results in a number of advantages, disadvantages and risks. The minimum cost saving a company needs to have before it may consider outsourcing as an attractive option represents an important and interesting item of information for a manager faced with this option. As shown in Table 9.4 below, our study revealed that the median cost saving needed for companies to outsource domestically was 20 per cent. However, of those companies willing to consider outsourcing globally the median cost saving needed to outsource globally was placed at 30 per cent.

Concerning the question of who initiated the outsourcing decision, only 2.1 per cent of the sample companies claimed it was solely the top management's idea to explore the possibility of outsourcing (see Table 9.5). According to our sample, 58.3 per cent of respondents said that an MIS executive first proposed it. Often several people—CEOs, MIS executives, and executives of user departments—looked into outsourcing alternatives at the same time. It is also interesting to note that a total of 79.2 per cent of the decisions to explore MIS outsourcing included the MIS executive.

Table 9.4 *Minimum Savings Needed to Justify Outsourcing Domestically and Globally**

Minimum Median Saving Needed to Outsource (%)	Domestically(%)	Globally(%)
10	16.7	6.3
20	39.6	22.9
30	29.2	18.8
40	2.1	6.3
50	4.2	2.1
60	0	10.4
No answer or won't consider outsourcing	8.4	33.4

*Domestically is defined as within the USA and Globally is defined as outside the USA.

Table 9.5 *Outsourcing Design*

Whose initial idea was it to explore the possibility of outsourcing?	%	
Top management	2.1	
Outside consultant	2.1	
MIS executive	58.3	
MIS executive and User dept	6.3	79.2
MIS executive and top mgmt	8.3	
All three	6.3	
No answer	16.7	
If you currently outsource MIS functions, who was most important in making the outsourcing decision?	**%**	
Top management	12.5	
Outside consultant	2.1	
MIS executive	52.1	
MIS executive and User dept	6.3	64.7
MIS executive and top mgmt	4.2	
All three	2.1	
No answer	20.7	
Total	100	

In identifying the person who played the most important role in making outsourcing decisions, top management was solely credited with such role in 12.5 per cent of the companies. MIS executives played important roles, alone or together with top management and/or user department executives, in a total of 64.7 per cent of cases. The roles different executives play in outsourcing decisions is still an open question. An interesting conjecture that deserves further research is that the CEO sets the proportion of expenditure on outsourcing while the CIO chooses what functions to outsource.

Relationship Between Outsourcing and the Firm Characteristics

Having studied the descriptive questions pertaining to the types of IS functions being outsourced, the reasons for and against outsourcing, the identity of the decision makers, and the differences and similarities between global and domestic outsourcing, we now investigate the relationship between IS outsourcing and the characteristics of the firm. We shall organize and present the result of our analysis through tests of a series of hypotheses which have been derived through basic economic theory and trade-off considerations.

IS Outsourcing in Manufacturing Versus Service Firms

Information systems functions are generally viewed as not being central to the mission of many manufacturing firms. In contrast, services are more information-intensive (Apte and Mason, 1995b), and many service firms use information systems as an integral (and at times even strategic) part of their operation. Considering this relative importance of information resources, as McFarlan and Nolan (1995) conclude, for economic and strategic reasons service firms may not be as interested in outsourcing IS functions as manufacturing firms.

Hypothesis I: Manufacturing firms are more likely to outsource than service firms

Our sample indicates that while manufacturing firms are more likely than service firms to outsource domestically (81.5 per cent versus 70.0 per cent respectively), this difference is not significant at the 0.005 level. Similarly, for global outsourcing, manufacturing companies are somewhat more likely to outsource globally (19.2 per cent) than service industries (15.0 per cent). But again, this is not significant. However, manufacturing firms require a significantly higher savings to outsource as 48 per cent need a savings payoff of 30 per cent or more while only 21 per cent of service firms require savings this large.

IS Outsourcing in Small versus Large Firms

Outsourcing can lead to lower production costs (i.e. the cost of delivering IS function) due to the economies of scale the vendor can enjoy (but see Chapter 4). However, the transaction costs (the costs of negotiating, monitoring and enforcing a contract) for outsourcing tend to be higher than that for the insourcing option (Apte, 1992). Depending on the relative sizes of these costs one option may be preferable to the other, and hence, it may be difficult to draw any generalized conclusion that relates size of the firm (small or large) to the outsourcing decision. However, to look for a pattern that may be present in the data, we formulate and test the following hypothesis.

Hypothesis II: Firms with smaller MIS budgets are less likely to outsource than larger firms, and small budget firms need bigger savings to outsource domestically and globally

The firms were divided into two groups by the size of their MIS budgets. Each group had 24 firms and the cut-off point was MIS budgets of $65 million a year. Considering the extent of IS outsourcing being practiced,

64 per cent of firms with small MIS budgets (those with annual budgets of $65 million or less) outsourced domestically, while 88 per cent of those with large MIS budgets (i.e., above $65 million per year) outsourced domestically. Similarly, in the case of global outsourcing, 8 per cent of the small budget firms outsourced globally while 24 per cent of the firms with large MIS budgets outsourced globally. These differences are significant at the 0.005 level. Thus it seems true that larger firms are more likely to outsource both domestically and globally.

One possible explanation may be that the larger firms have more power over vendors and therefore are less likely to be the victims of vendor opportunism. Hence, larger firms are more likely to outsource than smaller firms. Due to volume discount considerations, larger firms may be more able to attract better vendor bids than smaller firms. Other possible explanations involve the relative nature of costs. Production costs tend to be more variable in nature (i.e., they vary with respect to the size of the activity being outsourced), while transaction costs are relatively fixed in nature. Hence, it is likely that larger firms with larger outsourcing contracts may enjoy larger savings in production costs, which may outweigh the transaction costs, thus leading to their preference for outsourcing as opposed to insourcing.

Concerning the cost saving required to outsource domestically, 43 per cent of firms with small MIS budgets required savings of 30 per cent or more to outsource, while only 25 per cent of those with larger MIS budgets stated that they needed such a high savings to outsource. A possible reason for this difference is the fixed nature of costs of negotiating and monitoring outsourcing contract. To recoup this fixed cost, small firms may need a larger percentage of saving as compared to large firms. However, this explanation should be seen as only a preliminary conjecture. We are presently unaware of any studies which investigate the nature of outsourcing costs or which relate firm size to savings desired in order to outsource. This may be an interesting subject for further study.

When we come to global outsourcing the results are similar—those with large budgets need significantly less savings. None of the firms with small MIS budgets were willing to outsource for a savings of 10 per cent while 18.8% per cent of the firms with large MIS budgets were willing to outsource at this savings rate. All these differences were significant at the 0.005 level.

IS Outsourcing and Centralized or Decentralized Organization

The impact of centralized or decentralized organization on the relative sizes of production savings and the increased costs of negotiating and monitoring outsourcing contracts is unclear. However, with some demise in centralized IS departments as predicted by Deardon (1987), one can postulate that the practice of decentralized organization and outsourcing are both more likely since decentralized groups need more outside MIS expertise.

Hypothesis III: Firms where MIS functions tend to be centralized in the MIS department rather than being dispersed in the functional departments of the firm, are less likely to outsource domestically and globally

Table 9.6 shows an interesting result. Firms with decentralized MIS (i.e., where IS responsibility is dispersed throughout the functional departments of the firm) are more likely to outsource domestically but are less likely to outsource globally than those firms with more centralized MIS functions. Perhaps the global outsourcing decision requires an even stronger MIS department to negotiate and monitor necessary outsourcing contracts, and incurs higher transaction costs of global outsourcing, while the domestic outsourcing decision can be managed more easily by the functional departments.

Table 9.6 *Comparison of Centralization of MIS Functions in MIS Department and Global and Domestic Outsourcing**

	Level of Centralization**		
	Low	Medium	High
Outsource (%) Domestically?			
Yes	93.3	68.4	66.7
No	6.7	31.6	33.3
Number of firms	15	19	12
Outsource (%) Globally?			
Yes	7.1	21.0	16.7
No	92.9	79.0	83.3
Number of firms	14	19	12

*Domestic is defined as within the USA, and global is defined as outside the USA.
**For each of nine functions—software development, software maintenance, development of integrated systems, computer operation, data communication networks, support operations, disaster recovery, training and education, telephone support of customers—respondents were asked to rank whether 0, 20, 40, 60, 80 or 100 per cent of the functions were carried out in the MIS department. Each of these percentages were assigned weights of 1, 2, 3, 4, 5, 6 respectively. Then the weights were summed. Thus the scores for each company were ranged from 0 to 54. Then the scores were broken into three approximately equal groups—low, medium and high centralization (most of the tasks carried out in the MIS department).

IS Outsourcing and Spending on Strategic MIS

An often-cited advantage of outsourcing, which also surfaced in a secondary position in our survey, is that it allows management to focus the available IS talent on strategic IS activities, promoting competitiveness rather than utilizing resources for routine activities of software maintenance or operations (McFarlan and Nolan, 1995). On the other hand, the more IT contributes to strategy, the less likely the firm may be to outsource because it is losing its core capabilities (Lei and Slocum, 1992). Again, to uncover any underlying patterns in the data, we test the following hypothesis to see if any relationship exists between outsourcing and spending on strategic MIS by the firm.

Hypothesis IV: The firms that spent a high proportion of their MIS budget to support strategic policy would be more likely to outsource than firms that spend a smaller proportion of MIS budget on strategic policy

Surveyed firms spent a surprisingly high proportion of budget on strategic policy. As shown in Table 9.7, at least half of the firms spent 20 per cent or more of their IS budget on strategic policy. Were the strategic policy spenders more likely to outsource? Of those firms who spent less than 20 per cent of their budget on strategic policy, 67 per cent outsourced domestically while for those who spent 20 per cent or more on strategic policy, 75 per cent outsourced domestically. This difference was not statistically significant. Similarly 7 per cent of those who spent less than 20 per cent of their budget on strategic policy outsourced globally compared to 21 per cent of those spending 20 per cent or more of the budget on strategic policy. This result was not significant either. Possibly because there are pulls in both directions as suggested earlier, it appears that outsourcing and spending on strategic MIS policy are not significantly related.

Table 9.7 *Strategic Use of MIS Budget*

Percentage of MIS Budget Spent on Strategic Policy	Percentage of Firms Spending this Amount
Less than 10%	12.8
10 but less than 20%	25.7
20 but less than 30%	25.1
30 but less than 50%	10.5
Over 50%	14.6
No Answer	11.3

Outsourced IS Functions and Reasons For and Against Outsourcing

Finally, we investigate the relationship between the reasons for and against outsourcing cited by a firm and the type of IS function outsourced by a firm. We believe that these two are related. For example, outsourcing that involves professional help would be done by companies who give a high rating to the advantage of reduced need for IS professionals under an outsourcing option.

There is strong evidence (see Table 9.8) that there is a correlation between the type/s of savings that are important and the type/s of outsourcing that is done. For example, those who ranked savings of professional help very high were most likely to outsource integrated systems development (90 per cent) and data communications networks (89 per cent), both highly professional tasks. Those most interested in cost reduction were likely to outsource support operations (82 per cent), data entry (82 per cent), disaster recovery (79 per cent), education and training (65 per cent), and data communication networks (89 per cent). For those who were most interested in cost prediction, disaster recovery was most frequently outsourced (74 per cent). For those ranking more time for strategic policy as being very important, a high proportion outsourced software maintenance (72 per cent) and integrated systems development (70 per cent), allowing more professional time for strategic policy investments.

For those ranking access to leading edge technology and software as being important, software maintenance was the function most likely to be outsourced. A possible explanation—such outsourcing can allow firms to concentrate on leading edge software as they don't have to devote scarce resources to maintain or upgrade old software. Fifty seven per cent of the respondents in this category outsourced software maintenance. Those that viewed the reduction in capital investment as a very important advantage of outsourcing, tended to rank outsourcing of integrated system development (50 per cent), data centers (50 per cent) or support operations (48 per cent) as important. Finally, those who said that it was important that an increasing number of vendors be available, were most likely to outsource data entry (55 per cent) and support operations (47 per cent). The results indicate that outsourcing decisions are logically "thought out" by these effective users of IS. Moreover, in the decision to outsource IS functions, the underlying reasons are well related to actual types of outsourcing done.

The relationship between the reasons for/against outsourcing, and whether a firm has considered or is considering global outsourcing sheds some interesting light on the decision-making process as it relates to global outsourcing (see Table 9.9). For those who have global

Table 9.8 *Important Reasons for Outsourcing by Type of Outsourcing Done*

Firms ranking these reasons for outsourcing as very important (7–9)	Percentage Using Type of Outsourcing								
	Software Develop-ment	Data Entry	Software Main-tenance	Integrated Systems Develop-ment	Data Center	Data Network Commun-ications	Support Opera-tions	Disaster Recovery	Training & Education
1. Cost reduction	75*	82	57	50	67	78	82	79	78
2. Cost production	31	45	29	40	33	56	47	74	48
3. Less professional staff	68	55	72	90	67	89	66	58	65
4. More time for strategic policy	44	36	72	70	33	44	48	52	43
5. Access to leading edge technology	38	27	57	50	50	44	22	36	26
6. Reduce capital investment	31	36	43	50	50	44	48	42	43
7. Increased vendors available	19	55	29	40	17	22	47	42	35

*To read this cell: 75% of those who considered cost reduction as an important reason for outsourcing have outsourced software development.

Table 9.9 *Reasons For and Against Global Outsourcing*

	Policy Towards Global* Outsourcing (percentages)		
Firms Ranking These Reasons for Outsourcing as Very Important (7–9)	Have global outsourcing	Considering global outsourcing	Don't have global outsourcing
Cost reduction	25**	70***	56
Access to larger pool of professionals	86***	70***	44
Reduces cycle time	43	40	41
Improves access to global markets	72***	11	29
Difficulty communicating verbally	38	40	78***
Difficulty with data communication	38	40	72***
Unclear foreign govt. attitudes	50	33	89***
Violates intellectual property rights	50	13	50
Time differences in working hours	13	22	50
Cultural differences with a foreign vendor	13	22	33

*Global means outside the USA.
**To read this cell: 25% of those who consider cost reduction very important have global outsourcing.
***Most important functions in group.

outsourcing, access to a larger pool of professionals (86 per cent) and to global markets (72 per cent) are very important reasons for global outsourcing. For those who don't outsource globally, unclear foreign government attitude (89 per cent) and difficulties of verbal and data communication (72 per cent) are the prime reasons for not outsourcing globally. For those who are currently not outsourcing globally but are considering doing so, the primary reasons are cost reduction and access to a larger pool of professionals, although at least 40 per cent have considered the drawback of verbal and data communication. Thus it seems that for most usage, firms prefer to outsource domestically. The only time CIOs seem enthusiastic about global outsourcing is when it gives them access to foreign markets for their products or to a larger pool of IS professionals.

SUMMARY AND CONCLUSIONS

As one of the earlier exploratory studies to investigate empirically the domestic and global outsourcing of IS functions, the primary contribution of this research is to begin developing a better understanding of the outsourcing phenomenon. Specifically:

- the research provides empirical evidence for a number of conclusions concerning IS outsourcing, such as functions being outsourced, and advantages and disadvantages of outsourcing, that are presently found mostly in anecdotal write-ups in industry journals;
- representing the views and practices of companies that are considered to be the most effective users of MIS, the results of this research are likely to be of significant benefit to both: (i) other companies in their outsourcing decisions and practice, and (ii) researchers in developing a further understanding of the phenomenon.

The analysis of survey data sheds some interesting light on the outsourcing of information systems functions. The major conclusions are:

- A significant number (77.1%) of US firms surveyed are engaged in domestic outsourcing of one or more IS functions. Global outsourcing is adopted by a far smaller percentage of companies (16.7 per cent). However, this practice is likely to increase given that two-thirds of the companies were willing to consider global outsourcing as a valid option.
- Median cost saving needed for US-based outsourcing is 20 per cent, while for global outsourcing it is 30 per cent. Presumably, this reflects the higher risks associated with global outsourcing.
- While a larger percentage of manufacturing firms outsourced IS functions as compared to the service firms, the difference was not statistically significant. Hence, one may conclude that the rate of outsourcing is similar in both manufacturing and service firms. However, it was noted that manufacturers expected higher savings before they were ready to outsource.
- MIS executives play a very important role, and are involved in a large majority (64.7 per cent) of IS outsourcing decisions.
- Companies with relatively smaller MIS budgets are less likely to outsource than those with larger MIS budgets. Consistent with this observation, smaller companies do require larger savings to make outsourcing worthwhile.
- Firms with more decentralized MIS functions are more likely to outsource domestically than firms with more centralized MIS functions. On the other hand, firms with centralized MIS functions are more likely to outsource globally.
- The outsourcing decision and a firm's spending on strategic MIS policy seem not to be related. This may suggest that outsourcing is undertaken mainly for cost-saving, short-term purposes.

As the practice of outsourcing gains a stronger foothold in the future, it would be pertinent to study the views and practices of a large number of firms sampled from a broader spectrum. With the accelerating trend towards globalization, the issues and practices concerning global outsourcing of IS will also become more important in the future. Hence a study of global outsourcing practices would be of great interest and importance. The sample of this study consisted of US-based companies, but many of these companies studied were also large multinationals. Hence, the results of this survey may also be indicative of the views and practices of non-US-based companies. However, for better accuracy and reliability, it would be important to study and compare the outsourcing practices of firms in a number of countries. Such a study, which the authors plan to undertake in the near future, will investigate if the attitudes and practices related to outsourcing differ in different parts of the world. Finally, an evaluation of the relative efficiency of domestic versus global outsourcing decisions can be a very important topic for future empirical studies.

REFERENCES

Ang, S. (1993) *The Etiology of Information Systems Outsourcing*, Unpublished Ph.D. Dissertation, University of Minnesota, Minneapolis.

Apte, U. M. (1992) Global Outsourcing of Information Systems and Processing Services, *The Information Society*, **7**, 287–303.

Apte U. M. and Mason, R. O. (1995a) Global Outsourcing of Information Processing Services, in Harker, P. (ed.), *The Service Productivity and Quality Challenge*, Norwell, M: Kluwer Academic Publishers, 169–202.

Apte, U. M. and Mason, R. O. (1995b) Global Disaggregation of Information-Intensive Services, *Management Science*, **41**, 7, July, 1250–1262.

Arnett, K. and Jones, M. (1994) Firms That Choose Outsourcing: A Profile, *Information and Management*, **26**, 179–188.

Chaudhury, A., Nam, K. and Rao, H. R. (1992) Information Systems Outsourcing: A Mixed Integer Programming Analysis, *Proceedings of the 13th International Conference on Information Systems*, December, New York, 263 et seq.

Computerworld (1991) How We Rank the Premier 100, *Computerworld Premier 100*, 30 September, 13.

Computerworld (1992) How We Measure Effectiveness, *Computerworld Premier 100*, 14 Septembe, 53.

Deardon, J. (1987) The Withering Away of the IS Organization, *Sloan Management Review*, Summer, 87–91.

Foxman, N. (1994) Succeeding in Outsourcing, *Information Systems Management*, **11** , 1, Winter, 77–80.

Grover, V., Cheon, M. J. and Teng, J. T. C. (1994) A Descriptive Study on the Outsourcing of Information Systems Functions, *Information and Management*, **27**, 1 July, 33–44.

Jarvenpaa, S. and Ives, B. (1991) Applications of Global Information Technology: Key Issues for Management, *MIS Quarterly*, March, 32-43.

Lacity, M., Hirschheim, R. and Willcocks, L. (1994) Realizing Outsourcing Expectations, *Information Systems Management*, *11*, 4, Fall, 7–18.

Lacity, M. and Hirschheim, R. (1993) *Information Systems Outsourcing: Myths, Metaphors and Realities*, New York: John Wiley and Sons.

Lacity, M. and Willcocks, L. (1996) *Best Practices in Information Technology Sourcing*, Oxford Executive Research Briefing, Templeton College, Oxford.

Lacity, M., Willcocks, L. and Feeny, D. (1995) IT Outsourcing: Maximize Flexibility and Control, *Harvard Business Review*, May–June, 84–93.

Lei, D. and Slocum, J. (1992) Global Strategy, Competence-building and Strategic Alliances. *California Management Review*, Fall, 81–97.

Loh, L. and Venkatraman (1992a) Diffusion of Information Technology Outsourcing: Influence Sources and the Kodak Effect, *Information Systems Research*, **3**, 4, 334–358.

Meyer, N. D. (1994) A Sensible Approach to Outsourcing. *Information Systems Management*, **11**, 4, 23–27.

McFarlan, W. and Nolan, R. (1995) How to Manage an IT Outsourcing Alliance, *Sloan Management Review*, Winter, 9–23.

McMullen, J. (1990) New Allies: IS and Service Suppliers, *Datamation*, 1 March.

Patane, J. R. and Jurison, J. (1994) Is Global Outsourcing Diminishing the Prospects for American Programmers? *Journal of Systems Management*, **45**, 6, 6–10.

Richmond, W. B., Seidmann, A. and Whinston, A. B. (1993) Incomplete Contracting Issues in Information Systems Development Outsourcing, *International Journal of Decision Support Systems*, **8**, 5, 459–477.

Strassman, P. (1994) How We Evaluated Productivity, *Computerworld Premier 100*, 19 September, 45–53.

Walker, G., (1985) Strategic Sourcing, Vertical Integration and Transaction Costs, *Interfaces*, **18**, 3, 62–73.

Williamson, O. E. (1986) *Economic Organization*, New York: New York University Press.

10
The Management of Partnering Development in IS Outsourcing

ROBERT KLEPPER

INTRODUCTION

As at 1997 the Information Systems literature has begun to reflect an increased interest not just in outsourcing IS, but also in the processes of partnering with vendor firms (see, for example, McFarlan and Nolan, 1995; Willcocks, 1994; Willcocks and Kern, 1997). This is not always easy to accomplish, although, as other chapters have indicated (see especially Chapters 11 and 12), its importance is widely recognized. In this chapter we select a model of partnership development from the management literature and apply it to IS partnering. Here the emphasis is on the manageable aspects of partnership development and the actions that IS managers can take to speed partnership development and deepen relationships with vendors. Two case studies of IS partnership development are used to test and illustrate the concepts developed from the model of partnering behaviour.

As earlier chapters have demonstrated, outsourcing has become a very important way of meeting information systems needs in organizations. But one critical question that remains once the decision to outsource has been made is: What are the mechanisms for the development of long-term relationships between clients and vendors in IT outsourcing, or what are sometimes called partnering relationships (Oltman, 1990)? This chapter starts from the assumption that partner-

Strategic Sourcing of Information Systems.

ing relationships are advantageous under some circumstances. Often these circumstances come down to the provision of services by a vendor to a client where multiple, sequential contracts are called for and where the vendor becomes a more productive provider of services through investment in knowledge of the client firm's business (Klepper, 1994). The benefits of partnering derive from decreased cost and increased quality of the services produced in the exchange (Stralkowski and Billon, 1988).

The chapter approaches the development of partnerships from the client firm's perspective. It investigates the possibilities for managing the partnering process. These include screening to increase the chances of finding vendors suitable as future partners and the management of pre-partnering exchanges to increase the probability and speed of developing a partnering relationship. Suggestions for appropriate management action are then developed.

The plan of this chapter is as follows. First, the literature on the development of partnerships is reviewed. Second, theoretical issues and management initiatives in the screening of vendors and management of proto-partnership relationships are explored. Finally, the management of partnership development is illustrated with several brief case studies.

THE LITERATURE ON PARTNERING RELATIONSHIPS

Partnering is not new to the information systems literature; and it is taken up in a number of contexts. Table 10.1 presents a summary of some of the partnering literature in the Information Systems field. This literature does not provide a good basis for a study of the sort undertaken here—the process by which partnerships can be actively managed from the beginnings of a relationship to its culmination in a close, ongoing alliance. Much of the IS literature on partnering has taken a non-theoretical approach, as Table 10.1 shows. Only the Lasher, Ives and Jarvenpaa (1991) study addresses the beginnings of a partnership relationship. None of these earlier contributions is strong on the processes by which partnerships develop, though there is increasing evidence in the IS literature that this issue is beginning to be more seriously addressed (see Willcocks and Kern, 1997).

The development of partnering has been studied elsewhere in the management literature, particularly in marketing, and a number of models have been proposed for the building and sustaining of these

Table 10.1 *I/S Papers on Partnership*

Study	I/T Appliction area	Theory	Research Method	Address Partnership Beginnings?	Address Process of Development?
Elam (1988)	interfirm co-operation	none	non-empirical	no	no
Konsynski and McFarlan (1990)	interfirm co-operation	none	non-empirical	no	no
Henderson (1990)	I/S & line managers	none	non-empirical	no	some
Lasher, Ives and Jarvenpaa (1991)	interfirm co-operation (with vendor)	none	one case study	yes	some
Clemons and Row (1992)	interfirm co-operation	transaction cost theory	non-empirical	no	no
Gulati, Khama and Nohria (1994)	interfirm co-operation	game theory	non-empirical	no	no

relationships. Social exchange theory underlies many of the contributions outside the IS literature. Table 10.2 presents a summary of some of the management literature.

Three contributions all deal with continuity in already established partnering relationships, but do not provide an understanding of partnership beginnings and development which is the focus of this study. Anderson and Narus (1990) put forward a model to explain the level of satisfaction a manufacturer and distributor experience in a partnership. Satisfaction depends on a number of interacting variables, including perceived outcomes, dependence on the other firm, influence over the other firm, resolution of conflict, communication, trust and co-operation. Anderson and Weitz (1989) investigated the role of pledges in building and sustaining commitment between clients and vendors. One form of pledge that binds the parties to a relationship is investments in assets that are worth more inside the relationship than outside it. Another form of pledge is the submission to contract provisions that commit one partner to undertake actions that benefit the other partner. By "tying its hands" a firm demonstrates its trustworthiness and binds the other firm to the relationship. The relationship deepens through successive rounds of pledges by both parties.

Levinthal and Fichman (1988) argue that inter-organizational commitments grow over time primarily through two mechanisms. One is investments in knowledge of the other firm that result from learning by doing. The other is increased trust and increased ability to communicate that result from the development of personal relationships between persons in the client and the vendor firms who have boundary-spanning roles and whose responsibility it is to manage the relationship with the other firm.

Ring and Van de Ven (1994) developed a conceptual model for the development of co-operative inter-organizational relationships. They stress the importance of both equity and efficiency in the development and success of such relationships and the crucial role that boundary-spanning individuals play in the establishment and maintenance of partnerships, alliances, coalitions and joint ventures. They do address the beginnings of partnering relationships and explain the deepening of relationships through a cyclical stage model of negotiations, commitments, execution and assessment of agreements.

Dwyer, Schurr and Oh (1987) developed a sequential stage model of partnership development where the stages are awareness, exploration, expansion and commitment. They also posit subprocesses that work within the exploration, expansion and commitment phases that either move the parties closer to or further from the next stage. These subprocesses of attraction, communication, bargaining, power, norms and

Table 10.2 *Studies of Partnering from the Management Literature*

Study	Context	Theory	Research Method	Significant Aspects	Address Risks?	Management of Partnering?	Address Beginnings of Partnering
Anderson & Narus (1990)	manufacturer and distributor	social exchange theory	non-empirical	continuity of relationships	implicitly	implicitly	no
Levinthal and Fichman (1988)	auditor and client	transaction cost theory	event history analysis	continuity of relationships	yes	no	no
Anderson and Weitz (1989)	manufacturer and sales agent	social exchange, bargaining and negotiation theory	simultaneous equations	continuity of relationships	implicitly	implicitly	no
Ring and Van de Ven (1994)	interfirm co-operation	social exchange theory	non-empirical	cyclical stages	yes	implicitly	yes
Dwyer, Schurr and Oh (1987)	buyers and sellers	social exchange theory	non-empirical	sequential stages with subprocesses	yes	yes	yes

expectations are, at least in part, levers that managers can use to actively manage the development of partnerships.

Both the Ring and Van de Ven and the Dwyer, Schurr and Oh models are attractive for a study of this sort. Both address the beginnings of partnerships, and both develop theory that can guide managers who desire to build partnerships. The author chose the Dwyer, Schurr and Oh approach for this chapter because of the model's elaboration of the stages of partnership development to a subprocess level. Subprocesses allowed more detailed analysis of management action that can foster partnerships and provided a better vehicle for understanding how partnerships can be developed and managed.

MANAGEMENT ACTION IN SUPPORT OF PARTNERING

Throughout this chapter the reader should keep in mind that the achievement of a partnership is not assured and that partnerships, once culminated, are always subject to dissolution. Client and vendor objectives may not be sufficiently aligned to bring the relationship to one of partnership. Either the client or the vendor may fail to make the investments in relationship-specific capabilities expected by the other. Client and vendor may find that they are unable to resolve smoothly the inevitable differences and disputes that arise along the way. Either party may lose the confidence of the other by taking advantage of the relationship. Investments made in expectation of a deeper and more rewarding relationship may come to naught. While non-partnering inter-firm arrangements are the norm and partnering is the exception, the purpose of this paper is to explore what managers might do to promote partnerships, when underlying circumstances favour them.

The management literature that addresses the development of partnerships and co-operative arrangements between firms is united on the point that partnerships can only evolve through a progression of exchanges with steadily increasing trust in and commitment to an ongoing relationship by both client and vendor. The client and vendor must invest in the establishment of a deeper relationship. In circumstances in which partnership arrangements could be mutually beneficial to client and vendor, management actions that either reduce the investment needed to establish a partnership or clear the roadblocks that arise to successful partnering will further the development of partnering and help secure gains to both firms. Appropriate timing of management action may speed the process of partnering, and this may also act to reduce the cost of establishing partnerships.

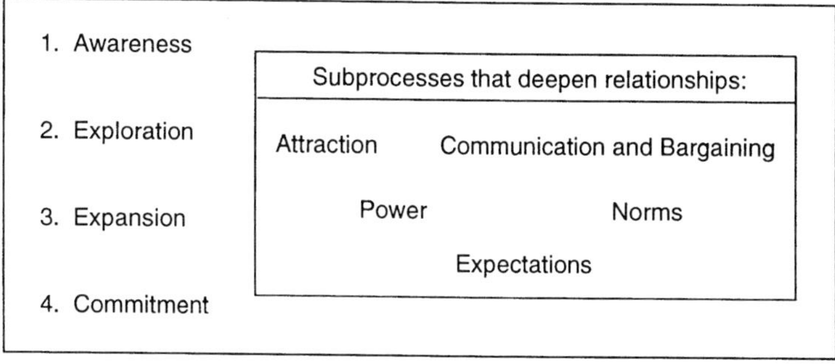

Source: Dwyer, Schurr and Oh (1987).

Figure 10.1 *The Dwyer, Schurr and Oh Model of Partnership Development*

Dwyer, Schurr and Oh's (1987) model of partnership or relational exchange development is a starting point for understanding the managerial interventions a client firm might make to further the partnering process. The model consists of four stages: awareness, exploration, expansion and commitment (see Figure 10.1).

Awareness consists of recognition that the other party may be a suitable exchange partner, but with no exchange at this point. Exchange begins in the second stage of exploration. It is in the exploration phase, after experience with exchanges, that the two parties first appreciate that a deeper, longer lasting relationship might be possible. In the expansion phase, benefits mount for both partners to the exchange and they become increasingly interdependent. In the commitment phase, the exchange partners receive such great benefits from their exchange that they agree, explicitly or implicitly, to continue the relationship and partnership is cemented. Indicators of commitment are high levels of input to building and sustaining the relationship by both partners, consistency in the application of inputs, and durability of a strong relationship over time.

The first, albeit somewhat obvious, principle for developing partnering relationships is to begin the process with vendors with whom the client firm has already done business. Narrowing the search in this way substantially reduces the information costs associated with the exploration stage by utilizing information from past work done for the client. It also speeds the process by skipping the awareness stage altogether.

Guides for management action can also be constructed from five subprocesses that come into play in the exploration phase of the Dwyer, Schurr and Oh model (Figure 10.1). The subprocesses are factors that work in the three stages of exploration, expansion and commitment to deepen (or weaken) the bonds between two interacting firms. The subprocesses are:

1. attraction
2. communication and bargaining
3. development and exercise of power
4. norm development and
5. expectation development.

Each of the sub-processes has implications for management action.

Attraction

This is the first subprocess which has to do with rewards provided directly to the client by the vendor and rewards inherent in the characteristics of the vendor. Direct rewards are the benefits the client receives from work done for it by the vendor in the past and currently, during the exploration stage. Vendors that carry out high quality work within time and budget constraints offer higher direct rewards than vendors who do not. Vendors whose personnel work easily and co-operatively with personnel of the client firm offer higher direct rewards than vendors who do not.

The characteristics of the vendor are also predictors of benefits to the client in the future. These characteristics include vendor objectives, beliefs, values, service capabilities, financial viability, managerial capabilities and status or reputation. Vendors that share the client's objectives, beliefs and values are more likely to be suitable as partners. Vendors with service capabilities complementary to the client's are more likely partners. Vendors with good management capabilities are more likely to have consistent, good performance and are better candidates for partnering arrangements. And vendors that have good reputations in the information systems field and are financially viable will more likely survive to be partners than vendors who are not.

In the exploration stage, most of the information necessary to inform the client firm of the attractiveness of a vendor as a possible partner may be available, but often it is scattered among the managers of the client firm. Perhaps a vendor has done three projects for the client firm and is currently doing a fourth, but each project has been co-ordinated by a different manager in the client firm. The first step is to systematically gather and centralize the information on direct rewards of the vendor.

The second management action related to the attraction process is to develop and implement methods for collecting data on the characteristics of vendors, that relate to inherent rewards. Again, managers of the client firm will already have much information on the objectives, beliefs, capabilities and other characteristics related to inherent rewards. But these data will be gathered and stored even less systematically than data on direct rewards and will usually only be retrievable as impressions and opinions of client firm managers, with many gaps and contradictions. Proactive data collection from client firm managers and data collection directly from vendors, after development of appropriate data collection instruments, will insure that reasonably valid and complete data are collected. These data can be used to help focus the investment in development of partnering arrangements through a screening process that eliminates some vendors from future consideration as partners.

In the expansion and commitment stages data collection can be used to explore further the avenues for co-operation that might be pursued and to check on and document the performance of a vendor firm.

Communication and Bargaining

This is the second subprocess involved in the exploratory stage. Communication is more than day-to-day exchange of project-related information between client and vendor. Communication is also concerned with open revelation of needs and resources related to the future of the relationship. Vendors who are willing to openly discuss their directions for the future, their capabilities, their strengths and weaknesses and who expect to receive like information from the client are better candidates for partnering. This information should be gathered as part of the data collection discussed in the previous section. The concern here goes beyond mere collection of data to the willingness of the vendor to make these data available and the sincerity with which the vendor engages in this process. Bargaining arises as part of contract negotiations with every project undertaken by a vendor, and often arises again when unforeseen mid-project circumstances require an adjustment of requirements and performance. Bargaining is critical to conflict resolution which is important in several of the models of partnership development reviewed above. Vendors with whom the client more easily and successfully resolves disputes through bargaining are better potential partners than vendors who are difficult to deal with. Vendors can be rated by client managers who bargain with them, and the ratings can, again, be used to screen vendors.

Later, in the expansion and commitment stages, further improvements in communication and demonstrated good faith in bargaining act to deepen the relationship between client and vendor.

Expectations Development

This is a third subprocess of the exploration stage. In a partnership, each party has expectations of the behaviour of the other. A party makes investments and takes actions that are beneficial to the other party in expectation that the second party will reciprocate. These expectations and the actions that stem from them are based on trust. Expectations that are fulfilled build trust, and trust allows expectations to rise, which when fulfilled builds more trust. The spiralling relationship between expectations and trust is a critical element in partnership development and is a necessary foundation for investment by both parties in assets and capabilities that are specific to the relationship. One can easily conceive of a sequence of contracts between client and vendor over time with steadily increasing expectations and trust and increasing investment in relationship-specific assets. However, nothing guarantees this outcome, and an end result of high trust, high expectations and a stock of relationship-specific assets could be entirely serendipitous.

Can the process of expectations development be directed or accelerated? In the largest sense it cannot. In a market economy with multiple clients and vendors, no client or vendor has sufficient power to completely direct the actions of another. But a client firm can move this process along by developing sets of expectations to which it will hold any partner-vendor, and by providing incentives for vendors who meet these expectations. For example, a client may have a quality improvement program that is integral to its functioning. To develop a long-term, partnering relationship the vendor must invest in the client's quality work process and use it successfully to produce good quality work for the client. Clients who clearly state expectations with regard to quality work processes and who rate vendors based on their ability to do work according to the guidelines, and who reward vendors with additional contracts based on past performance with respect to quality work will accelerate movement up the expectations-trust-expectations spiral. Vendors who do not meet these expectations can be eliminated as good candidates for partnership or can be put on hold until such time as they *do* meet expectations. If other, significant expectations can be identified and promoted in similar ways, the end result will be faster and lower cost development of expectations and trust.

In the expansion and commitment stages, expectations are increased and the enlarged expectations, when met, deepen trust.

Norm Development

A fourth subprocess in the exploration phase, has to do with expected patterns of behaviour in a relationship. Norms guide the actions of the client and vendor and set the stage for further interaction. An example of a norm is the way in which the vendor reacts to a request by the client for contract programming labour. Suppose the client requests three COBOL programmers to supplement its own labour on a project. It requests programmers with a skill level equivalent to eight years of experience. The vendor filling this request could respond with programmers having exactly eight years of experience, but the vendor may see from the requirements accompanying the request that it can meet the need with three of its people who are currently available, one of whom has eight years of experience and two of whom have five years of experience. The vendor charges less for the programmers with five years of experience. The norm that begins to be established here is that the vendor will use its judgment to find the combination of resources that best meets the client's need at the lowest price. This norm, then, becomes an expected pattern of behaviour. The benefits to the client firm of this norm are strengthened over time as client and vendor share more information, know more and more about each other's capabilities and needs, and are better able to match resources to needs. The client firm can strengthen and promote norm development by identifying positive vendor actions as the basis for possible norms as they occur and communicating these expectations to the vendor.

Existing norms are strengthened and additional norms are developed in the expansion and commitment stages of partnership development.

Power and Justice

This is the final subprocess occurring during the exploration phase. One party has power over a second party if the second is dependent on the first for valued resources, and this power is enhanced if there are limited alternative sources available to the second party. Exercise of power can be classified as just or unjust. It is unjust if the first uses its power for its sole benefit, without the second party's consent or understanding. It is just if both parties benefit jointly from, or if the second party is adequately compensated for, the exercise of the first party's power. As power grows in a client-vendor relationship, the way in which it is exercised is of fundamental importance to the movement of the relationship toward or away from partnering. Relationships in which power is used to provide joint benefits will flourish and grow; relationships in which power is abused will wither and die.

Investment in knowledge, practices and assets that are specialized to the relationship between client and vendor present the greatest potential for exercise of power in information system outsourcing relations. The party that invests in things worth more inside the relationship than outside it subjects itself to the possible opportunistic exercise of power by the other party (Williamson, 1985; see also Chapter 4).

For example, the client firm might acquire a particular application generator package to run on its equipment that is a specialty of the vendor firm so that the vendor's personnel can do application development for the client on the client's premises. The investment is made on the expectation that the vendor will rapidly and efficiently develop systems for the client now and into the future. If the client had no relationship with the vendor, it would not have purchased this particular application generation software. None of its personnel have expertise with the software. In this case the vendor gains power over the client, and the client is subject to "hold-up" by the vendor when the next contract for development using the application generator is negotiated. Because the client has made an investment it can easily recoup only by continued association with the vendor, the vendor can demand a higher price for its services on the next and succeeding application development projects. To exercise its power by demanding a higher price would be seen as unjust by the client and would reduce the probability that the vendor would become a partner of the client. To exercise its power justly by bargaining for add-on tools that make the application development generator even more productive with gains shared between vendor and client will be viewed favourably by the client and move the firms closer to partnership.

Other opportunities for investment in relationship-specific assets arise in the expansion and commitment stages of the development of a partnership. Both client and vendor invest in some aspects of the technology, the methods and processes, the standards, and the firm-specific knowledge of the other party. The dual nature of every relationship-specific investment is the power it cedes to the other party. The just use of that power is a keystone in the construction and deepening of a partnering relationship.

The client can educate the vendor and set norms for relationship-specific assets and the use of power by example and by precept. As an illustration, the client can require the vendor to have its personnel trained by a third party in particular software, as a condition for obtaining a contract. The client pays the vendor at a rate that fully compensates the vendor for the investment in training only if an additional, future contract is also negotiated under which the software is used again. The client assures the vendor that a future contract will be forthcoming and delivers on that promise. Here the client puts itself in a position of power over the vendor and exercises the power justly. The client can also engineer the inverse and give the vendor power and the incentive to exercise it justly. For example, the client can invest in training the vendor's personnel, at the client's expense, in processes and standards it expects the vendor to use when doing work for the client. This gives the vendor power over the client in negotiations for future work requiring the same processes and standards. But the client states explicitly that it does so on the expectation and understanding that the vendor will not exploit this advantage in bargaining over future work, and it follows through by forgoing future work by the vendor if the vendor violates the trust. Violation of the trust may also remove the vendor from consideration as a partner.

As suggested above, the five subprocesses continue to operate in the expansion and commitment stages, as well as the exploration phase. Management can work through the subprocesses to speed the movement toward to full partnering relationship in the final stage of commitment and to maintain the partnership, once it is established.

CASE STUDY ONE—US MANUFACTURING COMPANY

Brief case studies from two organizations illustrate some of the management actions that can be taken to build partnership arrangements, as suggested by the above theory. In both case study organizations the author gathered data through face-to-face interviews with IS managers responsible for developing partnering relationships with vendors. Interviews lasted one and one-half to two hours with each manager. A list of questions, or interview protocol, was developed at the outset of the research and guided the interviews, but many opportunities for open-ended data gathering were exploited, as well. Interviews were recorded to free the author from note taking and to increase the accuracy of data collection. The recordings were later transcribed, and the data were organized and analysed by the categories of the research model. IS managers in the first case study organization had developed written guidelines for their partnership programme, and these were also obtained and analysed.

The first case involves an IS department in a *Fortune 500* manufacturing company headquartered in the Midwest. The firm has revenues of nearly $8 billion and 30 000 employees, including approximately 350 IS staff. Interviews of three IS managers involved in the partnership programme were conducted in the spring of 1992. These were the corporate CIO, the team leader for the partnership programme, and a partnership programme team member responsible for documentation in the partnership effort. Several years prior to the interviews, IS management in the study company decided to drastically prune the list of contract programming vendors with which it does business. This action was taken to reduce the cost of constant sales calls from scores of vendor sales representatives, and also to increase the quality of services from vendors. These actions are not unlike the preferred vendor programmes undertaken by many other IS departments in recent years. However, the study company intends to use its preferred vendor base as a stepping stone to building closer partnership-type relationships with vendors.

By building closer relationships with contract programming vendors the study company aims to:

- identify and employ vendors that are best qualified to work with the study company;
- increase the understanding of the study company's business on the part of the vendor and of the vendor's business on the part of the study company;
- lower the costs of business to both the study company and its vendors; and
- increase the quality of vendor work.

Attraction

To identify vendors that have the potential for a closer relationship, IS managers have developed instruments to measure various aspects of direct rewards and inherent rewards of vendors. The instruments are implemented in three questionnaires. The first questionnaire is completed by every study company manager who has supervised the contract programming personnel of a vendor firm. It gathers information on the vendor as a company. The questionnaire asks the supervisor to rate the overall quality of vendor personnel, the ease and professionalism with which business is done with the vendor company, the ability of the vendor company to match its personnel to the study company's needs on the first try, the cost effectiveness of vendor personnel, and vendor attention to and alignment with the safety, security and quality concerns of the study company.

The second questionnaire, also completed by study company managers who have supervised vendor contract programming personnel, asks about individual employees from vendor firms. It gathers ratings on the skills required for the assignment and on the technical and personal skills the vendor programmer brought to the job.

Finally, the third questionnaire is administered in an on-site visit to the vendor's offices. It deals with vendor finances and the systems the vendor has in place to assure quality. These include quality standards, training, monitoring processes, employee retention and so on.

The study company rated vendor companies using the results of the three questionnaires. It then used these ratings to cut the number of contracting firms with which it did business to one-third of the number a few years ago.

Developing Expectations and Norms

The study company has formed teams with representatives of its IS staff and representatives of each vendor firm to jointly investigate ways to improve quality and to improve the relationship between the study company and vendors. Through this team effort the study company intends to develop expectations and norms that will guide vendor company and vendor personnel behaviour. Teams were established to look into a variety of issues, including quality procedures, measures of the benefits of quality practices, the sharing of training resources and training facilities, and ways to improve the matching of vendor personnel to the study company's needs.

As the teams study the issues and develop recommendations and procedures, the study company hopes to build patterns of vendor behaviour that increase vendor effectiveness. Furthermore, the study company hopes that the team effort will act to bring vendors along at much the same pace and with better alignment with study company objectives than would otherwise be the case.

Power and Justice

In exchange for greater vendor attention to study company concerns, IS managers in the study company give preference to its preferred vendors in awarding programming contracts. Beyond channelling business, the study company treats its vendors more as equals, including them in planning for quality initiatives and programmes and sharing plans for its information technology architecture and applications portfolio.

Communication and Bargaining

Communication and a changed commercial relationship is at the heart of the study company's initiative to overhaul its relationships with vendors. Too often the old way of dealing with vendors involved a search through piles of programmer resumés submitted by vendors in search of the person who could do the work at the most reasonable price. The relationship was market-like and arm's length. The new relationship with contract programming vendors centres on getting the best possible quality job done in a commercial relationship in which both firms benefit. The study firm gets the right programmer who is attuned to its quality processes on the first try and at a reasonable price. The vendor gets the continuing business of the study company and is a partner in improving quality in the systems its personnel help to build. It represents a "win-win" situation for both parties.

Expansion and Commitment

The study company plans to update periodically the questionnaire data on its contract programming vendors, continue its team efforts with vendors as a way of shaping vendor expectations and norms, and continuously strengthen its communication with vendors. The purpose of these combined efforts is to develop eventual partnerships with a subset of its vendors.

CASE STUDY TWO—A LARGE US MIDWEST ORGANIZATION

The second case involves a medium-size IS department of about 30 persons in a Midwest organization of 3000 total employees and annual sales of $500 million. Data on IS department relationships with its equipment and software vendors were gathered from two IS managers—the MIS department head and the manager of applications development. Interviews were conducted in the spring of 1993. In the early 1980s, the case study IS department was charged with delivering high levels of service from systems operating on six CPUs under several operating systems. The complexity of the operation demanded a fairly high level of systems programming and technical support. But the IS department was severely resource constrained and could not hire all the systems personnel necessary to assure adequate service levels.

IS managers in the case study organization set upon a deliberate course of building close relationships with its equipment and software vendors as a way of obtaining extraordinary vendor systems and technical support to supplement its meager staff. Its strategy and technique illustrate a number of the theory-derived management interventions detailed above in the extension of the Dwyer, Schurr and Oh framework to information systems outsourcing.

Attraction

First, the IS department chose CPU, disk drive, network equipment and systems software produced by financially stable vendors whose current capabilities and objectives for the development of future capabilities were aligned with the organization's computing needs. At the same time the selected vendors had great depth in technical staff and were capable of high levels of support for their products. In other words, the case study IS department did an analysis of the inherent characteristics of vendors and chose vendors that had the potential for meeting the case study organization's needs and with high service levels.

In most instances these were vendors with whom the IS department had done business in the past, and in these cases past dealings with the vendors had been satisfactory. The IS department had already established relationships with the vendors and had good evidence of vendor capability to deliver rewards. The small size of the case study IS department and the small number of IS managers involved allowed it to gather these data with much less formalism and quantification than a large IS department might find necessary.

Communication and Bargaining; Power and Justice

To change the essential nature of the relationship with its vendors, the IS department began a programme of intense communication. It brought in each of the sales representatives with whom it was working and explained in great detail its strategic plans and its needs for equipment or software *and* accompanying service. It made clear its willingness to enter into a long-term relationship with the vendor in which it would give preference to the vendor in meeting future equipment or software needs in exchange for greatly augmented service by the vendor.

Several aspects of this initiative are noteworthy. IS managers in the case study organization recognized that special treatment by vendors could only be won by giving something in return, in this case the promise of future business. Both sides had to gain from the relationship through a just sharing of benefits. In place of the usual hiding of intentions and the playing of one vendor off against another, the IS managers were very straightforward and above board in communicating the strategy they were following in establishing a relationship and bargained openly and honestly.

Expectations Development and Norm Development

Many hardware and software vendors use sales representatives as the first line of contact for service calls from a client. From the outset, the IS managers in the case study organization made clear that that the usual arrangements for delivering service were not satisfactory. They demanded direct access to vendor firm technical personnel. They asked for, and got, meetings with vendor technical people and explained the method by which they would work with the vendor in obtaining service. They demanded changes in the vendors' standard service call escalation procedures, requiring faster response and quicker escalation to more skilled technical personnel for problems that were not immediately resolved.

Establishing personal relationships with vendor technical people was a key part of this strategy. Expectations and norms could only be developed with individuals in the vendor company, not with the company as a whole. Whenever a problem escalated to a more specialized technical person, special efforts were made to develop a personal relationship with the higher level technician. When the same or similar problem reoccurred, the IS managers went directly to the higher level technician after informing the sales representative that they were doing so.

The IS managers used every service problem that arose as an opportunity to pursue their strategy and deepen the relationship with vendor service personnel. When service was not delivered as expected, they brought in both the vendor sales representative and service person to explain the shortcomings of the service from their perspective and the expectations they had for service in the future.

In a number of instances the IS managers found flaws in the service procedures of vendors and demanded changes in basic maintenance procedures, or new norms for maintenance service. For example, a disk drive vendor's standard maintenance procedures allowed service personnel to swap boards out of a faulty drive and use them immediately in other drives if the board seemed to be unrelated to the problem. The IS department's managers were concerned that these procedures did not rule out the possibility that the swapped boards were involved in the problem and that swapping would propagate the problem to other drives. The vendor adopted new standard maintenance procedures on disk drive boards at the insistance of the IS managers.

Expansion and Commitment

The strategy of extraordinary service in exchange for continued purchases of vendor equipment and software has been pursued for more than a decade by the case study organization. IS managers have been faithful in their commitment to buy vendor equipment or software, although they insist that prices be competitive. And through constant effort directed toward building personal relationships inside vendor service organizations and constant follow-up of problems in service delivery, they have succeeded in setting expectations and norms for service that are very atypical in the industry.

Two examples illustrate the extraordinary nature of these relationships. Technical personnel from each vendor organization all attend a weekly meeting with the IS managers in the case study company to review service needs, to develop strategies for resolving problems that involve more than one vendor's equipment or software, and to review plans for changes in equipment and software and related service needs. This ongoing, co-ordinated effort of service people from a number of vendor organizations is highly unusual in an organization of the modest size of the case study organization. Second, one vendor agreed to locate and dispatch its service personnel from offices on the case study organization's site providing the case study organization with almost immediate response from vendor service personnel.

CONCLUSION

As some earlier chapters have suggested, partnering arrangements between IS departments and vendor firms like those described in this study are the exception, not the rule. The costs of developing and maintaining partnerships can be high. Despite the obstacles, when the conditions are favourable for partnerships and a partnering relationship has potential benefits for client and vendor, IS managers would be well served by having an understanding of the actions they might take to promote and develop partnering arrangements. This chapter has proposed management initiatives that can be taken by a client firm to lower the cost and speed the development of partnership relationships with vendors in the provision of information systems services. The analysis is based on an extension of Dwyer, Schurr and Oh's (1987) model of partnership development. This stage model was selected over possible candidates for its elaboration of subprocesses that work within stages that can be managed to speed and deepen partnership arrangements. Two case studies were developed—one for a firm just embarking on a conscious programme of partnership development with vendors and another for a firm that has successfully partnered with a vendor for nearly ten years. The analysis of both cases suggests that a client firm can be proactive in selecting vendors with potential to become partners and can take action to reduce the cost and speed the process of moving through the exploration and expansion stages of partnership development. The case studies illustrate the application of the concepts in the model in real world settings. In both cases IS managers were careful to choose vendors with abilities that made them attractive as potential partners. Both firms' IS managers were careful to communicate clearly their expectations of potential partners. They engaged in fair bargaining so that gains were captured by both sides. They exercised power judiciously and recognized the importance of establishing norms to guide partnership behaviour without active day-to-day oversight.

This study is limited in a number of ways. The literature review shows that the management field holds more than one promising theory of partnership development (see also the Introduction to this volume). In the future an effort should be made to combine elements of several theories to obtain a better understanding of the mechanisms by which partnerships evolve and how this process can be managed. Additional case study research is needed that explores different kinds of partnerships. Longitudinal work that follows the development (and failure) of partnership efforts will provide results that are more robust than the retrospective case study method used here. And work should expand into wider data gathering efforts that will support formal empirical testing of hypotheses related to partnership development in IS.

ACKNOWLEDGEMENTS

An earlier version of this chapter appeared in the *Journal of Information Technology*, **10**, 4. The author is grateful to the editor and anonymous reviewers for suggestions that strengthened this paper.

REFERENCES

Anderson, J. and Narus, J. (1990) A Model of Distributor Firm and Manufacturer Firm Working Partnerships, *Journal of Marketing* **54**, 42–58.

Anderson, E. and Weitz, B. (1989) Determinants of Continuity in Conventional Industrial Channel Dyads, *Marketing Scienc*, **8**, 4, 310–325.

Clemons, E. and Row, M. (1992) Information technology and industrial Cooperation, in Nunamaker, J. and Sprague, R. (eds), Proceedings of the 25th Annual Hawaii International Conferences on Systems Sciences, vol. IV, 644–653.

Dwyer, F., Schurr, P. and Oh, S. (1987) Developing Buyer-Seller Relationships, *Journal of Marketing*, **51**, 11–27.

Elam, J. (1988) Establishing Cooperative External Relationships, in Elam J., *et al.* (eds), *Transforming the I.S. Organization*, International Center for Information Technologies, Washington, DC.

Gulati, R., Khanna, T. and Nohria, N. (1994) Unilateral Commitments and the Importance of Process in Alliances, *Sloan Management Review*, **35**, 3, 61–69.

Henderson, J. C. (1990) Plugging into Strategic Partnerships: The Critical IS Connection, *Sloan Management Review*, **31**, 3, 7–18.

Klepper, R. (1994) Outsourcing Relationships. in Khosrowpour, M. (ed.), *Managing Information Technology with Outsourcing*, Harrisburg, PA: Idea Group Publishing.

Lacity, M. and Hirschheim, R. (1993) *Information Systems Outsourcing: Myths, Metaphors and Realities*, New York: John Wiley and Sons.

Lasher, D., Ives, B. and Jarvenpaa, S. (1991) USAA-IBM Partnerships in Information Technology: Managing the Image Project, *MIS Quarterly*, **15**, 4, 551–565.

Levinthal, D. and Fichman, M. (1988) Dynamics of Interorganizational Attachments: Auditor-client Relationships, *Administrative Science Quarterly*, **33**, 345–369.

McFarlan, W. and Nolan, R. (1995) How to Manage an IT Outsourcing Alliance, *Sloan Management Review*, 36, Winter, 9–23.

Oltman, J. (1990) 21st Century Outsourcing, *Computerworld*, **24**, April, 77–79.

Ring, P. and Van de Ven, A. (1994) Development Processes of Cooperative Interorganizational Relationships, *Academy of Management Review*, **19**, 1, 90–118.

Stralkowski, C. and Billon, S. (1988) Partnering: A Strategic Approach to Productivity Improvement, *National Productivity Review*, Spring, 145–151.

Waller, D. (1990) The Evolution of EDI Partnerships, *Production and Inventory Management Review and APICS News*, **10**, 11, 30–31.

Willcocks, L. (1994) Collaborating To Compete: Towards Strategic Partnerships in I.T. Outsourcing? Oxford Institute of Information Management Research and Discusssion Paper 94/11, Templeton College, Oxford.

Willcocks, L. and Kern, T. (1997) IT Outsourcing As Strategic Partnering: The Case of the UK Inland Revenue, Proceedings of the Fifth European Conference in Information Systems, Cork, June.

Williamson, O. (1985) *The Economic Institutions of Capitalism*, New York: Basic Books.

11
Setting Up Outsourced Information Technology Service Companies

TAPIO REPONEN

INTRODUCTION

Outsourcing of Information Technology (IT) services has, in recent discussion, become a key question in the field of Information Systems (Lacity, Willcocks and Feeny, 1996; McFarlan, 1992; McFarlan and Nolan, 1995). As argued in earlier chapters, outsourcing is one alternative for arranging IT/IS in organizations, but as such it is not a new phenomenon. In the early 1970s EDP service companies were founded using a similar kind of reasoning as lies behind today's outsourcing decisions (Grover, Cheon and Teng, 1994). The main objective then was to share computer resources and also later on, software development costs. Large user organizations decided to start new enterprises to provide them with these services and also to sell services outside. Some of these service companies are now large software houses offering a full range of products, from facilities management to consulting in the field of strategy. They are also potential partners in terms of outsourcing (see Michell and Fitzgerald, 1997 for a full discussion of types of vendor and services).

In Scandinavia in the mid-1980s, a second wave of service companies appeared, but this time as a result of data processing departments becoming commercial enterprises in their own right. This has not been

Strategic Sourcing of Information Systems.
Edited by L. P. Willcocks and M. C. Lacity.

an isolated phenomenon, but a very widely-used means of developing IT/IS operations. Interestingly, however, these developments have taken many different paths. Some of the new service enterprises have been successful, but there have also been mergers, some have ceased trading and in addition some "insourcing" has occurred, i.e. taking certain IT/IS services back into the user organizations.

Much previous research has concentrated on the advantages and disadvantages of outsourcing (see for example Loh and Venkatraman, 1992; Lacity and Hirschheim, 1993a; Ketler and Walstrom, 1993; Grover, Cheon, and Teng, 1994; Altinkemer, Chaturvedi and Gulati, 1994; Loh, 1994; Lacity, Hirschheim and Willcocks, 1994). A variety of reasons have been presented for outsourcing, and it seems that decisions are very contextual but in many cases based on a "bandwagon effect" (Lacity and Hirschheim, 1993b). There are also some critical points regarding outsourcing. For example, from detailed research Lacity and Hirschheim (1993a) present the following:

- outsourcing may cause a loss of competitive advantage because in-house expertise disappears;
- there is a threat of opportunism, in particular during contract renewals;
- there may be significant risk if placing the control of confidential information in the hands of vendors;
- vendors may take advantage of the contract by charging excessive fees for services the company assumes the contract covers;
- cost savings achieved by the vendors could have been produced internally.

IS management and professionals are expected to take more responsibility over the fit between business needs and information systems services (Rouse and Hartog, 1988; Earl, 1990; Jarvenpaa and Ives 1991; Blanton, Watson and Moody, 1992; Boynton, Jacobs and Zmud, 1992), otherwise users will take the information resource over (Martin, 1982; Holloway, 1986; Janson, 1989). Outsourcing is one alternative for them but it requires, of course, careful consideration on what to outsource and how (Buck-Lew, 1992). The demands for strong leadership skills, power and business expertise in IS managers have been presented (Applegate, Cash and Mills, 1988; Applegate and Elam, 1992). There has also been discussion on the "withering away of IS organization" (Dearden, 1987, and more recently Cross, 1995), serving to illustrate the pressure for change.

The main objective of the present study is to gain a deeper, grounded understanding of one special form of outsourcing, namely developing a new outsourcing enterprise from an internal IS department. Knowledge of how this can be effected can be usefully obtained from those organizations that have made such a decision. The research carried out in this chapter sought to answer the following questions:

- What are the main reasons for outsourcing?
- What are the main difficulties or obstacles?
- What are the consequences of outsourcing?
- Is outsourcing a final solution?

The longitudinal study in real life situations reported here took place in a number of case companies over several years.

THE CONCEPT OF OUTSOURCING

First we need to adopt a working definition of IS outsourcing. This will not be dissimilar from definitions in other chapters. Loh and Venkatraman (1992) define IT "outsourcing" in the following way:

> ". . . the significant contribution by external vendors in the physical and/or human resources associated with the entire or specific components of the IT infrastructure in the user organization."

In this definition outsourcing means partial or total use of outside providers of IT services. It may cover different services, such as systems operations, application development and maintenance, network management, and/or end-user support. There are different types of outsourcing. Grover, Cheon and Teng, (1994) have proposed the following taxonomy:

1. complete outsourcing
2. facilities management outsourcing
3. systems integration outsourcing
4. time sharing outsourcing
5. other types of outsourcing.

Complete outsourcing involves the transfer of the entire computer or communications centre, together with related IS personnel, from the service receiver to the service provider. Starting a new company is one way of transferring technology or personnel outside the user organization. In most cases it is either complete outsourcing or facilities management. In this study the main objective is to find the reasons for making the decision to start a new service company. The other objectives are to observe the success of outsourcing decisions and to identify the possible factors that lie behind failure. The starting point is a suspicion concerning the role of outsourcing: Is it really a final or best solution for taking care of IT services? The study also presents examples of partial taking back of the outsourced IT services and analyses the reasons for this.

RESEARCH SETTING AND METHODS USED

The idea for the research originated from working as a facilitator in a large IS-strategy project in Finland in 1985. The organization of the IS function seemed to be one of the key issues in managing information resources (see also Willcocks, Feeny and Islei, 1997). At that time there were several examples of companies that had founded separate service organizations based on their data processing department, which had raised the question of why this had been done and whether or not these initiatives had been successful. This in turn led to the following research process (Table 11.1).

First, a decision was made to concentrate on situations where a new enterprise had been formed from an existing data processing depart-

Table 11.1 *Outline Description of the Research Process*

	Research Method	Result
1985	Actor in an outsourcing process	Interest in the phenomenon and problematic
1986	Informal discussions with experts in practice and a literature review	A model of outsourcing (Figure 11.1) and a questionnaire to study the objectives and implementation process of one kind of outsourcing: forming a new enterprise (Appendix 1)
1987	Semi-structured interviews of IS managers and user managers in six case companies	Empirical evidence for the importance of the different determinants of the process
1987	Drawing conclusions from above	A revised model of the objectives, means and results of forming a new enterprise
1988	Observations made of the case companies (newspapers, journals, discussions)	Information about several reorganizations in case companies
1993	Interviews in two of the case companies	Tentative reasons for insourcing previously outsourced parts of IT/IS services

ment. Then, a preliminary understanding of the subject was obtained via some informal discussions with IS managers, user managers and IS professionals. Based on these discussions and on the review literature (Adams, W., 1972; Gibson and Nolan, 1974; Ein-Dor and Segev, 1978; Nolan, 1979; Martin, 1982; Zuboff, 1982; McFarlan and McKenney, 1983; EDP Analyzer, 1983; Davies, 1984; Butler Cox, 1986; Brancheau and Wetherby, 1987; Lederer and Mendelow, 1988), a tentative model and a questionnaire were developed concerning the key reasons for outsourcing. Next, an investigation was undertaken to find those firms that had made these changes during the second wave of outsourcing, but that had at least two years experience of the new arrangement.

As a result six potential cases in Finland were identified. The next step was to contact them and to seek their collaboration in case research. Since all were co-operative, a study was designed and carried out in 1987. The research was based on semi-structured interviews. The managing director of each outsourced service firm and one manager in the user organization were interviewed. Twelve interviews were therefore carried out and while this is not a very large number, the interviews were carried out in depth. All the interviewees had wide experience in the field, and they had been driving forces in the change processes.

After a number of years of operating the new model, it is still unclear whether or not the experiment has been a success. Since 1987, in each case, there have been reorganizations and changes. The situation became very interesting when two of the case companies made a partial taking-back decision. As a result of this a follow-up study was undertaken in 1993 to find opinions regarding the relative success of the original outsourcing decision and the reasons for reverting to internal systems development. This study consisted of interviews with the user companies' IS managers.

The following section reports on the outsourcing phenomenon based on in-depth knowledge of selected organizations as a result of the involvement described above. The research methodology is a combination of case studies and action research (Argyris, Putnam and McLain Smith 1985; Calloway and Ariav, 1991; Jonsson, 1991). The results are based both on interviews made in case companies and on acting as a facilitator in two outsourcing decisions.

ARGUMENTS FOR OUTSOURCING

In the discussions designed to obtain an understanding of the outsourcing phenomenon the following arguments were presented. Business managers expressed considerable doubts as to the efficiency and effectiveness of data processing departments. Their opinion was that even small changes took a long time and large projects often lasted for years. At the same time, however, expectations were high due to the promises of easy-to-use, high-benefit IT by academics and practitioners in journals and at seminars. As a result, there was a wide gap between the vision and reality.

In addition, managers found it very difficult to evaluate the productivity of their IS professionals, and were somewhat suspicious of them. They wanted more control over IT/IS issues, but did not know how to achieve it. In principle, the need for links between business and IS was understood and accepted, but the differences in thinking and difficulties in communication were evident. In reality, therefore, this linkage did not work very well.

Managers and users also thought that data processing services were very expensive, at least in those organizations that used internal charging mechanisms. The users saw the costs of data processing very clearly, but had difficulties in evaluating the benefits. They found it very hard to understand why new investment was made so frequently in information systems or computers, especially given the claims made regarding the lower costs and increased power of IT. Despite this, data processing departments continued to make new investment proposals and arguments which threatened the collapse of whole systems, if investment was not accepted. Most of the projects seemed to be necessary, based on the priorities set in the IS department, and this led to even more confusion as to what was really happening.

There were also problems relating to the IS staff themselves. Systems designers and programmers are often portrayed as, and in the case studies were often found to be, logical thinkers, mathematically oriented, introvert, and difficult to approach. They are enthusiastic about their own solutions to technical problems, their innovations and the experience they have gained by doing things. They have a tendency to come up with their own unique solutions which others might not share. This presents a problem from the users' perspective, given their wish to have simple, operational solutions. Because of these problems, there seemed to be many reasons for investigating new organizational forms for data processing, and outsourcing was seen as one relevant alternative. The key point was the market mechanism between users and suppliers. Internal charging seemed to be artificial, and the market concept did not really work, but with a service company surely it would be different?

As a synthesis of the discussions and the author's own experience as actor in an outsourcing process the following list of determinants was inferred. In 1986 frameworks or theory on outsourcing were scarce and the list was therefore rather tentative:

- *Personnel*: Better professional motivation
  Less turnover
  Greater customer orientation
  Improved efficiency
- *Economic*: Better cost control
  Increased understanding of costs
  Cost reduction
  Less fixed costs
  More careful investment planning
  Greater responsibility at the point of production
- *Organization:* Smaller order backlog
  Better user support
  Faster decision making
  Greater cumulative experience

The next question facing senior executives in setting up a new enterprise related to how to achieve the objects listed above. Using the same procedure as described above, the following means were identified:

- *Personnel:* Greater personal responsibility given to DP professionals
  Flexible salary programmes
  Career alternatives
  Education programmes
  Flexible working hours
- *Economic*: Profit responsibility
  Charging mechanisms
  Price-lists for services
  Improved financial and accounting systems
  Alternative operational forms
- *Organization*: Decentralized decision making
  State-of-the-art working methods
  Product-like services
  Outside sales
  Marketing function.

After the change it was expected that in the IT/IS organization personnel motivation would be higher, costs under better control, and organizational skills good. But there were also some likely obstacles to the outsourcing process, such as:

- possible high turnover in personnel;
- increased costs because of new marketing and accounting departments;
- links to users may suffer because they were now trading with an outside company;
- new personnel may be needed because of outside sales and new products.

Outsourcing decisions have been based on expectations that many of the problems and difficulties in IT/IS management may be solved by externalizing those services, i.e. by creating markets for them. Based on the discussions described above a model has been created for the most important objectives of outsourcing, and the means that outsourcing offers to meet these objectives (see Figure 11.1, from Reponen, 1988).

The conceptual model for outsourcing is an overall framework for making and implementing outsourcing decisions. It states three areas of objectives: personnel, economic and organization. Each of these areas is important and should be considered during an outsourcing decision process. The model also describes the means for meeting the objectives set. Outsourcing IT/IS services is a change process which takes several years to stabilize, at least in the case of starting a new enterprise. The management problem is to make this change happen. The rationale behind outsourcing is that it offers better control than other organizational forms over the use of IT/IS resources. Since the control mechanism is the market itself, it is assumed that very little bureaucracy is involved therein (see the earlier chapters on transaction cost theory).

The questionnaire was designed to contain approximately sixty questions relating to the reasons for and means and consequences of outsourcing. Appendix 1 presents some examples of the types of questions used. The next step was to test if these factors really were relevant in practice.

TESTING THE ARGUMENTS

As indicated above, this study concentrates on cases where a new firm had been established from an existing data processing department to provide IT services. Six new firms were identified as having operated for more than two years and the following test was based upon them. They are described in Table 11.2.

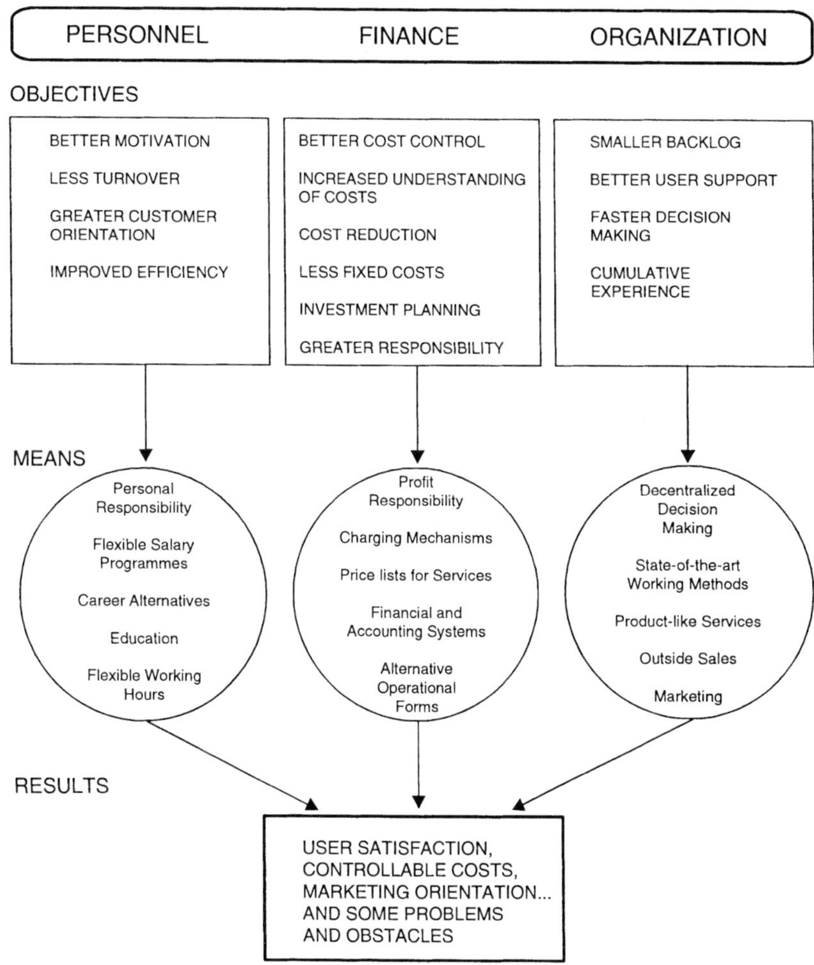

Figure 11.1 *Conceptual Model for Outsourcing*

As mentioned earlier at least two persons were interviewed in each case: the managing director of the IS firm and one user manager. The interviews were semi-structured and quite detailed, each lasting two to three hours. The interviewees were asked to evaluate the reasons, means and consequences of outsourcing as described above, using a Likert-like scale from 1 to 5 (see Appendix 1).

Table 11.3 provides the mean evaluations of both IT managers and user managers in relation to the factors identified above. As the number

Table 11.2 *Case Organizations*

Case A	Paper Mill and Saw Mill Company. Data Processing firm was founded in 1984 with 50 per cent ownership. In 1987 it had 130 employees, and a turnover of $15m. The firm offered all services from computer operation to consulting.
Case B	Retail-wholesale chain. Data Processing firm founded in 1985, 100 per cent ownership. In 1987 it had 150 employees, and a turnover of $8m. The main services were mainframe operation and maintenance of the existing software.
Case C	A conglomerate of shipyard, metal industry and paper mills. In 1985 the company moved its IS operations to a software house, which was founded in 1981, forming a partnership with them.
Case D	Construction company. Data Processing firm founded in 1984, 50 per cent ownership. In 1987 it had around 100 employees and a turnover of $10m. Its services included mainframe operations, software development and maintenance and software package sales.
Case E	Telephone operator for a large city. Data processing company started in 1986, 50 per cent ownership with 20 professionals, a turnover of $8m. The principal services were mainframe operations and systems development
Case F	A jointly owned software house for banks and insurance companies, founded in 1985, 74 people and a turnover of $4m. Software development and maintenance for banks and insurance companies.

Table 11.3 *The Main Reasons for Outsourcing*

	IT	Users
Personnel		
Motivation	3.8	4.7
Turnover	1.8	2.3
Customer orientation	4.0	4.2
Efficiency	3.6	4.2
Economic		
Cost control	2.2	2.8
Understanding costs	2.3	2.9
Cost reduction	1.4	2.2
Cost structures	2.6	2.2
Investment planning	4.0	1.8
Responsibility	3.2	3.2
Organization		
Order backlog	3.2	2.4
User support	2.8	3.2
Decision making	2.6	2.8
Outside sales	4.2	2.6
Cumulative experience	4.3	3.6

of interviewees was relatively small, the results give an overall picture of the situation in the case organizations, but they are not statistically representative and therefore no statistical tests have been done. The interviews confirmed that most of the listed factors had some importance as an objective in the outsourcing process, that there were only a small number of other factors that had not been previously identified, and that these were not, in comparison, potentially important.

Based on the mean evaluations the following factors were identified as the most important ones:

- motivation of IT professionals
- customer orientation of IT professionals
- cumulative experience
- efficiency of IT professionals
- outside sales.

Four of the above related to personnel (motivation, customer orientation, cumulative experience and efficiency), and one to organization factors. It may be that economic aspects were less emphasized, as it was expected that the market mechanism would take care of all such problems.

Although the sample was too small to be able to draw statistical significance from the results, we can see some differences in the answers of IT and user managers. The main differences were in the evaluation of the profitability of IT projects and in outside sales. IT managers regarded both factors as very important reasons for outsourcing, but to the user managers they did not seem to be particularly important. IT managers may have seen difficulties in IT evaluation more clearly than user managers and therefore they expected a new company to provide a solution to the measurement problems. The other major difference was that IT managers wanted to have a clear opportunity for outside sales and thus expanding their business. Conversely, user managers may have seen this in more negative terms, fearing the loss of their bargaining power. User managers expected more from increased motivation and efficiency than did IT managers. From their point of view better motivation was the single most important reason to start the outsourcing process. As a whole the interviews confirmed the structure of the outsourcing model described in Figure 11.1.

OPEN QUESTION ANALYSIS

Next, some comments will be presented on the results of the open discussions with the interviewees, which provide a deeper insight as to the reasons for and success of outsourcing. The objective was to find similarities and also originalities in the opinions.

The interviewees regarded all the factors presented in the questionnaire as important goals in their own organizations, but their importance depended on contingent factors. It seems that in the mid 1980s there was a widely-held belief in increasing the market orientation of services, including IT. Managers found it difficult to control IT. Outsourcing those services provided some relief for business managers, and at the same time they really believed this to be a solution to many of their IT problems. The CEO of Case B described the situation as follows:

> "Information is power. Even the information that might not be needed is collected. This makes IT/IS projects much larger and more complex than they would otherwise be. Outsourcing makes the users think more about what they really need."

Outsourcing was seen as one solution to the problem of unnecessary over-demand on services and large backlogs. It was expected to result in a better balance between user needs and development resources. Internal charging mechanisms did not fully meet this objective. But now all the projects would be based on written agreement, which made the situation clearer than before. In many cases, one important objective in outsourcing was to make sure that technological knowledge was sufficiently high. Some user managers were suspicious as to the level of professionalism in their own organization. As one manager said:

> "Our main objective was to increase the level of skills in the IT function. The outsourcing process draws the professionals out of the everyday routine of maintaining existing systems and helps them to concentrate more on new development. In a service company they will have to study and use new tools and even adopt new thinking. This may require some changes in personnel."

Another important factor was securing future resources in systems development:

> "Business strategies and plans are changing and systems need to support new operating models. Developing new systems requires both resources and knowledge. The present situation may look good, but demands are increasing. The IT service company can much better secure the quantity and quality of resources."

Profitability was also an important objective. The business managers were convinced that by outsourcing the use of IT, resources would be much more efficient and controllable. The main means of increasing service levels and profitability in all the new IT/IS companies were the following:

- more personal responsibility
- flexible salary structures
- more product-like services, with price lists
- education of personnel in marketing and customer service.

It was evident from the interviews that it took around two years for operations to be stabilized. There were a number of transition problems:

- some turnover in personnel;
- some deterioration in relationships with established users;
- in some instances, customer organizations learn faster to negotiate new projects than did the IT professionals in the new company;
- in the early stages, there were both nominal and real increases in costs;
- the new service companies found increased competition in the market,
- decision making was faster in the newly-formed IT companies, but still slow in user organizations.

Overall, in 1987 it seemed that user managements were satisfied with the outsourcing solution after a couple of years of operation. Many of the original objectives had been achieved, albeit slowly. But since 1987, there have been many reorganizations in these companies and outsourcing did not prove to be the solution to meet their changing IT needs. As a result two organizations were studied more closely in 1993 to find out the reasons for the changes.

CAN OUTSOURCING BE A FINAL SOLUTION?— A FOLLOW-UP STUDY

One of the objectives of this chapter is to show that outsourcing is not always a final decision. As mentioned above, there has been some reorganization since 1987 in each of the six cases. The return to in-house status was most evident in two of them, namely cases B and D. In what follows we shall concentrate on those two cases to find out how and why they did some insourcing of earlier outsourced operations.

Case B: A Wholesale-Retail Chain

In case B outsourcing met the demands of users very well for several years. The outsourced company had specialized in operating the mainframe computer and in maintaining the existing software. In the beginning there was enthusiasm for the new solution, but this began to turn to conflict over time. The users soon learned to negotiate for IT services, and their thinking became more open to other outside purchases.

However, during 1988, a new IS strategy was developed for the whole chain. The development in the business environment required a new operating model. The traditional wholesale business experienced difficulties, because of increased potential to create direct links between producers and customers. There was a need to adapt to this new situation. Consequently, the company changed its business strategy in order to meet these new demands. In the IS strategy it was decided that a new generation of software would be needed for the new operating model. A decision was also made to decentralize data processing in a co-ordinated way. The outsourced IT company had its main skills in operating mainframe computers and associated application software. They found it difficult to accept the new strategy, and did not adapt themselves very well to the new situation. They remained almost totally in the part of the business that was diminishing. Their mode of thinking seemed to be quite different from that of people they had been serving.

A new IS strategy was accepted in Autumn 1989. It led to a move from mainframe applications towards more distributed ones. The IT company's market decreased and a new role was designed for it. It was asked to specialize in developing and maintaining the information network needed for new operations. They started doing this work and even built some EDI applications. In 1991 there was a merger with another wholesale chain, resulting in a major rationalization of material flows and leading to a 40 per cent reduction in demand for services from the IT company. At the same time the parent company started thinking about alternative means of obtaining IT services. The following were considered:

- Adapting the IT company to the new situation.
- Starting joint ventures with other partners.
- Selling the IT companyto a software house.

After considering these alternatives, a decision was made in late 1991 to outsource the IT company for a second time. This outsourcing decision meant selling the company to a large software house with the intention to gradually withdraw from mainframe services. An agreement was entered into for annual purchases of mainframe services from the software house, but on a decreasing scale. The mainframe solution was replaced by a network of minicomputers and workstations; interestingly, network management was also to be outsourced. The objectives were twofold: to run down the mainframe but to buy network services competitively.

By 1995 the IS structure was such that the planning of systems and operating minicomputers was internal, but mainframe operations and network management had been outsourced. Outsourcing seemed to be working well, service was as good as before, and more controllable.

This offers evidence for the fact that outsourcing and insourcing can be equally relevant ways of organizing IT services. The contingent factors are decisive to choosing the solution in each specific case. In this case they were: new IS strategy, IT company's inability to adapt itself to the new situation, and higher than expected costs of IT services.

Case D—A Construction Company

Since outsourcing in 1984 there had been several stages of further development. The main reason for outsourcing had been to improve the level of IT services. The users thought that the skills of their IT function were lagging behind and that it was not ready for modern systems development. Outsourcing, with a 50 per cent partnership, seemed to be a very promising solution. Expectations were very high at the beginning.

The IS department had around 50 staff, but one of the targets for the new firm was rapid growth. In 1987 the staffing level had grown to almost 100, and outside sales had been achieved, but not to the required level. The new company did not have any clear business idea, and there was a conflict of interests between serving the parent company and increasing outside sales. There were some financial problems with the intended growth, which resulted in rationalization of the operations and a decrease in personnel. However, during this period new competencies had been achieved, but within a narrow sector. The core personnel had good contacts with the parent company, and their services were well received. The problem for the parent company was to utilize this good service, but to avoid the problems arising from too much effort going into outside services. Their solution was to re-integrate the expertise they needed and to outsource the other services provided by their IT company.

In 1990 a new operating model was created. The construction company insourced network services, and some of the financial services from the IT company, and they sold the other parts to a large software house. By this arrangement they released themselves from the software business and its problems. The process of selling was not easy, but the final solution was satisfactory.

The new internal unit faced its first real challenge in 1992. The construction company was party to a major merger with another company, which had completely different systems, architecture and philosophy. A comparison was made between the two IT organizations concerning technology, cost efficiency, skills and services. The results were favourable to the case company's unit, with the result that it was given responsibility for the integration of the two systems. After this successful implementation the credibility of the unit was restored and they were now no longer under attack. By 1994 the basic thinking was that systems engineering, project management, training, user support and application software should be handled internally, while programming and computer operation services would be obtained externally.

This is another example of both outsourcing and insourcing IT services over time. The contingent factors this time were the failure of the IT/IS company to meet expectations regarding outside sales, higher than expected costs of IT services and a desire to utilize the core skills of the IT service company internally.

Reasons for Partial Taking Back of Outsourcing Decisions

As pointed out in the Introduction and several earlier chapters, outsourcing is a very widely used form of organizing Information Systems services, and in terms of its growth in the 1990s one might even speak of a bandwagon effect (Lacity and Hirschheim, 1993b; Loh and Venkatraman, 1992). It has often been characterized as a final solution, that it is an almost irrevocable decision. However, in this study there are two examples of taking back some of the previously outsourced services. This evidence shows that to a certain degree it is possible to develop and make changes in the strategy for organizing IS (see also Lacity, Willcocks and Feeny, 1995).

The empirical evidence from these two examples shows that the following determinants might be considered obstacles to outsourcing:

- higher than expected costs of external IT/IS services;
- IT service company's inability to adapt itself to new and changing situations;
- desire to use the core IT skills internally;
- new IS strategy and its implications for new software development.

Literature presents more arguments why outsourcing is not an appropriate solutions in all situations (Blair, 1990; Loh and Venkatraman, 1992; Lacity and Hirschheim, 1993c; 1995; Apte and Mason, 1993; Willcocks and Fitzgerald, 1993; 1994). One new and interesting feature was found in this study that had not been clearly identified before. If an organization changes its strategic thinking or redesigns its operations, information technology is so closely linked to most of the changes needed that internal IT development is almost a necessity.

Changes in business strategy very often require the generation of a new IS strategy. A successful strategy generation process is an internal, interactive learning process where the role of internal competence is decisive. Consequently the importance of internal IT competence is increasing and most design tasks should be done internally. Outsourcing then plays a supportive role.

CONCLUSIONS

This study has empirically examined one set of outsourcing decisions, i.e. those related to forming an enterprise from a IS department. At first, the main determinants of outsourcing were sought from the empirical world. According to the study personnel, economic and organization factors all play an important part in outsourcing decisions. From this basis, a model has been constructed to describe the whole process: objectives, means and results. The model might also be applicable to other forms of outsourcing.

The original objective was to establish reasons for externalizing IT/IS services, which tended in the early phases of the research to emphasize the positive aspects of outsourcing. But later it became evident that outsourcing decisions are a tradeoff between many contingent factors, some favouring outsourcing and others insourcing. The determinants of the model designed are, however, valid for the consideration of both solutions. The organization decisions should be examined as two-way dynamic processes, where external and internal solutions are both possible and their priorities vary by time, as has been seen in the two case studies above.

As we have seen in earlier chapters, the conventional guideline is that all new and strategically important tasks should be performed internally. Those IT services which are closely linked to creating or maintaining the core competence of the organization should be internal. But the nature of tasks will change over time and strategic factors may be different in each case. For example, networking is one of the main trends of today but there are, however, examples of the successful outsourcing of IT network management. On outsourcing there is no general solution that can be applied to each and every specific case, but as argued here (and as we saw in Chapters 5 and 8), there are frameworks and models to analyse the specifics of a situation.

Organizations should consider a combination of different alternatives along the spectrum of total outsourcing or insourcing. Organizational decisions should be made consciously, and they should be based on the company's IS strategy. Careful consideration is needed, because major changes in organizations take around two years to stabilize.

Stating this we can develop further the model in Figure 11.1. It seems evident that the same factors are relevant in both alternatives, external and internal ones. These factors are: personnel factors, economic and organizational factors. The aims of organizing IS services is to get the services at a competitive price, to have highly motivated professionals, and to link IS services closely to the business processes of the organization.

It is very difficult to say definitively which of the alternatives, internal or external, leads to a better solution of the problems in the utilizing technology in operations. The factors influencing the decision are very contextual. First theories on outsourcing decisions have, however, been developed (Lacity, Willcocks and Feeny, 1995; Loh and Venkatraman, 1992; McFarlan and Nolan, 1995). The main objective of the organizational decisions is to find a good fit between the operations of the organization and its information systems. The concept of fit has been extensively studied in Iivari (1991). But, as have been seen in earlier literature, there are both merits and problems in different alternatives: the fit is not definitively better in either of them.

Based on the study described above, the tentative model of Figure 11.2 has been created. External and internal solutions are in a way two sides of the same phenomenon, organizing efficient and effective information services to users. Therefore the factors in decision making are

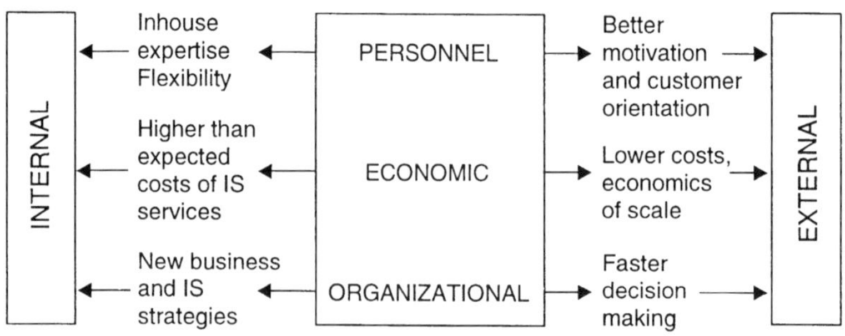

Figure 11.2 *Organizing IS Services*

the same (Ketler and Wahlstrom, 1993). The objectives are to have highly motivated IS professionals, low costs of information services and good user support.

These objectives may be met with both alternatives, external and internal. Now the question that remains: Is it possible to find general guidelines for making the decisions? My conclusion from this research adds to the picture supplied by other studies. The key elements in this decision would seem to be the need for inhouse expertise, the nature of user requirements and the complexity of the service offered.

Internal solutions are appropriate when inhouse expertise is genuinely needed, when users have special needs and when services are complex. External solutions are suitable for standard services, whose cost structures are easily understandable and the user involvement is not essential in creating and maintaining applications.

REFERENCES

Adams, W. (1972) New Role for Top Management in Computer Applications, *Financial Executive*, April, 54–66.

Altinkemer, K., Chaturvedi, A. and Gulati R. (1994) Information Systems Outsourcing: Issues and Evidence, *International Journal of Information Management*, 14, 252–268.

Applegate, L., Cash, J. and Mills, D. (1988) Information Technology and Tomorrow's Manager, *Harvard Business Review*, November–December, 128–136.

Applegate, L. and Elam, J. (1992) New Information Systems Leaders: A Changing Role in a Changing World, *MIS Quarterly*, December, 469–488.

Apte, U. and Mason R. (1933) Global Disaggregation of Information-intensive Services, Working paper 92-1201, Edwin L. Cox School of Business, Southern Methodist University, Dallas, Texas 75275.

Argyris, C., Putnam, R. and McLain Smith, D. (1985) *Action Science—Concepts, Methods and Skills for Research and Intervention*, San Francisco: Jossey-Bass.

Blair, D. (1990) I Survived Outsourcing, *CIO*, **3**, 10, July, 20–24.

Blanton, E., Watson, H. and Moody, J. (1992) Toward a Better Understanding of Information Technology Organization: A Comparative Case Study, *MIS Quarterly*, December, 531–555.

Boynton, A., Jacobs, G. and Zmud, R. (1992) Whose Responsibility Is IT Management? *Sloan Management Review*, Summer, 32–38.

Brancheau, J. and Wetherby, J. (1987) Key Issues in Information Systems Management, *MIS Quarterly*, March, 23–45.

Buck-Lew, M. (1992) To Outsource or Not? *International Journal of Information Management*, **12**, 1, 3–20.

Butler Cox Foundation (1982) Organizing the Systems Department, Research Report 52, July.

Calloway, L. and Ariav, G. (1991) Developing and Using a Qualitative Methodology to Study Relationships Among Designers and Tools, in Nissen, H.-E., Klein, H. and Hirschheim, R. (eds), IFIP Proceedings on Information Systems Research, Elsevier, North Holland, 175–193.

Cross, J. (1995) IT Outsourcing: British Petroleums Competitive Approach, *Harvard Business Review*, May–June, 94–104.

Davies, G. (1984) Management of the Information Systems Resource: Introduction, in McFarlan, W. (ed.), *The Information Systems Research Challenge*, Boston: Harvard Business School Press, 191–195.

Dearden, J. (1987) The Withering Away of IS Organization, *Sloan Management Review*, Summer, **28**, 4, 87–91.

Earl, Michael J. (1990) Putting IT in its Place: A Polemic for the Nineties, Oxford Institute of Information Management, Research and Discussion Paper 90/2, Templeton College, Oxford.

EDP-Analyzer (1983) How Work Will Change? **21**, 5.

Ein-Dor, P. and Segev, E. (1978) Organizational Context and the Success of Management Information Systems, *Management Science*, **24**, 10, 1064–1077.

Fitzgerald, G. and Willcocks, L. (1994), Contracts and Partnership in the Outsourcing of IT, Proceedings of the Fifteenth International Conference on Information Systems, 14–17 December, Vancouver.

Gibson, C. and Nolan, R. (1974) Managing the Four Stages of EDP Growth, *Harvard Business Review*, January–February.

Grover, V, Cheon, M. and Teng, J. (1994) A Descriptive Study on the Outsourcing of Information Systems Functions, *Information and Management*, 27, 33–44.

Holloway, S. (1986) Data Administration in the Organization, *Data Processing*, May, 195–198.

Iivari, J. (1991) The Organizational Fit of Information Systems: A Literature Review and Framework for Future Research, Research Paper Series A 13, Department of Information Processing Science, University of Oulu, Finland.

Janson, M. (1989) Evidence to Support the Continuing Role of the Information Systems Development in Organizations, *Journal of Management Information Systems*, Fall, **6**, 2, 21–31.

Jarvenpaa, S. and Ives, B. (1991) Executive Involvement and Participation in the Management of Information Technology, *MIS Quarterly*, June, 205–227.

Jonsson, S. (1991). Action Research, in Nissen, H., Klein, H. and Hirschheim, R. (eds), IFIP Proceedings on Information Systems Research, Elsevier, North Holland, 371–396.

Ketler, K. and Wahlstrom J. (1993) The Outsourcing Decision, *International Journal of Information Management*, December, 449–459.

Klepper, R. (1992) A Model of the Evolution of IS Outsourcing Relationships, Proceedings of the 13th International Conference on Information Systems, 13–16 December, Dallas, 262.

Lacity, M. and Hirschheim, R. (1993a) *Information Systems Outsourcing*, Chichester: John Wiley and Sons.

Lacity, M. and Hirschheim, R. (1993b) The Information Systems Outsourcing Bandwagon, *Sloan Management Review*, Fall, 73–86.

Lacity, M. and Hirschheim, R. (1993c) Implementing Information Systems Outsourcing: Key Issues and Experiences of an Early Adopter. OUT'93 Conference—Outsourcing of Information Systems Services, 20–22 May, University of Twente, The Netherlands.

Lacity, M. and Hirschheim, R. (1995) *Beyond The Information Systems Outsourcing Bandwagon: The Insourcing Response*, Chichester: John Wiley and Sons.

Lacity, M., Hirschheim, R. and Willcocks, L. (1994) Realizing Outsourcing Expectations: Incredible Expectations, *Information Systems Management*, Fall, 14, 7–18.

Lacity, M., Willcocks, L. and Feeny, D. (1995) IT Outsourcing: Maximize Flexibility and Control, *Harvard Business Review*, May–June, 84–93.
Lacity, M., Willcocks, L. and Feeny, D. (1996) The Value of Selective IT Sourcing, *Sloan Management Review*, **37**, 3, 13–25.
Lederer, A. L. and Mendelow, A. (1988) Information Systems Planning: Top Management Takes Control, *Business Horizons*, May–June, 73–78.
Loh, L. (1994) An Organizational-economic Blueprint for Information Technology Outsourcing: Concepts and Evidence, Proceedings of the Fifteenth International Conference on Information Systems, 14–17 December, Vancouver.
Loh, L. and Venkatraman, N. (1992) Determinants of Information Technology Outsourcing: A Cross-Sectional Analysis, *Journal of Management Information Systems*, **9**, Summer, 2–24.
Martin, J. (1982) Application Development without Programmers, Englewood Cliffs, N.J: Prentice-Hall.
McFarlan, W. (1992) Keynote Address, Proceedings of the 13th International Conference on Information Systems, 13–16 December, Dallas.
McFarlan, W. and McKenney, J. (1983) *Corporate Information Systems*, USA: Richard Irwin.
McFarlan, W. and Nolan, R. (1995) How to Manage an IT Outsourcing Alliance, *Sloan Management Review*, 36, 9–23.
Michell, V. and Fitzgerald, G. (1997) The IT Outsourcing Marketplace: Vendors and Their Selection. *Journal of Information Technology*, **12**, 3, 130–148.
Nolan, R. (1979) Managing the Crises in Data Processing, *Harvard Business Review*, March–April.
Reponen, T. (1988) Atk-osaston muuttaminen yritykseksi, Hallittu tietotekniikka—Menestyksen kulmakivi, Turku.
Reponen, T. (1993) Outsourcing or Insourcing? Proceedings of the 14th International Conference on Information Systems, Orlando.
Rouse, R. A. and Hartog, C. (1988) The New IS Professional—Part 1, *Journal of Systems Management*, May, **41**, 5, 6–10, and Part 2: *Journal of Systems Management, June,* **41**, 6, 19–21.
Willcocks, L., Feeny, D. and Islei, G. (eds) (1997) *Managing IT as a Strategic Resource*, Maidenhead: McGraw Hill.
Willcocks, L. and Fitzgerald, G. (1993) Market As Opportunity? Case Studies in Outsourcing Information Technology and Services, *Journal of Strategic Information Systems*, September 1993, 223–237.
Willcocks, L. and Fitzgerald, G. (1994) A Business Guide to IT Outsourcing: A Study of European Best Practice in the Selection, Management and Use of External IT Services, *Business Intelligence*, London.
Zuboff, S. (1982) New Worlds of Computer-mediated Work, *Harvard Business Review*, September–October.

APPENDIX 1—THE STRUCTURE OF THE QUESTIONNAIRE

Questionnaire: Forming an IT/IS Enterprise from IS Department

Name:
Position:
Organization:
Turnover:
Personnel:

I Objectives for Outsourcing

How important have the following objectives been in establishing a new enterprise?

Scale: 1 = not important
 2 = of little importance
 3 = important
 4 = very important
 5 = extremely important

1. Personnel
   - 1.1. Improving the working motivation of IS professionals
   - 1.2. Decreasing the turnover of IS professionals
   - 1.3. Increasing the customer orientation of IS professionals
   - 1.4. Developing salary policies
     - 1.4.1. Performance-based salaries
     - 1.4.2. Other benefits
     - 1.4.3. Above average salaries
     - 1.4.4. Salary raises
   - 1.5. Improving the efficiency of IS professionals
   - 1.6. Other objectives: List

2. Economic objectives
Questions about pricing policy, cost structures, profitability and personal responsibility

3. Other objectives
Questions about order backlog, decision making, user support and external sales

II Products and Services of the New Enterprise

Questions about products and services, product development, focus of business, market surveys, competitive position and customers

III The Implementation Process of the New Enterprise Concept

Questions about the initiative for outsourcing, prior organization, changes in personnel, salary structures, length of the implementation period, problems in implementation and relationships to parent companies

IV User Satisfaction

Questions about serviceability, application development, user support, links to business

V Open Questions

e.g.
Have the objectives been met?
Was the IS department a profit centre before the change?
Which kind of charging mechanism did it use?
Which kind of motivation means have been used?
What is the new organization of IS services like? Why is it organized in that way?

Abstract

This study concentrates on situations where a new enterprise has been formed from an existing data processing department, and where IS services have been moved to this new company, but some of them taken back into the parent company a few years later.

First, reasons for the original outsourcing decisions are identified by semi-structured interviews in six Finnish organizations. A model of the determinants of outsourcing has been developed. A follow-up study was conducted six years later in two of the case organizations showing "taking back" decisions, whose contingent factors are presented.

The main conclusion is that external and internal solutions are both equally relevant alternatives for organizing IT/IS services. There is no general solution to the outsourcing decision itself, but the determinants of the decision process are now well known. This paper identifies a growing trend towards a mixed mode of operation, combining both external and internal solutions, where IT services are being integrated into the parent company.

The main reason for having internal IT services is shown to be the fact that changes in business strategy or in organizational forms require internal IT analysis and design. Linking IT to business needs internal skills and competence. That linking may also be one source of core competence.

12
Failure in Software Outsourcing: A Case Analysis

SOON ANG AND SEE-KIAT TOH

INTRODUCTION

In recent years, outsourcing of information services has become a pervasive phenomenon. Increasingly, firms rely on external service providers for IT. Not only are firms outsourcing I/S operations, they are also outsourcing IS development (Altinkemer, Chaturvedi and Gulati, 1994; Lacity and Hirschheim, 1993; Mylott 1995).

Anecdotes from trade journals and prior research report many advantages associated with outsourcing. Through outsourcing, firms can reduce costs of developing or managing IS, gain access to specialized IS skills otherwise not found within the organization, and jettison peripheral activities to focus on core competences (see Chapters 1 and 7).

As Jaak Jurison argues in Chapter 6, outsourcing also carries risks. Perhaps the greatest risk of outsourcing is the loss of control (Lacity, Willcocks and Feeny 1995; McFarlan and Nolan 1995). Particularly vulnerable is software outsourcing. Even when software was developed in-house, organizations experienced problems. The complex, dynamic and political nature of software development often translates into time delays, cost overruns, or simply defective systems (Markus, 1983; Abdel-Hamid and Madnick 1991; Davis *et al.* 1992; Lyytinen and Hirschheim 1987). Outsourcing software exacerbates complexities of development (Whang, 1992; Richmond, Seidmann and Whinston 1992).

Strategic Sourcing of Information Systems.
Edited by L. P. Willcocks and M. C. Lacity.

Outsourcing increases the transaction costs of software development by involving external parties and incurring additional legal contractual obligations. Firms bear search costs for sourcing appropriate external software developers, negotiation costs for arriving at mutually agreed upon contract, and monitoring costs for ensuring that legal contractual obligations are fulfilled. As cautioned by Lacity, Willcocks and Feeny (1995), and McFarlan and Nolan (1995), unless properly managed, teething problems and failures in such arrangements can and do occur.

The purpose of this chapter is to demonstrate the additional complexity of developing an information systems externally. Chapter 13 will add the additional complicating factor of software development offshore. Here we focus on diagnosing a failed outsourcing case. Failed endeavours are not widely publicized. Firms restrict access to such information because failures can potentially damage their image, reputation and credibility (Sitkin, 1992). Consequently, research and the public press tend to report more of successes and less of failures. With lopsided research and reporting, organizations may unwittingly assume that failures are rare. Consequently, they forego important lessons of learning from failure. As Sitkin (1992) argues, research that over-emphasizes successes to the extent of avoiding failure is dangerous.

We believe in the control theory of negative feedback that failures provide equal, if not more diagnostic information than do successes. Studying failures is preventive because it helps firms reduce the probability of failures in future. Performance failure and implementation errors provide clear signals that something is amiss and must be changed. Accordingly, the motivation of this study is to provide a careful diagnosis of a failed outsourcing case.

To accomplish our objective, we rely on the diagnostic framework developed in Ang and Beath (1993). The framework rests on Stinchcombe's (1990) argument for the need to embed sufficient hierarchical elements in contracts to overcome shortcomings of outsourcing. The major sections of the chapter run as follows. In the next section, we present briefly the hierarchical elements framework as it applies to software outsourcing. In the next section we present the chronology of events culminating in contract failure. Then we apply the framework to the failed contract and interpret the events based on hierarchical elements analyses. We conclude in the final section with lessons learned and implications for future research and practice.

HIERARCHICAL ELEMENTS FRAMEWORK

The hierarchical elements framework (Ang and Beath 1993) is based on Stinchcombe's (1990) analysis of contracts as hierarchical elements. In his paper, Stinchcombe (1990) raised an interesting puzzle for transaction cost logic. According to transaction costs analysis, firms will refrain from outsourcing when they experience difficulty in specifying requirements in advance, when they are uncertain about prices, costs or quantities, when they require specific assets, or when they cannot control the behaviour of agents. However, in reality, we still observe firms outsourcing even under such adverse conditions. The outsourcing examples that contradict transaction cost analyses include complex R&D projects for weapons development by the government and automobile franchises in private industries (Stinchcombe 1990).

If we apply transaction cost logic to software development, we too will conclude that software should be developed internally because of the inherent uncertainties in specifying requirements determination, high investments in specific assets between the client and contractor, and performance unobservability. When we outsource software development, we should expect additional problems associated with opportunism and excessive co-ordination costs that will eventually lead to failure. In effect, software outsourcing raises the probability of failure over and above the traditional causes of failure of internally developed systems (Markus 1983; Lyytinen and Hirschheim 1987; Davis *et al.* 1992).

According to Stinchcombe, highly uncertain and high asset-specific projects survive outsourcing because firms consciously embed sufficient flexibility into the contractual relation. Flexibility is afforded by incorporating elements that are commonly found as if the activity was governed internally or hierarchically. In effect, with hierarchical elements, outsourcing will emulate hierarchical or internal governance to the extent that outsourcing contracts incorporate the flexibility and necessary control functions afforded by hierarchies. Based on Stinchcombe (1990), Ang and Beath (1993) developed a hierarchical elements framework for analysing software outsourcing. The framework comprises five major types of hierarchical controls:

1. command structures and authority systems;
2. rule-based incentive systems;
3. standard operating procedures;
4. non-market-based pricing systems; and
5. alternative dispute resolution mechanisms.

Command Structures and Authority Systems

According to Stinchcombe (1990), command structures and authority systems are information flows certified as legitimate or authoritative. Command and authority clauses substitute for complete predefinition of contingencies and contingent action. In software outsourcing, command structures assign explicitly decision rights and responsibilities to the contractual parties. Command structures in software include:

1. clauses authorizing certain parties to the contract the right to issue orders or to demand performance;
2. clauses assigning the client, contractor, or both, the power to change project scope without reneging or breaching contract;
3. clauses granting client the right to audit work-in-progress;
4. clauses granting client to choose and change contractor personnel, a privilege generally restricted to hierarchical governance; and
5. clauses granting client the right to cancel project at specified points in the outsourcing contract.

These command structures, together with sample clauses prescribed from various legal handbooks and software management publications, are elaborated in Ang and Beath (1993; 336–337).

Rule-based Incentive Systems

Rule-based incentive systems refer to systems of rewards and punishments tied to behaviour or outcomes and not to the market. Market incentives work well under conditions of certainty where all performance contingencies are considered *ex ante*. In contrast, rule-based incentive systems dissociate market-determined forces. Rule-based systems reflect locally determined inducements for desirable future performance. For example, if timely delivery is vital, penalties for delays beyond agreed completion date and rewards or bonus for early completion can be incorporated into the contract.

Standard Operating Procedures

Standard operating procedures refer to routines describing specific, well-understood actions to be followed by parties in the contract. Standard operating procedures constrain opportunistic behaviour. They facilitate monitoring and reduce uncertainties arising from performance unobservability. Standard operating procedures require contractors to produce formal progress reports to clients, and hold regular face-to-face meetings so that contractual parties can discuss potential problems arising from the project.

Non-market-based Pricing Systems

A non-market-based pricing system works on the principle of cost recovery or a combination of cost recovery and market prices. Generally, clients prefer market-based prices while contractors prefer cost recovery pricing. Market-based pricing is fixed at the onset of the contract. In contrast, cost-recovery pricing is not determined until the project is completed. Market-based pricing therefore reduces uncertainty on the cost of software outsourcing. When development cost is difficult to estimate, a cost recovery system removes risks of uncertainty from the contractor. To mitigate price uncertainty, a client may insist on fixing part of the price for systems delivery at the outset of the contract with a cost recovery-based system allowing clients to modify requirements midstream without necessarily shifting the consequences of change, (i.e. additional costs) onto the contractor. Clauses that mix fixed pricing together with cost recovery attempt to strike a reasonable balance between price risk for the client and compensation risk for the contractor.

Alternative Dispute Resolution Mechanisms

Alternative dispute resolution mechanisms refer to procedures used in resolving conflicts without having recourse to direct court sanctions. When companies resort to court sanctions, conflicts are resolved but relationships between contractual parties are severely impaired. Alternative mechanisms for dispute resolution serve to resolve conflicts with the objective of allowing contractual parties to survive conflicts and even complete the project in hand.

Alternative mechanisms are embedded in contracts, either in the form of private grievance procedures or third-party mediation or arbitration. Private grievance procedures comprise two levels of management. First, project managers from the client and contractor firms meet, discuss and resolve conflicts arising from the transaction. In the event that a resolution is not achieved at that level, senior management teams from both firms may be asked to intervene and negotiate the dispute directly.

In the event that private grievance procedures fail, parties may agree to third-party mediation. In such cases, contractual parties submit the dispute to non-binding mediation by a mutually agreed-upon computer professional. On the other hand, the parties may agree on arbitration to reach a final and binding solution. Under circumstances when both private grievance procedures and third-party mediation or arbitration fail, parties then pursue remedies available to them in formal legal litigation.

The five major categories of elements described above characterize hierarchical controls that have been prescribed to mitigate the risks of outsourcing. In the next section, we describe the chronology of events leading to a failure in software outsourcing.

SOFTWARE OUTSOURCING FAILURE: A CASE STUDY

We gathered facts of the case from secondary sources. The contract, together with notes of meetings, faxes and letters of correspondence between the two parties, and project documentation, form primary sources of evidence.

Table 12.1 gives an overview of the major milestones and events relating to the case. Dates and names of the companies have been disguised to ensure anonymity and confidentiality of the case.

Parties Involved

In June 19x1, Alpha, a company in the business services industry, approached Omega, a software consultancy firm, for assistance in software development. Omega was a reputable firm. In Omega's own words, they offered:

> "consultancy services to numerous companies for the computerization of their information. These companies are from a wide spectrum of services."

employed competent consultants:

> "Our consultants were well versed in the tasks of developing, evaluating, and implementing computer systems."

regarded highly their professional attitude and efforts:

> "Our approach to successfully assisting you is primarily based on providing experienced consultants who are familiar with your industry, and have a wide range of EDP systems development experience; and who provide an independent and objective appraisal of your requirements and suitable alternatives."

and took pride in their tried and tested systems development methodology:

> "Method X (disguised), is a comprehensive guide to computer planning, development, implementation, and operations. Standard project planning and control forms, checklists, and documentations ensure a thorough, consistent and effective approach to system development. Method was developed by Omega based on worldwide experience gained while conducting hundreds of thousands of hours of systems projects."

Based on Omega's reputation, Alpha negotiated directly with Omega to undertake the project, without open tender.

The Project

In the late 1980s, Alpha recognized the need to computerize. The company possessed no knowledge about information technology, and had been operating in a manual environment. Due to an unprecedented surge in business, Alpha became severely handicapped because of this. Management felt it imperative that they sought automation to relieve mounting paperwork. The firm faced difficulty keeping track of accounts receivables. In some cases, customers were issued invoices later than due payment dates. The bottleneck of writing out individual invoices manually to debtors triggered off a need for a computerized billing system that would remove the mundane tasks of generating invoices by hand.

Alpha approached Omega with a request for proposal 1 June 19x1. In their request for proposal to Omega, Alpha sought assistance from Omega for the following two objectives:

1. to identify detailed requirements for a computerized management system; and
2. to develop a billing system which should be simple to operate. The system should generate debit and credit notes based on the billing cycle and automatically compute the interests based on given rates.

Initial Negotiation

On 18 June, Omega presented the first proposal for a billing system. Omega estimated the project would take eight weeks to complete. Omega assigned four consultants to the project: V1, a senior consultant overall responsible for the project; V2, a mid-ranked consultant, and V3 and V4, two junior-ranked, associate consultants. The estimated cost of the system was between US$4000–$5000.

After hearing the first proposal, Alpha began to appreciate the potential power of computerization. Intense negotiations continued for four months. The continual dialogue and negotiation ultimately culminated

Table 12.1 Chronology of Events Culminating in a Failure

19x1	Major Events
1 June	• Alpha, a company in the services industry approached Omega, a management consultancy firm for consultancy assistance and software development for a billing system
18 June	• Omega offered first proposal: a system analysis and software development of billing system with user manual • Estimated time frame: 8 weeks • Estimated price: US$4–5K • Identified key personnel: V1–V4 (V1 senior consultant; V2 consultant; V3–V4 associate consultants)
6 July	• Omega offered second proposal • Scope increased to include additional two systems providing MIS exception reporting facilities to two other departments. In total three systems including data conversion from manual to computerized system • Time frame: 10 weeks • Estimated price: US$8–9K with out of pocket expenses capped at US$250
8 Aug	• Omega offered third proposal • Scope increased to include three more MIS systems for three other departments. In total six systems including data conversion from manual to computerized system • Estimated price: US$10–11K • No change in time frame
15 Aug	• Omega offered fourth proposal • No change in scope, but the five MIS systems plus the original billing systems were broken down to 10 separate modules • Time frame: 18 weeks • Estimated price remained at US$10–11K • V4 left, V5 joined
23 Oct	• Alpha confirmed acceptance of terms of Omega's proposals dated 6 July–15 Aug. 19x1 • Payment schedule: 70 per cent over five equal instalments on monthly basis effective Sept. 19x1. 20 per cent payable upon completion of assignment; 10 per cent payable after three months warranty period • Estimated time frame silent; estimated pricing unchanged at $20–22K
30 Nov	• Omega revised delivery schedule
19x2	
1 Jan	• V2 left; V6 joined
23 Jan	• Omega reported cost overruns amounting to US$65K • Suggested ex-gratia compensation
7 Feb	• Alpha clarifies position on direct compensation: will consider ex-gratia compensation only at end of contract
June–Aug	• Two trainees, undergraduate students on industrial attachment, were assigned to develop project

Table 12.1 (cont.)

19x2	Major Events
15 Nov	• Omega waiting for Alpha to sign off two modules
1 Dec	• Omega waiting for Alpha to sign off two more modules
28 Dec	• Alpha informed Omega of problems in some of the modules
	• Alpha refused sign-off
31 Dec	• V1 left. V6 took charge
19x3	
2 Jan	• Omega brought to Alpha attention outstanding sign-offs and deliverables
1 Mar	• V6 left, and V7 took charge
15 Mar	• V7 left and V8 took charge
	• Omega identified a total of 19 modules, 10 more than the original number
	• Omega delivered 14 modules all awaiting sign-off (commissioning)
	• Five modules yet to be delivered
31 Mar	• Omega issued stern warning letter demanding payment
	• Omega billed Alpha for about US$120 000, more than ten times the original contracted price

in a fourth proposal which expanded the original scope considerably. Added to a simple billing system were five MIS offering exception reporting facilities in each of the five major divisions of the firm. Omega then divided the six systems into ten separate software modules.

By October 19x1, four months after the initial proposal, the two parties signed an agreement for the project. Omega estimated that the project based on the fourth proposal would be completed within an 18 week time frame (i.e., around mid-February 19x2). Alpha was pleased with the time frame. It meant that they would be able to automate their internal operations by the first quarter of 19x2.

The estimated cost of the fourth proposal was around US$11 000. Alpha agreed to a staggered payment schedule. Alpha would pay 70 per cent of the cost over five equal instalments on a monthly basis with effect from September 19x1; 20 per cent payable upon completion of the assignment, and 10 per cent payable after three months warranty period.

Major Events Leading to Estrangement of Relationship

Three major events occurred between October 19x1 and March 19x3, the period between the original agreement and the final estrangement of the contractual relation.

First, on 30 November 19x1, about a month after the original agreement, Omega informed Alpha that they would not be able to deliver within the 18 week time frame. No concrete deadline was negotiated between the two parties.

Second, on 23 January 19x2, three months into the analysis and design of the system, Omega reported to Alpha substantial cost overruns amounting to US$65 000, about six times the cost stated in the original agreement. Omega demanded *ex-gratia* compensation. On 7 February 19x2, Alpha replied that it would consider *ex-gratia* compensation only at the end of the contract when Omega delivered a workable system.

Third, two key personnel on the project, V1 and V2, resigned from Omega leaving a vacuum in the leadership for the project. They were replaced by less experienced staff. During the summer months of June to August, two undergraduate students were employed on a temporary basis to expedite the development of the system.

Towards the end of 19x2, Omega finally delivered a number of completed modules to Alpha for commissioning or sign-offs. However, Alpha refused to sign off on any of the modules because none of them were fully operational.

The Estrangement

In March 19x3, some 18 months later, Omega issued a stern notice to Alpha demanding compensation for work completed. The bill amounted to around US$120 000, more than ten times the original agreed-upon amount of US$11 000.

As part of its justification for the revised fee, Omega claimed that Alpha continued to expand project scope beyond the original agreed upon specifications. Omega claimed to have developed a total of 19 system modules, nine more than the ten modules originally agreed upon. The notice also blamed Alpha for the colossal time slippage. According to Omega, Alpha was extremely non-committal and very tardy in signing off or commissioning modules that had been completed.

INTERPRETATION OF THE CASE

The case brought to the surface critical hierarchical elements missing in the contract that led to the demise of the outsourcing project. Table 12.2 applies the hierarchical elements framework to the case. Below we discuss in greater detail missing elements and their implications.

Table 12.2 *Case Diagnosis*

Hierarchical Elements	Case Diagnosis
Authority Relations	
(a) Explicit assignment of responsibilities of both Alpha, the client, and Omega, the contractor	None
(b) Explicit assignment of authority for authorizing scope changes	None. Alpha users continue to demand more modules. By March 19x3, Omega claimed a total of 19 system modules requested by Alpha, as opposed to the 10 agreed upon in the original contract
(c) Authority over price adjustments in projects	Alpha agreed verbally to *ex-gratia* payments after delivery to compensate for severe cost-overruns
(d) Authority over assignment of specific personnel and change in personnel	None. Project suffered serious turnover problems from Omega consultants. Three of the four original team members left within the 21 month period (see Figure 12.1)
(e) Right to audit work-in-progress	None. Alpha had no knowledge of right to audit work-in-progress
(f) Right to cancel project	None
Rule-based Incentive Systems	
Rules for punishing delays or giving bonuses for early completion	None
Standard Operating Procedures	
(a) Progress reports	Sporadic
(b) Regular meetings to discuss problems	Rare. A major meeting was convened between senior members of Omega and Alpha on 23 Jan 19x2. Omega reported cost overruns amounting to five times the original cost
Non-market Based Pricing Systems	
Pricing based on cost recovery considerations	The major fee for the major systems developed was computed on a fixed price basis. Cost recovery only for a small sum of incidental expenses such as travel. A cap of US$250 was placed for incidental expenses
Dispute Resolution Mechanism	
Informal (private grievances and third-party mediation/arbitration)	Omega raised attention of Alpha to non-payment, but Alpha continued to withhold payment for incomplete and unworkable system. Omega then served formal notice as first step towards legal recourse

Authority Relations

Based on the case, three major authority elements surfaced as being highly critical:

1. *Assignment of duties and responsibilities.* Explicit delineation of roles, duties, and responsibilities between Alpha and Omega was glaringly missing. Given that Alpha had had no prior working relationship with Omega, it is paramount that parties lay down clear lines of authority, accountability and responsibilities.
2. *Project scope.* Given the unwieldy and inevitable evolution of any system, a care and systematic authority system for approving scope changes is important. Changing scope generates rippling effects on cost structure and time schedules. In outsourcing contracts, clients should monitor scope changes carefully, otherwise they face the consequences of delayed schedules and escalating costs.
3. *Authority over personnel changes.* Contractors in outsourcing services often adopt a strategy of putting forward the best, most experienced people for contract proposal. As the project progresses, the experienced people are pulled out of the projects to pursue or deliver new business. In their place less experienced staff are assigned to complete existing projects.

In software outsourcing, a client's right to monitor and authorize personnel changes to the outsourcing team is vital because productivity of good and bad IT professionals can vary in the order of magnitude of 1:25 (Jones, 1985).

In this case, turnover was especially high—Figure 12.1 illustrates the excessive staff changes. Except for V3, a junior associate consultant, all original team members, including the senior consultant V1, left the project. At the peak of development, Omega resorted to deploying two student trainees to develop the system.

Alpha needed to ensure that Omega continued to provide the best people in the project. If the primary objective of outsourcing is to tap the distinctive competences of Omega, Alpha must ensure the quality of personnel on the project, and scrutinize any changes made to the project team. This requirement was also noted by Lacity and Hirschheim (1993).

Rule-based Incentive System

When successfully implemented, rule-based incentives act either to reward or punish the contractor to ensure timely delivery of system. In

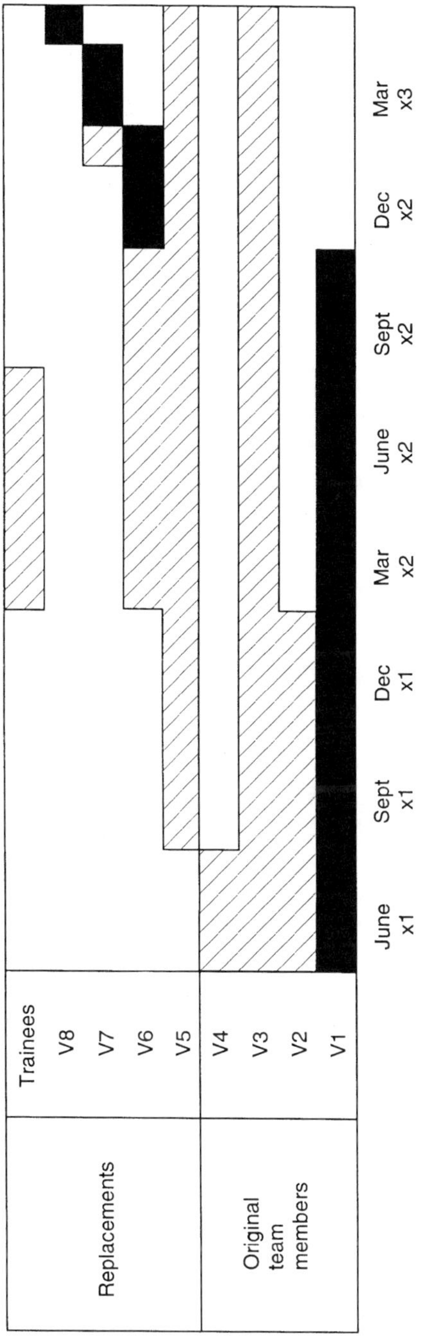

Replacements: Trainees, V8, V7, V6, V5

Original team members: V4, V3, V2, V1

June x1 | Sept x1 | Dec x1 | Mar x2 | June x2 | Sept x2 | Dec x2 | Mar x3

Key:

Shaded: duration of tenure of project members
Black: project leader

Figure 12.1 *Omega Staff Turnover Profile*

this case, Alpha and Omega had originally agreed upon a rule-based system based on instalment payment. However, the instalment plan was ineffective. First, the incentive plan was tied more to behaviour (rewarding Omega for time put into the project) rather than to outcome (rewarding for delivering modules). Based on the plan, Omega would be paid 70 per cent of the total cost over five equal instalments effective September 19x1, regardless of delivery of completed modules. Second, the instalment plan lost its effectiveness as an incentive when project costs soared and time schedules slipped badly. Even if Alpha had paid according to schedule, the payment amounting to 70 per cent of the original cost were minuscule compared to the colossal cost overruns. Alpha had wanted the cut-over of the computerization effort by the beginning of 19x2. If the cut-over deadline was critical, sufficient rewards and punishments should have been put in place to tie directly to outcome—the timely delivery of completed systems. In an extreme case, Omega may be asked to reduce the purchase price of the system at a certain rate as liquidated damages to Alpha.

Standard Operating Procedures

Outsourcing projects do not enjoy the luxury of hierarchies and bureaucracies. Conscious effort must be made to document all decisions so that someone else can examine the documents and reconstruct these decisions, especially when those working on the project leave.

Omega was confident that its proven methodology would offer routines necessary for conducting, monitoring and regulating the projects. However, Alpha did not understand the role they played in the methodology. Especially in the case where neither party has had prior mutual working relations, it is important that routines be institutionalized and made explicit. Procedures embedded in the methodology would possess no disciplining muscle if Alpha neglected their responsibilities out of ignorance of the methodology. Ignorance of the purpose and procedures of the methodology also meant that Alpha could not gauge whether Omega had breached procedures laid out by the methodology.

Non-market-based Pricing System

This case demonstrates how a poorly estimated project can go awry. Omega grossly underestimated the cost of the project. Although project scope increased at least fivefold (from a billing system to six major MIS systems), the fees increased only slightly over twofold (from an original US$4000–5000 to US$11 000).

In retrospect, Alpha should have ensured a better way of estimating the cost of the project by requesting for more than one bid from various vendors. Bids from various vendors provide valuable benchmarking data. For example, some companies use bids from leading consulting firms as industry benchmarks. They then adjust the fees proportionately in line with those signalled by the benchmark firm.

Parties to the contract must also adopt non-market pricing or cost recovery mechanisms so that the contractor can recoup its costs as project scope expands. To mitigate price uncertainty, Alpha and Omega could have specified an upper limit for costs exceeding the original fixed price of the system. An example of such a clause reads as follows:

> "If the verifiable actual cost of developing the System exceeds $25 000, GTC shall invoice MMRF for half of such cost exceeding $25 000, up to a maximum of $18 000, upon MMRF's accepting the system. ..." (American Bar Association 1987, p. 982).

In the context of expected scope changes, the above clause would strike a reasonable balance between price risk for Alpha and compensation risk for Omega. A mixed fixed price and cost recovery mechanism would provide sufficient inducement for both Alpha and Omega to enter into and to survive the outsourcing contract.

Alternative Dispute Resolution Mechanisms

Omega and Alpha had resorted to private grievance redress before the final estrangement of their business relationship. Sporadic formal meetings were called by the leader of the project team from Omega to discuss with Alpha issues concerning non-payment and escalating costs.

Unfortunately, private grievance procedures were not very effective because the frequent and abrupt changes of Omega personnel in authority impeded the development of mutual understanding. Generally, mutual understanding and adaptation occur through the social interaction that accompanies sustained joint work activities by the same members of an interorganizational team. As social interaction intensifies, members develop implicit standards of expected behaviour and mutual understanding. This overlay of social relations on a purely contractual relationship plays a crucial role in promoting alternative dispute resolution mechanisms.

Omega leadership changed hands four times during the course of the outsourcing contract (see Figure 12.1). Consequently, the contractual relationship between Omega and Alpha did not have the opportunity to develop into the good, trustworthy, socially embedded relationship necessary to fend off potential misunderstandings and disagreements. In fact, the final stern notice originated from a new senior consultant of Omega (V8) who was assigned primary responsibility for the Alpha project two weeks before the notice was served. V8 had had no prior contact with Alpha and did not empathize with the complexities of the project.

Team rebuilding and sustained effort on recommitment in the light of turnover cannot be over emphasized. In the landmark outsourcing contract between Kodak and IBM, the partnership had appointed two new CIOs and experienced an almost total turnover of the co-ordination team from both Kodak and IBM. According to McFarlan and Nolan (1995), the key success factor of the Kodak-IBM partnership is its emphasis on team building. The team interacts frequently and attends team-building retreats to ensure that turnover of personnel does not erode the stable relations of trust, obligations, customs and values of the outsourcing team (Willcocks and Kern, 1997). The issue of partnering was pursued in more detail by Robert Klepper in Chapter 10.

CONCLUSION

The purpose of this chapter was to describe and diagnose a failed contract to illuminate the added complexities of software outsourcing. To accomplish our objective, we relied on a diagnostic framework developed by Ang and Beath (1993) which prescribes embedding hierarchical elements in outsourcing contracts to overcome the shortcomings of outsourcing.

The analysis of the Alpha-Omega case shows that the outsourcing failure can be attributed to the lack of attention by the outsourcing parties to critical hierarchical elements. Major oversights included lack of clear lines of authority over sanctioning changes in project scope; lack of client authority over selection and changes in team members from the consulting firm; lack of punitive incentive systems for delays; lack of communication of the importance of standard operating procedures such as formal sign-offs and client audit; and unrealistic market-based, fixed pricing for a project of uncertain and uncontrollable scope.

The chapter contributes to outsourcing practice by demonstrating how one can conduct a diagnosis, analysis and postmortem on failed external software contracts. However, it behoves practitioners to recognize that although hierarchical or control elements mitigate the risk of outsourcing failure, they do not of themselves necessarily lead to outsourcing success.

In terms of future research, the application of the framework to the case surfaced critical contingencies that may derail outsourcing projects. One significant contingency is the high turnover rate experienced in the software industry. This makes it even more important to carry out the sort of extended vendor analysis detailed in Michell and Fitzgerald (1997). Future research should also examine the impact of personnel turnover on contractual parties ability to learn and improve outsourcing performance. The challenge is to identify and put in place mechanisms that foster inter-organizational learning, that is, the ability to translate largely tacit knowledge in software development to explicit routines and procedures available to both parties in the outsourcing relation. This, of course, gives an additional twist to the argument detailed earlier in Chapter 4.

REFERENCES

Abdel-Hamid, T. and Madnick, S. E. (1991) *Software Project Dynamics: An Integrated Approach*, Englewood, NJ: Prentice Hall.

Altinkemer, J., Chaturvedi, A. and Gulati, R. (1994) Information Systems Outsourcing: Issues and Evidence, *International Journal of Information Management*, 14, 252–268.

American Bar Association (1987) Software Contract Forms, American Bar Association, Section of Science and Technology, Chicago.

Ang, S. and Beath, C. M. (1993) Hierarchical Elements in Software Contracts, *Journal of Organizational Computing*, **3**, 3, 329–362.

Davis, G. B. *et al.* (1992) Diagnosis of an Information Systems Failure: A Framework and Interpretive Process, *Information and Management*, **23**, 293–318.

Jones, C. (1985) *Programmer Productivity*, New York: McGraw-Hill.

Lacity, M. and Hirschheim, R. (1993) *Information Systems Outsourcing: Myths, Metaphors, and Realities*, Chichester: John Wiley and Sons.

Lacity, M., Willcocks, L. and Feeny, D. (1995) IT Outsourcing: Maximize Flexibility and Control, *Harvard Business Review*, May–June, 84–93.

Lyytinen, J. and Hirschheim, R. (1987) Information Systems Failures—A Survey and Classification of the Empirical Literature, in Zorkoczy, P. I. (ed.), *Oxford Surveys in Information Technology*, 4, Oxford University Press, Oxford, 257–309.

Markus, M. L. (1983) Power, Politics, and MIS Implementation, *Communications of the ACM*, **26**, 6, 430–444.

McFarlan, F. W. and Nolan, R. L. (1995) How to Manage an IT Outsourcing Alliance, *Sloan Management Review*, Winter, 9–23.

Michell, V. and Fitzgerald, G. (1997) The IT Outsourcing Marketplace: Vendors and Their Selection, *Journal of Information Technology*, **12**, 3, 130–148.

Mylott, T. R., III (1995) *Computer Outsourcing: Managing the Transfer of Informa-*

tion Systems, Englewood Cliffs: Prentice Hall.

Richmond, W. B., Seidmann, A. and Whinston, A. (1992) Contract Theory and Information Technology Outsourcing, *Decision Support Systems*, **8**, 5, 459–477.

Sitkin, S. B. (1992) Learning Through Failure: The Strategy of Small Losses, in Cummings, L. L. and Staw, B.M. (eds), *Research in Organizational Behavior*, Greenwich, CT: JAI Press, Inc.

Stinchcombe, A. L. (1990) Contracts as Hierarchical Documents, in Stinchcombe, A. and Heimer, C. (eds), *Organizational Theory and Project Management*, Oslo, Norway: Norwegian University Press, 1985; reprinted in Stinchcombe, A. (1990) *Information and Organizations*, Berkeley, CA: University of California Press, Chapter 6.

Whang, S. (1992) Contracting for Software Development, *Management Science*, **38**, 3, March, 307–324.

Willcocks, L. and Kern, T. (1997) IT Outsourcing as Strategic Partnering: The Case of The Inland Revenue, Proceedings of The Fifth European Conference in Information Systems, Cork, Ireland, June.

13
Problems and Issues in Offshore Development of Software

T. M. RAJKUMAR AND DONALD L. DAWLEY

INTRODUCTION

Information Systems Outsourcing is here defined as the significant contribution by external vendors in the physical and/or human resources associated with the entire or specific components of the information technology infrastructure in the organization (Loh and Venkatraman, 1992). As earlier chapters indicate, software development, systems design, integration and data centre operations are areas that are commonly outsourced. Outsourcing may be project based such as the modification of a software product by a third party, or period based such as support for a product over a period of time by a third party.

In-house software development is beset with problems, particularly with the delivery of products that are late and over budget (see for example Abdel-Hamid and Madnick, 1989). This leads to user dissatisfaction with the IS department and in the 1990s has been one reason why companies have frequently sought to outsource some of their system development work. Woodring and Colony (1990) reported that 38 per cent of companies performed decentralized application development and an additional 22 per cent were evaluating this. Once a decision is made to outsource application development, the application may be developed by suppliers either in the US or in other countries. Salaries in less developed countries (LDC) are typically five to ten times

Strategic Sourcing of Information Systems.
Edited by L. P. Willcocks and M. C. Lacity.

lower for the comparable quality of output than in the United States (Aeh, 1990; Yourdon, 1996). For example, talented and experienced programmers in India and Argentina earn about $3000–$3600 per year. Such salaries make offshore software development attractive to the bottom line.

High labour costs and the shortage of qualified engineers in the US coupled with available and inexpensive engineering talent in other countries such as Ireland, India, Singapore and the Philippines, make offshore product development attractive to US companies and those in other developed economies. In particular, India has often proved to be a preferred choice for outsourcing because:

1. It is possible to resolve software problems within a 24-hour period due to the ten-hour time difference between the US and India;
2. Indian software experts are well versed in the English language; hence there is no communication gap;
3. In India computer engineers are very competitive.

India's software export has grown from US$24 million in 1985 to over US$350 million in 1994 (Kohli, 1994). After Ireland, India has the second largest share of software development for US companies (Mahabharat, 1992a). The objective of this chapter is to investigate and provide an overview of offshore development to one country, namely India. Specifically, here we will investigate the strategies used by companies; the benefits, problems and the key issues associated with offshore development in India. Other investigations (Aeh, 1990; Ravichandran and Ahmed 1993; Press, 1993) look at offshore development from the perspective of the western or US company. In contrast, we take the approach of looking at the offshore development process both from the perspective of the US company and that of the Indian development company.

FORMS OF PROGRAMMING SERVICES PROVIDED IN INDIA

Basically there are two types of programming services provided by Indian software companies: exporting personnel (body shopping) and offshore services.

- *Exporting personnel*: Akin to the contract employee, developing countries recruit and send development personnel to work at the client's site. For example, in 1989 nearly 80 per cent of Indian software export revenue was from providing contract personnel (Yourdon, 1989). This continued to be the case in 1993 with nearly 59 per cent of the revenue to Indian companies coming from providing on-site programming (Soota, 1994). The quintessential type of work performed was the conversion of application software from one mainframe to another (Soota, 1994). This leads to competing on price only (Press, 1993) and also provides the opportunity for the software developer to leave the parent company.

- *Offshore Services*: Offshore services include performing systems analysis and design at the customer's site while programming services are provided from India. A subset of these programs are developed in India and delivered using 64 KBps dedicated satellite links. Installation and testing is then performed at the US site. This type of service has become more popular with the Indian companies and accounted for roughly 40–50 per cent of the Indian software export of $350 million in 1994 (Soota, 1994). Indian companies have the expertise and experience to work on all platforms and software including CASE, relational database management systems, graphical user interfaces and object-oriented technologies (Soota, 1994).

STRATEGIES OF US COMPANIES IN OFFSHORE DEVELOPMENT

We will focus throughout on offshore development from the USA to India. We classify the strategies used by US companies in using offshore services into four categories:

1. direct outsourcing to Indian companies;
2. sub-contract to a US agent of the Indian company;
3. wholly-owned Indian subsidiary; and
4. joint ventures with Indian companies.

For a detailed case study of such offshore outsourcing see Kumar and Willcocks (1996).

Direct Outsourcing to Indian Companies:

Major Indian software companies such as HCL America, Tata Consultancy Services and Wipro Systems Limited US employ marketing managers in the US; many others also have offices in the US The personnel based in the US then deal with the US company. They get new contracts and also administer and provide maintenance support for the old ones.

These personnel take the initiative of defining the need for undertaking the prospective project at the client's office and develop the functional specifications. The design and development is undertaken in India. A few members of the development team from India then come to the US company to install and obtain acceptance certification. In most cases the IS managers in the US company have a single source of contact in the US through whom all problems can be cleared.

Sub-contract to a US Agent of the Indian Company

Some Indian companies have marketing relationships with companies in the US. For example, Mastech is a Pittsburgh firm that handles all contacts with the client company in the US, while shipping the program development to India, and ensuring the quality of the services from the Indian company (Krepchin, 1993). Through such firms, IS managers in the US avoid the difficult task of dealing with different languages and cultures.

Wholly-owned Indian Subsidiary

US companies such as Texas Instruments (TI) and Verifone have established subsidiaries in India. These subsidiaries provide programming, maintenance and other services to the parent company using company owned dedicated satellite links. TI (India) for example, re-engineers, develops, maintains and exports proprietary CAD software to its parent company using TI's CASE technology, the Information Engineering Facility (Harding, 1991).

Joint Ventures with Indian Companies

Companies such as Hewlett Packard and Sun MicroSystems have joint ventures with Indian companies. For example, Wipro Systems Ltd. provides maintenance and help facilities for Sun's Solaris operating systems. These strategic alliances lead to increased co-operation, and resource sharing between companies.

Strategies for Outsourcing

Puryear (1993) recommends that US companies look at a multisourcing option, i.e., selectively outsourcing the software process. In this method, the client is delegating the responsibility for a particular service, but the overall management remains with the company (Riccuiti, 1994). In most cases when the work is done the outsourcer will eventually hand the responsibility back to the customer. The advantage is that the IS organization within the company is intact and is not scattered like traditional outsourcing of the data centre (Rice, 1994). The types of outsourcing provided with this method are as follows (Puryear, 1993):

- *Rehabilitation and Return*: With this approach, temporary outsourcing takes place where the outsourcer is charged with improving the software and returning control to the company.
- *Capability Development*: Here the outsourcer develops the software and turns the software over to the in-house staff.
- *Transition Assistance*: Here the outsourcer takes over legacy systems while the in-house staff focus on new technology.

Puryear (1993) further recommends that each software project be handled independently, with the US company selecting the type of outsourcing that is appropriate for each project.

Four main benefits from offshore development are often expected amongst US companies (see also Chapter 9). These are reduced IS costs, improved morale, round-the-clock maintenance and access to new markets. Let us look at each of these in turn.

Reduced IS Costs

Because the average cost of a programmer is much lower in India, the cost of developing and maintaining applications is reduced. A cost saving of up to 40–50 per cent has been realized by companies (Anthes, 1993). In addition, the quality of the code written by Indian programmers is at least equivalent in quality to that turned out by their US counterparts (Anthes, 1993; Yourdon, 1996). Outsourcing systems development also gives small US firms access to economies of scale that would be virtually impossible to develop internally (Clemons and Row, 1992).

Improved Morale

By outsourcing the development of software, the in-house IS staff can be released from the mundane and routine tasks of coding and maintenance. It allows them to concentrate on analysis and design and to apply their knowledge of business to the development of newer and better systems. It also allows the IS staff to update their knowledge by acquiring and being trained in new skills and technology. Even in countries that have open trade policies, there is a time lag of a year or two before a new technology is introduced because the vendor may not have the resources available to quickly adapt the product documentation and support to the local countries' condition (Ives and Jarvenpaa, 1991). This time lag is greater for LDC such as India. IS personnel thus get to work with better technologies and solve more important business problems.

Round-the-Clock Maintenance

A time zone difference of 10 hours between Eastern Standard Time (EST) and Indian Standard Time (IST) enables a fault that is logged at the US site in the evening to be debugged and solved remotely during Indian working hours. Thus the fault is solved by the next morning (EST) without the loss of sleep for anyone (see Kumar and Willcocks, 1996, for a practical example of this).

Access to New Markets

Besides software development in India slated for export, the US companies in India want to gain ground within the growing Indian market, which for example in 1993 was US $1 billion (Kohli, 1994). India also has a large middle class population (250 million; *Economist* 1991) with discretionary funds that US companies might want to target.

On the other hand a number of benefits from offshore development can flow to Indian companies. These include the following (Mani, 1993):

- *Exposure to New Methods*: Indian on-shore personnel in US companies benefit from a higher level of exposure to other business systems, rigorous systems development methodologies and management techniques. This knowledge is then absorbed, transferred and adopted in the Indian industry.
- *Changes in attitude*: IS shops in India still need to improve their concept of service to their Indian domestic customers. The service attitude that "the customer is right" is not persistent. IS shops in India still "live in a glass house" with respect to their own domestic customers. Business ties with US companies teach Indian companies the importance of the customer and bring about needed changes in attitude. The attitude change toward service along with the focus on meeting customer needs will enable the Indian company to better meet the demands of the domestic Indian customer. Other attitude changes towards Western knowledge and culture may be diffused to the domestic Indian industry.
- *Technology transfer*: The on-shore personnel may also be exposed to new technologies and the software development needs of the new

technologies. For example, cellular phone services are not widely prevalent in India today. The needs of this industry can then be analysed by Indian companies and the knowledge gained can be used to (i) transfer the technology to domestic Indian customers, and (ii) diversify into new markets.

- *Morale*: The Indian computer industry has been a protected market from 1977 (when IBM left India) until recently. Success in developing world-class quality software products for export and visits to advanced nations boosts the pride and morale of Indian software developers; and is of great value in retaining the programmer/developers within the Indian companies.
- *Foreign exchange*: The Indian government has erected huge trade barriers to importing advanced technology. For example, the import tax on personal computers is 150 per cent. Some of these barriers are being dismantled by the present government. However, these barriers do not exist if the company generates its own foreign exchange. Developing software for export to the US and other Western countries generates much needed foreign exchange. This foreign exchange can then be used to import advanced technologies and enable the Indian companies to keep pace with the developments in the computer industry.

KEY ISSUES FOR MANAGEMENT

Key Issues for American Companies

Porter (1986) argues that the global competitor will locate activities where competitive advantages lie; decoupling comparative advantages from the firms' home base. For a company to become a truly global enterprise, employees have to change the way they think and act; progressively taking on a more global responsibility and initiative without the CEO cracking the whip (Maruca, 1994). This involves several aspects.

The first is possessing an integrated strategy. A company should consider whether software development is a key component of the businesss core operation. If it is not a core business component then software can possibly be outsourced either domestically or offshore (Jones, 1994). Hence, for offshore development to be successful, it is essential that this be integrated with the regular development processes within the company. The risks associated with any offshore development must be carefully considered and analysed. A cost-benefit analysis must be done before deciding to ship a project offshore. Not only must the cost benefits be analysed, but the sensitivities of the employees in the IS department must also be addressed. They must be educated to recognize the benefits of outsourcing so that there is no significant loss of morale or productivity.

The second is the need for a software co-ordinator. The use of a software co-ordinator has been found to be important to successful offshore development programs in large companies such as GE (Krepchin, 1993). The software co-ordinator can identify projects that are suitable for offshore development; can perform the risk analysis associated with such development; can train and sensitize managers and employees to the benefits of offshore development. The co-ordinator can also be the point of contact for offshore suppliers.

Thirdly, proper implementation is essential for the success of any project. This is even more important when a company outsources its projects; to ensure that its business needs are met. Ensuring that business needs are met, requires that the following three considerations be intertwined to link to the business strategy (Suh, 1992):

1. *Business knowledge*: Information technology should be chosen and developed with the business needs and requirements in mind. The offshore vendor should have expertise in your companys industry and in the kinds of software the company uses (Jones, 1994). With offshore development, it becomes essential to concentrate resources on monitoring the design and development process to ensure that the business issues are the focus of the development effort.
2. *Flexibility*: The system must respond to changing business and user needs. Offshore development can aid flexibility because the supplier may be able to bring in new expertise and technology which the company does not possess to adapt to changing needs.
3. *Decisiveness*: The company must ensure that the systems can respond to the needs of the user. It becomes essential to ensure that the supplier understands and aligns the project goals with the corporate goals.

In addition, Suh (1992) suggests that the following strategies support project success: a clear understanding of the risks and benefits of a project; rewarding suppliers for achieving the benefits; clear and concise goals and building a reward/penalty contract that directly supports these goals; key users be included in the early stages of the project.

Key Issues for Indian Companies

For Indian companies to succeed they must understand the business needs of the customer (US company). The first step is to focus on *why* the customer wants the software developed. Once that is understood, the second step is to focus on *what* software to build (Zultner, 1993). If the Indian companies can convince the US companies that their service helps achieve the customers' corporate goals and business needs, it is easier for the Indian company to obtain the contract.

The *process of developing the software* is as important as the product itself. As Rice (1994) points out, U.S. companies are very interested in not only building the right system but also in *building the system right*. Continuous improvement in the process is a key element of total quality management. This focus on process will enable the Indian company to keep pace with technological advances and enable it to deliver the right system. In order to do this, it is essential that Indian companies perform the following (adapted from Ives and Jarvenpaa, 1991):

1. Identify skill competencies or weaknesses present in their company.
2. Provide opportunities for global learning for their personnel related to these areas of competencies or weaknesses.
3. Seek new ways to sensitize Indian personnel sent to the US to cultural, religious and political differences.

With global competition, particular attention has to be paid to quality and quality certification. (See also the evidence in chapter 9 on this point.) It has been shown that certification helps assure the customer of the supplier's qualifications and helps the supplier make it to the customer short list (Jobber *et al.*, 1989). This enhances the acceptance rate of a supplier. Hence, it is necessary for firms to become certified under ISO 9001. This certification covers the design, development, re-engineering and maintenance of software (Kohli, 1994). However, certification under ISO 9001, although necessary, is not a sufficient condition in todays' market conditions: it has recently come under criticism.

Coallier (1994) states that software, unlike hardware, is a product that is constantly modified and expanded; is inherently complex; and is challenging to scope, develop, validate and maintain. Hence, there must be an approach that focuses on a strong total-quality approach; on customer satisfaction and on continuous improvement. Unfortunately, ISO 9001 lacks any support for continuous improvement. In contrast, the Software Engineering Institutes' Capability Maturity Model (CMM) is a better approach (Collier, 1994). CMM is a comprehensive model that measures software development capability, is committed to continuous process improvement, and has a five level rating scheme. Each level of the CMM process lays a foundation for the next level (Paulk, *et al.*, 1993). Level 1 is in the initial stage. With a disciplined process, it

Table 13.1 *CMM Model of Software Quality*

Level	Characteristics	Steps to Move to Next Level
Initial	Maturity of individual employees, not organization	Disciplined process
Repeatable	Project planning and tracking are stable, with repeatable success	Standard consistent process
Defined	Both software engineering and management are stable. Organization wide understanding of roles, activities and processes	Predictable process
Managed	Process is measured and operates within measurable limits	Continously improving process
Optimizing	Technology and management are planned and managed as ordinary business activities	

leads to level 2 or the repeatable level. With a standard consistent process it leads to level 3 or the defined level. With predicted processes, it leads to level 4 or the managed level. With continuously improving process, it reaches level 5 or the optimizing level. CMM, in addition, can be self-assessed. ISO 9001 certification translates mostly to level 2 of the CMM model. Hence, Indian companies must strive to meet the CMM standards. A summary of the CMM model is shown in Table 13.1.

Though a few companies such as Motorola India self-assess at level 5 of the CMM model (Sims, 1992), most Indian companies operate at a much lower level. Raju (1993) reports that a pilot study of Indian software quality measured process maturity in five companies and 25 projects using the Bootstrap method revealed that the quality was comparable to that of developers of similar software in Europe and the US. Indian developers placed at level 1 (third quartile) and two at level 2 (first quartile) maturity. A majority of the products were evaluated at level 1 third quartile. A comparative study placed 57 per cent of Japanese companies at level 1 maturity. However, the Indian study sample was too small for statistical significance. Hence, this highlights a trend showing that Indian companies are beginning to be aware of, and are taking process improvements very seriously. Indian companies, however, have to engage in continuous process improvement to bring them to the higher levels of the CMM model. This is essential if they are to maintain their current rate of growth in the software development industry in the US market.

Key Issues for Both Supplier and Customer

It has been shown through research that computer networks alone are not sufficient for organizational trust to develop (Nohria and Eccles, 1992). It is necessary for initial face-to-face contact to take place (Davenport, 1994). Symantec, for example, concluded that E-mail communication is not sufficient for development teams; and it is necessary for people in geographically far-flung groups to see each other (Davenport, 1994). E-mail can only help maintain, but not necessarily create, personal relationships (Ives, Jarvenpaa and Mason, 1993). Video conferencing is also of limited use (Fish *et al.*, 1993), such as checking on project status, keeping in touch and exchanging information of various types. Video conferencing, unless it is task specific, does not allow the user to share work and does not build trust. In addition, the time difference between the countries (India and the US) requires that video conferencing will be done only on an essential basis. It is recommended that the initial contacts be face-to-face, with later project status checks taking place via video conferencing or E-mail.

Total Quality Management (TQM) principles emphasize the need for TQM principles to be followed throughout the customer and supplier organizational infrastructures. In many places suppliers are now required to show that they are committed to the total quality movement. It is necessary to invest in a long-term relationship so that the companies can better understand and help each other in achieving their goals (Zells, 1992). In addition, long-term relationships help foster the continuous process improvements that are necessary to ensure that TQM permeates their entire organizations. A long-term commitment also facilitates the development of global systems that enables them to more effectively share their data across international borders more co-operatively and efficiently (Karimi and Konsynski, 1991) and enables the companies to benefit from global economies of scale. It will also allow both companies to track down defects in the software development process more effectively.

With offshore development, international data flows will necessarily take place. It is essential that the two companies agree on the standardization of data flows. Agreements must be made as to the nature of data that will be transferred and to ensure the security of the business rules that are encoded within the programs; both at the offshore site, and during the transmission of the programs.

Projects have to be chosen carefully for success in offshore development. The following are some factors that need to be considered. McFarlan (1981) divides the risks of global systems development into four categories: size, structure, technology and user factors.

- *Size and Complexity*. The length of projects is a vital factor in the success of offshore development. Long developmental cycles introduce problems. Even though Indian companies have done 100–250 man-year projects, Indian companies do not necessarily have the resources to do programming projects that large (Yourdon, 1992). A large project will have better success if it can be broken down into phased deliverables that are manageable and measurable (Harding, 1991). Only in this way should a large project be outsourced to offshore developers.
- *Structure*. Choose projects that can be well specified. If the projects are structured and well specified through analysis and design they have a greater chance of success. If the project is not well specified, it becomes necessary for an on-shore person to interact with the client continuously; thus making it difficult for the Indian company to shift the programming services back to India to achieve the cost advantage.
- *Technology*. Unfamiliar technology can lead to drastic results. Technological solutions that work in one country or company do not necessarily work well for another company or in another country. If the offshore developer (the Indian Company) is using technology that is not in line with company policy, such as a UNIX-based solution when the US company is an IBM mainframe shop, then the result can be disastrous. The technology chosen for implementing and delivering the outsourced project must be one that has a comfort level for both the supplier and the customer. For example, the use of CASE software lends itself to good offshore development, since its use leads to a highly structured and well-specified project (Harding, 1991).
- *User Factors*. The number of user interactions and number of user sites is another issue that needs to be considered (Ravichandran and Ahmed, 1993). If the level of interactivity with users is high, such as with developing client-server systems which call for graphical user interfaces; then there is increased need for communications between user and developer, making such projects less acceptable for offshore development. If the users are dispersed at a wide variety of sites within the US, the projects are less suitable for offshore development, and, again, communication needs to increase.

The core of a software contract is dependent on three components: product definition, intellectual property protection and a payment structure (Whang, 1992). The companies must resolve each of these three parts to their mutual satisfaction. With offshore software development there are complexities introduced in each of these three components

1. *Product definition*: This component defines in great detail the definition of the product, services and delivery conditions. It is to be noted in US practice the product definition is left open as to whether the delivery of offshore software should be treated as a good or service (Whang, 1992). In contrast, international law or the offshore country law may specify whether it is a good or service. It is essential that this ambiguity be resolved prior to writing the contract. The resolution should be consistent with the laws of the country that will apply to the software contract.
2. *Intellectual property protection*: Since information is shared between supplier and developer, there is a potential for conflicts of ownership or the license of intellectual properties (Whang, 1992). When a requirement to update or modify the software occurs, opportunities for dissension should not arise. Hence, delineation of these rights from the beginning is critical to the success of contracts. In addition, even though all necessary laws to protect intellectual property are encoded in India's Copyright Act of 1984, intellectual property rights are poorly enforced in India and other similar third world countries (Kohli, 1994; Zorpette, 1994). Care must be taken to ensure that a proper understanding is reached between the offshore developer and the US company.
3. *Payment structure*: The structure of payment for various services rendered must be identified early. Companies in India generally face difficulty in obtaining financial credit as banks hesitate to lend to a software firm whose assets are hard to repossess (Nidumolu and Goodman, 1993). Indian companies work because of the attractiveness of the US dollar and foreign exchange receipts. Hence, payment schedules that are tied to the development cycle paying a fixed portion of the total fee at completion of each cycle will be more attractive for Indian companies.

KEY POLICY ISSUES FOR GOVERNMENTS

Government Policies for the USA

Software professionals working at the customer's site in the US are generally provided temporary work visas. Currently the US government is looking at several measures to restrict the issuance of these visas (Anthes, 1993). Most of the restrictions are geared towards reducing the number of imported personnel. However, the government must ensure that temporary B-1 business visitors, visas be easily available to encourage personnel to test and install the software at the US site. Even without the new proposed restrictions, it costs the Indian company an average of $1500–$2000 to complete the necessary legal paperwork to obtain a temporary B-1 visa. This represents a huge outlay for the temporary placement of personnel from Indian companies and discourages them from sending personnel unless there is an absolute need for personnel to be stationed in the US. Some of these factors were seen to operate in the case study described in Chapter 13. If easier access is provided to personnel, it will ensure that the installation, test and delivery phases of the projects are completed with consistently high quality and in a timely manner.

Offshore development is critically dependent on satellite and long-distance communication services for its success. It is necessary that the US government ensure competition among these service providers. They should also lower barriers of entry and trade to alternative and newly emerging technologies such as cellular communication technologies and low-orbit satellite communications. Anti-trust policies should be vigorously enforced to prevent market dominance by vertically integrated monopolies (US ACM, 1994).

Trans-border data flows of program code may contain significant business knowledge and rules of the companies involved. Communication services are more highly valued when privacy can be assured (Rotenberg, 1993). When privacy cannot be assured, the value of a communications service is diminished and users seek other avenues of information exchange. Hence, the US must ensure that privacy of the data is not violated through satellite observation and other methods. The US government must develop a comprehensive set of policies to ensure that the privacy of all people is adequately protected (US ACM, 1994).

Government Policies in India

Countries with national computer policies and those that achieve a national consensus on the economic importance of computer systems are making measurable progress in managing the software development needed to provide systems (Zucconi, 1990). A world bank study recommends that a software development board (SDB) be formed with specific responsibilities for marketing software (Mahabharat, 1992). The SDB should then rent space at trade conventions to provide exhibit space for individual suppliers (Press, 1993). International marketing will allow Indian companies to capitalize on their software expertise and project a better image (Udell, 1993).

In working with offshore development, it is essential that communication links and facilities be provided so that the supplier and the client can communicate reliably and securely to co-ordinate the software project. Citing the low-cost communication facilities in India and Ireland, Press (1993) advocates that less developed countries subsidize satellite and other communication links as a matter of policy to enhance exports. India, for example, has seventy 64 Kbyte links to provide data communication links (Soota, 1994). Links should be expanded to handle not only data, but also video conferencing and voice transmission. Some of these links are point-to-point links and can handle software exports.

Reducing import barriers such as import taxes will enhance the ability of companies to keep pace with modern technology and allow the exporters to build the necessary infrastructure. The Indian government has introduced a concept of Software Technology Parks (STP) which have the benefit of reduced customs regulations/levies. The STP's located in Export Zones are geared towards exporting their products. To take advantage of this, many firms have established their own STPs.

A strong educational infrastructure ensures the supply of qualified personnel to meet growing demands in the software industry. Not only does the Indian government need to focus on universities but also on the private institutions that prepare computer personnel that meet quality standards. Accreditation of these private institutions must take place so that they meet the Department of Electronics' standards on accreditation (Mahabharat, 1992a). Coupled with this is the need for a research and development infrastructure. If the gifted students, with the knowledge gained from universities, cannot apply and improve their knowledge and skills they will inevitably migrate to the West. The end result will be a "brain drain" (Press, 1993).

CONCLUSIONS

In the US, the pressure to reduce IS costs coupled with the high demand for IS applications puts pressure on firms to consider alternatives to in-house application development. The availability of highly skilled, low-cost engineers in countries like India make offshore development an attractive alternative to inhouse development. India is a particularly attractive alternative since their engineers are proficient in English, are acclimated to a democratic government, are in a complementary time zone that is well suited to US operational IS needs, and place continuous emphasis and commitment to total quality management. India also represents a large potential market for US business.

Successful offshore development must be mutually beneficial to the companies and governments concerned. India is receptive to offshore development and had the goal of reaching $1 billion in software exports by the year 1996 and surpassing this in subsequent years. India's benefits from offshore relationships include the exposure to new methodologies and technologies, the further development and retention of their highly skilled engineers, and a gain of critically needed funds for importing technology.

The key to successful offshore projects requires clear linkages with corporate goals and objectives, well-defined modular deliverables, effective communications, comprehensive standards and certification, and effective delivery and payment systems. Offshore arrangements should be considered from a long-term perspective. These relationships must be characterized by a single focal point for each company, flexibility, a spirit of co-operation, a customer orientation, and facilitating government policy. Temporary business travel must be facilitated by the government policies of both countries.

Given the technological trends and the expanded emphasis on global competition, outsourcing has a bright future and India will most likely reach its 1997/8 goals. However, both Indian and US companies must work co-operatively to help each other attain their respective goals. In addition, the governments of the two largest democracies must work together to remove restrictions to trade and allow a more free exchange of goods and services between the two countries.

REFERENCES

Abdel-Hamid, T. and Madnick, S. (1989) Lessons Learned from Modeling the Dynamics of Software Development *Communications of the ACM*, 32, 12 December, 1426–1438.

Aeh, R. (1990) OffShore Development: Looking into the Future, *Journal of Systems Management*, **41**, 6, June, 17–20.

Anthes, G. (1993) In Depth; Not Made in the USA, *Computerworld*, 6 December, 123.

Coallier, F. (1994) How ISO 9001 Fits into the Software World, *IEEE Software*, January, 98–100.

Clemons, E. and Row, M. (1992) Information Technology and Industrial Cooperation: The Changing Economics of Coordination and Ownership, *Journal of Management Information Systems*, **9** 2, 9–28.

Davenport, T. (1994) Saving IT's Soul: Human-Centered Information Management, *Harvard Business Review*, **72**, 2, 119–131.

Economist, (1991) Survey of India, 4 May.
Fish, R. et al. (1993) Video as a Technology for Informal Communication, *Communications of the ACM*, 36, January, 48–61.
Harding, E. (1991) US Companies Find CASE Travels Well in India, *Software*, **11** 14, 24–28.
Ives, B. and Jarvenpaa, S. (1991) Applications of Global Information Technology: Key Issues for Management, *MIS Quarterly*, **15**, 1, 33–49.
Ives, B., Jarvenpaa, S., and Mason, B. (1993) Global Business Drivers: Aligning Information Technology to Global Business Strategy, *IBM Systems Journal*, **32**, 1, 143–161.
Jones, C. (1994) Evaluating Software Outsourcing Options, *Information Systems Management*, Fall, 28–33.
Jobber, D. *et al.* (1989) Assessing the Value of a Quality Assurance Certificate for Software: An Exploratory Investigation, *Management Information Systems Quarterly*, March, 19–31.
Karimi, J. and Konsynski, B. (1991) Globalization and Information Management Strategies, *Journal of Management Information Systems*, **7**, 4, 7–26.
Kohli, F. (1994) A Bonafide Industry With a Long Way to Go, *IEEE Spectrum*, March, 32–34.
Krepchin, I. (1993) When Offshore Programming Works, *Datamation*, **39**, 14, July, 55–57.
Kumar, K. and Willcocks, L. (1996) Offshore Outsourcing: A Country Too Far? Proceedings Of The Fourth European Conference in Information Systems, June, Lisbon.
Loh, L. and Venkatraman, N. (1992) Determinants of Information Technology Outsourcing: A Cross-Sectional Analysis, *Journal of Management Information Systems*, 8, 7–24.
Mahabharat, C. (1992a) Indian Technology Exports set for Boom Period, *Newsbytes*, 28 July.
Mahabharat, C. (1992b) Indian Government Tries to Improve Computer Training Institutions, *Newsbytes*, 17 September.
Mani, R., Personal Correspondence/Interview with the authors, Manager, Software Exports (Database Group), Datamatics, India.
Maruca, R. (1994) The Right Way to Go Global: An Interview with Whirlpool CEO David Whitham, *Harvard Business Review*, March–April, 134–145.
McFarlan, W. (1981) Portfolio Approach to Information Systems, *Harvard Business Review*, 59 September–October, 142–150.
Nidumolu, S. and Goodman, S. (1993) Computing in India: An Asian Elephant Learning to Dance, *Communications of the ACM*, 36, June, 15–22.
Nohria, N. and Eccles, R. (1992) Face to Face: Making Network Organizations Work, in Nohria, N. and Eccles, R. (eds), *Networks and Organizations*, Boston: Harvard Business School Press.
Paulk, M. *et al.* (1993). Capability Maturity Model, Version 1.1, *IEEE Software*, July, 18–26.
Porter, M. (1986) *Competition in Global Industries*, Boston: Harvard Business School Press.
Press, L. (1993) Software Export from Developing Nations, *IEEE Computer*, December, 62–67.
Puryear, R. (1993) IS Explores Multisourcing, *Software*, June, 28–30.
Raju, J. (1993) Study Takes First Look at Indian Maturity Levels, *IEEE Software*, March, 96–97.

Ravichandran, R. and Ahmed, N. (1993) Offshore Systems Development, *Information and Management*, 24, 24–40.
Rice, R. (1994) Building Quality Applications in a Changing Technology World, *Enterprise Systems Journal*, January, 36–40.
Riccuiti, M. (1994) Outsourcing as a Survival Tactic, *Datamation*, 15 April, 48–52.
Rotenberg, M. (1993) Communications Privacy: Implications for Network Design, *Communications of the ACM*, **36**, 8, 61–68.
Sims, D. (1992) Motorola India Self-Assesses at Level 5. *IEEE Software*, March.
Soota, A. (1994. A Partner on the Other Side of the Globe, *IEEE Spectrum*, March, 34–36.
Suh, R. (1992) Guaranteeing That Outsourcing Serves Your Business Strategy, *Information Strategy*, Spring, 39–42.
US ACM (1994) Renewing the Commitment to a Public Interest Telecommunications Policy, *Communications of the ACM*, **37**, 1, 106–108.
Udell, J. (1993) India's Software Edge, *Byte*, September, 55–60.
Whang, S. (1992) Contracting for Software Development, *Management Science*, **38** 3, 307–324.
Woodring, S. and Colony, G. (1990) How Software Will be Managed, *Forester Strategy Report*, June.
Yourdon, E. (1989) *India American Programmer*, 3–26.
Yourdon, E. (1992) *Decline and Fall of the American Programmer*, Englewood Cliffs, New Jersey: Yourdon Press.
Yourdon, E. (1996) *Rise and Resurrection of the American Programmer*, Englewood Cliffs, New Jersey: Yourdon Press.
Zells, L. (1992) Learning from Japanese TQM applications to Software Engineering, in Schulmeyer, G. G. and McManus (eds), *Total Quality Management for Software*, New York: Van Nostrand Reinhold.
Zorpette, G. (1994) Technology in India, *IEEE Spectrum*, March, 25–32.
Zucconi, L. (1990) U.S. Technology: We're Losing the Edge in Software, *Journal of Systems Software*, 12, 71–77.
Zultner, R. (1993) TQM for Technical Teams *Communications of the ACM*, **36**, 10, 79–91.

Index

Note: Page references in *italics* refer to Figures; those in **bold** refer to Tables